MILLER'S

20th-century design

MILLER'S 20th-CENTURY DESIGN BUYER'S GUIDE

Created and designed by
Miller's Publications
The Cellars, High Street
Tenterden, Kent TN30 6BN
Telephone: 01580 766411
Fax: 01580 766100

Consultant Editor: Paul Rennie
Project Co-ordinators: Gillian Charles, Deborah Wanstall
Editorial Assistants: Joanna Hill, Maureen Horner
Designers: Philip Hannath, Kari Reeves
Advertisement Designer: Simon Cook
Jacket Design: Victoria Bevan
Advertising Executive: Jill Jackson
Advertising Co-ordinator & Administrator: Melinda Williams
Production Assistants: Helen Clarkson, Léonie Sidgwick, Ethne Tragett
Additional Photography: Robin Saker
Indexer: Hilary Bird
US Advertising Representative: Katharine Buckley,
Buckley Pell Associates, 34 East 64th Street, New York, NY 10021
Tel: 212 223 4996 Fax: 212 223 4997 E-mail: buckley@moveworld.com

First published in Great Britain in 2003
by Miller's, a division of Mitchell Beazley,
imprints of Octopus Publishing Group Ltd,
2–4 Heron Quays, London E14 4JP

© 2003 Octopus Publishing Group Ltd

A CIP catalogue record for this book is
available from the British Library

ISBN 1 84000 694 3

Some images have appeared in previous editions of
Miller's Antiques Price Guide and Miller's Collectables Price Guide

Illustrations and film output by CK Litho, Whitstable, Kent
Printed and bound by Toppan Printing Co (HK) Ltd, China

Front Cover Illustration:
A zinc-wire cone chair, by Verner Panton, for Plus-Linje
(a later Fritz Hansen edition), designed 1960.
£700–1,200/$1,000–1,800
© OPG Photograph by Tim Ridley

MILLER'S

20th-century design

Paul Rennie

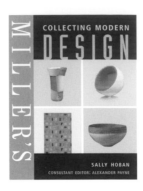
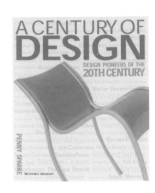

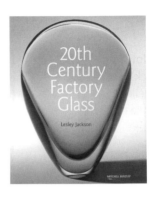

Contents

6

How to use this book

I t is our aim to make this book easy to use. In order to find a particular item, consult the contents list on page 5 to find the main heading – for example, Furniture. Having located your area of interest, you will find that larger sections have been sub-divided. If you are looking for a particular factory, designer or craftsman, consult the index which starts on page 299.

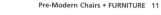

Pre-Modern Chairs

A beechwood and pressed board bentwood rocking chair, by Thonet, Austrian, c1890.
£600–750
$870–1,100 ⊞ UC

An Edwardian bentwood rocking chair, with canework back and seat panels, together with a similar rocking footstool.
£250–300
$350–450 ↗ DDM

A bentwood side chair, by Michel Thonet, model No. 511, Austrian, c1905.
£2,000–2,500
$3,000–3,500 ↗ BB(L)

Thonet & Bentwood

Michel Thonet (1796-1871) was a pioneer industrialist in furniture-making. After training as a cabinet maker he began to experiment with the new process of making curved wooden shapes using laminates – thin strips of wood which can be bent easily. The strips are glued together to give the curved structure strength. This method for making curved structures in wood is far cheaper that hand cutting or carving. Thonet's first patents date from 1840 and are evidence of his status as pioneer Modernist. The patents defend his industrial processes and methods and are far removed from the traditional craft defences of secrecy and guild membership.
Thonet's simple café chair, made from just six elements bolted together, is a classic of industrial production and has been made by the million. Its simplicity hides a design of great engineering sophistication. During the 1920s and '30s the Thonet firm applied its expertise to making tubular metal furniture.

A stained bent solid beech armchair, by Josef Hoffman, model No. 728/F, with red vinyl-covered padded seat, designed 1905–06, manufactured by Jacob & Josef Kohn, Austrian, c1915.
£320–380
$450–550 ↗ Bon

A set of three mahogany-framed sun loungers, by Dryad, with caned seats and backs, outswept scroll arms and rubber-tyred wheels, c1938, 63in (160cm) long.
£4,400–5,200
$6,400–7,600 ↗ P
The Dryad firm was established in 1907 by Harry Peach and is known for its association with the Omega Workshops.

Further reading

Miller's Collecting Modern Design, Miller's Publications, 2001

A wooden side chair, by Josef Hoffman, manufactured by Jacob & Josef Kohn, Austrian, c1905.
£1,500–2,000
$2,000–3,000 ↗ BB(L)

A pair of oak open armchairs, by Koloman Moser for Prag Rudniker, with plaited rush seats and high chequerboard backs, worn, c1903.
£2,500–3,500
$3,600–5,000 ↗ S

Price Guide
this is based on actual prices realized. Remember that Miller's is a price guide not a price list and prices are affected by many variables such as location, condition, desirability and so on. Don't forget that if you are selling it is quite likely you will be offered less than the price range. Price ranges for items sold at auction tend to include the buyer's premium and VAT if applicable.

Information Box
covers relevant collecting information on factories, makers, fakes and alterations, period styles and designers.

Caption
provides a brief description of the item including the maker's name, medium, year it was made and in some cases condition.

Further Reading
directs the reader towards additional sources of information.

Source Code
refers to the Key to Illustrations on page 296 that lists the details of where the item was photographed. The ↗ icon indicates the item was sold at auction. The ⊞ icon indicates the item originated from a dealer.

Introduction

This Buyer's Guide is intended to provide an introduction to buyers and collectors of modern design from the 20th century. The auction market for post-WWII design is, relatively speaking, of quite recent origin and has expanded quickly to cover various aspects of the development of Modernism since 1945. Modernism and design are terms used to describe different aspects of the same processes and movement. Within the context of the auction market the distinction is quite clear – *Modernism* is before WWII, *design* after. The difficulty with this arbitrary distinction is that it emphasizes the ruptures and discontinuities rather than its continuities. The war was an accelerator of social changes and, perhaps, an inevitable consequence of the project itself.

Modernism is driven by the industrial capacity of developed capitalism and in the enlightened belief in the progress of society and the emancipation of people through education and knowledge. It is therefore natural that Modernism, in whatever its form, should be about making better things available to more people by using technology and new materials. The Modernist and design project is thus fundamentally utopian in its objectives. The emancipation of peoples and the creation of mass markets are therefore inextricably linked. It's not surprising, given the progressive trajectory of these ideas, that Modernism has tended to attract political radicals and the creative avant-gardists to its cause. A large number of architects have distinguished themselves by contributing to this debate and by designing furniture that exemplifies the desire to live differently. The 20th-century tendency to embrace mechanization, technology and science as progressive virtues is in marked contrast to that of the 19th century which viewed these same developments with suspicion. More recently we have tried to distinguish politically between the project and those planned elements within it, largely as a consequence of the relative failure of post-war economic and political planning.

The Arts and Crafts philosophies of William Morris lasted well into the 20th century. The utilitarian utopianism of Morris, which hoped that beautiful things, carefully made, would enrich the world has foundered on the inability of beautifully handmade objects to be produced in sufficient volume to be available to the mass of the population at reasonable prices. The integration of machine production into the manufacture of furniture and other artefacts has been the defining characteristic of the 20th century, but this has not entirely killed off the desire in people to make and to own beautiful things.

The modern house was famously described by Le Corbusier as a machine for living in. While we would agree, from our 21st century viewpoint, that houses should be economical, convenient and efficient, we remain suspicious of the alienating and de-humanizing associations of the machine. This has opened a space, within the rhetoric of Modernist design, for the handmade and the craft tradition, for the primitive and visceral and for the continuation of local traditions. Collecting artefacts from the past has often been about the psychological desire to create a private ordered world. Nowadays this is done not just through classification and completion but by balancing these very powerful narratives within the context of a personal selection of object that offer the possibility of a Modernism that is as comfortable and personal as it is dynamic. In Britain this has manifest itself in a jaunty style that is often as much about the beach hut and garden shed as about anything more grandiose.

The inclusion in this Guide of advertising material is representative of the mainstream position of this material in contemporary society. The development of the mass market, which has been a fundamental part of the Modernist project, is unrealizable without the intervention of advertising as both information and as a manifestation of salesmanship. At the beginning of the 20th century advertising art was, broadly speaking, realistic; nowadays it is more about desire and fantasy – about tomorrow rather than today. The posters produced to sell products, information and films throughout the 20th century have been a dramatic collaboration between artists and between printing and marketing technicians. The creation of advertising images was a natural development of both the economic development of the market and in the artistic development of Modernism which demanded an engagement, on behalf of the artist, beyond the limited confines of the gallery space. Nowadays these posters are collected as historical artefacts and as documentary evidence of the ideas that shaped the 20th century.

The book also extends its scope towards the phenomenon of collecting celebrity memorabilia – whether from the worlds of sport, fashion or entertainment. This is both a reflection of the significance of these objects and of the part these stories play in our experience of the modern world. It is no coincidence that the appeal of celebrity personalities has been used, and is increasingly used, to make sense of both the past and the future in relation to contemporary society.

The objects included throughout have been selected to reflect both the international nature of this market and its local characteristics. The scope and scale of the book reflect its intention to be used primarily as an introduction to this new field of collecting.

Rather than approaching Modernism and design as self-contained categories, this book attempts to reconcile the industrial and craft traditions as they play off one another throughout the 20th century. The sections of the book are arranged thematically and each has an introduction which outlines the main thrust of effort and ideas within that context, supported by information boxes on the defining movements, artsists and designers of this story.

Paul Rennie

Date	World events	USA	Germany
1900	**WWI**	ARTS & CRAFTS *Gustav Stickley (fl. 1905–1916)*	ARTS & CRAFTS
1920	**Wall Street Crash**	MACHINE AGE	BAUHAUS FUNCTIONALISM Tubular Metal furniture widely available
1930	**Age of Mass Media** **Cinema became popular**	STREAMLINE New York World's Fair 1939	
1940	**WWII** **Cold War**	ORGANIC MODERN BAUHAUS USA Case Study Houses (end 1940s–50s)	INTERNATIONAL STYLE RECONSTRUCTION
1950	**TV became popular**	*Charles & Ray Eames (fl. 1950s–60s)*	
1960	**Vietnam War**	BIG MODERN (CORPORATE) New York World's Fair 1964	Technical excellence in workmanship
1970	**Counter Cultural Youth Movement**		FUNCTIONALISM
1980		POST-MODERN	
1990	**End of Soviet era**		
2000	**Globalization**	ECLECTICISM	

UK	France	Scandinavia	Italy
ARTS & CRAFTS	ARTS & CRAFTS	ARTS & CRAFTS	ARTS & CRAFTS
Homes Fit for Heroes		Bentwood furniture widely available	
Wembley Empire Exhibition 1924			
	Art Deco Paris Exhibition 1925	*Alvar Aalto (fl. 1920s–50s)*	
TIMBER-FRAMED MODERN			
ART DECO	ART DECO	*Plywood furniture widely available*	*Gio Ponti (fl. 1930–early 60s)*
Gordon Russell (fl. 1930s)	*Jean Prouvé (fl. 1930s–60s)*		
UTILITY	Paris International Exhibition 1937		*Piero Fornasetti (fl. 1940s–60s)*
Ernest Race (fl. mid 1940s–50s)	RECONSTRUCTION	ORGANIC MODERN	
		Hans Wegner (fl. mid 1940s)	
Festival of Britain 1951 Festival Style			*Verner Panton (fl. 1950s–60s)*
Robin & Lucienne Day (fl. 1950–mid 70s)		*Arne Jacobsen (fl. 1950s–60s)*	
INDEPENDENT GROUP ART MOVEMENT	Student Riots in Paris 1968		ANTI DESIGN
POP ART			*Ettore Sottsass (fl. 1960s–80s)*
SWINGING LONDON & PSYCHEDELIA			
PUNK			
POST-MODERN	POST-MODERN		POST-MODERN
			Memphis Group (fl. 1980s)
ECLECTICISM	ECLECTICISM		ECLECTICISM

Furniture

Looking back at the 20th century it is easy to forget that the relative abundance of the contemporary market place is so recent. In home furnishings this has been made possible by the introduction of new materials and by new manufacturing techniques supplementing traditional methods.

Mass production is not new in furniture design. The Thonet bentwood dining chair (see p11) was the fruit of industrial experiments carried out in the 1820s and 1830s. Thonet's chairs were included by Le Corbusier in his *Pavillon de L'Esprit Nouveau* (1925). Le Corbusier recognized Thonet's logic as that of a pioneer Modernist and his chairs were claimed as the proper antecedents to the Functionalist logic of the tubular metal furniture of the 1920s and 30s. Another source of inspiration for Le Corbusier and other designers was in the manufacturing technologies of boat builders, and the lightweight materials available to the developing aviation industry.

The key materials of the inter-war years were tubular metal, aluminium and plywood. The use of tubular metal, often chromed, was pioneered in the design experiments of the German Bauhaus school. After WWI a new architecture and design logic called Modernism emerged, particularly in Europe, reflecting dissatisfaction with the bankrupt ideas and styles of former Imperial regimes. It is not surprising that Modernist design should associate itself with socially progressive political ideas in Europe – particularly as part of a strategy to resist the spread of communism from Soviet Russia. After WWII the Modernist project was taken up by America, which underwrote the global expansion of its economy by appealling to technology, science and design. The organization of the furniture section is, broadly speaking, in two sections. These sections are subdivided to take account of different evolutions of Modernism.

The Victorian powers of WWI offered a very different context to emergent Modernism from that of central Europe. In Britain and France ideas of national identity were recast around, among other things, local craft traditions and a feeling for landscape so that the 1920s became a period of revival for the Arts and Crafts ideals of the previous century. In England this took the form of the tudorbethan suburban home for the returning hero or stockbroker complete with limed oak dining furniture. During the inter-war years in Britain it became clear that the question of Empire would require consideration and national identity was built around a cluster of identifiably Anglo-Saxon values.

In France the respsonse was altogether more grandiose with the Art Deco style becoming a continuation of the 18th century *ébénistes* and *style de luxe*. The style was launched at the Paris Exhibition of 1925 and is at its finest in the work of the Rhulman workshops. It reached its apotheosis in the luxurious décor of the Compagnie Transatlantique's *Normandie* ocean liner.

The German Bauhaus school of design and architecture was founded by Walter Gropius in 1918. Gropius and his colleagues set out to identify a new process of design that was independent of historical and political legacies that would qualify as Internationalist and Functionalist. The Bauhaus school was responsible for the development of eduction in the creative sector. It was closed by the Nazis in 1933 and so began the creative spread from Europe, through Britain, to America.

Many refugees from Europe were able to establish themselves in Britain and Modernism, far from being rejected, was enthusiastically embraced by the British. The period of war and its immediate aftermath was characterized by great austerity. It was, nevertheless, a period of great technolgical innovation and development

After WWII the USA became the powerhouse economy of the world. The great story of post-war design is, therefore, mostly an American one. As in the aftermath of WWI, the war had resulted in new materials, new technologies and in an expanded potential of industrial output. The Museum of Modern Art in New York was at the forefront of the post-war debate about swords and ploughshares.

The design partnership of Charles and Ray Eames initially worked on experiments in moulding ply for first aid material for the US military. These experiments were put to good use after WWII by the development of a series of plywood chairs and, subsequently, of moulded fibreglass furniture. Eames' designs became part of the Knoll range of furniture and their Aluminium Group designs became the staple of corporate America. By the 1960s the Eames had created the frame of their most famous and widely recognized piece of furniture, the Lounge Chair and Ottoman. This is featured in many contemporary loft spaces.

The Eames' legacy was the sense that design and Modernism could be fun. The transition from an economy of scarcity to one of abundance has transformed late 20th century design into an activity that is about desire and fun. The heroic Modernist period, (1918–1960), was characterized by a belief that design could make the world a better place. The post-war experience of Vietnam, nuclear power and the space race has tended to point to the limitations of technology and science as far as human happiness is concerned. The ever increasing cost of small advances in technology dented the momentum of the Modernist project at the end of the 20th century. It should be noted that the Modernism that is popular today is not contemporary Modernism but the Modernism of 50 years ago at least. Modernism and design has never been so easily available but it is now simply one consumer choice out of many retro-chic style options.

Pre-Modern Chairs

A beechwood and pressed board bentwood rocking chair, by Thonet, Austrian, c1890.
£600–750
$870–1,100 ⊞ UC

An Edwardian bentwood rocking chair, with canework back and seat panels, together with a similar rocking footstool.
£250–300
$350–450 ↗ DDM

A bentwood side chair, by Michel Thonet, model No. 511, Austrian, c1905.
£2,000–2,500
$3,000–3,500 ↗ BB(L)

Thonet and Bentwood

Michel Thonet (1796-1871) was a pioneer industrialist in furniture-making. After training as a cabinet maker he began to experiment with the new process of making curved wooden shapes using laminates – thin strips of wood which can be bent easily. The strips are glued together to give the curved structure strength. This method for making curved structures in wood is far cheaper that hand cutting or carving. Thonet's first patents date from 1840 and are evidence of his status as pioneer Modernist. The patents defend his industrial processes and methods and are far removed from the traditional craft defences of secrecy and guild membership.

Thonet's simple café chair, made from just six elements bolted together, is a classic of industrial production and has been made by the million. Its simplicity hides a design of great engineering sophistication. During the 1920s and '30s the Thonet firm applied its expertise to making tubular metal furniture.

A stained bent solid beech armchair, by Josef Hoffman, model No. 728/F, with red vinyl-covered padded seat, designed 1905–06, manufactured by Jacob & Josef Kohn, Austrian, c1915.
£320–380
$450–550 ↗ Bon

A six-piece bent beechwood salon suite, attributed to Josef Hoffman, early 20thC, settee 46½in (118cm) wide.
£4,000–4,500
$5,800–6,500 ↗ S(NY)

Pre-Modern

The roots of Modernism can be discerned, in experimental form, in the 19th century. The development, through science and education, of new materials and their applications to industry and commerce are what drove the industrial revolution forward. The bentwood furniture experiments of Michael Thonet and the cast-iron architecture of Paxman are key elements in the early history of Modernism.

A wooden side chair, by Josef Hoffman, manufactured by Jacob & Josef Kohn, Austrian, c1905.
£1,500–2,000
$2,000–3,000 ↗ BB(L)

A pair of oak open armchairs, by Koloman Moser for Prag Rudniker, with plaited rush seats and high chequerboard backs, worn, c1903.
£2,500–3,500
$3,600–5,000 ↗ S

A pair of brown-painted wicker armchairs, the curved backs leading to rolled arms above caned seats, on circular banded legs joined by a X-stretchers, c1900.
£1,500–1,600
$2,000–2,300 ↗ S(NY)

Modernism and history

The relationship between 20th-century Modernism and history is complex. There is a significant element of Modernism that rejects historical precedent and seeks to locate Modernism in the logic of industrial production, form and function as a singularly 20th-century phenomenon. This is especially true of the post WWI German Modernism associated with the Bauhaus school. Others, however, lay claim to historical precedents to lend the project authority or authenticity through tradition and materials. The antecedents of the Modernist project are to be found throughout the 19th century in the development of new materials, new technologies of mass production, and in the progressive ideologies of social democratic movements. In Britain, the most widely found form of Modernism is as an archaic styled, but technologically mediated, extension of the metropolis; otherwise called the suburbs or, more affectionately, metroland.

◀ **A set of three mahogany-framed sun loungers,** by Dryad, with caned seats and backs, outswept scroll arms and rubber-tyred wheels, c1938, 63in (160cm) long.
£4,400–5,200
$6,400–7,600 ↗ P
The Dryad firm was established in 1907 by Harry Peach and is known for its association with the Omega Workshops.

▶ **A Lloyd Loom miniature chair,** painted green, 1930s.
£60–65
$90–95 ⊞ SWN

Arts & Crafts Chairs

▶ **An Arts and Crafts oak and elm swivel deskchair,** c1900.
£270–300
$400–450
⊞ COLL

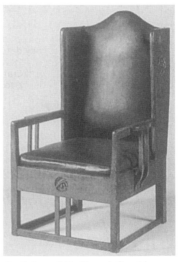

An Arts and Crafts oak fireside chair, with carved wing panels and front apron, labelled Baker & Co, Oxford, c1905.
£500–600
$720–870 ↗ C

An inlaid mahogany chair, the plain top-rail and carved splats above a padded seat, c1900.
£250–350
$360–500 ⊞ APO

Cross Reference
See Colour Review
(page 65–80)

◀ **A set of eight stained ash Clissett chairs,** by Ernest Gimson, with rush seats, c1910.
£2,200–2,500
$3,200–3,600 ↗ S

An oak rocking armchair, by L. & J. G. Stickley, with brown leather drop-in seat and trade label, c1912.
£550–600
$800–870 ⊞ B&B

A limed-oak part dining room suite, by Heal's, London, comprising eight dining chairs, a sideboard and side table, early 20thC, side table 36in (91.5cm) wide.
£2,300–2,750
$3,350–4,000 🔨 S(S)

A set of six ash ladderback chairs, by Gordon Russell, with leather lattice seats, five with metal labels, 1925.
£700–800
$1,000–1,150 🔨 Bri

A limed-oak armchair, c1930.
£150–180
$220–260 ⊞ AnSh

A set of six oak single dining chairs, by Robert (Mouseman) Thompson, with panelled backs and hide seats, c1953.
£1,800–2,000
$2,600–3,000 🔨 TMA

A set of 20 mahogany and holly-strung dining chairs, by Edward Barnsley, made by Herbert Upton, George Taylor, Leal Wyatt and Oskar Dawson, including a pair of open armchairs, the over-scrolled back rails above inset padded backs and drop-in seats, 1956.
£7,200–8,600
$10,500–12,500 🔨 P

Arts and Crafts

The relationship between the Arts and Crafts movement and Modernism in design is problematic. Indeed, the rhetoric of Modernism has tended to identify with the metropolitan and industrial values of consumption. The same values that William Morris considered to be the most alienating and morally deforming aspects of contemporary society in the 19th century. The foundations of the Arts and Crafts movement have their origin in the desire to reconnect people with the integrity of labour and materials. Unfortunately, the priority attached to handicrafts and traditional materials undermined the potential impact of the movement. Without mass production, the alliance of ideas and objects could never reach critical mass. However, the ideas of William Morris and his followers have been, and remain, influential. The relative affluence of this following has given, in Britain at least, a disproportionate significance to the Arts and Crafts legacy and its claim on local traditions and materials. Interestingly, much of the Arts and Crafts vocabulary of honesty, truth and materials, is now used in relation to products of the machine age.

An oak settle, by Gustav Stickley, with slatted back and arms, worn, c1910, 77in (196cm) wide.
£4,200–4,600
$6,000–6,750 🔨 S(NY)

An Arts and Crafts Lifetime oak sofa, No. 719¾, the wide back crest rail above slats, American, c1910, 75½in (192cm) wide.
£1,000–1,500
$1,500–2,150 🔨 SK

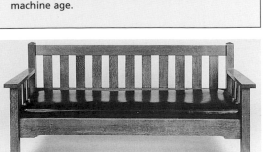

◀ **An oak settle,** with sprung cushion seat, American, c1912, 81in (205.5cm) wide.
£700–800
$1,000–1,150 🔨 SK

Art Deco Chairs

A pair of mahogany armchairs, by André Sornay, upholstered in taupe leather, A. Sornay mark, French, c1930.
£5,250–6,500
$7,500–9,500 ➤ S(NY)

A satinwood and upholstered three-piece suite, comprising sofa and two armchairs, French, c1930, sofa 67¾in (172cm) wide.
£1,000–1,500
$1,500–2,200 ➤ S(O)

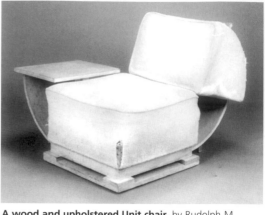

A wood and upholstered Unit chair, by Rudolph M. Schindler, custom manufactured, designed 1930s, 26in (66cm) high with seat back attached.
£26,000–31,000
$37,700–45,000 ➤ BB(L)
This piece is designed to allow the addition of a table and seat back, or for use as a stand-alone ottoman.

Art deco

The Art Deco style of the 1920s and '30s is most closely associated with France after the launch of the style at the 1925 *Exposition des Arts Décoratifs* from which it gets its shortened name. After the austerity and trauma of WWI, the style marked a return to the essential French values of quality materials and traditional execution by skilled artisan craftsmen.

These qualities are enshrined in French culture by the tradition of training in *arts et metiers* which goes back to the beginning of the 19th century. The Art Deco style was therefore part of a project to recast French society along traditional lines.

The style has since become associated more with cinema and the marine architecture of ocean liners. By emphasizing the qualities of tradition, skill and materials the movement has some similarities to the Anglo-Saxon Arts and Crafts tradition. However, the French movement is more forward-looking in its ideas and more flexible in its class associations than its English counterpart.

A six-piece beechwood salon suite, c1930, settee 50in (127cm) wide.
£3,000–3,500
$4,500–5,000 ⊞ B&B

A pair of walnut and leather-upholstered Cloud chairs, 1930s.
£850–950
$1,250–1,400 ➤ S(NY)

A set of four walnut-veneered dining chairs, French, 1930s.
£850–950
$1,250–1,400 ➤ P(B)

◄ **A walnut and leather three-piece suite,** re-covered, 1940, sofa 74in (188cm) wide.
£1,700–1,900
$2,500–2,750 ⊞ JAZZ

A pair of birchwood upholstered armchairs, Swedish, early 1930s.
£3,000–3,400
$4,500–5,000 ⊞ CAV

A pair of maple-veneered tub armchairs, by Ray Hille, c1930.
£700–800
$1,000–1,150 ⊞ MoS

A child's desk and chair, design attributed to H. Wouda, painted in red and black, Dutch, c1930, table 19in (48.5cm) high.
£750–900
$1,100–1,300 ⚒ S(Am)

Gerrit Rietveld

Gerrit Rietveld (1888–1964) was a Dutch architect and furniture designer associated with the Modernist group De Stijl, of which the Modern painter Mondrian was also a member. Rietveld's furniture has a geometric austerity and transparency that are the result of a programmatic approach to design. The Red/Blue chair is probably one of the most famous – and least sat on – chairs of the 20th century. Very few early examples survive and they command a high value as museum-quality objects. However, the chair has been widely reproduced and later examples are available.

An white-patinated elm Zigzag chair, by Gerrit Rietveld, manufactured by Gerard van de Groenekan, Dutch, 1940s.
£2,200–2,500
$3,200–3,600 ⚒ S(Am)

A painted deal Berlin chair, by Gerrit Rietveld, with trade label, designed 1923, manufactured by Gerard van de Groenekan, Dutch, c1960.
£10,000–12,000
$14,500–17,500 ⚒ S(NY)

Functionalist Chairs

A birch-veneered moulded plywood armchair, by Gerald Summers for Makers of Simple Furniture, with a drop-in sprung seat, designed 1933–34.
£4,000–4,500
$5,800–6,500 ⚒ Bon

Cross Reference

For more Chairs see Dining Room (page 59–64)

▶ **A laminated wood chair,** by Gerald Summers for Makers of Simple Furniture, c1935.
£1,800–2,000
$2,600–3,000 ⚒ S

Plywood

Plywood has its origin in the laminate experiments of the 19th century. The creation of large sheets of this material opened the way for creating three-dimensional designs from a two-dimensional sheet by cutting and folding. These are procedures that could be made completely mechanical and lend themselves to industrial-style production. The pioneer designer of plywood furniture was the Finnish architect Alvar Aalto. His designs were imported to Britain by Jack Pritchard's Isokon and the range was developed to include further designs by the German emigré architect Walter Gropius. Plywood furniture was well received in Britain where it seemed to combine well with the nautical emphasis of much modern design. Other names associated with plywood include Gerald Summers, Charles Eames and Ernest Race.

A pair of moulded plywood side chairs, by Gerald Summers for Makers of Simple Furniture,1930s.
£4,000–4,500
$5,800–6,500 ↗ Bon

A child's pressure-formed birch plywood chair, by Alvar Aalto for Artek, worn, Finnish, 1930s.
£1,000–1,200
$1,500–1,750 ↗ BUK

A laminated birch dining chair, by Alvar Aalto for Finmar, with maker's label, 1930s.
£150–180
$220–260 ↗ DORO

An ebonized plywood and birch-framed 403 side chair, by Alvar Aalto for Finmar, model No. 51, with Finmar retail label, c1930.
£600–720
$870–1,000 ↗ Bon

A plywood and birch-framed 403 armchair, by Alvar Aalto for Finmar, model No. 51, with remnants of Finmar label, c1930.
£500–600
$720–870 ↗ B(Ba)

◄ **A laminated birch cantilver-framed armchair,** by Alvar Aalto, model No. 400, Finnish, 1935–36.
£3,200–3,800
$4,500–5,500 ↗ S

A plywood and laminated Springleaf armchair, by Alvar Aalto, model No. 379, 1932.
£1,600–2,000
$2,300–3,000 ↗ Bon

▶ **A laminated birch and upholstered easy chair,** by Alvar Aalto for Finmar, model No 400, with sprung seat and back, c1935.
£1,200–1,400
$1,750–2,000
↗ Bon

Modernism and chairs

Chair design holds a special place in the development of modern furniture and design. It is true to say that the chair is the totem object of Modernism and a number of chairs have achieved iconic status within the Modernist story. The origins of this status are to found in the reduced architecture of the Modernist interior – functional, small, economic and with fitted storage – the chair becoming the single most significant object within a minimalist setting. The material and structural complexities of chair design also give this problem a specific appeal to architects and designers who considered themselves, at least in the middle part of the 20th century, as problem solvers foremost.

In addition to the usual appeal of materials, craft and structure, the modern chair may be seen as a piece of sculpture. Indeed, the chair lends itself to the contemporary taste for collecting iconic pieces as stand-alone objects.

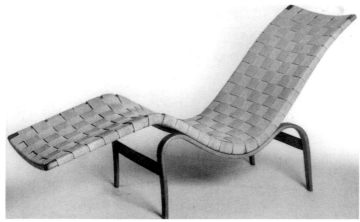

A moulded beech-framed Pernilla chaise longue, by Bruno Mathsson for Karl Mathsson, Swedish, with hemp webbing, stamped maker's mark, c1934.
£750–900
$1,100–1,300 ⚒ Bon

A laminated wood chaise longue, by Marcel Breuer for Isokon, damaged, c1935.
£1,000–1,200
$1,500–1,750 ⚒ P

A plywood long chair, by Marcel Breuer for Isokon, 1936.
£3,000–3,500
$4,500–5,000 ⚒ RBB

Isokon

Jack Pritchard (b.1899) established Isokon as both a manufacturing company of plywood furniture in the 1930s and as a cultural conduit for the introduction of radical ideas into Britain. Pritchard's background was in building materials where he began to appreciate the potential of plywood for moulding into furniture. He was instrumental in commissioning avant-garde architects to design for Isokon and in making their products available in Britain. Marcel Breuer's 'chaise longue' is probably the most famous Isokon product. The firm was re-established recently and continues to commission new furniture designs as well as manufacturing their classic range.

A set of four dark-stained pine garden chairs, by Alvar Aalto, Finnish, 1938–39.
£5,000–5,500
$7,250–8,000 ⚒ S

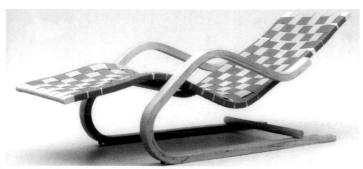

A laminated bent beechwood recliner, by Alvar Aalto for Artek, model No. 39, with red and beige webbing, slight damage, Finnish, c1940.
£3,000–3,600
$4,500–5,000 ⚒ BUK

A wood and webbing lounge chair, by Alvar Aalto, model No. 406, Finnish, 1946.
£400–450
$580–650 ⊞ PLB

◄ **A dark-stained oak-veneered plywood chair,** by Harry Rosenthal, with dark brown stain, some restoration, German, 1926.
£2,000–2,200
$3,000–3,200 ⚒ DORO

A set of six beech dining chairs, by Sir Basil Spence for Thonet, 1930s.
£1,700–2,000
$2,500–3,000 ⚒ P(Ed)

A beechwood and upholstered armchair, by Heal & Son, 1930s.
£250–300
$360–440 ⊞ BTB

A wood and upholstered lounge chair, by Frank Lloyd Wright, 1940–41.
£7,000–8,400
$4,700–12,300 ⚒ BB(L)

A beech-veneered plywood chair, by Erich Menzel, model No. 50 642, German, 1949–50.
£1,375–1,700
$2,000–2,500 ⚒ DORO

◄ **A birch-veneered plywood chair,** by Kaes Braakman for UMS Pastoe, Dutch, 1950.
£450–550
$650–800 ⚒ DORO

A set of four plywood side chairs, by Max Bill, Swiss, c1950.
£1,500–1,800
$2,200–2,600 ⚒ BB(L)

A pair of plywood and upholstered chairs, by John Wright, laminated plywood shell cut from the drum, with brown leather-covered padded seats and backs, one chair seat missing, one stamped Peacock Room, 1960.
£3,000–3,500
$4,500–5,000 ⚒ P
These chairs were designed for the *Canberra* cruise liner, the interior of which is significant from a design perspective as it presented a rare opportunity for British architects and designers of the period to show their talents. On *Canberra*, the largest team of designers ever to be assembled for a British ship created a modern look, with experimental lighting, cutting edge furniture designs and architectural ploys. These chairs were designed for the Peacock Room café/lounge area. Variants of Wright's cut-out plywood chair appear in other communal areas onboard.

A tubular metal-framed stool, by Le Corbusier, Pierre Jeanneret and Charlotte Perriand for Thonet, original metal label, Austrian, c1930, 18½in (47cm) high.
£3,500–4,000
$5,000–5,800 ⚒ S

A chromed tubular steel and plywood armchair, attributed to Mart Stam, c1930.
£400–500
$580–720 ⚒ P(Ba)

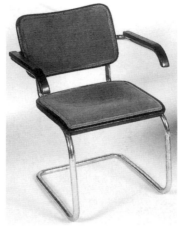

A pair of tubular steel armchairs, by Thonet, with upholstered seats, backs with enamel Thonet badge, Austrian, c1930.
£100–120
$145–175 ⚒ B(B)

A pair of chromium-plated club chairs, by Mart Stam for Thonet, with cantilever frames, the seats and backs covered in green dogtooth check Rexine, Austrian, c1930.
£1,000–1,200
$1,500–1,750 ⚒ P(Ba)
Made for the staff recreation club of the BATA factory, these two chairs were part of a shipment brought to Britain when BATA, a Czechoslovakian company, re-located to Tilbury, Essex to escape the Nazis in 1938. This design is the first formal armchair of Stam's using the cantilever principle.

◄ **A tubular steel and ebonized plywood armchair,** Czechoslovakian, c1930.
£200–250
$290–360 ⚒ Bon

A pair of tubular chromed steel and wood B64 armchairs, by Marcel Breuer for Thonet, c1930.
£200–250
$290–360 ⚒ B(B)

Tubular metal

Tubular metal became widely available after WWI and was quickly recognized by furniture designers as a material that lent itself to industrial manufacture. The shapes of tubular metal furniture are simpler than those of Michel Thonet's bentwood creations – they aspire to the minimalist excitement of cantilever engineering.
It was an obvious extension of the Thonet firm's activities to begin manufacturing metal furniture during the 1920s. In chromium-plated form the metal structures reflect light and achieve a weightless transparency that is the apotheosis of machine-age modern.
The architects of the Bauhaus school in Germany are associated with its most avant-garde use. In Britain, PEL manufactured tubular furniture in great quantity and their products became popular in England after WWII.

◄ **A tubular steel and canvas beach lounger,** by Battista and Gino Giudici, the arms bound with plastic, c1930.
£1,300–1,500
$1,900–2,200 ⚒ DORO

► **A tubular steel folding lounger,** by Embru/Schweiz with fabric seating, 15¾in (40cm) high.
£440–500
$630–720 ⚒ DORO

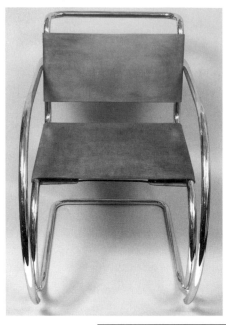

A tubular metal MR10 chair, designed by Ludwig Mies van der Rohe for Berliner Metallgewerbe, 1927–31.
£1,200–1,350
$1,800–2,000 ⊞ ORI

◀ A tubular metal MR20 chair, by Ludwig Mies van der Rohe, with leather seat and back, 1927.
£200–225
$290–320 ⊞ ZOOM

A tubular metal MR10 chair, designed by Ludwig Mies van der Rohe for Knoll International, American, c1970.
£250–275
$360–400 ⊞ PLB

▶ A tubular anodized aluminium chaise longue, by Warren McArthur, with rubber webbing, c1930, 64½in (162.5cm) long.
£17,500–21,000
$25,500–30,500
⚒ BB(L)

A chromed tubular steel and bent plywood upholstered chair, by Jean Royère, c1936.
£5,500–6,200
$8,000–9,000 ⊞ MI

A pair of tubular steel and leather cantilever lounge chairs, with padded seats and ebonized wood armrests, c1930.
£300–350
$440–500 ⚒ Bon

A set of six chromed tubular steel and Rexine SP9 dining chairs, by Rowland Wilton-Cox for PEL, stamped brass labels, 1932–34.
£700–800
$1,000–1,150 ⚒ P(Ba)

A chrome and vinyl diner bar stool, on a later iron base, 1950s.
£40–45
$60–65 ⊞ TRA

A tubular steel Wassily chair, designed by Marcel Breuer for Habitat, c1960.
£110–125
$160–180 ⊞ MARK

A chrome and plastic bar stool, Italian, 1970.
£40-45
$60-65 ⊞ Har

A pair of steel-framed Brno side chairs, by Ludwig Mies van der Rohe for Knoll International, the flattened steel frame with leather seat and back, 1929–30.
£500–600
$720–870 ✗ B(Ba)

A pair of chrome-plated metal and leather Brno chairs, by Ludwig Mies van der Rohe for Knoll International, American, designed, 1929–30.
£1,400–1,600
$2,000–2,300 ✗ S(Am)

Folded metal

The chief exponent of folded metal furniture design was the French radical designer Jean Prouvé. Prouvé was keen to apply industrial processes to the manufacture of simple furniture and borrowed from the aviation and automotive industries. His designs were widely used by the educational and public sector in France during the 1940s and '50s. His designs are functional and have a mid-century utopian quality that is derived from the relentless logic of Prouvés experiments with materials and production.

▶ **A set of four chrome-plated flat steel Brno chairs,** designed by Ludwig Mies van der Rohe for Knoll Associates, the cantilever frame with padded leather seat and back, c1960.
£950–1,150
$1,400–1,600
✗ Bon

◀ **A pair of chrome-plated steel and leather Basculant armchairs,** by Le Corbusier, Charlotte Perriand and Pierre Jeanneret for Aram, back rail stamped, late 1960s.
£650–750
$950–1,100
✗ Bon

A pair of stainless steel and leather Barcelona chairs, by Ludwig Mies van der Rohe for Knoll Associates, with padded leather cushions on saddle-leather straps, label on underside of cushion, c1960.
£1,600–1,800
$2,300–2,600 ✗ Bon

A chrome-plated tubular steel and leather LC2 sofa, by Le Corbusier c1925, 50in (127cm) wide.
£1,000–1,200
$1,500–1,700 ✗ BB(L)

A mahogany and suede sofa, designed by Ludwig Mies van der Rohe for Jerry Griffith, American, c1940, 91in (231cm) wide.
£3,200–3,500
$4,650–5,000 ✗ BB(L)
This piece was owned by the noted architect James DeForrest Ferris, who studied at the Illinois Institute of Technology under the personal tutelage of Ludwig Mies van der Rohe. While a student, he obtained a suite of 13 pieces from the Mies van der Rohe workshop in Chicago. This rare pre-production sofa from the suite retains its original suede upholstery.

Mid-Century Chairs

A fibreglass La Chaise chair, by Charles and Ray Eames, with iron rods on a wooden base, designed 1940s.
£3,200–3,500
$4,650–5,000 ➚ Bon
This chair was originally designed in the 1940s as a proposal for the Museum of Modern Art International Competition for Furniture Design. Although La Chaise was not one of the prize-winning designs, its elegant form made it one of the most notable competition entries, appearing in both the catalogue and the exhibition of 1950.

A bent plywood LCW chair, by Charles and Ray Eames, designed 1940s, manufactured c1970.
£700–800
$1,000–1,150 ⊞ MARK

A moulded plywood and chrome DCW chair, c1950.
£380–425
$560–620 ⊞ PLB

Fibreglass and plastics

The possibility of manufacturing furniture from plastics and fibreglass emerged after WWII. In America, Charles (1907–78) and Ray Eames (1912–88) had begun experimenting with moulded structures during WWII and produced a leg-splint design in plywood. These early experiments were put to use in the 1950s for the design of fibreglass chairs. Many variations of the designs were produced. During the late 1960s and early '70s plastic was adopted by designers in a self-conscious attempt to get away from the beaux-arts aesthetics of hand-made furniture, and from the sleek corporatist associations of metal and leather furniture. The spirit of fun and invention in the use of plastics for furniture was diminished by later environmental concerns and by the relative fragility of the material.

A fibreglass DAR chair, by Charles and Ray Eames for Herman Miller, on an Eiffel Tower base, marked Herman Miller, designed 1948–50, manufactured 1950–53.
£270–350
$400–500 ➚ BUK

A set of four fibreglass DSR chairs, by Charles and Ray Eames for Herman Miller, on tubular metal Eiffel Tower bases, marked Herman Miller, c1950.
£620–700
$900–1,000 ➚ BUK

A fibreglass chair, by Charles Eames for Herman Miller, with plastic-coated metal frame and vinyl seat, c1950.
£230–260
$330–380 ➚ S

Mid-century

The turn of Modernism after WWII was very different in the USA and in Europe.
In America, the war effort had produced a victorious and booming economy. New mass production techniques and new materials were put into service providing comfort and convenience through technology and science.
The atomic age was understood to be an age of progress.
In Europe, the period of reconstruction was an anxious one. Modernism embraced a social democtatic project and found expression in the infrastructure of the welfare state and social housing. This often looks small and a bit unworthy in relation to its shiny American cousin.

◀ A pair of fibreglass DAR chairs, by Charles and Ray Eames, on Eiffel Tower bases, first edition, 1957.
£675–750
$975–$1,100 ⊞ MARK

Design and the affluent society

Western economies have enjoyed a long period of stability and growth during the second half of the 20th century. This has resulted in the emergence of what J.K. Galbraith has called 'the affluent society' driven by the consumption of an ever-increasing abundance of goods and services. Design serves the affluent society by creating new products. The concepts of Modernism provide a framework for the ideas of progress and convenience that support our desire for the new. We are so wealthy now that new products may be consumed regardless of material need – we may replace our furniture, as part of a makeover – long before it wears out. The affluent society transforms consumption into a series of lifestyle choices.

▶ **A fibreglass DAR chair,** by Charles and Ray Eames, on a wire rod base, c1955.
£400–450
$580–650 ⊞ **MARK**

A wire rod and vinyl DKR chair, by Charles and Ray Eames, first edition, c1953.
£280–350
$400–500 ⊞ **MARK**

A pair of wire rod and vinyl DKR-2 chairs, by Charles and Ray Eames for Herman Miller, c1953.
£360–420
$520–620 ⚒ **BB(L)**

A chrome-plated DKR chair, by Charles and Ray Eames, with vinyl bikini pads, American, designed 1951, manufactured from 1980s.
£250–300
$350–450 ⊞ **MARK**

A DKR chair, by Charles and Ray Eames for Herman Miller, on a bent wire frame with stove-enamelled and black vinyl finish, beige wool-covered bikini, designed 1951, manufactured c1952.
£450–550
$650–800 ⚒ **Bon**

A DAR rocking chair, by Charles and Ray Eames for Herman Miller, with grey fibreglass seat, 1950.
£650–750
$950–1,100 ⚒ **Bon**

A brown fibreglass rocking chair, by Charles and Ray Eames for Herman Miller, with wooden rocker and Eiffel Tower metal base, late 1950s.
£350–425
$500–625 ⊞ **PLB**

◀ **A pair of blue swivel side chairs,** by Charles and Ray Eames for Herman Miller, c1953.
£350–420
$500–600 ⚒ **BB(L)**

▶ **A white fibreglass DAR chair,** by Charles Eames, with Eiffel Tower chrome base, 1970s.
£200–250
$300–350 ⊞ **PLB**

An Aluminium Group armchair and stool, by Charles and Ray Eames for Herman Miller, c1960.
£900–1,100
$1,300–1,600 ⚒ S

A chrome chair, by Charles Eames, with black upholstery, c1960.
£550–650
$800–1,000 ⊞ ZOOM

An Aluminium Group armchair, by Charles and Ray Eames for Herman Miller, c1960.
£200–250
$300–350 ⊞ MARK

An aluminium Soft Pad chair, by Charles and Ray Eames for Herman Miller, with brown leather-covered padded seat and back, 1960s.
£200–250
$300–360 ⚒ Bon

An Aluminium Group chair and stool, by Charles and Ray Eames for Herman Miller, c1960.
£600–700
$870–1,000 ⚒ SLN

An aluminium Soft Pad desk chair, by Charles and Ray Eames for Herman Miller, with black leather-covered padded seat and back, swivel/tilt mechanism, designed 1960s, manufactured 1970s.
£900–1,000
$1,300–1,500 ⚒ Bon

◄ **A Tandem Sling seating unit,** by Charles and Ray Eames for Herman Miller, the two pairs of seats separated by a table, with cast-aluminium steel frame and charcoal grey vinyl seats, c1960.
£1,000–1,200
$1,500–1,750 ⚒ Bon

An Aluminium Group armchair, by Charles Eames for Herman Miller, with ribbed red fabric on a five-support swivel base with casters, c1960.
£500–575
$720–820 ⚒ Bri

A Time Life lobby chair, by Charles and Ray Eames for Herman Miller, with black leather-covered padded seat and back, on a cast-aluminium frame with white nylon glides, c1960.
£400–500
$580–720 ⚒ Bon

A Time Life lounge chair, by Charles and Ray Eames for Herman Miller, with pale tan leather-covered padded seat and back, on a cast-aluminium base, c1960.
£1,000–1,200
$1,500–1,750 ⚒ Bon

► **A rosewood 670 lounge chair,** by Charles and Ray Eames for Herman Miller, with black leather-covered padding, on an aluminium pedestal, American, 1956.
£1,600–1,800
$2,300–2,600
➴ Bon

A rosewood 670 lounge chair, by Charles and Ray Eames for Herman Miller, with black leather-covered padding, on an aluminium pedestal, armrests restored, American, 1956.
£1,150–1,300
$1,650–1,900 ➴ Bon

A laminated plywood and black leather Lounge Chair and Ottoman, by Charles and Ray Eames for Herman Miller for Hille, model Nos. A670 and A671, restored, labelled, 1956.
£800–1,000
$1,150–1,500 ➴ Bon

A plywood and steel Compact sofa, by Charles and Ray Eames for Herman Miller, with vinyl upholstery, c1965.
£1,000–1,200
$1,500–1,700 ➴ BB(L)

LOCATE THE SOURCE
The source of each illustration in Miller's can be found by checking the code letters below each caption with the Key to Illustrations, pages 296–298.

► **A walnut valet chair,** by Johannes Hansen, model No. PP250, the seat hinged to reveal a well, c1953.
£1,500–1,800
$2,200–2,600 ➴ SK

A black-enamelled steel Sofa Compact, by Charles and Ray Eames for Herman Miller, upholstery by Alexander Girard, on chrome-plated steel legs, 1954.
£2,200–2,600
$3,200–3,800 ➴ Bon

A set of four oak chairs, by Hans J. Wegner, with cane seats, wear and minor cane damage, marked C. M. Madsens, 1960.
£550–650
$800–950 ➴ BUK

A teak and woven cane armchair, by Hans J. Wegner for Johannes Hansen, Danish, 1949.
£525–625
$750–900 ↗ BUK

A teak armchair, by Hans J. Wegner for Johannes Hansen, with black leather seat, Danish, 1949.
£750–1,000
$1,100–1,500 ↗ DORO

A pair of teak and woven cane armchairs, by Hans J. Wegner for Johannes Hansen, Danish, 1949.
£1,600–2,000
$2,300–3,000 ↗ BUK

An oak-veneered pressure-formed plywood armchair, by Hans J. Wegner for Carl Hansen & Sons, with branded stamp, Danish, 1950s.
£1,200–1,400
$1,750–2,000 ↗ DORO

A copper Sjuan tube chair, by Arne Jacobsen for Fritz Hansen, Model No. 3107, covered in brown leather, torn and printmarked, 1950s.
£200–250
$300–350 ↗ BUK

A steel and pine Swivel chair, by Hans J. Wegner for Johannes Hansen, with brown leather seat, the steel frame with central split strut with steel feet and later casters, wear and tear, metal tag, 1960.
£8,750–10,000
$12,500–14,500 ↗ BUK

Craft traditions and mass production

Post-WWII Scandinavian furniture design achieved world-wide recognition. The Scandinavian furniture manufacturers were early exponents of flat-pack export and their designs were ideally suited to the new residential architectures of European reconstruction and, later, of affluence. The designs are rooted in the fine cabinet-making traditions of the Scandinavian furniture workshops. The industry made wide use of teak and rosewood as materials.

A teak Easy chair and footstool, by Hans J. Wegner for Johannes Hansen, with leather and wool upholstery, c1953, footstool 27½in (70cm) wide.
£2,800–3,200
$4,000–4,600 ↗ BB(L)

An ash and teak Peacock chair, by Hans J. Wegner for Johannes Hansen, Danish, c1947.
£4,500–5,000
$6,500–7,250 ↗ WDG

A pale oak plank sofa, by Hans J. Wegner for Getama, with leather-covered back and seat cushions, on sprung webbing, Danish, 1955.
£580–700
$850–1,000 ⚒ Bon

A pair of pale oak plank armchairs, by Hans J. Wegner, with tan leather-covered seat and back cushions, on sprung rubber webbing, Danish, Getama, c1955.
£800–1,000
$1,150–1,500 ⚒ Bon

A set of six Ant chairs, by Arne Jacobsen for Fritz Hansen, 1952.
£850–1,000
$1,250–1,500 ⊞ MARK

An oak sawback chair, by Hans J. Wegner for Carl Hansen, the cream fabric padded seat and back within a turned and carved oak frame, ink stamp to underside, designed 1951, manufactured 1960s.
£800–1,000
$1,150–1,500 ⚒ Bon

An aluminium prototype chair, by Arne Jacobsen, c1960.
£6,250–7,250
$8,750–10,500 ⚒ BB(L)

Miller's is a price GUIDE not a price LIST

▶ **An armchair,** by Arne Jacobsen for Fritz Hansen, model No. 3107, 1955.
£450–550
$650–800 ⚒ BB(L)

A metal and plywood Seagull chair, by Arne Jacobsen for Fritz Hansen, Model No. 3108, with pale olive green lacquer finish, the back legs extending upwards to support the elliptical armrests, moulded marks, designed 1970, manufactured 1971.
£1,200–1,400
$1,750–2,000 ⚒ P(Ba)

A set of six chairs, by Arne Jacobsen for Fritz Hansen, Danish, designed 1952, manufactured 1965.
£475–575
$700–850 ⚒ DORO

An Ant chair, by Arne Jacobsen for Fritz Hansen, Series 3103, 1955.
£90–110
$130–160 ⊞ ORI

A black wood and metal Grandprix chair, by Arne Jacobsen for Fritz Hansen, 1972.
£75–85
$110–125 ⊞ PLB

A chrome-plated tubular steel Drop side chair, by Arne Jacobsen, with vinyl-covered padded seat and back, c1960.
£900–1,100
$1,300–1,600 ⚲ Bon
This is one of 300 chairs designed and manufactured exclusively for the SAS Royal Hotel, Copenhagen.

▶ **A leather Egg chair,** by Arne Jacobsen for Fritz Hansen, with tan leather-covered padded shell and seat pad, on a cast-aluminium pedestal, c1960.
£4,000–5,000
$5,800–7,250 ⚲ Bon

A Pot chair, by Arne Jacobsen for Fritz Hansen, model No. 3318, c1960.
£750–1,000
$1,100–1,500 ⚲ BB(L)

A cast-aluminium Swan chair, by Arne Jacobsen for Fritz Hansen, with turquoise upholstery, marked, c1960.
£250–280
$350–400 ⚲ DN

An Egg chair, by Arne Jacobsen, on an aluminium swivel base, c1960.
£450–550
$650–800 ⚲ S(O)

◀ **An Egg chair,** by Arne Jacobsen for Fritz Hansen, with pale green hop-sack upholstery, on an aluminium pedestal foot, c1960.
£750–1,000
$1,100–1,500 ⚲ Bon

▶ **An Egg chair,** by Arne Jacobsen for Fritz Hansen, c1960.
£850–1,000
$1,250–1,500 ⚲ Bon

Mid-Century USA

After WWII the USA took up the lead in modern design and developed a style that reflected the affluence and optimism of society. Several key strands in design came together to give mid-20th century American design a distinctive appeal. The high design of metropolitan East and West coasts is epitomized in the work of the Eames and of George Nelson. This high-end design was adopted by American corporate culture and became the look of an expansive global capitalism. At the same time American factories mass produced furnishings and home goods for the mass market – this 'diner design' is robust, large-scaled and calls to mind the styling of American cars of the 1950s.

◀ **A laminated beech and white enamelled-steel school desk and chair,** by Jean Prouvé, the desk lid in solid beech, 1930s, 24½in (62cm) wide.
£1,000–1,100
$1,500–1,600 ⚲ DORO

A Biltmore armchair, by Warren McArthur, 1933.
£4,000–5,000
$5,800–7,250 ⚒ BB(L)

An aluminium and vinyl folding chair, by Warren McArthur, 1933.
£145–175
$210–250 ⚒ BB(L)

A set of cast re-smelted aluminium dining chairs, by Edwin Clinch for Good Earl Brothers, the seats and backs upholstered in textured green Rexine, on detachable cast-aluminium legs with black rubber caps, stamped mark to underside of seat, designed 1945, manufactured 1946.
£750–850
$1,100–1,250 ⚒ P

A Goodform aluminium side chair, with undulating back, c1950.
£525–625
$750–900 ⚒ BB(L)

A photographer's portrait chair, American, 1950s.
£350–400
$500–580 ⚒ BB(L)

▶ **A chrome SE 40 chair,** by Egon Eiermann for Wilde & Spieth, with black leather back, seat and armrest, on four casters, 1952.
£800–950
$1,150–1,350 ⚒ DORO

A pair of theatre armchairs, by Poul Henningsen, with black-lacquered tubular steel frames and copper back splats, 1957.
£600–700
$870–1,000 ⚒ BUK

▶ **A bar stool,** by Zoftig, Bude, Cornwall, 1960s.
£300–350
$440–500 ⊞ ZOOM

A set of three stainless steel adjustable stools, American, 1960s.
£260–300
$380–350 ⚒ BB(L)

A teak stool, by Mogens Lassen for K. Thomsen, Danish, 1942, 20in (51cm) high.
£2,200–2,600
$3,200–3,800 ⚹ BB(L)

A bent rosewood-veneered plywood Butterfly stool, designed by Sori Yanagi for Tendo Mokko, with a brass rod, 1954.
£850–1,000
$1,250–1,500 ⚹ Bon

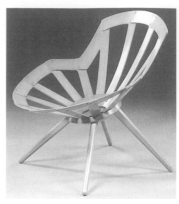

A plywood chair, by Gregotti, Meneghetti and Stoppino for SIM, 1954.
£4,800–5,200
$7,000–7,500 ⚹ S

◀ **A beech, brass and leather folding chair,** by Mogens Koch, for Interna, Rud Rasmussens Snedkerier Aps, designed 1932, manufactured 1960.
£220–250
$320–360 ⚹ WDG
The concept for this chair was influenced by the Safari chairs designed by Kaare Klint. Considered too avant-garde to be produced in 1932, this design was not manufactured until 1960, since when it has become an icon in the history of Danish chair design.

▶ **A set of three rosewood and black hide high stools,** Danish, c1960, 20in (51cm) high.
£500–575
$720–850 ⊞ MARK

▶ **A rocking lounger,** by Franco Albini, with a stretched canvas seat, c1940, 63in (160cm) long.
£4,200–4,800
$6,000–7,000 ⚹ S(NY)

Further reading
Miller's Collecting Modern Design,
Miller's Publications, 2001

A wicker and metal bar stool, 1950s, 32in (81.5cm) high.
£25–30
$35–45 ⊞ Har

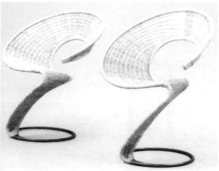

A pair of wicker armchairs, by Vittorio Bonacina, repaired, Italian, 1963.
£475–575
$700–850 ⚹ BUK

◀ **A chocolate cake pop art stool,** c1970s.
£150–165
$220–235 ⊞ PLB

A pair of tubular armchairs, after Carlo Mollino, 1950s.
£450–500
$650–720 ✗ WBH

◄ A steel, bronze and leatherette side chair, by Jean Royère, 1940s.
£20,000–25,000
$30,000–37,000 ✗ BB(L)

A birch and chromed-steel rocking stool, by Isamu Noguchi for Knoll Associates, designed c1953, manufactured c1955, seat 14in (35.5cm) diam.
£3,500–4,000
$5,000–5,800 ✗ B&B

A painted wood, aluminium and plywood side chair, by Richard Neutra, with upholstered seat and back, pencil mark, c1938.
£2,000–2,500
$3,000–3,500 ✗ BB(L)

Terence Conran

The 1960s and '70s saw the development of a new style of furniture retailing pioneered in Britain by Terence Conran's Habitat store. Conran (b1931) had visited France and Italy during the 1950s and saw the potential In their traditions of manufacturing and display. The store format grouped furniture together in lifestyle areas and complemented them with stacked displays of smaller items. The effect was to create an exciting feeling of abundance – borrowed from the market stalls of Provence – to entice the consumer. This approach was very different from the conservative and insular strategies adopted by the established furniture trade with their 'ideal home' aesthetics. The growth of popular travel, particularly to the Mediterranean, supported the sophistication of Conran's presentation. The store format continues today.

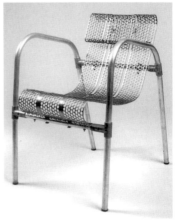

A pierced metal armchair, by Adrien Claude for Meubles Artistiques Modernes, 1950.
£1,500–1,800
$2,200–2,600 ✗ DORO

A pair of beech armchairs, upholstered in cream vinyl, on swept-back legs and short splayed tapering front legs, 1950s.
£1,200–1,400
$1,750–2,000 ✗ P(B)

A wicker chair, by Terence Conran, on metal hairpin legs, 1960s.
£85–95
$125–140 ⊞ MARK

A teak-faced S88 folding chair, by Osvaldo Borsani for Tecno, on articulated black-enamelled tubular steel frame with rubber insulators, with manufacturer's metal disc, designed 1957, manufactured 1960s.
£750–1,000
$1,000–1,500 ✗ Bon

A Modern Art chair,
Canadian, 1950s.
£280–320
$400–460 ⚒ BB(L)

**A polished steel table
and four chairs,** with Lloyd
Loom seats, 1950s.
£3,200–3,500
$4,700–5,000 ▦ ZOOM

A dining room suite, by
Brattrud & Richardson,
comprising a rosewood
extending table on a
pedestal base, and eight
laminated palisander and
chromium-plated chairs
with wooden splats, on
metal supports, c1958.
£350–450
$500–650 ⚒ P(B)

A wooden side chair, by
Piero Fornasetti, transfer-
printed with a design of a
capital, 1950s.
£2,000–2,500
$3,000–3,500 ⚒ BB(L)

A wooden Sedia chair, by
Piero Fornasetti, with
transfer-printed back and
detachable seat,
manufacturer's paper label,
Italian, 1950s.
£750–1,000
$1,000–1,500 ⚒ Bon

**A black-lacquered
Leggera chair,** by Gio
Ponti, with rush seat,
Italian, designed 1957,
manufactured 1960s.
£550–650
$800–950 ⚒ DORO

▶ **A teak-
laminated side
chair,** by Grete
Jalk for Paul
Jeppesen, Danish,
1963.
£4,750–5,250
$7,000–7,500
⚒ CSK
**This chair is a
very important
designer piece,
hence its high
value.**

▶ **A set of four side chairs,** by Nathan Lerner, c1950.
£1,200–1,500
$1,750–2,200 ⚒ BB(L)

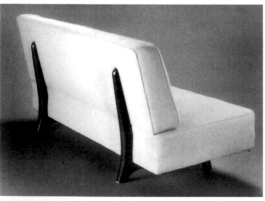

A couch, by Edward Wormley for Dunbar Furniture Co, 1948.
£2,800–3,300
$4,000–4,800 ⚒ BB(L)

▶ **An oak and white-painted tubular metal chaise
longue,** by Jean Prouvé, c1950, 60in (152.5cm) long.
£8,500–10,000
$12,500–14,500 ⚒ S(NY)

Four steel and plywood Antelope chairs, by Ernest Race, c1950.
£120–140
$175–225 ⚑ L
These chairs were originally designed for the Festival of Britain in 1951.

Ernest Race

Ernest Race (1913–64) is a little-known, but influential, British furniture designer. Working from the 1940s onwards, Race developed a system for making furniture from the materials at hand after WWII. Thus he pioneered the use of steel rod frame construction for seating furniture but this was only possible with the development of foam to fill the frame. His most famous chair is probably the 'Antelope' chair designed for outside use and shown at the Festival of Britain in 1951. The chair complemented the architecture of the Festival perfectly and helped to develop the idea of a public space for leisure with café seating – a hitherto mostly Continental concept. Race furniture is functional, restrained and robust.

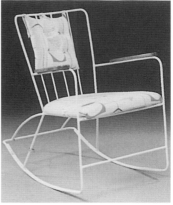

A white-painted metal rod rocking chair, by Ernest Race for Race Furniture, with mahogany armrests, c1950.
£350–400
$500–580 ⚑ S

A white-painted metal rod rocking chair, by Ernest Race for Race Furniture, with oak arm rests, crewelwork upholstered seat and back cushion, c1950.
£100–120
$145–175 ⚑ M

A hardwood reclining chair, by Robin Day for Hille, the one-piece frame with button-back and adjustable headrest, with ash table arms, 1952.
£800–1,000
$1,150–1,500 ⚑ Bon

A Form Group unit four-seat seating system, by Robin Day for Hille, each with ebonized plywood back with grey, cream and black striped tweed fabric, with a coffee table and pad seat, on black-enamelled squared steel frames, 1961, each frame 83in (211cm) wide.
£1,000–1,200
$1,500–1,750 ⚑ P(Ba)

◀ **A beech plywood Jason chair,** by Karl Jacobs for Kandya, c1950.
£140–160
$200–230 ⊞ PLB

A pair of lounge chairs, by Robin Day for Hille, with slatted stick backs and shaped single-piece back and arm rails, on turned uprights, with white vinyl-covered squab cushions, designed 1950, manufactured 1956.
£700–850
$1,000–1,250 ⚑ B(Ba)

▶ **A folding Samson chair,** by Russel Wright for Samsonite, c1955.
£200–220
$300–320 ⊞ ORI

A wooden stool, by Karl Schwanzer, 1958.
£3,800–4,200
$5,500–6,000 ⚑ Doro

A green-painted sofa, by Børge Mogensen for Fritz Hansen, with spindle back and sides, one side adjustable, Danish, c1945, 63in (160cm) wide.
£1,400–1,600
$2,000–2,300 🔨 **WDG**

A beech workchair and stool, by Bruno Mathsson for Karl Mathsson, model No. 41, the chair with woven upholstery, chair and stool with later reversible sheepskin cover, worn, repaired, maker's marks, Swedish, designed c1940, manufactured 1941.
£800–1,000
$1,150–1,500 🔨 **BUK**

A wooden lounge chair, by Jens Risom for Knoll International, with cotton fibre strap seat, c1946.
£375–425
$550–620 🔨 **BB(L)**

◄ **A teak armchair,** by Finn Juhl for Niels Vodder, model No. 53, c1953.
£875–975
$1,250–1,450 ⊞ **MARK**

A Lamino chair, by Yngve Eckstrom for Swedese, with sheepskin seat, 1950s.
£525–575
$750–850 ⊞ **MARK**

► **A beech Easy Chair No. 133,** by Finn Juhl for France & Son, upholstered in black fabric, maker's mark and 6907693, Danish, 1954.
£115–130
$170–200 🔨 **BUK**

A teak armchair, by Paar Armsessel for Hans Grünbeck, Danish, designed c1960, manufactured 1967.
£320–380
$450–575 🔨 **DORO**

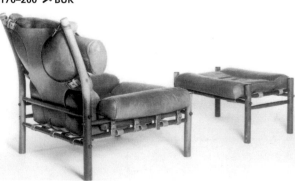

A turned and stained beech lounge chair and footstool, by Arne Norell, upholstered in mid-brown bison hide on leather strapping, with matching detachable cylindrical head cushions, 1960s.
£400–500
$580–720 🔨 **Bon**

A Constanze sofa, by Johannes Spalt for Franz Wittmann, with blue woollen upholstery, on teak feet, designed 1961, manufactured 1967, 77¼in (196cm) wide.
£475–575
$700–850 🔨 **DORO**

A pair of armchairs, by Hans J. Wegner for Getama, with removable cushions, 1951.
£600–700
$870–1,000 🔨 Bon

A rosewood Modous easy chair and footstool, by Kristian Solmer Vedel for Soren Willadsen, upholstered in black leather, 1960s.
£300–350
$450–500 🔨 Bon

A teak and steel flat-pack sofa, by Peter Hvidt and Olga Molgaard Nielsen for John Stuart, with detachable arms, upholstered in wool, c1959.
£1,500–1,800
$2,200–2,600 🔨 BB(L)

A pair of teak lounge chairs, by Finn Juhl for France & Sons, with upholstered seat and back, c1950.
£1,000–1,200
$1,500–1,750 🔨 BB(L)

A laminated ash rocking chair, by Robin Williams, with tan leather-covered padded seat and back, c1980.
£1,200–1,500
$1,750–2,200 🔨 P

◄ **A teak armchair,** by Finn Johl for Niels Vodder, with leather seat and back, maker's stamp, c1948.
£700–850
$1,000–1,250 🔨 BB(L)

An oak-framed Corona chair, by Paul Volther for Eric Jörgensen, Danish, 1961.
£2,500–3,000
$3,500–4,500 🔨 BUK

> **Cross Reference**
> For more Chairs see Dining Furniture (page 59–64)

A matt chrome and sprung steel folding metal PK41 stool, by Poul Kjaerholm for E. Kold Christensen, with beige canvas seat, worn, Danish, 1961.
£900–1,100
$1,300–1,600 🔨 BUK

A walnut R bench, by George Nakashima, signed, c1965.
£7,000–8,500
$10,000–12,500 🔨 S(NY)

A chrome and sprung steel PK22 lounge chair, by Poul Kjaerholm for Fritz Hansen, with black leather seat, maker's label, Danish, designed 1955-6.
£700–850
$1,000–1,250 ⚲ BUK

Design and consumption

During the 1950s, Britain's Design Council had a special showroom in London's Haymarket where the best contemporary products were displayed and could be seen by a curious public. The idea that 'design' could be a special feature which added value began to take hold. This idea held to the belief that the input of a designer – in terms of materials and styling – could make a product function better and last longer and would, therefore, improve quality of life. By the 1960s the role of designer was beginning to change. Nowadays, design assures the steady flow of an ever-increasing range of goods onto the market; design helps us recognize those products in terms of styling and price point.

A pair of steel-framed and leather PK22 lounge chairs, by Poul Kjaerholm for E. Kold Christensen, 1957.
£2,200–2,500
$3,200–3,500 ⚲ Bon

A steel-framed PK22 lounge chair, by Poul Kjaerholm for E. Kold Christensen, with canework seat and back, manufacturer's stamp to stretcher, designed 1955–56, manufactured 1956–70.
£850–1,000
$1,250–1,500 ⚲ Bon

A pair of flat steel-framed PK22 lounge chairs, by Poul Kjaerhol for E. Kold Christiansen, with tan leather-covered seats and backs, manufacturer's stamp, designed 1955–56, manufactured 1956–70.
£2,200–2,600
$3,200–3,800 ⚲ Bon

A set of six matt chrome, sprung steel and ash PK11 chairs, by Poul Kjaerholm for E. Kold Christensen, with brown leather seats, signed, leather marked, designed 1957, manufactured 1957–82.
£5,300–6,000
$7,750–8,750 ⚲ BUK

A matt chrome and steel PK33 seat, by Poul Kjaerholm for E. Kold Christensen, with brown leather cushion, worn, rubber stoppers missing, signed, designed 1959, manufactured 1960s.
£1,150–1,300
$1,700–2,000 ⚲ BUK

A pair of tubular chromed-steel T chairs, by William Katavolos for ICF, model No. 3LC, with black leather upholstery, damaged, leather worn, 1952.
£475–575
$700–850 ⚲ BUK

◀ A steel-framed lounge chair, by Arne Norell, with ribbed black leather-covered padded seat and back, secured by leather straps, c1970.
£1,000–1,200
$1,500–1,750 ⚲ Bon

A pair of lurashell plastic egg-style chairs, after Arne Jacobsen, 1956–60.
£250–300
$350–450 ⚲ WilP
These were produced for the Scandinavian airline system, Royal Hotel and air terminal.

A pair of teak lounge chairs, by Peter Hvidt and Orla Molgaard Nielsen for France & Son, with black vinyl-upholstered sprung seat cushions, on detachable brass uprights with articulated brass glides, manufacturer's badges to frames, 1950s.
£600–700
$870–1,000 ✗ Bon

◄ **A teak lounge suite,** by Peter Hvidt and Orla Molgaard Nielsen for France & Son, comprising a long and short sofa, two coffee tables, one forming a corner piece to the sofas, the sprung cushions covered in green tweed fabric, 1950s.
£800–900
$1,150–1,300 ✗ Bon

A rosewood easy chair, by Ole Wanscher for P. Jeppesen, model No. 149, with a woven cane seat and leather-covered cushions, Danish, c1950s.
£750–900
$1,100–1,300 ✗ TREA

A wood, steel and plastic laminate modular sofa, by George Nelson for Herman Miller, with cream vinyl cushions, 1950s.
£700–850
$1,000–1,200 ✗ BB(L)

A moulded sheet-metal and foam Orange-slice chair, by Pierre Paulin for Artifort, designed 1950s, manufactured 1980s.
£600–700
$870–1,000 ⊞ MARK

► **A Lady suite,** by Marco Zanuso for Arflex, foam rubber upholstery renewed 1980s, marked, 1950s, 78¾in (200cm) long.
£2,000–2,200
$3,000–3,200 ✗ WBH

► **A steel Diamond chair,** by Henry Bertoia for Knoll Associates, black-varnished wire mesh body and tubing legs, covered with brown and black fabric, 1950s.
£120–145
$175–210 ✗ BUK

A black-enamelled metal and chrome-framed Marshmallow sofa, by George Nelson for Herman Miller, 18 round cushions upholstered in black leather, signed with paper label, re-upholstered, 1950s, 53in (134.5cm) long.
£5,500–6,000
$8,000–8,700 ✗ TREA

A pair of rattan chairs, by Nanna and Jorgen Ditzel, on turned teak uprights joined by stretchers, Danish, 1950s.
£300–350
$450–500 ✗ P(Ed)

A cast-aluminium and wool fabric sofa, designed by Morrison & Hannah for Knoll International, mid-1970s, 70 in (178cm) long.
£300–350
$440–500 ⊞ MAR

A set of four children's chairs, designed by Harry Bertoia, designed c1950, produced 1970s.
£400–450
$580–650 ⊞ MARK

A chromed-wire side chair, by Harry Bertoia for Knoll Associates, designed c1950, manufactured 1970s.
£65–75
$95–110 ⊞ MARK

A steel Bird chair, by Harry Bertoia for Knoll Associates, with black plastic welded coated frame, c1950.
£250–300
$360–440 ⚲ Bon

► **A pair of Bird chairs and a footstool,** by Harry Bertoia, for Knoll Associates, model No. 423LU, manufacturer's label, c1958.
£600–700
870–1,000
⚲ SK

A steel Diamond chair, by Harry Bertoia, for Knoll Associates, with chrome-plated wire rod frame, rubber shock mounts, on a steel rod understructure, designed 1950, produced c1970.
£650–800
$950–1,150 ⚲ Bon

◄ **A leather and matt chromed steel PK31 armchair,** by Poul Kjaerholm for E. Kold Christensen, signed, designed 1958, 1960s.
£175–200
$250–290
⚲ BUK

A pair of chrome-plated steel lounge chairs, by Florence Knoll for Knoll Associates, with tan leather-covered padded seat and back, c1960.
£1,100–1,300
$1,600–1,900 ⚲ Bon

An aluminium Arkana chair, with white plastic seat and cushion, 1960–70.
£180–220
$260–320 ⊞ ZOOM

◄ **A pair of steel-framed 042 lounge chairs,** by Geoffrey Harcourt for Artifort, with black vinyl upholstered padded bucket seats, c1968.
£350–400
$500–580 ♫ Bon

A flat steel-framed chaise longue, by Merrow Associates, with tan leather-covered padded seat with detachable bolster cushion, c1965, 65in (165cm) long.
£1,600–1,800
$2,300–2,600 ♫ Bon

◄ **A pair of white varnished fibreglass Tulip armchairs,** by Eero Saarinen for Knoll International, on aluminium central stands, minor tears, c1955–56.
£360–420
$520–620 ♫ BUK

Pop Modern Chairs

A set of four white metal and plastic chairs, by Pierre Paulin for Artifort, c1960, with a wool circular rug.
£720–800
$1,000–1,150 ♫ S

A set of six Zanotta leather and chrome chairs, Italian.
£160–200
$230–290 ♫ CAu

A Perspex and metal Champagne chair, by Erwin and Estelle Leverne, 1957.
£400–450
$580–650 ⊞ MARK

Pop Modern

In the late 1950s, television brought American popular culture into British homes. It was an instant hit with the emerging youth culture and a focus of their developing consumerism. It heralded a period of hedonism and fun, and symbolized a rejection of Establishment values. Pop was evident in fashion magazines and mass-produced art which explored industrial production methods, and went beyond the boundaries of traditional taste.

Modern designers used new materials and processes to produce radical experimental designs which were expressions of post-Modern disengagement from the European political agenda.

A Perspex and aluminium Castelli edition Plona chair, by Giancarlo Piretti, 1970s.
£185–235
$270–340 ⊞ PLB

A set of four chrome airport chairs, upholstered in green plastic, Italian, c1967.
£40–50
$60–75 ♫ P(B)

A set of four chrome and white plastic chairs, by Giancarlo Piretti, 1960s.
£350–400
$500–580 ⊞ OOLA

An ABS plastic side chair, by Joe Colombo for Kartel, 1960s.
£700–850
$1,000–1,200 ⚒ BB(L)

A plastic Selene chair, by Magistretti, Italian, c1970.
£80–100
$115–145 ⊞ PLB

Prices

The price ranges quoted in this book reflect the average price a purchaser might expect to pay for a similar item. The price will vary according to the condition, rarity, size, popularity, provenance, colour and restoration of the item, and this must be taken into account when assessing values. Don't forget that if you are selling it is quite likely that you will be offered less than the price range.

◄ **A Perspex and chrome Plona chair,** by Giancarlo Piretti, Italian, 1969.
£225–250
$325–360 ⊞ PLB

An aluminium and leather chair, by Asko, Finnish, c1965.
£375–425
$560–620 ⊞ MARK

► **Six moulded-plastic chairs,** by Bruno Bodo Rasch, 1960s.
£2,250–2,500
3,300–3,600 ⊞ ZOOM

A fibreglass sofa, with black leather-covered padded seat and back, Italian, late 1960s.
£900–1,100
$1,300–1,600 ⚒ Bon

A pair of dark green plastic Shell chairs, by Steen Ostergaard for Cado, upholstered in yellow, maker's mark, Norwegian, 1972.
£130–150
$190–220 ⚒ DORO

► **A plastic Mushroom stool,** by Arkana, with black fabric seat, 1960s.
£60–75
$90–95 ⊞ MARK

◄ **A bronze wire chair and stool,** designed by Warren Platner for Knoll, with wool fabric upholstery, 1966.
£1,600–1,800
$2,300–2,600 ⚒ TREA

Two Top Hat chairs, by Evans Furniture, 1960s.
£220–250 each
$320–350 ✦ WBH

Design and Pop

The increasing importance of popular culture in contemporary society, mediated by powerful channels of communication, has opened up the possibility of a design rhetoric informed by the playfulness, transience and economy of much popular consumption. This trend began in the 1950s and accelerated during the 1960s and '70s. The trend helped to undermine the accepted singular notion of good taste based on aristocratic or bourgeois norms. Designers opposed the classic notion of good taste with the development of lifestyle consumer choice as the engine of demand.

A Djinn series suite, by Olivier Mourgue for Airbourne, comprising two chairs, a chaise longue and two twin-back sofas, one sofa and chair with later loose covers over the original fabric, 1965, sofa 50½in (128cm) wide.
£2,700–3,200
$3,900–4,700 ✦ S(O)

A moulded sheet metal Cone chair, by Verner Panton, with fabric covered foam upholstery, Danish, designed 1958, manufactured 1960s.
£700–800
$1,000–1,150 ⊞ PLB

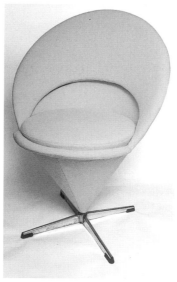

A yellow fabric Cone chair, designed by Verner Panton for Plus-Linje, manufactured by Fritz Hansen, 1960.
£650–750
$950–1,100 ⊞ PLB

An injection moulded black plastic stacking chair, by Verner Panton for Herman Miller, designed c1960, manufactured 1968–79.
£300–350
$440–500 ⊞ MARK

◄ **A pair of System 1-2-3 chairs,** by Verner Panton for Fritz Hansen, with black removable seat covers, on a chrome steel foot, stained, Danish, 1973.
£500–600
$720–870 ✦ BUK

► **A red reinforced polyester Pastilli chair,** designed by Eero Aarnio for Asko, in two parts, 1967.
£400–500
$580–720 ✦ WBH

A chrome and red plastic lounge chair, Italian, 1960s, 29 in (73.5cm) long.
£225–265
$325–385 ⊞ PAB

A fibreglass chair, with cream leather upholstery, probably by Airborne Industries, French, late 1960s.
£350–450
$500–600 ⊞ MARK

A black PVC Primate stool, by Achille Castiglioni for Zanotta, on grey plastic base, designed c1969.
£720–800
$1,000–1,150 ⚒ S

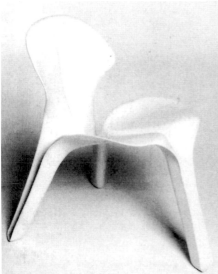

LOCATE THE SOURCE

The source of each illustration in Miller's can be found by checking the code letters below each caption with the Key to Illustrations, pages 296–298.

◄ **A red plastic anthropomorphic Floris chair,** by Günter Beltzig for Beltzig Bros, from an edition issued by Wolfgang F. Maurer, Munich, signed and marked 38/100, German, 1990.
£1,150–1,300
$1,700–1,900 ⚒ DORO

◄ **A moulded fibreglass and reinforced polyester Floris chair,** by Günter Beltzig, with pale cream finish, designed 1967, manufactured c1970.
£700–900
$1,000–1,300 ⚒ Bon

A malacca and reed 692 rocking chair, by Franco Bettonica for Vittorio Bonacina, 1964.
£300–350
$440–500 ⚒ S

A clear Perspex hanging bubble chair, designed by Eero Aarnio for Asko, 1966.
£3,500–4,000
$5,000–5,800 ⚒ S

A chromed-steel Papegojan armchair, by Ib Arberg for Rocksjöverken, with black lacquered metal support and upholstered in beige corduroy, Swedish, c1970, 63¾in (162cm) high.
£650–720
$950–1,000 ⚒ BUK

◄ **A red fibreglass garden Egg chair,** by Peter Ghyczy for Reuter Product, with orange fabric interior, designed 1968.
£250–300
$360–440 ⊞ W

► **A red glass-reinforced polyester Castle chair,** by Wendell Castle, American, c1969.
£500–600
$720–870 ⚒ Bon

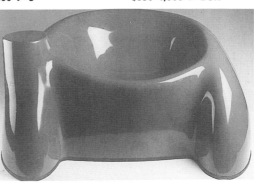

A child's polyurethane Zocker chair/desk, designed by Luigi Colani for Top System, 1972.
£180–200
$260–290 ⚲ S

A white fibreglass footstool, the cushion upholstered in pale yellow and white Marimekko fabric, Finnish, c1970.
£260–300
$380–440 ⚲ Bon

A child's red and cream corduroy bean bag, by Hobart Rose, in the shape of a boxing glove, 1970s, 40in (101.5cm) long.
£65–75
$95–110 ⊞ PLB

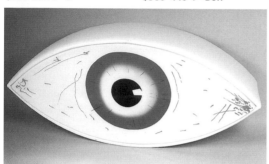

A Le Témoin seat, designed by Man Ray for Gavina, made for the Ultramobile Exhibition, 1971.
£1,350–1,500
$2,000–2,200 ⊞ MARK

Disposable furniture

The architecture and design of Modernism embraces the idea of a fast and dynamic society. The concept of a multi-function interior calls for fewer, more versatile, pieces of furniture. This is how Modernism and minimalism are so often combined. Accordingly, the modern interior is full of gadgets and electrical goods but has less furniture than, say, an interior from the beginning of the 20th century. During the 1960s, various experiments were tried to create disposable furniture – paper was a favourite material – or to make furniture out of recycled products. Disposable furniture was usually replaced with a more enduring product and the trend withered – however, it helped condition consumers towards a more dynamic consumption of design.

A moulded black plastic modular seating system, by Cini Boeri for Knoll International, comprising one sofa, two settees and two telescopic tables, with leather upholstery, manufactured by Gavina, 1972, sofa 91½in (232.5cm) wide.
£10,000–12,000
$14,500–17,500 ⚲ P(PL)

◄ **A clear Perspex stool,** with leopard-skin covered sprung seat, 1960s, 25in (63.5cm) high.
£450–500
$650–720 ⊞ ZOOM

► **An inflatable chair,** by Zanotta, the clear plastic seat including a foot pump, Italian, 1967.
£250–300
$360–440 ⚲ CSK
Inflatable chairs were subject to punctures and were never intended to be durable. Condition is all important and collectors today prefer to buy old stock, unused and still boxed.

A black plastic and aluminium chair, Italian, 1970s.
£280–300
$410–440 ⊞ ZOOM

A pair of System 1-2-3 de Luxe armchairs, by Verner Panton for Fritz Hansen, upholstered in beige fabric and with aluminium bases, 1970s.
£800–900
$1,150–1,300 ⚒ BUK

A pair of metal-framed Jan lounge chairs, by Jan Ekselius for Stendig, with foam upholstered orange fabric, c1970.
£600–700
$870–1,000 ⚒ P(Ba)

A tubular metal Fiocco chair, by Group 14 for Busnelli, upholstered with yellow synthetic stretch fabric, 1970.
£2,000–2,250
$2,900–3,300 ⚒ S

A flat steel-framed Reigate rocking chair and footstool, by William Plunkett, the black vinyl-coated frame with orange tweed-upholstered foam seat and back, on Pirelli webbing, designed c1969, manufactured c1970.
£500–600
$720–870 ⚒ Bon

A smoked-Perspex and chrome chair, by Tabacoff, with cream vinyl padded covers, Belgian, early 1970s.
£200–240
$290–350 ⊞ MARK

► **A Maralunga sofa,** designed by Vico Magistretti for Cassina, upholstered in black leather with adjustable back and head rest, Italian, 1973, 64½in (165cm) long.
£1,600–2,000
$2,300–2,900
⚒ LJ

◄ **A brushed-steel-framed two-seater sofa,** with brown leather-covered cushions, Scandinavian, c1970, 49½in (125.5cm) long.
£400–480
$580–700 ⚒ Bon

► **A chrome and leather adjustable arm chair,** 1970s.
£120–140
$175–200 ⊞ Har

A set of eight leather and steel armchairs, by Eero Aarnio, covered in plum red leather, on polished steel supports, labelled 'Mobel Italia, design: Eero Aarnio', Italian, 1970s.
£620–750
$900–1,100 ⚷ S(S)

A day bed, by De Sede, the grey-painted slatted wooden bench with tan leather upholstered mattress cushion, together with two brown leather-covered bolster cushions and four shaded brown leather patchwork cushions, manufactured c1975, 73¼in (186cm) long.
£950–1,150
$1,400–1,700 ⚷ Bon

Contemporary designer furniture

During the 1980s, various designers began to make a name for themselves by creating modern furniture designs in limited editions. The cult of the designer assured them of celebrity. Among the best known of these are Ron Arad and Philippe Starck – both of whom have developed their own names into brands. In the 1990s, fashion houses began to launch their own home product ranges – this continued the development of lifestyle consumerism and, at the same time, speeds up the fashion cycle in home furnishings.

◀ **A set of four leather and aluminium armchairs,** Continental, 1970s.
£1,200–1,500
$1,750–2,200
⊞ ZOOM

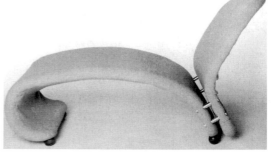

A System 1-2-3 chaise, by Verner Panton, for Fritz Hansen, the organic two-part form with beige tweed upholstery, on stained wood spherical feet, 1970s.
£250–300
$360–440 ⚷ Bon

◀ **A pink leather Karelia easy chair,** by Liisi Beckman for Zanotta, damaged, c1960.
£350–425
$500–620 ⚷ BUK

Post Modern Chairs

◀ **A pair of black-painted Seconda chairs,** by Mario Botta for Alias, with mesh seats and ribbed drum backs, c1982.
£450–550
$650–800 ⚷ L&T

▶ **A Silver chair,** by Vico Magistretti, for de Padova, Italian, 1989.
£95–110
$140–150 ⚷ BB(L)

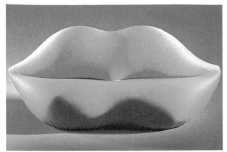

A polyurethane foam Marilyn sofa, by Studio 65 for Gufram, designed 1972, manufactured 1986, Italian, 1986, 82¾in (210cm) wide.
£2,400–2,750
$3,500–3,950 ⚒ DORO

A polyurethane foam Marilyn sofa, by Studio 65 for Gufram, covered in red stretch fabric, 1972.
£1,800–2,200
$2,600–3,200 ⚒ BUK
Model 'Marilyn' was produced by the Italian design group Studio 65 in 1972, as a homage to Salvador Dali's 1936 'Mae West' sofa.

A pair of white plastic-moulded chairs, in the style of Joe Colombo, with pink upholstered seats on moulded circular bases, 1960s.
£125–150
$180–220 ⚒ WilP

A corrugated cardboard and Masonite Easy Edges side chair, by Frank Gehry, c1970.
£900–1,000
$1,300–1,550 ⚒ BB(L)

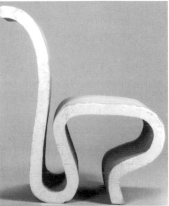

A dining chair prototype, hand made by Frank Gehry, Robert Irwin and Jack Brogan, 1970.
£18,000–21,000
$26,000–30,000 ⚒ BB(L)

A pair of black painted wood and steel armchairs, by Philippe Stark for Driade, the cushions covered with black leather, some damage, 1980s.
£575–700
$850–1,000 ⚒ BUK

▶ **A metal and black laminate suite,** by Gerd Mayr-Keber, comprising a table and three armchairs, the chairs with chromed-steel legs, 1988, table 30in (76cm) high.
£480–550
$700–800 ⚒ DORO
This suite was manufactured for the domed room at the History of Art Museum, Vienna.

Retro Modern

By the end of the 20th century, lifestyle consumption had evolved into a pick-and-mix process. The 1990s fashion for minimalism was underpinned by the requirement, among Western consumers, to clear out their things and to start again. The functionalism of first-period Modern (1930s) design was rediscovered and appropriated as part of the contemporary minimalism. The size and scale of these consumer trends around the world means that there is now more Modernism than ever, and the style has become the staple of advertising aesthetics and estate agents' brochures. The relative abundance of retro-style Modern should not obscure the fact that, during the 1930s in Britain, Modernism was hugely significant but limited to a smallish circle of intellectuals.

Tables

An Art Nouveau coffee table, by Heal's, with undershelf, on six triangular-section legs, c1900, 28½in (72cm) wide.
£400–500
$580–720 ♪ P

A work table, the top with stencilled decoration, 1900–10, 19in (48.5cm) diam.
£275–325
$400–470 ⊞ NET

A beech table and stool, with original grey paint, Austrian, 1920, table 29½in (75cm) high.
£1,500–1,800
$2,200–2,600 ♪ DORO

An oak side table, by Gordon Russell, 1920s, 36in (91.5cm) wide.
£600–650
$870–1,000 ♪ SWO

An Art Deco oak three-tier coffee table, on block feet, c1930, 41¼in (105cm) high.
£50–60
$75–100 ♪ P(B)

The trouble with tables

The engineering and material constraints on designing tables have resulted in a relatively diminished range of developments in table design – at least compared with chair design. This trend also reflects the fewer opportunities offered for tables within the multi-function interior with integrated storage areas and surfaces. Experiments with metal have had the most impact on this branch of furniture design. Heavy, more robust, metals have tended to be used. These often appeal to handicraft tradition rather than to high-tech production. Only where engineering and construction techniques have been borrowed from the aviation industry have lighter, wing-shaped, structures resulted.

◄ **An oak tiered occasional table,** retailed by Bowman, 1930s, 23in (58.5cm) high.
£180–200
$250–300 ⊞ BTB

◄ **A walnut occasional table,** with crossbanded inlay, on a square base, c1930, 21in (53.5cm) diam.
£150–180
$220–260 ⊞ BTB

A birch-veneered two-tier table, No. 70, 1930s, 21¾in (55.5cm) high.
£1,800–2,200
$2,600–3,200 ♪ S

A burled wood-veneered cocktail table, by Russel Wright for Heywood-Wakefield, with chrome-plated handles, c1934, 21in (53cm) high.
£2,500–3,000
$3,500–4,500 ♪ BB(L)

◄ **A blonde wood corner table,** manufactured by Heywood-Wakefield, model No. 311, marked, c1955, 44in (112cm) wide.
£300–350
$450–500 ♪ SK

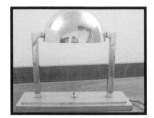  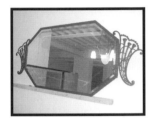

A pair of Art Deco calamander and satinwood occasional tables, stamped mark, French, c1930, 24in (61cm) wide.
£1,000–1,100
$1,500–1,600 🔨 P

An Art Deco bird's-eye maple console table, attributed to Ray Hille, the top inset with pink mirror tiles, c1935, 21in 953.5cm) wide.
£500–600
$720–870 🔨 P

A fruitwood two-tier table, by Gerald Summers, with black-painted edges, 1930s, 29in (73.5cm) diam.
£2,000–2,200
$3,000–3,200 🔨 S

An Art Deco walnut and satinwood sewing table, the removable top with concealing another removable tray, with ebonized pull, c1930, 22¾in (57.5cm) diam.
£380–420
$570–620 🔨 P

An Art Deco nest of three walnut tables, Austrian, c1935, largest 28in (71m) high.
£800–880
$1,200–1,300 ⊞ MTay

A nest of four oak tables, on block feet, 1930s, 21in (53.5cm) square.
£250–300
$360–440 🔨 P

A wooden sewing table, by Gerrit Thomas Rietveld, c1936, 21½in (54.5cm) high.
£3,500–4,000
$5,000–5,800 🔨 S(Am)

An Art Deco sycamore and walnut two-tier occasional table, c1935, 26¾in (68cm) diam.
£1,000–1,200
$1,500–1,750 🔨 P

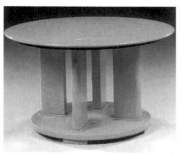

A red-lacquered occasional table, by Jules Leleu, the top raised on four bowfronted block legs, branded 3212, c1930, 35¼in (89.5cm) diam.
£7,000–8,000
$10,000–11,500 🔨 S

▶ **A walnut occasional table,** by Gordon Russell, with ebony feet, 1930s, 23in (58cm) wide.
£900–1,100
$1,300–1,600 🔨 C

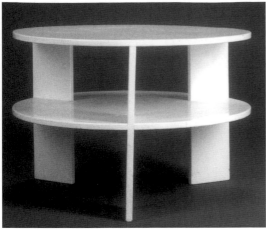

A laminated wood occasional table, by Gerald Summers for Makers of Simple Furniture, c1934, 20in (51cm) high.
£1,200–1,400
$1,750–2,000 ⚷ BB(L)

A mahogany breakfast table, by Dick Russell for Gordon Russell, the top with a central inset illuminated glazed panel, on a cylindrical support on a slightly domed plinth base, c1934, 54in (137cm) diam.
£4,000–4,800
$5,800–7,000 ⚷ P

◄ **A chrome and marble-topped console table,** 1930s, 38in (96.5cm) high.
£380–420
$570–650 ⊞ NET

LOCATE THE SOURCE
The source of each illustration in Miller's can be found by checking the code letters below each caption with the Key to Illustrations, pages 296–298.

An Art Deco nest of tables, 30in (76cm) diam.
£300–350
$450–500 ⊞ ARF

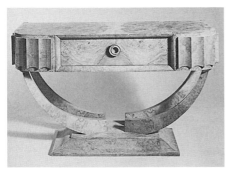

A walnut serving table, by Hille, with glass back panels, on four curved and angled supports, c1935, 54in (137cm) wide.
£759–900
$1,100–1,300 ⚷ P

A maple-veneered two-tier occasional table, on three square tapering splayed legs, 1950s, 31½in (80cm) diam.
£175–200
$250–300 ⚷ P(B)

A burr-walnut occasional table, by Edward Barnsley, the top with ebony stringing, on four curved supports, stamped mark, c1990, 29in (73.5cm) diam.
£900–1,100
$1.300–1,600 ⚷ Bon

An Art Deco silvered-bronze and marble console table, French, c1925, 40in (101.5cm) wide.
£30,000–35,000
$43,000–50,000 ⚒ S(NY)

▶ **A padouk dining table,** by Joseph Emberton, the end supports on stepped bases, 1930s, 105in (266.5cm) wide.
£2,000–2,200
$3,000–3,200
⚒ S

A lacquered wood and gilt-iron console table, by André Arbus, c1939, 46¼in (117.5cm) wide.
£11,000–13,000
$16,000–19,000 ⚒ P(PL)

A parchment, lacquered wood and bronze table, by Jacques Quinet, French, c1941, 45in (114.5cm) wide.
£15,500–18,000
$22,500–26,000 ⚒ S(NY)

◀ **A gilt-bronze and travertine marble table,** by Jacques Quinet, French, c1947, 42in (106.5cm) wide.
£13,000–15,000
$19,000–22,000 ⚒ S(NY)

A chrome and glass coffee table, in the modernist style, 1940s, 24in (61.5cm) diam.
£400–450
$580–650 ⚒ S

◀ **An ebonized wood and chromium-plated steel occasional table,** by Donald Deskey for S. Karpen & Bros Furniture Co, American, 1930s, 20in (51cm) high.
£3,800–4,500
$5,500–6,500 ⚒ P(PL)

An Art Deco rosewood folding breakfast table,
the hinged top on U-shaped supports, French, c1930,
39½in (100.5cm) wide.
£950–1,150
$1,400–1,700 🔨 B

An Art Deco palisander fold-over breakfast table, the
hinged sliding top on a column with a hinged door and a
plinth base, on ebonized block feet, French, c1930,
31¼in (80cm) wide.
£900–1,100
$1,300–1,600 🔨 B

Two plywood nesting tables, by Marcel Breuer for
Isokon, the larger moulded birch-faced plywood, stamped
mark, the smaller moulded beech-faced plywood, Estonian,
designed 1935–36, manufactured 1940s–50s,
larger 24in (61cm) wide.
£1,200–1,400
$1,750–2,000 🔨 Bon
**The blockade of eastern European ports by Nazi
Germany prevented pre-ordered plywood sheets
being obtained by Isokon. During the war period and
beyond, Isokon, London, had to develop the
technology with which to produce the plywood shells
for Marcel Breuer's designs. The lack of access to birch
in unoccupied western Europe led Isokon to develop
the use of beech as an alternative.**

Flat pack

Flat pack furniture is not a new concept but its
integration into logistics and retailing have greatly
increased its impact during the second half of the
20th century. The reduction of the supporting
structure of a table to four separate leg elements
makes for much easier transport. Nowadays, flat
pack is usually associated with user assembly.
Tales of the difficulties of self assembly have
passed into the folklore of contemporary life.

During the post-war period it was the furniture
industry of Scandinavia that promoted the design
and manufacture of flat pack. Its enthusiastic
endorsement by big retailers has ensured that it
will continue.

A stained beech nest of tables, by Gustave Gautier,
the tops with removable glass plates, French,
44in (112cm) wide.
£3,500–4,000
$5,000–5,800 🔨 S

A white-lacquered plywood nesting table, by Marcel
Breuer for Isokon, 1936, 24in (61cm) wide.
£950–1,150
$1,400–1,700 🔨 DORO

**A chrome-plated steel-
framed Table B10,** by
Marcel Breuer for Thonet,
with blue lacquered pine
top, damaged, 1930s,
29in (73.5cm) wide.
£2,300–2,750
$3,300–4,000 🔨 BUK

**A green anodized
aluminium illuminated
table,** by Artlight, 1940s,
24in (61cm) diam.
£350–400
$500–580 ⊞ BTB

A green anodized aluminium illuminated table, by Artlight, 1940s, 24in (61cm) diam.
£350–400
$500–580 ⊞ BTB

A holoplast and aluminium occasional table, by Ernest Race at Race Furniture, with manufacturer's Horse logo transfer table, 1940s–50s, 42in (61cm) wide.
£260–300
$380–450 ⚒ Bon

A holoplast and aluminium dining table, by Ernest Race at Race Furniture, 1940s–50s, 78in (198cm) wide.
£1,000–1,200
$1,500–1,750 ⚒ Bon

A stained poplar and glass coffee table, by Isamu Noguchi, probably for Herman Miller, c1947, 50¾in (129cm) wide.
£1,200–1,400
$1,750–2,000 ⚒ BUK

A laminated cherry wood-faced breakfast suite, by Robin Day for Hille, comprising table and four Hillestack chairs, the table with a solid beech under frame and hinged top, 1951.
£500–600
$720–870 ⚒ Bon

▶ **A leather, glass and painted iron card table,** by Jacques Adnet, c1950, 41in (104cm) diam.
£10,000–12,000
$14,500–17,500 ⚒ S(NY)

A white-laminated and tubular steel writing desk, by George Nelson for Herman Miller. c1947, 59in (150cm) wide.
£700–850
$1,000–1,250 ⚒ BB(L)

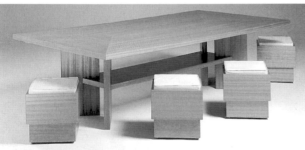

A mahogany table and four stools, by Frank Lloyd Wright, the stools with inset yellow vinyl cushions, c1954, table 95½in (242.5cm) wide.
£6,500–7,250
$9,500–10,500 ⚒ S(NY)

Cross Reference
See Colour Review (pages 113–121)

A wrought-iron, wood and black glass Boomerang table, by Jean Royère, on yo-yo legs, c1953, 33in (84cm) wide.
£13,000–15,000
$19,000–22,000 ⚒ S(NY)

▶ **A mahogany 2000 Series coffee table and six stools,** by Frank Lloyd Wright, c1956, table 47in (119.5cm) wide.
£2,200–2,500
$3,000–3,500 ⚒ BB(L)

A beech AX sofa table, by Peter Hvidt and Olga Molgaard Nielsen for Fritz Hansen, the legs with mahogany inlay, 1950, 43in (109cm) wide.
£375–450
$550–650 ⚒ DORO

▶ **A set of four Aluminium Group armchairs and a table,** by Charles and Ray Eames, the chairs covered with ribbed black fabric, the table with laminated top with vinyl edging, American, c1958, table 60¼in (153cm) diam.
£1,600–2,000
$2,300–3,000
⚒ Bri

▶ **A solid and laminated oak FH4103 dining suite,** by Hans Wegner for Fritz Hansen, comprising a table and six chairs, Danish, 1952, table 47in (119.5cm) diam.
£1,200–1,400
$1,750–2,000 ⚒ Bon

A walnut Time Life stool, by Charles and Ray Eames for Herman Miller, American, c1955, 13in (33cm) high.
£400–450
$580–650 ⊞ MARK

▶ **A teak-faced plywood Series 301 dining suite,** by Arne Jacobsen for Fritz Hansen, with grey-painted and ribbed grey vinyl coated tubular metal legs, manufacturer's stamp, c1955.
£750–900
$1,100–1,300 ⚒ Bon

A pair of laminated plywood and aluminium occasional tables, 1960s, 20in (51cm) wide.
£160–180
$230–260 ⚒ BB(L)

A blue reinforced polyester resin and chromed-metal dining table, by Ferrieri and Gardella for Kartell, 1967.
£250–300
$350–450 ⚒ S

A teak sewing table, the half-hinged top with rotating shelf, with leather-lined material store, Norwegian, c1960, 23in (58.5cm) diam.
£200–240
$300–350 ⚒ TRL

A sycamore nest of tables, Japanese, c1960, largest 23¾in (60.5cm) wide.
£180–220
$260–320 ⚒ P(Ba)

A two-tier teak and cane table, by Peter Hvidt and Olga Molgaard, for France & Sons, Danish, c1960, 29in (73.5cm) high.
£330–360
$470–525 ⊞ GOH

A pair of laminated beech and teak AX chairs and matching coffee table, by Peter Hvidt and Olga Molgaard Nielsen for Fritz Hansen, the table with teak-faced laminated top and laminated teak and beech uprights, Danish, 1950s, table 43½in (110cm) wide.
£850–1,000
$1,250–1,500 ⚒ Bon

A chromium-plated PK61 table, by Poul Kjaerholm, with detachable grey and black-veined alabaster top, marked, 1956, 31½in (80cm) square.
£1,400–1,600
$2,000–2,300 ⚒ S

A white-painted cast-aluminium Tulip dining suite, by Eero Saarinen for Knoll Associates, comprising white-painted table with white Formica top and six matching chairs with blue tweed-covered padded seats, manufacturer's label, American, 1956, table 47½in (121cm) diam.
£1,700–2,000
$2,500–3,000 ⚒ Bon

A set of three white-painted cast aluminium Tulip occasional tables, by Eero Saarinen for Knoll Associates, with white Formica top, American, 1955–56, together with a Tulip stool.
£320–385
$470–575 ⚒ Bon

A miniature plastic Tulip table and four chairs, in the style of Eero Saarinen, c1960, 4in (10cm) high.
£55–65
$80–100 ⊞ PLB

A marble-topped Tulip table, by Eero Saarinen for Knoll International, on a white-lacquered aluminium base, American, c1960, 41¾in (106cm) diam.
£450–550
$650–1,000 ⚒ BUK

A red marble-topped Tulip table, by Eero Saarinen for Knoll International, on a white-lacquered aluminium base, American, 1960, 19¾in (50cm) diam.
£200–240
$300–350 ✎ BUK

A red marble-topped Tulip table, by Eero Saarinen for Knoll International, on a white-lacquered aluminium base, American, 1960, 19¾in (50cm) diam.
£235–280
$335–400 ✎ BUK

A table, by Arkana, with white moulded top on a white pedestal base, 1970s, 41½in (105.5cm) diam.
£400–450
$580–650 ⊞ ZOOM

A Perspex dining table, comprising a series of flat Perspex planes joined by brass bolts, late 1960s, 82in (208.5cm) long.
£2,000–2,400
$3,000–3,500 ✎ Bon

Tables and systems

A good deal of effort in furniture design goes into producing specialized office and work environments. These designs are often built up out of parts into a coherent, integrated environment. These systems are not really domestic in scale and office furniture cannot always be integrated into the home except as part of a high-tech interior. Norman Foster's experiments in this field are among the most likely to succeed beyond the niche market. The appeal of system furniture is in its design logic of inter-connecting parts and in its machine-driven aesthetics.

A rosewood desk/dining table, by Richard Schultz for Knoll Associates, with chrome-plated uprights, American, designed c1965, manufactured 1970s, 76in (193cm) wide.
£850–1,000
$1,250–1,500 ✎ Bon

◀ **A chrome-plated steel and glass coffee table,** by Florence Knoll for Knoll Associates, American, c1965, 29½in (75cm) square.
£250–300
$350–450 ✎ Bon

A chrome-plated steel and glass coffee table, by Florence Knoll for Knoll Associates, American, c1965, 45in (114.5cm) wide.
£220–260
$320–380 ✎ Bon

A brushed steel and glass Selsdon coffee table, by William Plunkett at William Plunkett Furniture, c1969.
£500–600
$720–870 🔨 Bon

A chromed-metal table, by Florence Knoll for Knoll International, model No. 2481, with a marble top, American, 1961, 78¼in (199cm) wide.
£1,600–1,900
$2,300–2,750 🔨 BUK

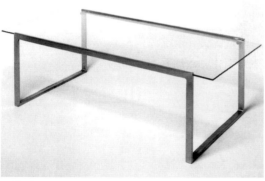

A flat brushed-steel and glass coffee table, by William Plunkett at William Plunkett Furniture, c1965, 40¼in (102cm) wide.
£400–480
$580–700 🔨 P

A metal and glass dining table, 1970s, 29½in (75cm) high.
£1,800–2,000
$2,500–3,000 ⊞ ZOOM

A chrome and glass three-tier revolving coffee table, 1960–70, 17in (43cm) high.
£700–800
$1,000–1,150 ⊞ ZOOM

A metal and glass coffee table, 1970s, 15½in (39.5cm) diam.
£450–500
$650–720 ⊞ ZOOM

A rosewood-veneered and cast-metal coffee table, c1970.
£350–420
$500–600 🔨 Bon

A rosewood-veneered and aluminium occasional table, by Michael Sodeau, c1990.
£280–330
$400–480 🔨 Bon

A stainless steel poker table, by Joe Colombo for Zanotta, the white Formica top with swing-out counter trays, 1968, 39in (99cm) square.
£700–850
$1,000–1,250 ✤ **Bon**

A chrome and tile-topped coffee table, the tiles probably Poole and with abstract slip-glaze decoration, 1960s–70s.
£140–170
$200–250 ✤ **WiLP**

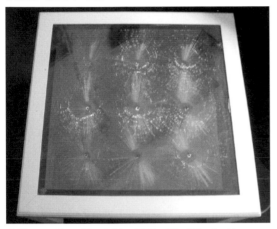

A fibre-optic coffee table, 1970s, 26in (66cm) wide.
£750–850
$1,100–1,250 ⊞ **PLB**

A galvanized steel and Formica occasional table, by Sir Norman Foster, limited production, 49in (124cm) long.
£2,100–2,500
$3,000–3,500 ✤ **Bon**
This table was hand-made for use in the Renault headquarters building, London.

◄ **A black marble End Table,** by Ettore Sottsass, Jr for Up & Up, c1980, 19½in (49.5cm) diam.
£1,100–1,300
$1,600–2,000 ✤ **BB(L)**

A steel and resin Open Sky Series breakfast table, by Gaetano Pesce, 1990s, 36in (91.5cm) diam.
£400–480
$580–700 ✤ **Bon**

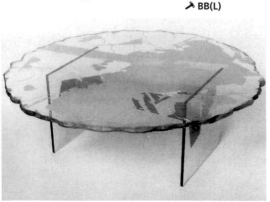

◄ **An iron and toughened sheet glass occasional table,** by Danny Lane and Ron Arad for One-Off, the underside with incised abstract line decoration, late 1980s.
£450–550
$650–800 ✤ **Bon**

Sideboards & Dining Furniture

A set of four walnut and hickory chairs and a walnut table, by George Nakashima, table 54in (137cm) diam.

Chairs	£1,800–2,000
	$2,600–3,000
Table	£3,800–4,500
	$5,500–6,500 ⚒ S(NY)

A walnut sideboard, by Betty Joel for Token Handmade Furniture, with glass top and three drawers over two cupboards, manufactured by W. Older, 1928, 46in (117cm) wide.
£2,200–2,400
$3,200–3,500 ⊞ RUSK

An Art Deco dining room suite, by Heal's, comprising table, four single chairs, two carvers and a sideboard, c1930, table 60¼in (153cm) wide.
£2,600–3,000
$3,800–4,400 ⚒ B(B)

Domestic Modern

The Modernist transformation of the domestic interior has been led by the desire for convenience – with every object and facility within easy reach. The modern interior is designed so that it can be looked after without the large staff requirements of the Edwardian or Victorian home. Many of the secondary furnishings of the home are incorporated into its design in the form of fitted storage spaces and surfaces. This makes for economical and convenient uses of space – particularly in bedrooms and kitchens. The dining room has practically disappeared from the modern home as a separate space and is now part of a larger cooking, eating and living space.

An oak sideboard, by Arthur Simpson, the centre section fitted with two long drawers below two short drawers, flanked by two pairs of panel doors, the base carved with pomegranates, grapes, leaves and flowers, 66¼in (168.5cm) wide.
£2,000–2,400
$3,000–3,500 ⚒ B(B)

A satinwood sideboard, by Jules Leleu, with four central parchment-covered drawers with bronze pulls, flanked by two doors opening to reveal shelved interiors, c1930, 84in (218cm) wide.
£4,250–4,750
$6,200–7,000 ⚒ S(NY)

An adzed oak dresser, by Robert (Mouseman) Thompson, the five drawers with turned wood handles, flanked on each side by a six-panelled cupboard door with wrought-iron mounts, 1930s, 60in (152.5cm) wide.
£2,000–2,500
$3,000–3,500 ⚒ AH

An oak sideboard, by Robert (Mouseman) Thompson, the two doors enclosing three central drawers, with iron hinges and catches, 1930s, 72in (183cm) wide.
£3,800–4,500
$5,500–6,500 ⚒ S

A hardwood bowfronted sideboard, by A. Buckingham for Token Works, with shell-shaped handles, 1936, 55in (139.5cm) wide.
£2,000–2,200
$3,000–3,200 ⊞ RUSK

A silky oak and Macassar ebony serpentine-fronted sideboard, by Token Works, 1937, 69in (175.5cm) wide.
£3,500–3,800
$5,000–5,500 ⊞ RUSK

A pine sideboard, by Florence Knoll for Knoll Associates, with sliding doors and leather loop handles enclosing shelves and interior with sliding drawers, on black-painted steel uprights, 1952–78, 72in (183cm) wide.
£550–650
$800–950 ⚒ Bon

A birch and rosewood-veneered ebonized sideboard, attributed to Robin Day for Hille, on black-enamelled steel uprights, c1955, 84in (213.5cm) wide.
£550–650
$800–950 ⚒ Bon

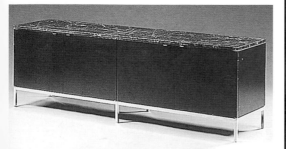

A black-painted wood credenza, by Florence Knoll for Knoll Associates, with white-veined black marble top, late 1950s, 74¾in (190cm) wide.
£2,500–2,750
$3,500–4,000 ⚒ S

A limed-oak side cabinet, by James Mont, the doors with hammered metal ring pulls, maker's mark, c1948, 52in (132cm) wide.
£2,500–3,000
$3,500–4,500 ⚒ S(NY)

Cross Reference
See Colour Review (page 122)

A limed-oak refectory dining table, with twin-barrel turned end supports, 1950s, 78in (198cm) wide, and six limed-oak dining chairs.
Table £2,700–3,000
$4,000–4,500
Chairs £2,500–2,800
$3,500–4,000 ⚒ WW

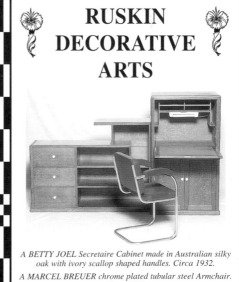

Sideboards

Long and low sideboards are recognizably modern. The low horizontal shape fits into the lower ceilinged interior of the modern apartment or home. Also, it provides a rare surface area for the display of objects. The favoured timbers are teak and rosewood. The long, low shape has tended to favour sliding doors on the front – a hinged door will require special, piano-style, hinges to support the levered weight of a deep door. Metal furnishings are also an anachronism with handles being incorporated into the design of the drawer and door fronts.

► **A two-tone Formica sideboard,** early 1950s, 60in (152.5cm) wide.
£120–150
$175–220
⊞ **RAT**

A two-tone Formica sideboard, 1950s, 66in (167.5cm) wide.
£120–150
$175–220 ⊞ **RAT**

A maple and satinwood inlay dining suite, comprising a table, six cream leather-upholstered dining chairs and a sideboard, 1930s, table 72in (183cm) wide.
£1,500–1,800
$2,200–2,600 ⚒ **AH**

► **A teak dining suite,** by Hans J Wegner for Fritz Hansen, comprising dining table and a set of six Nils Moller dining chairs with black leather seats, 1950s, table 110in (279.5cm) wide, fully extended.
£700–850
$1,000–1,250 ⚒ **Bon**

A white plastic dining suite, by Arkana, comprising a table and six chairs on steel pedestals, c1970, table 73in (185.5cm) wide.
£400–475
$580–700 ⚒ **L&T**

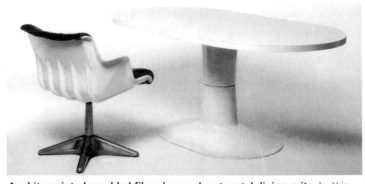

A white-painted moulded fibreglass and cast-metal dining suite, by Yrjo Kukkapuro for Haimi, comprising a table and seven chairs, the chairs with black leather-covered seats and backs, 1965, table 67in (170cm) wide.
£400–480
$580–700 ⚒ **Bon**

A Palm Springs dining table, by Ettore Sottsass, and a set of six First dining chairs by Michele de Lucchi for Memphis, 1983 and 1984, Italian, table 84in (213.5cm) wide.
£4,500–5,000
$6,500–7,250 ⊞ **B&B**

Cross Reference
See Chairs section (page 10–47)

► **A set of four chromed-steel dining chairs,** by Eileen Gray, with rosewood tips and brown suede-covered seats, designed 1927–28, manufactured c1965.
£60,000–70,000
$87,000–100,000 ⚒ **P(PL)**

A set of four steel and black-lacquered wood dining chairs, by Richard Neutra for Paul Williams, with white upholstery, American, c1937.
£9,000–11,000
$13,000–16,000 ⚒ P(PL)

A wall-mounted sideboard/bookcase, by Marcel Breuer for Isokon, with two rolling shutter doors opening to reveal a single compartment fitted with a shelf and fixing points for adjustable vertical supports, one handle and vertical supports missing, manufactured by P. E. Gane, manufacturer's plastic label, 1935–36, 92in (233.5cm) wide.
£11,000–13,000
$16,000–19,000 ⚒ S

An Art Deco oak and walnut table, with four oak tub chairs, c1930, table 72in (183cm) wide.
£1,600–1,800
$2,300–2,600 ⊞ JAZZ

A sycamore-veneered plywood wall-mounted hi-fi unit/sideboard, by Marcel Breuer for Isokon, with single door opening to reveal wireless control panel, speaker section with polished wire mesh front, hinged cover for gramophone above fall-front cabinet for gramophone records, with D-shaped chromium-plated metal handles and two tubular metal supports, 1935–36, 86in (219cm) wide.
£30,000–35,000
$43,500–50,500 ⚒ S

An oak draw-leaf dining table and six chairs, by Charles Dudouyt, branded signature, c1940, 127in (322.5cm) long, extended.
£5,000–6,000
$7,200–8,800 ⚒ S(NY)

A wood and laminated plywood dining suite, by T. H. Robsjohn-Gibbings for the Widdicomb Furniture Co, comprising a dining table with three leaves and six upholstered chairs, c1947, table 48in (122cm) diam.
£1,500–1,800
$2,200–2,500 ⚒ BB(L)

A **mahogany serving table,** by Jean-Michel Frank, stamped maker's mark, French, c1935, 71in (180.5cm) wide.
£16,000–19,000
$23,000–27,000 ⚒ **P(PL)**

A **walnut dining suite,** by T. H. Robsjohn-Gibbings for the Widdicomb Furniture Co, comprising a table and six upholstered chairs, the upholstery designed by George Farkas for Spectrum, American, c1948, table 72in (183cm) wide
£10,000–12,000
$14,500–17,500 ⚒ **P(PL)**

A **carved maple dining table,** by Franco Campo and Carlo Graffi for Carlo Mollino, with a glass top, the *Millepedi* skeleton base joined with brass screws, Italian, c1953, 84in (213.5cm) wide.
£93,000–112,000
$134,000–162,000 ⚒ **P(PL)**
This is a very good example of the Turinese Organic School, known as *Millepedi* by collectors.

An **adzed oak dining suite,** by Robert 'Mouseman' Thompson, comprising table, six dining chairs and two carvers, the chairs reupholstered with leopard-skin pattern fabric, 1930s, table 72in (183cm) wide.
£8,500–10,000
$12,500–14,500 ⚒ **S**

A **set of six carved maple side chairs,** by Franco Campo and Carlo Graffi for Carlo Mollino, upholstered in red leather, with brass tacks, Italian, c1953.
£16,000–19,000
$23,000–27,000 ⚒ **P(PL)**
The young architects Campo and Graffi worked under the tutelage of Mollino in the early 1950s, going on to design numerous Italian homes and interiors in the latter part of the decade.

A **polished metal and glass Les Dessous de Table dining suite,** by Yonel Lebovici, comprising a table, three fork chairs and three knife chairs, French, 1992, table 95in (241.5cm) wide.
£40,000–48,000
$60,000–70,000 ⚒ **P(PL)**

◀ A **wood, aluminium and moulded plastic cabinet,** by Charlotte Perriand, with two sliding doors, c1960, 71¼in (181cm) wide.
£14,000–17,000
$20,000–25,000 ⚒ **P(PL)**

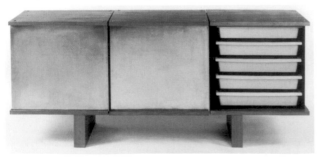

Colour Review

An orange-lacquered bentwood and plywood armchair, designed by Josef Hoffman or Adolf Schneck, made by Thonet-Mundus AG, remains of Thonet paper label, 1925.
£1,200–1,400
$1,750–2,000 ⚚ DORO

A bentwood side chair, by Thonet, c1870.
£400–480
$580–700 ⚚ BB(L)

A beech bentwood rocking chair, by Thonet, with footrest rail, stamped Thonet, with remains of paper label, early 20thC
£1,200–1,400
$1,750–2,000 ⚚ S(O)

An Arts and Crafts oak settle, attributed to Jung, early 20thC, 91in (231cm) wide.
£2,300–2,600
$3,350–3,800 ⚚ B&B

A stained beech bentwood and cane rocking chair, in the style of Antonio Volpe, Italian, c1910.
£5,250–6,250
$7,500–8,750 ⚚ S(NY)

A set of six bamboo, simulated bamboo and cane open armchairs, by Dryad of Leicester, with copper ashtrays to reverse of cresting rails, metal trade label to reverse.
£2,000–2,400
$3,000–3,500 ⚚ S(O)

A beech and deal Red/Blue chair, by Gerrit Rietveld, designed 1918, manufactured 1919.
£30,000–35,000
$43,000–50,000 ⚚ S(NY)

An Art Deco leather-upholstered club chair, French, early 20thC.
£600–700
$870–1,000 ↗ NOA

A pair of Ours Polaire armchairs, by Jean Royère, French, 1951.
£30,000–36,000
$43,000–53,000 ↗ S(P)

◄ **A set of six wooden stacking chairs,** by Alvar Aalto for Artek, c1932.
£5,250–6,250
$7,500–9,000 ↗ BB(L)

► **A wooden stacking stool,** by Alvar Aalto for Artek, model No. 60, 1930–33.
£1,000–1,200
$1,500–1,750 ↗ BB(L)

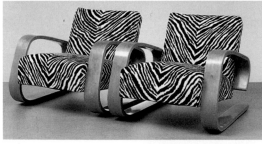

A birch-veneered pressure-formed plywood Paimio armchair, by Alvar Aalto for Artek, Finnish, some wear, 1945–55.
£2,800–3,300
$4,000–4,800 ↗ BUK

◄ **A pair of birch armchairs,** by Alvar Aalto for Artek, Finnish, designed 1935–36, manufactured 1945–55.
£4,500–5,500
$6,500–8,000 ↗ BUK

► **A laminated beech bentwood and canvas recliner,** by Alvar Aalto for Artek, model No. 39, Finnish, c1940.
£3,400–4,000
$5,000–5,800 ↗ BUK

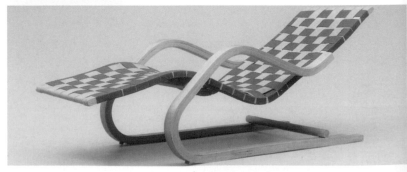

A bent plywood chaise longue, by Marcel Breuer for Isokon, designed c1938.
£2,800–3,500
$4,000–5,000 ⚒ BB(L)

▶ **A beech-framed Pernilla easy chair,** by Bruno Mathsson for Karl Mathsson, with woven paper cord body, cushion missing, Swedish, c1940.
£200–220
$290–320 ⚒ BUK

An oak-veneered plywood armchair, by Hans Pieck for Lawo, constructed from a single piece of pressure-formed plywood, stamped with serial No. c. 1500, Dutch, 1946.
£2,000–2,400
$3,000–3,500 ⚒ DORO

A sycamore-veneered plywood prototype armchair, by Marcel Breuer for Isokon, the armrests with integral cocktail shelves, 1935.
£40,000–48,000
$58,000–68,000 ⚒ S

A moulded plywood high-back chair, designed by Gerald Summers for makers of Simple Furniture, c1938.
£4,000–5,000
$5,800–7,200 ⚒ P(Ba)

A three-legged side chair, by Egon Eiermann, German, c1950.
£1,200–1,400
$1,750–2,000 ⚒ BB(L)

A beech-veneered pressure-formed plywood armchair, by Hans Pieck, minor damage, stamped 350, Dutch, 1946–47.
£1,750–2,000
$2,500–3,000 ⚒ BUK

A child's wooden chair, by Kit Nicholson for the Pioneer Health Centre, c1935.
£400–480
$580–700 ✗ BB(L)

A wooden side chair, by Jean Prouvé, c1950.
£2,000–2,400
$3,000–3,500 ✗ BB(L)

A wood and metal Standard chair, by Jean Prouvé, French, 1930.
£1,500–1,800
$2,200–2,600 ✗ BB(L)

A pair of child's plywood chairs, American, c1950.
£350–400
$500–580 ✗ BB(L)

▶ **An enamelled tubular-steel and fabric Wassily chair,** designed by Marcel Breuer for Thonet, model No. B3, c1928.
£12,500–15,000
$18,000–22,000
✗ S(NY)

▶ **A tubular metal and fabric armchair,** by Ludwig Mies van der Rohe for Thonet, model No. MR20, 1927.
£7,250–8,500
$10,500–12,500 ✗ BB(L)

▶ **An aluminium chaise longue,** designed by Marcel Breuer, the arm supports set with wooden handles, c1935, 53in (135cm) long.
£12,000–15,000
$17,500–22,000
✗ C(Am)

A chromium-plated tubular steel and wicker chair, designed by Marcel Breuer for Thonet/ Frankenberg, with wooden armrests, 1930.
£1,100–1,300
$1,600–2,000 ✗ DORO

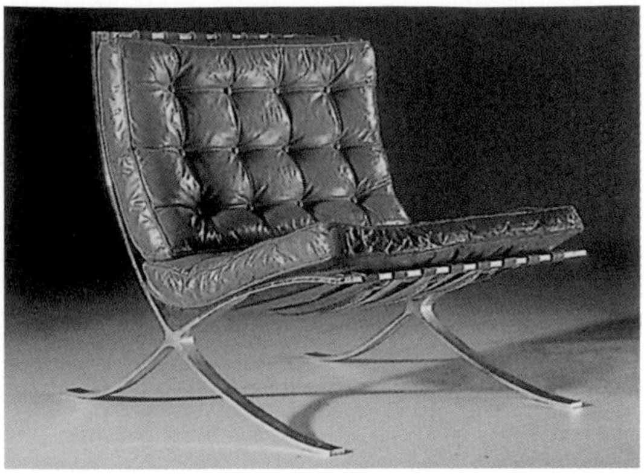

◄ **A metal-framed Barcelona Chair,** by Ludwig Mies van der Rohe, model No. MR90, c1931.
£60,000–80,000
$87,000–115,000 C(Am)

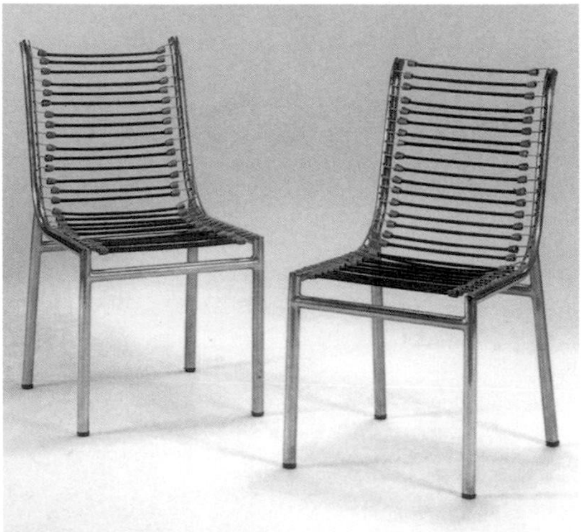

A set of six chromium-plated tubular steel frame chairs, by René Herbst, the backs and seats strung with elasticated straps, 1933.
£9,500–11,000
$14,000–16,000 S

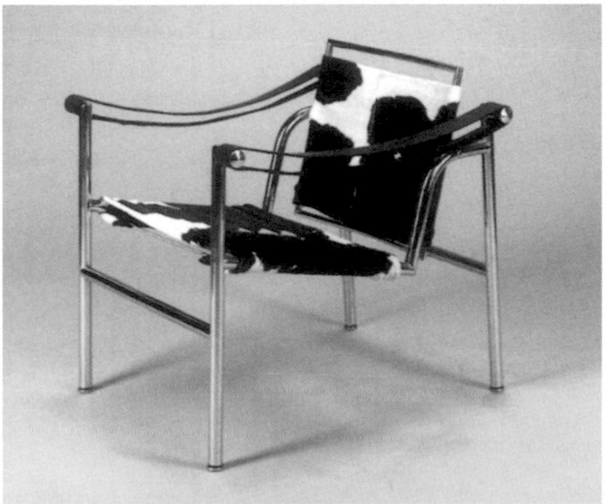

◄ **A metal-framed Basculant chair,** by Le Corbusier, Charlotte Perriand and Pierre Jeanneret for Cassina, model No. B301, c1960.
£950–1,150
$1,400–1,700 BB(L)

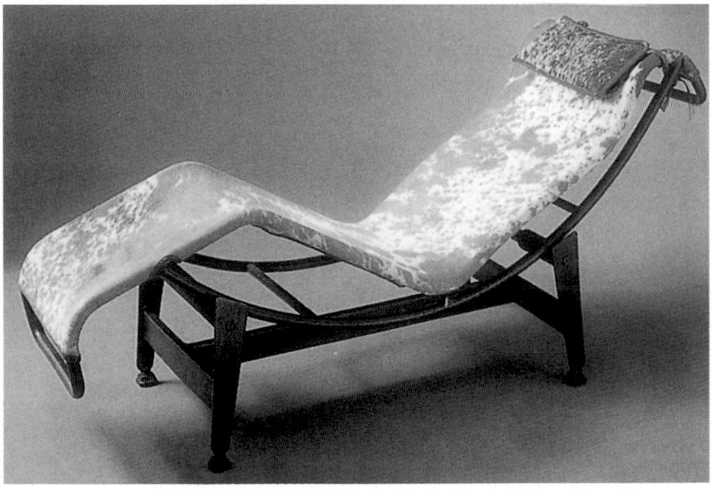

A black metal chaise longue, by Le Corbusier, Charlotte Perriand and Pierre Jeanneret, manufactured by Embru Corporation, Swiss, c1932.
£7,000–8,500
$10,200–12,200 S(NY)

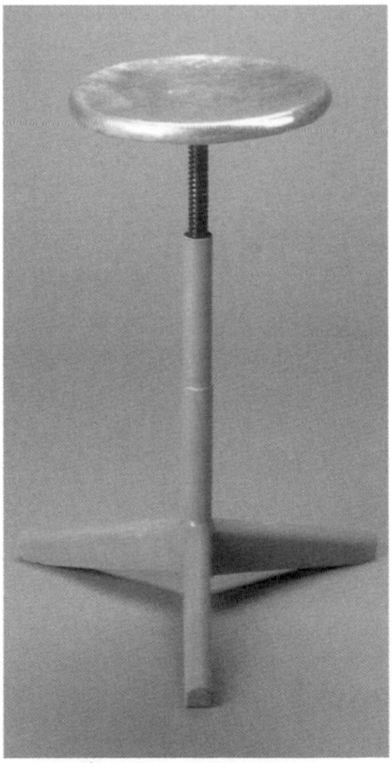

An aluminium and painted steel swivel stool, by Jean Prouvé, French, c1950.
£2,400–2,800
$3,500–4,000 BB(L)

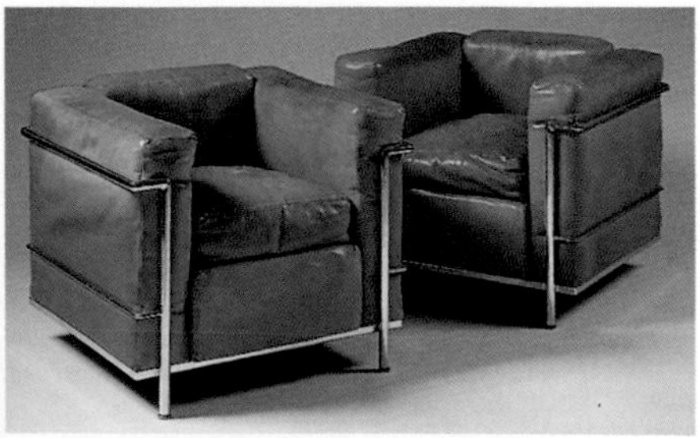

A pair of chromed-metal and leather Le Grand Comfort chairs, by Le Corbusier, Charlotte Perriand and Pierre Jeanneret for Heidi Webber, designed 1928, c1960.
£9,000–10,000
$13,000–14,500 S(NY)

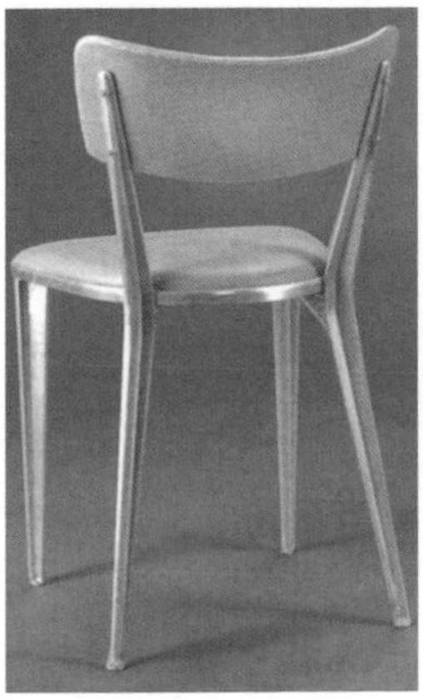

◄ **A pair of aluminium BA chairs,** by Ernest Race, 1945.
£600–700
$870–1,000 BB(L)

▶ **An ash-framed Hoop Chair,** by Hans J. Wegner for PP Møbler, the seat and backrest covered with wool, the back legs with casters, marked, Danish, 1965.
£750–900
$1,100–1,300 ↗ **BUK**

An ash and teak Peacock chair, by Hans J. Wegner for Johannes Hansen, with a paper cord seat, marked Johannes Hansen, Copenhagen, Denmark, 1947.
£1,550–1,850
$2,200–2,700 ↗ **BB(L)**

▶ **An ash and leather Safari chair,** by Kaare Klint, with brass hardware, designed c1933.
£1,150–1,350
$1,650–2,000 ↗ **BB(L)**

◀ **A pair of oak-framed Wishbone chairs,** by Hans J. Wegner for Carl Hansen, with rush seats, designed c1950.
£700–800
$1,000–1,275 ↗ **BB(L)**

A teak and woven cane The Chair armchair, by Hans J. Wegner for Johannes Hansen, cane renovated, 1949.
£600–720
$870–1,000 ↗ **BUK**

Prices

The price ranges quoted in this book reflect the average price a purchaser might expect to pay for a similar item. The price will vary according to the condition, rarity, size, popularity, provenance, colour and restoration of the item, and this must be taken into account when assessing values. Don't forget that if you are selling it is quite likely that you will be offered less than the price range.

A set of six teak and cane chairs, by Hans J. Wegner for Johannes Hansen, designed c1946.
£3,000–3,600
$4,400–5,200 ↗ **BB(L)**

A set of six pressure-formed plywood and teak chairs, by Arne Jacobsen for Fritz Hansen, model No. 3123, with black varnished steel legs, some damage, marked, Danish, 1967–76.
£400–480
$580–700 ↗ **BUK**

A pair of child's wood chairs, by Arne Jacobsen for Fritz Hansen, c1955.
£28,000–32,000
$40,000–46,000 ⚒ BB(L)

A fibreglass and aluminium Swan chair, by Arne Jacobsen for Fritz Hansen, model No. 3320, 1957–58.
£1,000–1,200
$1,400–1,700 ⚒ BB(L)

An aluminium-framed Swan sofa, by Arne Jacobsen for Fritz Hansen, with moulded fibreglass shell, Danish, 1957–58.
£2,200–2,600
$3,200–3,800 ⚒ BB(L)

An aluminium and leather Swan chair, by Arne Jacobsen for Fritz Hansen, slight surface damage, Danish, designed 1957–58.
£1,750–2,000
$2,500–3,000 ⚒ BUK

An aluminium and leather-covered Egg chair and footstool, by Arne Jacobsen for Fritz Hansen, model No. 3316, with moulded fibreglass shell, some surface damage, chair and stool marked, Danish, c1960.
£3,300–4,000
$4,800–5,800 ⚒ BUK

An aluminium-framed and leather-covered Egg chair, by Arne Jacobsen for Fritz Hansen, with moulded fibreglass shell, damaged, the leather stamped in white with the initials FH, with label, marked, Danish, c1960.
£1,500–1,800
$2,200–2,600 ⚒ BUK

An aluminium-framed and leather-covered Egg chair, by Arne Jacobsen for Fritz Hansen, minor damage, maker's label stamped FH Made in Denmark 1964 by Fritz Hansen.
£3,250–4,000
$4,800–5,800 ⚲ **BUK**

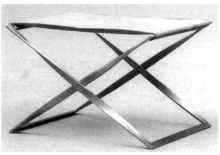

A matt chrome sprung steel PK-41 folding stool, by Poul Kjaerholm for E. Kold Christensen, with beige canvas seat, worn, c1960.
£1,750–2,000
$2,500–3,000 ⚲ **BUK**

A Love Seat, by Arne Jacobsen for Fritz Hansen, series No. 33, 1956, 50in (127cm) wide.
£1,200–1,400
$1,750–2,000 ⚲ **BUK**

A pair of chrome and leather PK-22 lounge chairs, by Poul Kjaerholm for E. Kold Christensen, marked with Kold Christensen's signature, 1957.
£1,000–1,200
$1,500–1,750 ⚲ **BB(L)**

▶ **A set of four chrome and plywood DCM chairs,** by Charles and Ray Eames for Herman Miller, two with maker's label, designed 1945–46.
£500–600
$720–870 ⚲ **BUK**

◀ **A moulded birch plywood LCW chair,** by Charles and Ray Eames for Evans Products Co, distributed by Herman Miller, with original wide mount, and Evans label.
£750–900
$1,100–1,300 ⚲ **TREA**

A metal-framed La Chaise easy chair, by Charles and Ray Eames for Vitra, with moulded fibreglass shell.
£2,000–2,400
$3,000–3,500 ⚲ **BUK**

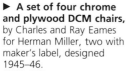

◄ **A moulded fibreglass and tubular metal RAR rocking chair,** by Charles and Ray Eames for Herman Miller, with wooden rockers, stamped, 1957.
£1,000–1,200
$1,500–1,750 ✗ BUK

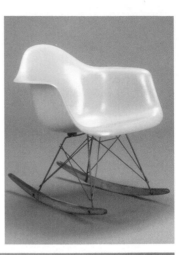

► **A RAR rocking chair,** by Charles and Ray Eames for Herman Miller, 1951.
£900–1,000
$1,300–1,500 ✗ BB(L)

A set of six side chairs, by Charles and Ray Eames for Herman Miller, c1953.
£1,600–1,900
$2,300–2,750 ✗ BB(L)

A pair of Aluminium Group lounge chairs, by Charles and Ray Eames for Herman Miller, 1958.
£1,400–1,700
$2,000–2,500 ✗ BB(L)

A DAR chair, by Charles and Ray Eames for Herman Miller, 1951.
£260–300
$380–440 ✗ BB(L)

◄ **A rosewood-veneered plywood Lounge Chair and Ottoman,** by Charles and Ray Eames, with leather upholstery, designed in 1956.
£1,500–1,800
$2,200–2,600 ✗ S(O)

A transfer-printed wood side chair, by Piero Fornasetti, designed c1950.
£2,200–2,600
$3,200–3,800 ✦ BB(L)

A metal and string side chair, by André Dupré for Knoll International, c1948.
£220–260
$320–380 ✦ BB(L)

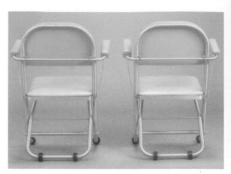

A pair of aluminium folding chairs, by Warren McArthur, c1935.
£475–575
$700–850 ✦ BB(L)

A steel and rope side chair, by Alan Gould, c1950.
£575–675
$850–1,000 ✦ BB(L)

A set of four Pretzel chairs, by ICF, Italian, c1986.
£1,350–1,500
$2,000–2,200
⊞ BTB

A side chair, by George Nelson Associates for Herman Miller, model No. 4671, c1948.
£2,000–2,400
$3,000–3,500 ✦ BB(L)

A pair of walnut and hickory Lounge Plus armchairs, by George Nakashima, American.
£5,000–6,000
$7,250–8,750 ✦ S(NY)

An ash and varnished wickerwork chair, by Pierre Jeanneret, canework not original, 1955.
£6,800–8,000
$10,000–11,500 ✦ S(P)

◀ **A wood-framed adjustable lounge chair,** in the style of Mollino, c1950.
£750–900
$1,100–1,350 ➹ BB(L)

A walnut and leather rocking chair, by Sam Maloof, stamped 44 668, with metal label 'Forty-Niner/Gerald M. Jennings/1968/Los Angeles Chapter', 1968.
£16,000–19,000
$23,000–27,000 ➹ BB(L)

A pair of maple-framed lounge chairs, attributed to Russell Wright, with upholstered cushions, designed c1950.
£1,000–1,200
$1,450–1,750 ➹ BB(L)

▶ **A pair of Lady lounge chairs,** by Marco Zanuso for Arflex, 1951.
£3,500–4,000
$5,000–6,000 ➹ BB(L)

A pair of white-varnished steel mesh Diamond Chair armchairs, by Harry Bertoia for Knoll International, with leather cushions, 1950–52.
£400–480
$580–700 ➹ BUK

A black-enamelled and chrome-framed Marshmallow sofa, by George Nelson for Herman Miller, with Alexander Girard's Mogul stripe upholstery, 1950s, 51in (129.5cm) wide.
£11,000–13,000
$16,000–19,000 ➹ TREA

A Tulip swivel stool, by Eero Saarinen for Knoll International, 1956, 16in (40.5cm) high.
£1,800–2,200
$2,600–3,200 ➹ BB(L)

A Tulip armchair, by Eero Saarinen for Knoll International, model No. 150, 1956.
£200–240
$300–350 ➹ BB(L)

◀ **A pair of chrome-plated wire rod Contour lounge chairs,** by David Colwell for 4's Company, with tinted heat-formed clear acrylic bucket seats, 1968.
£600–720
$870–1,000 ⚒ P

A steel-framed Coconut chair, by George Nelson for Herman Miller, American, 1955.
£2,500–3,000
$3,600–4,400 ⚒ P(Ba)

▶ **A Batchelor chair,** by Verner Panton for Fritz Hansen, 1955.
£325–375
$470–570 ⚒ BB(L)

A polyurethane foam armchair, by Gaetano Pesce for C & B, with original stretch fabric, Italian, 1969.
£1,400–1,600
$2,000–2,300 ⚒ DORO

▶ **A lounge chair,** by Pierre Paulin, model No. 555, 1958.
£970–1,100
$1,400–1,600 ⚒ BB(L)

A Tongue chair, by Pierre Paulin for Artifort, c1970.
£950–1,150
$1,400–1,700 ⊞ MARK

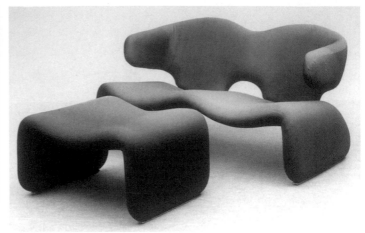

A stainless steel and foam Mushroom armchair, by Pierre Paulin, model No. 560, with spring suspension, covered in nylon jersey, on a lacquered wood base, numbered 1/35/60, French, 1963.
£1,000–1,200
$1,500–1,750 ⚒ S(P)

A steel-framed Djinn sofa and footstool, by Oliver Mourgue for Airborne, covered in nylon jersey, colour faded, c1960.
£575–650
$850–950 ⚒ BUK
The Djinn series can be seen in the interior of Stanley Kubrick's film *2001: A Space Odyssey.*

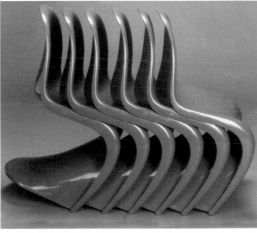

A steel-framed Ribbon Chair, by Pierre Paulin for Artifort, with a varnished wood foot, damaged, Dutch, c1965.
£1,450–1,700
$2,000–2,400 ⚒ BUK

A set of six Panton chairs, by Verner Panton for Herman Miller, 1959–60.
£2,600–3,000
$3,800–4,000 ⚒ BB(L)

Three Universale plastic chairs, by Joe Colombo, c1967.
£1,000–1,100
$1,500–1,600
⚒ S

► **A Cone chair,** by Verner Panton for Plus-Line, Danish, 1958.
£700–800
$1,000–1,150
⚒ BB(L)

A Panton chair, by Verner Panton for Herman Miller, 1959–60.
£240–280
$350–400 ⚒ BB(L)

A Tecno adjustable lounge chair, by Osvaldo Borsani for Tecno, model No. P40, Italian, 1954.
£2,200–2,500
$3,200–3,500 ↗ BB(L)

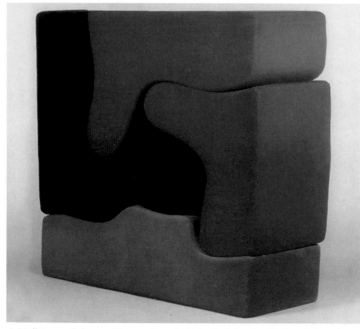

A Malitte modular seating system, by Roberto Sebastian Matta, designed to function as a sculptural wall when not in use, 1966.
£900–1,000
$1,300–1,500 ↗ S(O)

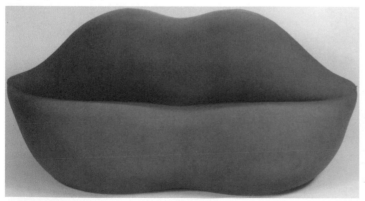

A polyurethane foam Marilyn sofa, by Studio 65 for Gufram, Turin, 1972.
£3,200–3,700
$4,700–5,400 ↗ DORO

▶ **A leather and fabric Tennis Ball chair,** by De Sede, c1980, 31in (78cm) high.
£850–1,000
$1,250–1,500 ↗ S

A set of six Cone chairs, designed for Fritz Hansen, Danish, 1959.
£2,000–2,400
$3,000–3,500 ↗ WBH

A moulded-steel and foam Living Tower, by Verner Panton for Panton Design, 1968.
£4,200–5,000
$6,000–7,250 ↗ BUK

A leather chair, in the shape of a boxing glove, 1960s.
£450–500
$650–720 ⊞ MARK

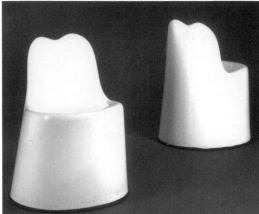

A pair of Molar chairs, by Wendell Castle for Beylerian, 1969.
£770–850
$1,100–1,250 ♪ BB(L)

◄ **A moulded fibreglass and polyester Ball chair,** by Eero Aarnio for Asko Lahti, on a painted aluminium foot, with wool interior.
£1,700–2,000
$2,500–3,000 ♪ Bon
This chair was originally used in the television series ***The Prisoner.***

A chaise longue, by Richard Schultz for Knoll International, c1968.
£900–1,100
$1,300–1,600 ♪ BB(L)

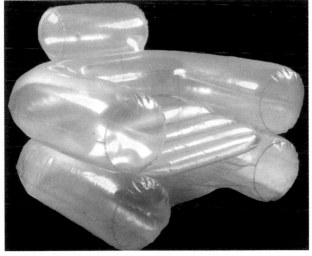

A transparent PVC Blow Armchair, by Donato d'Urbino, Paolo Lomazzi and Jonathon De Pas for Zanotta, Italian, 1967.
£700–850
$1,000–1,250 ♪ DORO

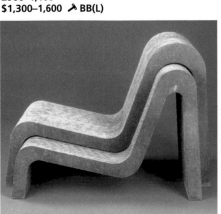

A pair of laminated corrugated cardboard Easy Edges nesting chairs, by Frank Gehry, American, 1971.
£3,200–3,800
$4,700–5,500 ♪ BB(L)

► **A cardboard Wiggle chair,** by Frank Gehry for Jack Brogan, 1970s.
£2,250–2,750
$3,250–4,000 ♪ TREA

A laminated corrugated cardboard Easy Edges chair, by Frank Gehry, American, c1970.
£950–1,100
$1,400–1,600 ♪ BB(L)

A steel mesh How High the Moon armchair, by Shiro Kuramata for Vitra, Japanese, 1986.
£4,500–5,500
$6,500–8,000 ↗ DORO

◄ **A welded mild steel Paris chair,** by André Dubreuil, 1998.
£1,800–2,200
$2,600–3,200 ↗ S(O)

A pair of birch-faced plywood side chairs, by Jasper Morrison, with narrow gauge enamelled steel frame, c1988.
£550–650
$800–950 ↗ P

Sets/pairs

Unless otherwise stated, any description which refers to 'a set' or 'a pair' includes a guide price for the entire set or the pair, even though the illustration may show only a single item.

A polished sheet steel Well Tempered chair, by Ron Arad for Vitra, 1986–93.
£7,500–9,000
$11,000–13,000 ↗ DORO

◄ **A pair of metal side chairs,** by Philippe Starck for Adelphi, c1990.
£2,200–2,500
$3,200–3,600 ↗ BB(L)

► **A set of three wood and metal side chairs,** by Philippe Starck for Adelphi, c1990.
£650–750
$900–1,100 ↗ BB(L)

A set of four painted steel bar stools, by Philippe Starck for Adelphi, c1990.
£700–800
$1,000–1,150 ↗ BB(L)

Desks & Work Tables

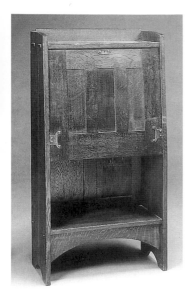

An oak desk, by Gustav Stickley, the panelled fall-front opening to a fitted interior, fall-front replaced and two drawers missing, c1904, 26in (66cm) wide.
£1,800–2,200
$2,600–3,200 ⊞ B&B

An oak double school desk, c1920, 40in (101.5cm) wide.
£100–120
$145–175 ⊞ WaH

An oak writing desk, by Ambrose Heal for Heal's, with fall flaps at each end, enclosing six file trays, printed label, 60in (152cm) wide.
£8,000–10,000
$11,500–14,500 ⋏ C

▶ **A silky oak secretaire with adjoining bookshelves,** by Betty Joel for Token Handmade Furniture, with ivory scallop-shaped handles, manufactured by W. G. Evans, 1932, 84in (214cm) wide.
£2,400–2,600
$3,500–4,800 ⊞ RUSK

An Arts and Crafts oak needlework table, Continental, c1910, 30in (76cm) high.
£400–500
$580–720 ⊞ PVD

An Edwardian lady's satinwood-crossbanded and boxwood-strung mahogany writing table, the hinged top opening and projecting the sliding writing surface to reveal a morocco leather-fitted interior, stamped mark, 31in (79cm) wide.
£800–900
$1,150–1,300 ⋏ P(NW)

A desk and a pair of bookshelves, the desk veneered in large chequer pattern of pale and dark woods, with central frieze drawer, the bookshelves edged with conforming chequer veneer, Austrian, early 1900s, desk 73¼in (186cm) wide.
£28,000–33,000
$40,000–48,000 ⋏ S

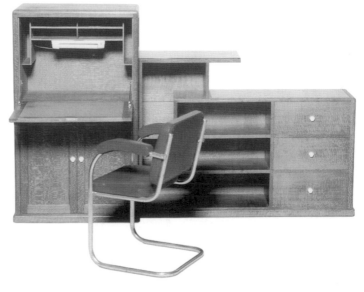

A sycamore-veneered and chromium-plated tubular metal desk, by Marcel Breuer for Isokon, with glass top and five drawers, manufactured by P. E. Gane, manufacturer's label, 1935–36, 48in (122cm) wide.
£32,000–38,000
$45,000–55,000 ⚒ S

An adzed oak writing table, by Robert (Mouseman) Thompson, 1930s, 66in (167.5cm) wide.
£9,000–10,500
$13,000–15,000 ⚒ S

A tubular anodized aluminium and black Formica desk, by Warren McArthur, American, 1930s, 50½in (127cm) wide.
£21,000–25,000
$30,000–36,000 ⚒ P(PL)

▶ **An oak and Fibrosil trestle table,** by Carlo Mollino, the oak trestle legs supporting a Fibrosil simulated oak grain writing surface, with an oak-veneered and Fibrosil pedestal, Italian, 1946, 75¼in (191cm) wide.
£6,200–9,000
$9,000–13,000 ⚒ P(PL)

A parchment-covered wood desk, by André Arbus, c1935, 43in (52.5cm) wide.
£6,200–6,800
$9,000–10,000 ⚒ S

A steel and wood Secretaire desk, by Jean Prouvé, French, 1941–43, 48½in (123cm) wide, together with a Standard chair.
£8,000–9,500
$11,500–13,500 ⚒ P(PL)

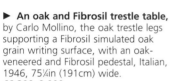

A birch and tubular steel drop-leaf desk, by George Nelson for Herman Miller, American, c1947, 40in (101.5cm) wide.
£700–850
$1,000–1,250 ⚒ BB(L)

▶ **A walnut-framed Home Desk,** by George Nelson for Herman Miller, model No. 4658, with a leather top, with typewriter compartment, storage unit with sliding doors and a steel mesh Pendaflex basket, on tubular metal legs, American, c1950, 54in (137cm) wide.
£12,500–15,000
$18,000–22,000 ⚒ P(PL)

◀ **A child's steel and wood desk and chair,** by Jean Prouvé, French, c1948, desk 19in (48.5cm) wide.
£2,500–3,000
$3,500–4,500 ⚒ P(PL)

A leather, brass and steel desk, by Jacques Adnet, with one drawer, c1950, 64in (162.5cm) long.
£13,000–15,000
$19,000–22,000 ⚒ BB(L)

An oak desk, by the Dunbar Furniture Co, with cream-coloured laminated writing surface, the central drawer flanked by further drawers, American, c1950, 50in (127cm) wide.
£300–350
$450–500 ⚒ SK

A blonde wood desk, by Charlotte Perriand and Pierre Jeanneret, c1944, 64¼in (163cm) wide, together with a steel and plywood Standard chair by Jean Prouvé, French, c1950.
£14,500–17,500
$21,000–25,500 ⚒ P(PL)

A laminated and solid wood writing desk, with a glass top and a single drawer, 1950s, 55in (139.5cm) wide.
£1,200–1,400
$1,800–2,000 ⚒ S

▶ **A chromium-plated desk,** by Warren Platner, with a rust-coloured leather writing surface and leather-covered frieze drawer, with conforming computer table, c1960, desk 89¾in (228cm) wide.
£1,300–1,500
$2,000–2,200 ⚒ S

A mahogany desk, by Hans J Wegner for P. P. Møbler, with three drawers, Danish, 1950, 54¼in (138cm) wide.
£500–600
$720–870 ⚒ DORO

A wood and steel-framed Action Office desk, by George Nelson for Herman Miller, with a stained wood roll top, American, 1964, 65¾in (167cm) wide.
£850–1,000
$1,150–1,500 ⚒ DORO

A rosewood Action Office 1 desk, by George Nelson for Herman Miller, on a green-painted aluminium base, damaged, American, 1964–70, 66¼in (168.5cm) wide, with a chair.
£1,800–2,200
$2,600–3,200 ⚒ BUK

A walnut and rosewood desk, by George Nakashima, each work surface supported on a pedestal with three drawers, with a third slab leg, signed, 1972, 76in (193cm) wide.
£17,500–21,000
$25,500–30,500 ⚒P(PL)
This L-shaped work station is a variant of Nakashima's two classic desk models, the Double Pedestal Desk and the Conoid (cross-legged with single pedestal) Desk. This prototype was designed with an option for a third pedestal with drawers, which would create two separate pieces, but the client preferred this original design.

Organic Modern

The use of large planks of timber in modern design, as used by George Nakashima, is an attempt to connect to the organic and natural within the context of a rational and planned interior. Furthermore, the plank construction brings to mind the simple homestead furnishings of the American pioneers. The artist Mondrian experimented with orange crate furnishings and Le Corbusier designed a multi-function stool/storage unit based on the packing crate. These experiments were driven by economy and Functionalism, but they were also part of a Modernist desire to distance itself from 19th-century conventions in design.

Bedroom Furniture

An Egyptian-style bed, the headboard with a beaten copper panel, 42in (107cm) wide.
£600–700
$870–1,000 ⚒ C

A carved walnut armoire, by Louis Majorelle, labelled, c1920, 78in (198cm) wide.
£2,500–2,750
$3,500–4,000 ⊞ B&B

A figured black walnut-veneered bed, c1928, 48in (122cm) wide.
£1,600–1,800
$2,300–2,600 ⊞ RUSK

An Art Deco walnut-veneered chest of drawers, the five graduated drawers with ebony handles, 1930s, 36in (91.5cm) high.
£900–1,000
$1,300–1,500 ⚒ P(LB)

A fruitwood and mahogany washstand, inlaid with mother-of-pearl, with inset marble top, with two side chairs, c1875, washstand 45in (114.5cm) wide.
£1,400–1,700
$2,000–2,500 ⚒ SK

◄ **A wardrobe,** with decorative panels and door mirror, late 19thC, 87in (221cm) high.
£300–350
$440–500 ⊞ NET

An oak and Macassar ebony Spirales divan, by Emile-Jacques Ruhlmann, upholstered in velvet, c1920, 72in (183cm) long.
£270,000–300,000
$390,000–435,000 ⚒ S

A walnut dressing table, by Betty Joel for Token Handmade Furniture, the mirror flanked by two banks of drawers, together with a matching stool, c1928, 61in (155cm) wide.
£1,350–1,650
$2,000–2,400 ⊞ RUSK

A pair of walnut bedside cabinets, with inset glass tops, 1928, 19in (48.5cm) wide.
£2,000–2,200
$3,000–3,200 ⊞ RUSK

◄ **An Art Deco gold-lacquered grand lit,** 1930s, 71in (180cm) wide.
£1,300–1,700
$2,000–2,500 ⚒ C

A limed-oak wardrobe, by Heal's, with central mirrored door flanked by panelled doors enclosing hanging space and drawers, c1930, 72½in (184cm) wide.
£480–520
$700–750 ➶ P

A satin birch bedroom suite, by Heal's, comprising double wardrobe, single wardrobe, double bed and a chest of drawers, c1930, chest of drawers 32in (81cm) high.
£700–850
$1,000–1,250 ➶ P(B)

An oak wardrobe, by Robert (Mouseman) Thompson, with beaten iron fittings, 48in (122cm) wide.
£3,000–4,000
$4,000–5,800 ➶ C

An Art Deco chromium-plated bed, probably by PEL, c1930, 54in (137cm) wide.
£450–500
$650–720 ➶ P(Ba)

A mirror, with pink glass side panels, some pitting to edges, c1930, 32in (81.5cm) high.
£80–100
$115–145 ⊞ JAZZ

A pair of ebonized wood and tubular steel bedside cabinets, attributed to Marcel Breuer, with fall-front doors.
£600–720
$870–1,000 ➶ Bon

A white birch and tubular anodized aluminium low chest, by Warren McArthur, with two short drawers above three long drawers, American, 1934, 48in (122cm) wide.
£6,500–7,500
$9,500–11,000 ➶ TREA

A tubular anodized aluminium and rubber stool, by Warren McCarthur, upholstered in cream-coloured fabric, American, 1930s, 17in (43cm) high.
£2,000–2,400
$2,750–3,500 ➶ P(PL)

◀ **A white birch and tubular anodized aluminium bedside table,** by Warren McArthur, manufacturer's label, American, 1934, 18in (45.5cm) wide.
£2,900–3,200
$4,200–4,700 ➶ TREA

A sycamore-veneered plywood wardrobe, by Marcel Breuer for Isokon, the top with rolling shutters each with chromium-plated handle, the double doors enclosing rails and shelves, manufactured by P. E. Gane, manufacturer's label, 1935–36, 106in (269cm) wide.
£6,000–7,000
$8,500–10,000 ⚒ **S**

A red-lacquered steel day bed, by Jean Prouvé, French, c1935, 35½in (90cm) wide.
£1,300–1,500
$2,000–2,200 ⚒ **P(PL)**

▶ **A walnut chest of drawers,** by Dick Russell for Gordon Russell, with three drawers, c1938, 35in (89cm) wide.
£350–450
$500–720 ⚒ **Bon**

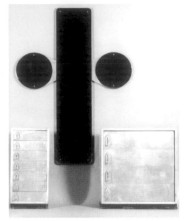

A sycamore-veneered plywood dressing table, by Marcel Breuer for Isokon, comprising wall-mounted mirror flanked by two hinged mirrors, one four-drawer unit and one seven-drawer unit with red laminated tops and chromium-plated metal handles, manufactured by P. E. Gane, veneer damaged, manufacturer's label, 1935–36, wall mirror 62in (157.5cm) high.
£43,000–50,000
$62,000–72,000 ⚒ **S**

A sycamore-veneered plywood cabinet, by Marcel Breuer for Isokon, with red laminated top, the double doors enclosing an adjustable shelf, with chromium-plated metal handle, manufactured by P. E. Gane, manufacturer's label, 1935–36, 36in (91.5cm) wide.
£3,500–4,000
$5,000–5,800 ⚒ **S**

> **Cross Reference**
> See Colour Review (page 126)

An oak and metal wardrobe, by Jean Prouvé, French, c1944, 62½in (159cm) wide.
£9,500–11,500
$13,800–16,800 ⚒ **P(PL)**

◀ **A painted and gilt gesso bed,** by Carlo Mollino for Casa Minola, with picture frame headboard upholstered in silk, Italian, 1944, 74in (188cm) wide.
£8,500–10,000
$12,000–14,500 ⚒ **P(PL)**

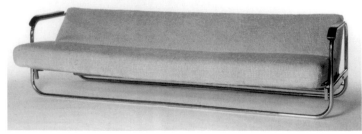

A chrome-plated tubular metal-framed convertible sofa, by Alvar Aalto, with ebonized wooden armrests and adjustable seat and back, Finnish, c1948, 25¼in (64cm) high.
£18,000–21,000
$26,000–30,000 ⚒ **P(PL)**

A wooden four-panel Farfalle screen, by Piero Fornasetti, transfer-printed, on casters, Italian, 1950s, 78½in (199.5cm) high.
£3,200–3,800
$4,600–5,500 ⚒ **P(PL)**

A chrome-plated tubular steel, wood and plastic sectional chaise longue and footstool, by Herman Miller for George Nelson Associates, upholstered in black wool, manufacturer's label, American 1950s, 64in (162.5cm) long, and a tray.
£4,500–5,500
$6,500–8,000 ⚒ P(PL)

A wood and lacquered aluminium armoire, by Jean Prouvé, 1950, 62¾in (159.5cm) wide.
£15,000–18,000
$22,000–26,000 ⚒ P(PL)

A gilt-iron-framed Starlet bed, by Jean Royère, c1956, 47¼in (120cm) wide.
£47,000–55,000
$68,000–80,000 ⚒ P(PL)

An oak-veneered and ebonized chest of drawers, by John and Sylvia Reid for Stag Cabinet Co, with detachable oak legs, c1958, 30in (76cm) wide.
£300–350
$450–500 ⊞ GRM

A birch-framed Berlin day bed, by Bruno Mathsson for Karl Mathsson, the mattress covered in a brown-grey fabric with leather buttons, marked, Swedish, c1970, 37½in (95.5cm) wide.
£1,100–1,300
$1,600–1,900 ⚒ BUK

A Dilly Dally dressing table, by Luigi Massoni for Poltrona Frau, comprising table with lift-up mirror, hinged stool and two pouffes, all covered in orange plastic, minor damage to table, Italian, c1970, table 25½in (65cm) diam.
£580–700
$870–1,000 ⚒ BUK

◄ **A pair of rosewood bedside cabinets,** by Jon Barnsley for Edward Barnsley Workshop, with frieze drawers and undertiers, 1987, 23in (58.5cm) high.
£1,300–1,500
$2,000–2,200 ⚒ Bon

► **A wood, glass and metal screen,** by Philippe Starck, with paper images, signed, c1990, 76in (193cm) high.
£3,000–3,600
$4,500–5,000 ⚒ BB(L)

Cabinets

An Arts and Crafts coromandel and ebony cabinet-on-stand, by Charles Spooner, c1910, 37½in (95.5cm) wide.
£9,500–10,500
$13,750–15,250 ⚒ P

An Art Nouveau mahogany display cabinet, 66in (167.5cm) high.
£850–950
$1,250–1,400 ⊞ BrL

An Arts and Crafts oak chest, attributed to Heal's, the cupboard doors with fielded chestnut panels, over three long drawers.
£1,500–1,800
$2,200–2,600 ⚒ P

LOCATE THE SOURCE
The source of each illustration in Miller's can be found by checking the code letters below each caption with the Key to Illustrations, pages 296–298.

◄ An adzed oak glazed cabinet, by Robert (Mouseman) Thompson, with leaded door panels and sides, three glass shelves and iron hinges and handles, 1930s, 42in (106.5cm) wide.
£3,300–4,000
$4,500–7,250 ⚒ S

An oak cabinet, by Ambrose Heal for Heal & Sons, manufacturer's label, 44in (113cm) wide.
£2,500–3,000
$3,500–4,500 ⚒ C

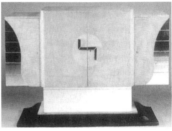

An Art Deco satin maple and ebonized cocktail cabinet, attributed to Hille, the breakfront with two doors enclosing a satin birch and mirrored interior, c1930, 63¾in (162cm) wide.
£1,700–2,000
$2,500–3,000 ⚒ P

◄ A wood cabinet, in the style of Dagobert Pêche, all-over decorated with a pale wood lattice on a dark ground with stylized leaf motifs, with a serrated pediment frieze above two doors opening to revel two adjustable shelves, Austrian, 1920s, 26¼in (66.5cm) wide.
£7,500–9,000
$11,000–13,000 ⚒ S

A cherry-veneered cupboard-on-chest, by Josef Frank for House & Garden, the cupboard with mahogany interior, Austrian, c1930, 56in (142cm) high.
£7,500–9,000
$11,000–13,000 ⚒ DORO

An Art Deco burr-maple cocktail cabinet, the upper doors enclosing mirrored interior and two rear shelves, the front slide above a further cupboard with a shelf and a drawer, c1930, 41¼in (105cm) wide.
£1,900–2,200
$2,750–3,200 ⚒ S(O)

An amboyna and blonde wood cocktail cabinet, by Maurice Adams, c1934, 48in (122cm) wide.
£3,700–4,000
$5,300–5,800 ⚒ S

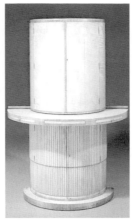

An Art Deco satin birch cocktail cabinet, attributed to Ray Hille, c1935, 46½in (118cm) wide.
£1,800–2,200
$2,600–3,200 ⚒ P

An Art Deco walnut bowfronted drinks cabinet, with roller doors, the upper section with mirrored interior, 1930s, 36in (91cm) wide.
£380–420
$550–600 ⚒ P(B)

An Art Deco walnut-veneered cocktail cabinet, with Bakelite and steel handles, 1930s, 65in (166cm) wide.
£160–180
$230–260 ⚒ P(B)

A wood storage unit, by Gilbert Rohde for Herman Miller, with one drawer, a fall-front cabinet and a bookshelf with four drawers and a door, manufacturer's label, 1935, 36in (91.5cm) wide.
£5,500–6,500
$8,000–9,500 ⚒ BB(L)

A birch cabinet, by Alvar Aalto for Artek, Finnish, 1935–40, 36in (91.5cm) wide.
£1,300–1,600
$1,900–2,300 ⊞ PLB

◄ **A teak and beech drinks cabinet,** by Tove and Edvard Kindt-Larsen, 1955, 32¼in (82cm) wide.
£1,250–1,500
$1,800–2,200
⚒ S

A walnut display cabinet, c1940, 50in (127cm) high.
£450–500
$580–720 ⊞ JAZZ

A birch, black-painted steel ESU 270-C storage unit, by Charles and Ray Eames for Herman Miller, with black and white Masonite panels, American, 1950, 24in (61cm) wide.
£8,500–10,000
$12,500–14,500 ⚒ **P(PL)**

A black-painted wood and zinc-finished steel ESU 251-C storage unit, by Charles and Ray Eames for Herman Miller, with red, white, blue and grey Masonite panels, American, 1950, 24in (61cm) wide.
£7,000–8,500
$10,000–12,000 ⚒ **P(PL)**

A wood and metal ESU 420-N storage unit, by Charles and Ray Eames for Herman Miller, American, 1953, 47in (119.5cm) wide.
£8,000–9,500
$11,500–13,500 ⚒ **BB(L)**

A steel and moulded plywood ESU storage unit, with painted Masonite panels, c1950, 47in (119.5cm) wide.
£5,500–6,000 ⚒ **S(NY)**

A birch and ebonized wood side cabinet, by George Nelson for Herman Miller, with sliding shelf, c1960, 17in (43cm) wide.
£300–360
$450–500 ⚒ **Bon**

A Formica, plastic, hardboard and white-enamelled steel side cabinet, by Raymond Loewy for DF2000, with shelved interior, the drawers shaded from brown to grey, French, c1970, 41½in (105.5cm) wide.
£1,000–1,200
$1,500–1,800 ⚒ **Bon**

A black and clear Plexiglass Highlight Hi-fi cabinet, by Kenneth Brozen, with compartments for record deck and records, American, 1970s, 48in (122cm) wide.
£350–420
$500–600 ⚒ **Bon**

▶ **A lacquered wood D'Antibes cabinet,** by George J. Sowden for Memphis, with blue top and yellow sides, American, 1981, 23in (58.5cm) wide.
£2,200–2,500
$3,200–3,500 ⚒ **Bon**

A lacquered wood and metal Gli Animali miniature cupboard, by Hans von Klier for Planula, c1970, 14in (35.5cm) wide.
£2,800–3,200
$4,000–4,500 ⚒ **S**

Hall Furniture

An oak plant stand, with studded metal bands, c1900, 36in (91.5cm) high.
£235–260
$330–380 ⊞ NAW

A copper-mounted wooden stick stand, by Wylie & Lockhead, retailed by Liberty, 1902, 29in (73.5cm) high.
£450–500
$650–720 ⊞ ANO

A rosewood three-tier *étagère*, by Edward Barnsley, stamped mark, c1990, 12½in (32cm) wide.
£600–720
$870–1,000 ⚒ Bon

Bookcases

A walnut hanging bookshelf, by Stanley W. Davies, with exposed dovetails and ebony tenons, carved mark, 1933, 36in (91.5cm) wide.
£1,000–1,200
$1,500–1,750 ⚒ M

A walnut library bookcase, by Peter Wals, with ebony and boxwood stringing, early 20thC, 76in (193cm) wide.
£12,000–15,000
$17,500–22,000 ⊞ L

An oak inlaid dwarf cabinet, by M. H. Baillie-Scott for J. P. White, the cupboard door with pewter and fruitwood inlay, c1904, 20in (51cm) wide.
£1,800–2,200
$2,600–3,200 ⚒ C

Cross Reference
See Colour Review (page 128)

▶ **A bookcase,** with drawers to centre cupboard, shelves and slides to outer cupboards, c1930s, 108in (274.5cm) wide.
£4,400–4,800
£6,500–7,000 ⊞ RUSK

◄ **An Art Deco walnut open bookshelf unit,** c1935, 36in (91.5cm) high.
£340–370
$350–550 ⊞ MTay

► **A moulded plywood bookshelf,** with adjustable black metal book ends, 1950s, 40in (101.5cm) wide.
£420–500
$620–700 ↗ TREA

A pine and painted aluminium bibliotèque, by Charlotte Perriand for Jean Prouvé Workshops, French, 1953, 71¾in (182.5cm) wide.
£36,000–43,000
$52,000–62,000 ↗ P(PL)

Chests Of Drawers

◄ **A light oak chest of drawers,** by the School of Cotswold Furniture Designers, 1920s, 35½in (90cm) wide.
£600–700
$870–1,000 ⊞ OOLA

► **An oak chest,** by Frank Wardel Knight, c1930, 49in (124.5cm) wide.
£1,500–1,750
$2,200–2,500 ↗ E

A wood and laminated bentwood chest of drawers, attributed to Alvar Aalto, possibly for Finmar, Finnish, 1930s.
£1,400–1,600
$2,000–2,300 ↗ BB(L)

A galuchat and ivory-inlaid commode, attributed to Jean-Michel Franck and Adolphe Chanaux, with green marble top, c1930, 46¾in (119cm) wide.
£22,000–25,000
$32,000–36,000 ↗ P(Z)

► **A walnut-veneered and chrome-plated steel credenza,** by George Nelson for Herman Miller, American, c1960, 74in (188cm) wide.
£2,200–2,600
$3,200–3,800 ↗ BB(L)

Tea Trolleys

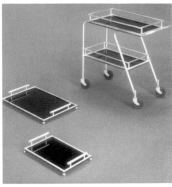

An aluminium and plastic two-tier trolley, by Aero Art, 1930s, 30½in (77.5cm) high.
£480–570
$700–850 ⚒ BB(L)

A chrome two-tier tea trolley with black Vitrolite shelves, on three casters, c1930, 30in (76cm) high.
£225–250
$325–360 ⊞ JAZZ

A chrome two-tier Savoy trolley, on three casters, 1930s, 30in (77cm) high.
£50–70
$75–100 ⚒ P(B)

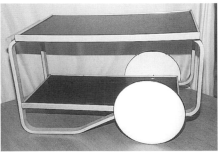

► **A birch and laminated birch serving trolley,** by Alvar Aalto for Artek, Finnish, 1934.
£2,900–3,400
$4,000–5,000
⚒ Bon

A blonde wood and laminate tea/serving trolley, by Alvar Aalto for Artek, model No. 98, with grey and black shelves, Finnish, 1935–36, 21½in (54.5cm) wide.
£550–600
$800–870 ⊞ PLB

► **A red-stained birch plywood Rolo serving trolley,** by Caes Braakman for Pastoe, model No. PB01, c1950, 26¾in (68cm) high.
£2,800–3,500
$4,000–5,000 ⚒ P(PL)

A tubular-steel and painted sheet steel two-tier trolley, in the style of Mathieu Mattegot, French, c1950.
£120–140
$175–200 ⚒ Bon

► **A wooden-framed tea trolley/serving cart,** with glass shelves, c1958, 17¾in (45cm) wide.
£90–100
$130–145
⊞ GRM

Magazine Racks

A Liberty mahogany magazine rack, c1900, 39in (99cm) high.
£450–550
$650–800 ⊞ ANO

A leather-bound metal-framed magazine rack, by Jacques Adnet with Hermès for *Compagnie des Art Français*, c1950, 18½in (47cm) high.
£3,000–3,600
$4,400–5,000 ⚖ P(PL)

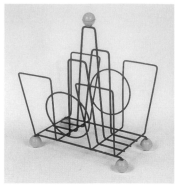

A black metal magazine rack, with yellow feet and handle, 1950s, 15in (38cm) high.
£15–20
$20–30 ⊞ TWa

A black bean canterbury, by Jon Barnsley for Edward Barnsley, with one drawer, 1996, 18in (45.5cm) wide.
£900–1,000
$1,300–1,500 ⚖ Bon

◄ A white plastic magazine rack, by Giotto Stoppino for Kartell, Italian, 1971–72, 18in (45.5cm) high.
£125–140
$180–200 ⊞ MARK

Storage

A storage tree, by Pastoe, Dutch, 1950s, 26¾in (68cm) high.
£1,300–1,500
$1,900–2,200 ⚖ BB(L)

Further reading
Miller's Collecting Modern Design,
Miller's Publications, 2001

► A plastic ABS stacking unit, by Anna Castelli Ferrieri for Kartell, 1968, 30in (76cm) high.
£140–160
$200–230 ⊞ PLB

An IBM Telestand, by Elliot Noyes, c1956, 23in (58.cm) high.
£500–600
$720–870 ⚖ BB(L)

► A plastic Boby office trolley, by Joe Colombo, designer's signature in relief on bottom shelf, 1970s, 29in (73.5cm) high.
£250–300
$350–450 ⊞ ZOOM

Miscellaneous

A teak sewing box, the hinged lid opening to reveal a storage tray, with pull-out wicker basket, Danish, c1960, 22¾in (58cm) high.
£300–350
$440–500 GRM

A painted black and gold iron fire screen, 1950s, 28in (71cm) high.
£40–50
$60–75 RAT

A moulded foam Giant Cactus coat rack, by Guido Drocco and Franco Mello for Gufram, slight wear, c1972, 64in (162.5cm) high.
£950–1,150
$1,400–1,700 TREA

A white ceramic and oiled walnut planter on stand, by La Gardo Tackett for Architecural Pottery, model No. SW-03, stamped maker's mark, American, 1950s, 21in (52.5cm) diam.
£3,800–4,500
$5,500–6,500 P(PL)

An unglazed ceramic planter, by Paul McCobb for Architecural Pottery, model No. M-3, stamped maker's mark, American, 1950s, 21½in (54.5cm) diam.
£3,800–4,500
$5,500–6,500 P(PL)

An unglazed ceramic planter, by Rex Goode and John Follis for Architectural Pottery, on a metal stand, stamped maker's mark, American, 1950s, 16½in (42cm) diam.
£6,500–7,500
$9,500–11,000 P(PL)

Inside/Outside Modern

A wall made out of glass is possible where the load-bearing requirements of the wall are separated from its shelter functions. This possibility has led designers to experiment with a more flexible approach to where inside and outside spaces occur in modern architecture. Light and space are prioritized in modern architecture by their appeal to healthy living and transparent Functionalism.

The popularity of metal furniture is based, in part, on its being suitable for indoor/outdoor use. From the 1950s onwards designers and architects began to use plants as organic elements within buildings – avoiding where possible the Victorian-style aspidistra with its Orwellian associations of petit-bourgeois suburbia.

A beige plastic and chrome ashtray, 1970s, 20½in (52cm) high.
£35–40
$45–75 ZOOM

A blue ABS plastic Pluvium umbrella stand, by Giancarlo Piretti for Castelli, the six umbrella holders rotate in stages around the base, Italian, 19¾in (50cm) high.
£225–250
$325–360 GRM

▶ **An oak log bin,** by Edward Barnsley, c1990, 28in (58cm) wide.
£320–380
$470–700 Bon

Fireplaces

An Arts and Crafts blue tiled fireplace, c1910, 24in (61cm) high.
£450–500
$650–720 ⊞ C20F

An Art Deco sienna marble fireplace, 1920s, 64in (162.5cm) wide.
£2,000–2,300
$2,900–3,300 ⊞ C20F

▶ **An Art Deco cream and black marble fireplace,** 1935, 56in (142cm) wide.
£1,100–1,275
$1,600–1,800 ⊞ C20F

An Art Deco-style cast-iron fireplace, 1920s, 42in (106.5cm) wide.
£700–800
$1,000–1,150 ⊞ C20F

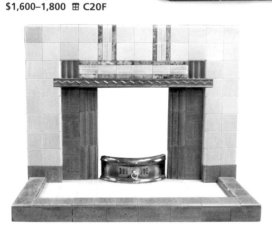

A brown and cream tiled fireplace, 1940s, 48in (122cm) wide.
£650–800
$950–1,150 ⊞ C20F

A tangerine and cream tiled fireplace, 1950s, 60in (152.5cm) wide.
£750–850
$1,100–1,250 ⊞ C20F

A grey and blue tiled fireplace, 1930s, 48in (122cm) wide.
£600–700
$870–1,000 ⊞ C20F

A brown and cream tiled fireplace, 1950s, 54in (137cm) wide.
£800–1,000
$1,150–1,500 ⊞ C20F

A tiled fireplace, 1950s, 54in (137cm) wide.
£600–700
$870–1,000 ⊞ C20F

Ceramics

This book can only give an overview of British collecting trends of 20th-century ceramics. The choice of material reflects the major interests of collectors in Britain, and while the emphasis is on British material, there are strong international connections with Europe, the Orient and North America.

In broad terms there are three main traditions that ceramic collectors have focused on: art pottery from the beginning of the century, studio pottery from the 1930s to the present, and the industrial tradition of manufacturing based in Stoke-on-Trent. The latter includes the output of factories such as Midwinter, Wedgwood and Doulton, and the work of designers such as Clarice Cliff and Susie Cooper. The wide range of products made in ceramic testify to its status as a wonder material of the 20th century and of the last two millennia!

The art pottery movement flourished in the early part of the 20th century and has its roots in the Arts and Crafts movement. It used Persian and Oriental decoration as its inspiration and attempted to rediscover the secrets of lustre glazing effects to create decorative wares. Art pottery manufacturers such as Ruskin also produced small parts for the jewellery manufacturing artisans of the Arts and Crafts movement. It should be noted that the art pottery movement was part of commercial, small-scale, manufacturing.

The studio ceramic tradition has its origins in the attempt, as part of the Arts and Crafts movement, to rediscover an English vernacular and authentic pottery tradition, and to create wares that aspire to an honesty and truth of materials allied to a fitness for purpose. The primary exponent of the tradition was Bernard Leach, who travelled to Japan and discovered a craft tradition that still connects artisan makers and local communities. He was determined to create a similar network of relationships in Britain and settled in St Ives where he established his studio. The Leach tradition was greatly reinvigorated by the advent of European émigré potters who were able, post WWII, to enrich the rather limited colour palette and extend the formal values of the English studio tradition.

Industrial ceramic manufacturing in Britain has been consolidated, throughout the 20th century, into a smaller number of larger concerns. Doulton and Wedgwood dominate the collectors' market. Wedgwood are still best known for the jasper wares which aspire to a timeless classical quality. However, during the 20th century they have produced a wide variety of products which are avidly collected. Fairyland lustre wares command high prices and the pieces which are decorated in the style of Eric Ravilious from the 1930s have an increasing following. Poole and Denby are probably the best known and most widely collected of the potteries outside Stoke-on-Trent.

Plates – Art Pottery

A Clarice Cliff plate, by Graham Sutherland, impressed mark, 1934, 9in (23cm) diam.
£125–150
$180–220 ⊞ AOS

▶ **A limited edition plate,** by John Cocteau, 'Chèvre-Pied au Long Cou', decorated with ceramic crayons and highlighted with slip, signed and dated, marked 11/40, 1957, 12¼in (31cm) diam, with certificate of origin.
£800–1,000
$1,150–1,500 ⚒ P(Ba)

Artists in industry

Many of the great artists of the 20th century have embraced the decorative arts. Picasso's experiments with clay at Valauris are now recognized as an important and distinctive phase of his career. Not all artists, though, become potters. A large number of English artists have worked with ceramic manufacturers to produce interesting and unusual designs. In the 1930s, Clarice Cliff and the Foley factory launched factory-produced wares with decorations by Paul Nash, Graham Sutherland and others but they were not successful. Wedgwood were more successful in their association with the watercolourist and wood-engraver, Eric Ravilious.

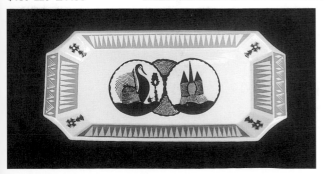

◀ **A Royal Worcester cake tray,** by Scottie Wilson, transfer-printed with an exotic bird and a castle in black and grey on a white ground, c1960, 13½in (34.5cm) wide.
£80–100
$115–145 ⊞ DAD
Scottie Wilson, who claimed to be illiterate, was 'discovered' working in a clockmaker's workshop in Toronto. He came to London and was at his most prolific in the 1960s, associating with Picasso and Miró. Apart from his work for Royal Worcester, he also made items in terracotta and produced silk scarves for Liberty.

Plates – Studio Pottery

A stoneware dish, by Geoffrey Whiting, impressed A seal, mid-20thC, 8¼in (21cm) wide.
£100–120
$145–175   ⚒ Bon

A blue and white tin-glazed bowl, by Alan Caiger-Smith, 1960, 10½in (26.5cm) diam.
£85–95
$125–140   ⊞ IW

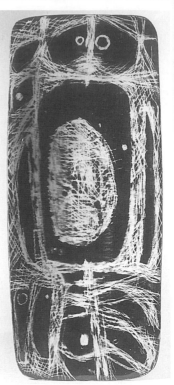

A pottery dish, by Michael Smith, decorated with brown flowers on a blue ground, Australian, c1960, 12in (30.5cm) wide.
£60–70
$90–100   ⊞ RAC

An earthenware dish, by James Tower, with shiny brown and cream glaze decoration, marked, 1953, 22in (56cm) long.
£600–700
$870–1,000   ⚒ Bon

◄ **A pottery plate,** by Keith Murray, signed, c1930, 10in (25.5cm) diam.
£70–80 / $100–115   ⊞ JAZZ

Plates – Factories

A Hollinshead & Kirkham fluted plate, decorated with Plums pattern, c1920, 10in (20.5cm) diam.
£140–160
$200–230   ⊞ AOT

A Grimwades Byzantaware plate, decorated with blue and orange enamels, c1930, 10in (25.5cm) wide.
£40–50
$60–75   ⊞ AOT

A Poole Pottery plate, decorated by Gwen Haskins after a 1930s design by Arthur Bradbury, c1974, 15½in (39.5cm') diam.
£500–600
$720–870   ⊞ HarC

A Gray's Pottery dish, painted with pink flowers and green leaves, 1930, 9½in (24cm) wide.
£60–70
$90–100   ⊞ CSA

A Carlton Ware dish, decorated in green, with gilt rim, 1950s, 12in (30.5cm) wide.
£25–30
$35–45   ⊞ CHU

A Royal Cauldon charger, by Edith Gater, tube-lined in green and yellow, c1938, 11½in (29cm) diam.
£125–150
$180–220 ⊞ AOT
A noted designer of the period, Edith Gater worked for Samson Hancock & Sons and Cauldon Potteries.

A Ridgways vegetable dish, by Enid Seeney, decorated with Homemaker pattern, 1955–57, 9in (23cm) diam.
£60–70
$90–100 ⊞ GIN

A pottery dish, with Lascaux-style decoration, c1950, 11½in (29c) diam.
£65–75
$95–110 ⊞ DSG

A Stavangerflint plate, painted in green, yellow and black with a bird, Norwegian, 1960s, 8in (20.5cm) diam.
£25–30
$35–45 ⊞ MARK

▶ **An Arabia dish,** by Birger Kaipiainen, decorated with a leaf pattern in green on a pale ground, signed, mid-20thC, Finnish, 15½in (39.5cm) wide.
£630–750
$900–1,100 ⋏ BUKF

A Paragon plate, commemorating the Coronation of George VI and Queen Elizabeth, 1937, 8½in (21.5cm) diam.
£90–100
$130–145 ⊞ W&S

▶ **A Rye Pottery avocado dish,** decorated with blue and grey stripes on a white ground, 1950s, 5½in (14cm) wide.
£25–30
$45–45 ⊞ NCA

A Rosenthal dish, by Raymond Peynet, decorated with a boy and a girl in a boat, in blue, pink, green and brown on a white ground, 1950s, 7¾in (19.5cm) wide.
£85–100
$125–145 ⊞ RDG

A Ridgways meat plate, by Enid Seeney, decorated with Homemaker pattern, c1957, 15in (38cm) wide.
£125–150
$180–220 ⊞ HarC
Homemaker tableware was sold exclusively through Woolworths between 1955 and 1967. The pattern features a range of easily identifiable 1950s objects including a Gordon Russell sideboard and a Robin Day chair.

◀ **Three Midwinter Stylecraft Fashion Tableware plates,** designed by Terence Conran, from the Collectors' series, printed in black on a white ground, c1955, 3¼in (8.5cm) wide.
£25–30
$35–45 each ⋏ AND

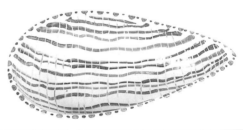

An Edelkeramix pottery plate, decorated with dancers in green, brown, yellow and black on a white ground, 1950s, 14in (35.5cm) wide.
£40–50
$60–90 ⊞ PrB

An Arabia stoneware plate, by Birger Kaipiainen, with raised bead decoration in a colours, under a lustre glaze, signed, 1970, 17½in (44.5cm) wide.
£550–600
$800–870 ⋏ BUK

Vases & Jugs – Art Pottery

An Elton ware vase, decorated with a gilt crackleware glaze, c1902, 7½in (19cm) high.
£400–450
$580–650 ↗ P(Ba)

A Pilkington vase, shape No. 2104, decorated with blue curdle and feathered glaze, c1906, 6in (15cm) high.
£200–225
$300–325 ⊞ PGA

A Baron Pottery vase, with sgraffito decoration and painted slip-glaze in green, brown and blue, 1900, 11¼in (28.5cm) high.
£130–160
$200–230 ⊞ COHU

An Upchurch Pottery jug, decorated in green, c1935, 7in (18cm) high.
£160–175
$230–250 ⊞ HUN

A Ruskin high-fired vase, with mottled purple, red and green glazes, impressed maker's mark, 1935, 8in (20.5cm) high.
£1,000–1,200
$1,500–1,750 ↗ S(O)

A Zsolnay Persian-style ewer, Hungarian, c1890, 9in (23cm) high.
£700–800
$1,000–1,150 ⊞ ANO

A Ruskin high-fired vase and cover, impressed maker's mark, 1901–05, 9¾in (25cm) high.
£2,200–2,500
$3,200–3,600 ↗ S(O)

A Ruskin high-fired vase, with coloured glazes, impressed maker's mark, 1905–10, 12½in (32cm) high.
£7,300–8,700
$10,500–12,500 ↗ S(O)

Experimental wares

The dissatisfaction with the homogenized products of industrial pottery manufacture provoked a revival of interest in the possibilities of a more eccentric process. The small-scale workshops that powered the revival of art wares were usually driven by experiments in glaze. The Ruskin, Royal Lancastrian and other factories associated with this tendency had flourished with successive fashions for the Arts and Crafts and for Art Nouveau. Flambé glaze effects are notoriously difficult to duplicate and the out put of these factories is often idiosyncratic and spectacular. A collection of art wares will never have two items exactly the same.

A Ruskin vase and cover, with lustre 'tea dust' glaze, incised manufacturer's mark, 1905, 10in (25.5cm) high.
£1,100–1,300
$1,750–2,000 ⚒ S(O)

A Ruskin vase, decorated with blue crystalline glazes, c1928, 12in (30.5cm) high.
£450–500
$650–720 ⊞ GAA

A Ruskin high-fired vase, with white veining on a moss green ground, impressed maker's mark, 1909, 11½in (29cm) high.
£2,200–2,600
$3,000–3,800 ⚒ S(O)

◀ **Ruskin high-fired vase,** decorated in green, black and purple, impressed maker's mark, c1906, 6½in (16.5cm) high.
£1,800–2,200
$2,600–3,200 ⚒ S(O)

A Ruskin high-fired vase, decorated in green on a lavender, purple and white ground, chips, impressed maker's mark, 1904–09, 8in (20.5cm) high.
£550–650
$800–950 ⚒ S(O)

▶ **A Ruskin high-fired vase,** decorated with lavender and green streaks over purple and blue, impressed maker's mark, c1905, 6in (15cm) high.
£1,300–1,500
$2,000–2,200 ⚒ S(O)

A Ruskin high-fired vase, with snakeskin glaze, impressed maker's mark and dated 1914, 11½in (29cm) high.
£2,200–2,600
$3,200–3,800 ⚒ S(O)

A Ruskin high-fired vase, with red, purple and green glazes, impressed maker's mark, 1933–35, 7¾in (19.5cm) high.
£1,600–1,900
$2,300–2,750 ⚒ S(O)

A Ruskin high-fired vase, with oxblood, purple and green spotted glaze, impressed maker's mark, 1926–33, 6¼in (16cm) high.
£1,600–1,900
$2,300–2,750 ⚒ S(O)

▶ **A Ruskin vase,** decorated with crystalline glazes, impressed maker's mark, c1930, 14¼in (36cm) high.
£950–1,150
$1,400–1,700 ⚒ S(O)

A Ruskin high-fired jar, with speckled decoration in green and black over a lavender and red ground, impressed maker's mark, c1909, 6in (15cm) high.
£1,300–1,500
$2,000–2,200 ⚒ S(O)

A Ruskin high-fired vase, decorated with a red glaze on a white ground with purple and green streaks and spots, impressed maker's mark, c1913, 10¼in (26cm) high.
£7,000–8,000
$10,000–11,500 ⚒ S(O)

A Ruskin high-fired vase, impressed maker's mark, 1927–33, 15¼in (38.5cm) high.
£8,200–9,800
$12,000–14,000 ⚒ S(O)

A Ruskin high-fired jar, cover and stand, impressed maker's mark, 1927, 8¼in (21cm) high.
£7,300–8,700
$10,500–12,500 ⚒ S(O)

▶ **A Ruskin ginger jar and stand,** decorated with blue and orange matt glazes, impressed and raised marks, c1930, 10½in (26.5cm) high.
£500–600
$720–870 ⚒ FHF

◄ **A Pilkington's Royal Lancastrian vase,** by W. Mycock, decorated in a streaky blue glaze, c1930, 9in (23cm) high.
£700–800
$1,000–1,200 ⊞ DSG

A Pilkington's Royal Lancastrian vase, model No. 3302, c1920, 8in (205cm) high.
£125–140
$180–200 ⊞ RUSK

A pair of Pilkington's Royal Lancastrian pottery vases, with mottled lavender glaze, c1975, 11in (28cm) high.
£425–475
$620–700 ⊞ HUN

A Royal Doulton Sung vase, by C. J. Noke, c1930, 14in (35.5cm) high.
£4,500–5,000
$6,500–7,250 ⊞ POW

► **A Moorcroft vase,** decorated with Watarah pattern under a flambé glaze, impressed facsimile signature and signed in blue 'W.M.', 1928–35, 8in (20.5cm) high
£5,000–6,000
$7,250–8,700 ⚒ S(O)

A Moorcroft vase, decorated with Pomegranate pattern, restored, impressed maker's mark, signed in green 'W Moorcroft', 1916-18, 12½in (32cm) high.
£500–600
$720–870 ⚒ S(O)

A Moorcroft vase, decorated with Peacock Feather pattern, impressed maker's mark and signed in blue 'W. Moorcroft', mid-1930s, 10½in (26.5cm) high.
£3,300–3,800
$4,750–5,500 ⚒ S(O)

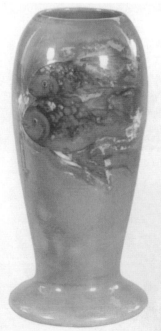

► **A Moorcroft vase,** tube-lined with swimming fish under a flambé glaze, impressed facsimile signature and signed in blue 'W. Moorcroft', c1938, 14¼in (37cm) high.
£1,750–2,000
$2,500–3,000 ⚒ S(O)

Vases & Jugs – Studio Pottery

◀ **A pottery jug,** in the style of Bernard Leach, with a fish-tail strap handle, c1950, 9½in (24cm) high.
£30–35
$45–50 ⚒ P(B)

Studio traditions

The revival of interest in the craft of pottery is part of the complex interaction between modern life and material culture. The huge advances in machine production have been accepted as part-and-parcel of 20th century life and progress. At the same time a desire for the authentic, local and handmade has fuelled the growth in small-scale pottery studio production. The pioneers of this revival in Britain were Bernard Leach and Michael Cardew. Leach was inspired by Japan and returned to St Ives to establish a pottery workshop alongside the artists' community in the Cornish fishing village. Leach worked with Shoji Hamada, the Japanese potter. Cardew is more closely associated with the pottery of Africa. These tendencies were rooted in traditional forms and practice. The post-war pottery from the studios of Hans Coper and Lucie Rie challenged these traditional forms by the development of a more contemporary aesthetic.

◀ **A stoneware jar,** by Shoji Hamada, ash glazed, with cobalt blue and brown decoration, 1955, 5¼in (13.5cm) high.
£2,800–3,000
$4,000–4,500 ⚒ Bon

▶ **A stoneware vase,** by Shoji Hamada, signed, c1967, 10in (25.5cm) high.
£6,200–6,800
$9,000–9,800 ⚒ Bon

◀ **A stoneware pot and cover,** by Katherine Pleydell-Bouverie, with a carved frieze, impressed marks, c1930, 3½in (9cm) diam.
£700–850
$1,000–1,250 ⚒ Bon

An Isle of Wight Pottery vase, by Ernest Saunders, with green and orange decoration, c1935, 7¼in (18.5cm) high.
£75–90
$110–130 ▦ DSG

▶ **A stoneware vase,** by Charles Vyse, decorated with reddish-brown foliage on a grey-green ground, incised mark, 1930s, 9½in (24cm) high.
£600–650
$870–1,000 ⚒ Bon

A stoneware jar, by William Staite Murray, the thick cream glaze with light blue and rust speckles, incised mark, 1922, 6¾in (17cm) high
£850–1,000
$1,250–1,500 ⚒ P

A pottery vase, by Dame Lucie Rie, c1930, 7in (18cm) high.
£5,250–6,000
$7,500–8,700 ⚒ S

A stoneware vase, by David Leach, decorated with an ash glaze, c1950, 9½in (24cm) high.
£250–300
$350–400 ⊞ RUSK

▶ **A stoneware pot,** by David Leach, impressed DL and St Ives seals, c1950, 10in (25.5cm) diam.
£550–600
$800–870 ⚒ P

A Rye Pottery vase, decorated with leaves, 1950s, 6½in (16cm) high.
£30–35
$45–50 ⊞ ADE

A celadon crackle-glazed vase, by James Walford, c1950, 4¼in (11cm) high.
£80–100
$115–145 ⊞ IW

▶ **A stoneware jug,** by Bernard Leach, decorated with a combed design under a green ash glaze, impressed BL and St Ives seals, 7½in (19cm) high.
£500–600
$720–870 ⚒ Bon

A stoneware vessel, by Hans Coper, the brown body with an incised white spiral, impressed mark, c1956, 14¾in (37.5cm) high.
£5,500–6,000
$8,000–8,700 ⚒ P

◀ **A stoneware vase,** by Hans Coper, decorated with mottled brown glaze, crazed and minor chip, impressed mark, early 1950s, 5¼in (13.5cm) high.
£600–700
$870–1,000 ⚒ RTo

▶ **A stoneware pot,** by Hans Coper, with textured buff body and dark brown neck and rim, impressed HC seal, c1952, 13½in (34.5cm) high.
£3,000–3,300
$4,400–4,800 ⚒ Bon

A stoneware vase, by Dame Lucie Rie, with all-over blue-green glaze with brown speckles, impressed LR seal, c1960, 11½in (29cm) high.
£700–850
$1,000–1,250 ↗ B(B)

A Cycladic black bud form, by Hans Coper, on square base, impressed HC seal, c1975, 9½in (24cm) high.
£35,000–40,000
$50,000–58,000 ↗ Bon

A stoneware vase, by David Leach, brown and white with a brown wax-resist motif, impressed DL seal, 9¼in (23.5cm) high.
£160–200
$230–300 ↗ Bon

A salt-glazed stoneware vase, by Tatsuzo Shimaoka, with a pierced lug above each corner, impressed seal, 9¾in (25cm) high,
£3,500–4,200
$5,000–6,000 ↗ B

A stoneware vase, by Dame Lucie Rie, 1960s, 7¾in (19.5cm) high.
£2,400–2,800
$3,500–4,000 ↗ PLY

▶ A stoneware pot, by Janet Leach, the grey-green glaze with vertical blue stripes, impressed marks, c1965, 5½in (14cm) high.
£350–420
$500–620 ↗ Bon

A stoneware vase, by William Ruscoe, with a black-painted design on a speckled grey ground, incised 'William Ruscoe 1965', 10in (25.5cm) diam.
£300–330
$440–480 ↗ Bon

▶ A Mushroom vase, by Joanna Constantinidis, 1990s, 7¾in (20cm) high.
£300–330
$440–480 ⊞ PGA

A composite Digswell form, by Hans Coper, impressed HC seal, c1963, 6in (15cm) high.
£7,000–8,500
$10,000–12,000 ↗ B

A stoneware ewer, by Michael Anderson, glazed in shades of brown, c1960, 6¼in (16cm) high.
£100–125
$145–180 ⊞ DSG

A vase, by John Maltby, in the shape of a spade, 1990s, 8½in (21.5cm) high.
£200–225
$300–325 ⊞ PGA

▶ **A stoneware vase,** by Sue Mundy, with horizontal impressed lines inlaid with porcelain, impressed SJM seal, 12½in (32cm) high.
£90–100
$130–145 ⚒ Bon

A vase, by Mary Rich, with gilded decoration, red mark, 1980s, 8¼in (21cm) high.
£350–375
$500–560 ⊞ PGA

A pottery vase, by Ray West, decorated with burgundy and blue crystalline effect glaze, American, c1900, 14¼in (37.5cm) high.
£650–700
$900–1,000 ⊞ PGA

A sculpted flat slab vase, by Gordon Cooke, decorated with feather patterning, seal mark, 1990s, 11½in (29cm) high.
£225–250
$325–360 ⊞ PGA

A burnished earthenware vase, by Christine Gittins, 1990, 7¾in (20cm) high.
£50–75
$75–110 ⊞ ELG

A vase, by Chris Carter, with yellow and brown mottled decoration, c1995, 22½in (57cm) high.
£650–800
$950–1,150 ⊞ DSG

A mother-of-pearl lustre vase, by Gebruder Henbach, decorated with an iris, c1900, 6in (15cm) high.
£220–250
$320–360 ⊞ ANO

A stoneware vase, by Otto Lindig, with beige and brown glaze, marked, German, c1935, 4¼in (11cm) high.
£900–1,000
$1,300–1,500 ⚒ P(Ba)

▶ **A pottery vase,** decorated in green and yellow, German, c1950, 17in (43cm) high.
£50–55
$75–80 ⊞ V&S

A sgraffito-effect pottery vase, decorated in blue and red on a black ground, Italian, c1950, 6in (15cm) high.
£45–55
$65–80 ⊞ **V&S**

A black pottery vase, hand-decorated with white stripes, German, 1950, 7in (18cm) high.
£40–45
$60–65 ⚲ **V&S**

A bottle vase, by Marcello Fantoni, with brown drip glaze over dark blue, Italian, c1960, 9in (23cm) wide.
£250–275
$350–400 ⊞ **DSG**

An earthenware goblet vase, by Ettore Sottsass for Bitossi, glazed red with a grey band, signed, Italian, c1960, 13in (33cm) high.
£2,600–3,000
$3,800–4,400 ⚲ **Bon**

A pottery vase, by Bernard Rooke, 1960s, 5in (12.5cm) high.
£50–55
$75–80 ⊞ **MARK**

A miniature vase, by Carl-Harry Stålhane, Swedish, c1960, 2in (5cm) high.
£40–45
$60–65 ⊞ **MARK**

◄ **A Longchamps terracotta jardinière,** decorated with blue, pink, white and green enamels, French, c1900, 12in (30.5cm) diam.
£300–325
$440–470 ⊞ **ANO**

A pottery vase, hand-painted with a glazed portrait in blue, green, white and brown on a red ground, Italian, c1950, 8in (20.5cm) high.
£45–55
$65–80 ⊞ **V&S**

A miniature jar, by Carl-Harry Stålhane, c1960, 1½in (4cm) high.
£40–45
$60–65 ⊞ **MARK**

A dark brown stoneware vase, by Gotlind Weigel, each side decorated with a black triangular web pattern, incised mark and seal and dated 1986, 8¼in (21cm) high.
£300–350
$450–500 ⚲ **Bon**

Vases & Jugs – Factories

A Clarice Cliff Bizarre vase, decorated with Carpet pattern in orange, grey and black, moulded No. 358, 1930, 7½in (19cm) high.
£3,400–3,800
$5,000–5,500 ✗ RBB

Clarice Cliff

The most widely recognized products of the 'jazz' age are probably Coco Chanel's fashion and Clarice Cliff's pottery. The Wilkinson pottery promoted Clarice Cliff as an art director of brightly coloured and angular patterned table wares and domestic china. These were mass-produced during the 1930s and aimed at a developing mass market. The range of products and patterns is huge. In consequence, when the revival of interest in Art Deco refocused attention onto Clarice Cliff there was an abundance of material. The growth in the popularity of this material for collectors is a reflection of its relative abundance and also of the careful documentation of the factory's output. Other, perhaps finer, wares from the same period or later are not collected in the same way. Clarice Cliff is a phenomenon.

A Clarice Cliff vase, shape No. 196, decorated with Sunrise pattern, with black printed mark, 1929–30, 6¼in (16.5cm) high.
£700–850
$1,000–1,250 ✗ S(O)

A Clarice Cliff Dover shape pot, decorated with Original Bizarre pattern, c1928, 6in (38cm) high.
£450–500
$650–720 ⊞ HEW

A Royal Winton vase, decorated with Hazel pattern, c1940, 5in (12.5cm) high.
£145–160
$200–230 ⊞ RH

A Crown Ducal vase, by Charlotte Rhead, decorated with blue and pale mauve stylized foliage on a mottled grey ground, 1930s, 8½in (21.5cm) high.
£120–130
$175–200 ✗ GAK

A Clarice Cliff Athens jug, decorated with Sliced Fruit pattern, 8in (20.5cm) high.
£425–500
$620–720 ⊞ RIC

A Midwinter pint jug, decorated with Yang pattern in yellow, green and brown, 1930s.
£18–20
$20–30 ✗ AND

▶ **A pair of Crown Ducal vases,** decorated with Stitch pattern, 1940s, 7in (18cm) high.
£45–50
$65–75 ⊞ RAC

Insurance values

Always insure your valuable antiques for the cost of replacing them with similar items, regardless of the original price paid. Both dealers and auctioneers can provide a valuation service for a fee.

A pair of vases, by Frederick Rhead, decorated in blue and with a trellis pattern, c1912, 13in (33cm) high.
£675–750
$1,000–1,000 ⊞ ANO

▶ A Wedgwood vase, by Keith Murray, decorated with a cream-coloured glaze, c1930, 6½in (16.5cm) high.
£400–450
$580–650 ⊞ PGA

A Wedgwood vase, by Keith Murray, with cream glaze, 1930–40, 6½in (16.5cm) high.
£250–300
$350–450 ⊞ BEV

A Carter, Stabler & Adams pottery vase, painted in buff, grey, black and blue with stylized flower and leaf motifs, marked with artist's initial H and pattern code LJ, c1925, 11¾in (30cm) high.
£1,300–1,500
$1,500–2,200 ⚒ RTo

A Wedgwood vase, by Keith Murray, with white glaze, early signature, 1930s, 7in (18cm) high.
£300–325
$440–470 ⊞ JAZZ

A Wedgwood stoneware vase, the brown body with glazed top and white spout, impressed mark for J. Dermer, mid-20thC, 11¼in (28.5cm) high.
£550–600
$800–1,000 ⚒ SK(B)

A Carter, Stabler & Adams pottery jug, by Truda Carter, decorated by Marjorie Bat, 1928–34, 8¾in (22cm) high.
£350–400
$500–580 ⊞ ADE

A Wedgwood Vase, by Keith Murray, finished in green matt glaze, 1930s, 7in (18cm) high.
£175–200
$250–300 ⊞ BET

Condition

The condition is absolutely vital when assessing the value of an antique. Damaged pieces on the whole appreciate much less than perfect examples. However a rare desirable piece may command a high price even when damaged.

A Carter & Co vase, decorated in underglaze blue in Seccessionist style with figures in panels, signed, c1915, 8in (205cm) high.
£400–450
$580–650 ⚒ P(B)

A Carter, Stabler & Adams pottery vase, decorated by Betty Gooby, 1955–59, 7½in (19cm) high.
£200–250
$300–350 ⊞ ADE

◀ **A Carter, Stabler & Adams pottery vase,** by Alfred Rhead and Guy Sydenham, decorated by Dianne Holloway, marked, 1955–59, 10in (25.5cm) high.
£450–500
$650–720 ⊞ ADE

Poole

Poole Pottery is an English pottery, based in Dorset, and is now widely recognized as one of the most singular and successful manufacturers of the post-war period in Britain. Poole were pioneers in developing a range of contemporary designs using bright colours to decorate pottery in an almost abstract way. This was a huge departure for a firm whose traditions lay in the production of floral-decorated functional wares. They also produced a series of illustrated tiles during the 1930s and onwards. The output of the firm is well documented which is an important factor in its popularity.

A Poole Pottery Delphis vase, by Guy Sydenham, decorated with semi-circles of mottled green, stamped, maker's mark, 1960s, 5¾in (14.5cm) high.
£150–170
$220–250 ⚚ P(B)

A Poole Pottery red earthenware vase, by Carol Cutler, shape No. A20/3, decorated with four carved green-glazed castellated bands, marked, c1975, 5in (12.5cm) high.
£100–120
$145–175 ⚚ RTo

A Poole Delphis vase, 1970s, 8in (20.5cm) diam.
£80–90
$115–130 ⊞ DSG

▶ **A Pearsons & Co vase,** with cream glaze, 1950s, 12in (30.5cm) high.
£65–75
$95–110 ⊞ DSG

A Spode Velamour vase, with light brown glaze, 1940–50, 10¾in (27.5cm) high.
£50–60
$75–100 ⊞ DSG

A Beswick double funnel vase, decorated in blue, black and yellow, c1950, 8in (20.5cm) high.
£35–40
$50–60 ⊞ GIN

A Burleigh Ware vase, hand-painted in grey and black with a turquoise interior, 1950s, 8in (20.5cm) high.
£65–75
$95–110 ⊞ RAT

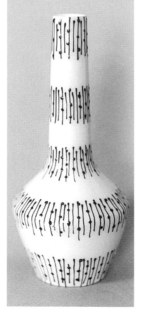

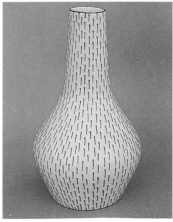

▶ **A Midwinter vase,** by Jessie Tait, tube-lined with Bands and Dots pattern, c1956, 6¾in (17cm) high.
£200–240
$300–350 ⊞ BDA

▶ **A Midwinter vase,** by Jessie Tait, tube-lined with Modern pattern in black and white, c1956, 9in (23cm) high.
£250–300
$350–450 ⊞ BDA

Prices

The price ranges quoted in this book reflect the average price a purchaser might expect to pay for a similar item. The price will vary according to the condition, rarity, size, popularity, provenance, colour and restoration of the item, and this must be taken into account when assessing values. Don't forget that if you are selling it is quite likely that you will be offered less than the price range.

A Hornsea Pottery vase, tube-lined in blue and white, 1950s, 5¼in (3.5cm) high.
£35–40
$50–60 ⊞ PrB

A wall vase, by Arthur Wood, decorated with hand and footprints in red and black, 1950s, 8in (20.5cm) diam.
£20–25
$30–35 ⊞ DAC

A Hornsea Pottery vase, decorated in black and white on a grey ground, 1950, 6½in (16.5cm) high.
£30–35
$45–50 ⊞ PrB

A Dennis China Works jug, by Sally Tuffin, decorated with daffodils, c1997, 10in (25.5cm) high.
£145–165
$200–250 ⊞ NP

A Troika pottery vase, with a speckled brown glaze, 1970s, 7¾in (19.5cm) high.
£75–85
$110–125 ⊞ MARK

LOCATE THE SOURCE

The source of each illustration in Miller's can be found by checking the code letters below each caption with the Key to Illustrations, pages 296–298.

An Alexandra Porcelain Works amphora vase, decorated with a Secessionist design, c1900, 9in (23cm) high.
£450–500
$650–720 ⊞ ANO

A Lallemant glazed earthenware vase, painted in black and rust on a cream ground with a dockside scene, marked, c1925, 13in (33cm) high.
£675–750
$1,000–1,100 ⊞ B&B

A Villeroy & Boch vase, decorated with a poppy design in yellow, blue and red, German, c1900, 12in (30.5cm) high.
£520–580
$750–850 ⊞ ANO

▶ An Arabia ceramic vase, by Francesca Mascitti-Lindh, with a multi-coloured glaze, signed, Finnish, 5¼in (13.5cm) high.
£100–120
$145–175 ⚲ BUKF

Colour Review

An Arts and Crafts oak dining table, by M. H. Baillie Scott for John P. White, Bedford, c1901, 71in (180.5cm) wide.
£10,500–12,000
$15,250–17,500 ⚒ S

An oak trestle dining table, by Gustav Stickley, model No. 631, top revarnished, c1904, 96in (244cm) wide.
£14,750–17,750
$21,500–25,500 ⚒ S(NY)

◀ **An oak refectory dining table,** by Robert (Mouseman) Thompson, c1953, 66in (167.5cm) wide.
£1,200–1,400
$1,750–2,000 ⚒ TMA

An oak occasional table, by Robert (Mouseman) Thompson, the shaped adzed top with scroll-carved corners, on octagonal baluster and block supports, c1930, 25½in (65cm) wide.
£1,500–1,800
$2,200–2,600 ⚒ DD

A painted wood table, by Gerrit Th. Rietveld for Gerard van de Groenekan, 1980s, 20¼in (51.5cm) wide.
£600–700
$870–1,000 ⚒ S(Am)

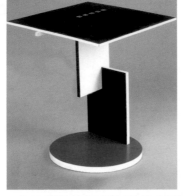

◀ **A painted wood Schroder House end table,** by Gerrit Th. Rietveld for Gerard van de Groenekan, 1924, manufactured c1960, 19¾in (50cm) wide.
£3,200–3,800
$4,700–5,500 ⚒ BB(L)

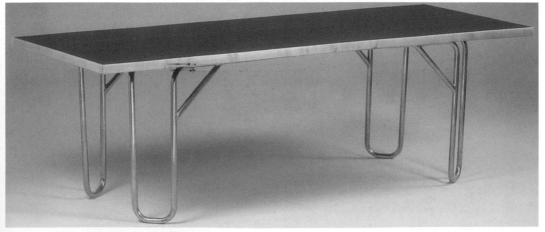

A chromium-plated tubular steel and maple table, by Cox & Co, Birmingham and London, with black linoleum-covered top, 1932, 88¾in (225.5cm) wide.
£1,000–1,200
$1,500–1,750 ⚒ DORO

A glass and iron-framed Modernist B 307 table, by Le Corbusier, Pierre Jeanneret and Charlotte Perriand for Thonet, with thick textured glass top, on chromium-plated metal legs, 1929, 30½in (77.5cm) wide.
£11,500–13,500
$16,500–19,500 ✗ S

A chromium-plated tubular steel and wood table, by Marcel Breuer for Thonet, with orange-painted top, designed 1927, manufactured 1930, 29½in (75cm) square.
£1,750–2,000
$2,500–3,000 ✗ DORO

A pair of tubular steel stacking tables, by Marcel Breuer for Thonet, German, 1927–28, 15½in (39.5cm) wide.
£900–1,000
$1,300–1,500 ✗ BB(L)

A steel Biltmore table, by Warren McArthur, American, c1930, 24in (61cm) wide.
£2,200–2,600
$3,200–3,800 ✗ BB(L)

An oak metal table, by Charlotte Perriand for the Jean Prouvé workshop, with circular pad feet, c1955, 34in (86.5cm) wide.
£12,000–14,000
$17,500–20,500 ✗ S

◄ **A pair of cream-lacquered stools,** in the style of Jean Michel Frank, the shaped rectangular tops on inswept supports joined by a solid base, c1935, 25½in (65cm) wide.
£1,000–1,200
$1,500–1,750 ✗ B

▶ **A burr-wood Faure pedestal dining table,** by Alfred Porteneuve, post-1933, 72in (183cm) diam.
£150,000–180,000
$218,000–260,000 ✗ S(NY)
This table is directly related to two desks designed by Ruhlmann in 1923 and 1930. In both desks Ruhlmann incorporated the unusual tripartable spool-shaped supports.

A plywood nesting table, by Marcel Breuer for Isokon, c1938, 24in (61cm) wide.
£700–850
$1,000–1,250 ✗ BB(L)

A plywood occasional table, by Eliel Saarinen for Johnson Furniture, c1939, 28¼in (72cm) wide.
£1,000–1,200
$1,500–1,750 ✗ BB(L)

A wooden Nimbus coffee table, by Neil Morris for Morris Furniture, with teak-faced laminated wood top, c1950, 39in (99cm) wide.
£450–550
$650–800 ✗ P

An Art Deco sycamore and golden oak dining table, the top veneered in large squares within a wide border, on large square section ends and solid platform base, c1930, 98½in (250cm) wide.
£2,000–2,300
$3,000–3,250 ✗ Bon

◀ A transfer-printed wood and painted-metal dining table, by Piero Fornasetti, with original paper label, Italian, c1955, 45in (114.5cm) diam.
£3,300–4,000
$4,800–5,800 ✗ S(NY)

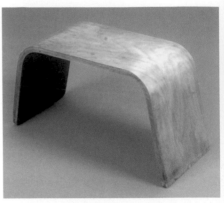

▶ A wooden office artifact, by Charles and Ray Eames for Herman Miller, c1945, 18½in (47cm) wide.
£350–420
$500–600 ✗ BB(L)

A prototype marble and plywood occasional table, by Charles and Ray Eames for Herman Miller, the marble top containing cross sections of fossilized sea creatures, on teak-faced plywood board with bevelled edges, with beech-faced plywood legs, 1946–52, 48in (122cm) wide.
£650–780
$950–1,150 ✗ Bon

A rosewood CTM table, by Charles and Ray Eames for Herman Miller, 1945, 34in (86.5cm) diam.
£2,200–2,600
$3,200–3,800 ✗ BB(L)
CTM stands for Coffee Table Metal.

A walnut-veneered plywood and steel DTM table, by Charles and Ray Eames for Herman Miller, with folding legs, Herman Miller label, c1946, 54in (137cm) wide.
£650–780
$950–1,150 ✗ BB(L)
DTM stands for Dining Table Metal.

A pair of wood and metal LTR tables by Charles and Ray Eames for Herman Miller, 1950, 15½in (39.5cm) wide.
£300–350
$450–500 ✗ BB(L)

A walnut-veneered plywood and metal LTR table, by Charles and Ray Eames for Herman Miller, with label, 1950, 13½in (33.5cm) wide.
£1,400–1,600
$2,000–2,300 ✗ BUK
LTR stands for Low Table Rod.

A wood and metal table, by Charles Eames, 1970–80, 41½in (105.5cm) diam.
£450–550
$650–800 ⊞ ZOOM

A walnut, steel and plastic laminate End Table, by Greta Grossman for Glen of California, c1954, 60½in (153.5cm) wide.
£2,000–2,200
$3,000–3,200 ✗ BB(L)

◄ **A wooden Rudder table,** by Isamu Noguchi for Herman Miller, 1949–50, 49in (124.5cm) wide.
£870–1,000
$1,300–1,500 ➤ BB(L)

An ebonized birch and glass coffee table, by Isamu Noguchi for Herman Miller, model No. IN-50, 50¼in (127.5cm) wide.
£1,600–2,000
$2,300–3,000 ➤ BB(L)

A walnut-framed Altimara console table, by Ico Parisi for Singer & Sons, with inset burr-walnut top, brass trim and brass-capped feet, c1950, 70¾in (179.5cm) wide.
£3,275–4,000
$4,800–5,800 ➤ TREA

An oak-framed sofa table, by Hans J. Wegner for Andreas Tuck, the teak top above a woven cane magazine shelf, stained, manufacturer's mark, Danish, 63in (160cm) wide.
£300–350
$450–500 ➤ BUK

An Oxford dining suite, by Arne Jacobsen for Fritz Hansen, c1960, table 57½in (146cm) diam.
£3,500–4,000
$5,000–5,800 ⚒ S

A beech-framed Maria Flap gate-leg table, by Bruno Mathsson, marked, Swedish, 1936, 35½in (90cm) wide.
£1,000–1,200
$1,500–1,750 ⚒ BUK

A teak dining suite, by Frem Røjle, comprising an extending table and four chairs, marked 1960s, table 41¼in (105cm) diam.
£600–650
$870–950 ⊞ ZOOM

A wood and metal Tulip table, by Eero Saarinen for Knoll International, the rosewood top above a white-varnished metal support, minor damage, 1957, 19¾in (50cm) diam.
£200–220
$300–320 ⚒ BUK

A steel and glass Spring side table, 1950s, 15in (38cm) diam.
£250–300
$360–440 ⚒ BB(L)

A polyester cast and moulded Samsone table, by Gaetano Pesce for Cassina, 1980, 63in (160cm) wide.
£7,000–8,000
$10,000–11,500 ⚒ Bon

A nest of epoxy and metal tables, by Gaetano Pesce for Fish Studios, 1990s, larger 16in (40.5cm) wide.
£750–900
$1,100–1,300 ⚒ TREA

Sets/pairs

Unless otherwise stated, any description which refers to 'a set' or 'a pair' includes a guide price for the entire set or the pair, even though the illustration may show only a single item.

▶ **A painted oak Oil Rig desk and chair,** by Stephen Owen, 1980s, table 52in (132cm) wide.
£1,500–1,800
$2,200–2,600 ⚒ P(Ed)

A Macassar ebony Dominique dining suite, comprising table and eight chairs, stamped, c1930, table 92½in (235cm) wide.
£7,000–8,500
$10,000–12,000 ↗ S(NY)

An Art Deco blonde wood and ebonized dining suite, by Ray Hille, the table with extension leaf, c1935, 83¾in (212.5cm) wide.
£2,200–2,400
$3,200–3,500 ↗ P

► **A coromandel dining room suite,** by Laszlo Hoenig, comprising 10 pieces, with label, c1930, table 67in (170.5cm) wide.
£2,800–3,200
$4,000–4,500 ↗ S(O)

An Art Deco burr-walnut dining suite, comprising 11 pieces, c1930, table 80in (203cm) wide.
£4,500–5,500
$6,500–8,000 ↗ S(NY)

A burr-walnut dining suite, by Epstein, comprising 11 pieces, the table on a U-shaped support joined by a shaped stretcher and two moulded plinth supports, the chairs with scroll-over top-rails, veneered backs and stuff-over seats, c1935, table 84¾in (215.5cm) wide.
£2,000–2,200
$3,000–3,200 ↗ B

► **An Art Deco walnut dining suite,** comprising nine pieces, quarter-veneered and crossbanded, c1930, table 73½in (186.5cm) wide.
£3,800–4,200
$5,500–6,000 ↗ AH

A **nickel- and chromium-plated metal and painted wood dining suite,** by Ludwig Mies van der Rohe, comprising nine pieces, including six MR10 chairs upholstered in leather, leather replaced, German, c1931, table 59in (150cm) wide.
£1,475–1,775
$2,150–2,500 ⚒ S(Am)
This suite, together with an MR20 chair was purchased at a furniture fair in Germany c1931 and was in the same private ownership until 1991. The table, sideboard and serving tables may be prototype designs by van der Rohe produced for the trade fair to complete a room setting, but never commercially produced.

A **Macassar ebony** *bureau plat,* by Emile-Jacques Ruhlmann, with ivory fittings and feet and extending side panels, c1925, 82in (208.5cm) wide, extended.
£145,000–175,000
$210,000–253,000 ⚒ S(NY)

▶ A **birch-veneered plywood desk and chair,** by Gerald Summers for Makers of Simple Furniture, the desk with original linoleum top, 1936, desk 53¼in (135.5cm) wide.
£9,500–11,500
$13,800–16,800 ⚒ DORO

◀ **An Art Deco sycamore and walnut dining suite,** comprising eight pieces, c1935, table 71¼in (181cm) wide.
£2,500–3,000
$3,500–4,500 ⚒ P

A **set of four moulded plastic Tulip armchairs and a table,** by Eero Saarinen for Knoll International, model No. 150, 1956, table 36in (91.5cm) diam.
£1,000–1,200
$1,500–1,750 ⚒ BB(L)

A **set of four Ed Archer chairs and an M table,** by Philippe Starck for Driade, the table with a mahogany top and chromed aluminium legs, the chairs with chromed aluminium frames and leather upholstery, stamped, Italian, 1986, table 53¼in (135.5cm) wide.
£1,000–1,200
$1,500–1,750 ⚒ BUK

A **red birch-veneered plywood, linoleum, steel, aluminium and painted wood Animation desk,** by K. E. M. Weber, with label, c1938, 72in (183cm) wide.
£6,500–7,800
$9,500–11,500 ⚒ BB(L)
This desk was custom made for Walt Disney Feature Animation.

◄ **A wood and metal Compass desk,** by Jean Prouvé, with three ABS plastic drawers, incised mark, French, c1950.
£6,500–8,000
$9,500–11,500   ⚷ BB(L)

A sycamore-veneered and chromium-plated tubular metal desk, by Marcel Breuer and made by P. E. Gane for Isokon, with glass top and five drawers, manufacturer's label, 1935–36, 48in (122cm) wide.
£32,000–38,000
$45,000–55,000   ⚷ S

◄ **A chrome-framed ESU desk and return,** by Charles and Ray Eames, with birch tops and Masonite panels, two black-enamelled file drawers and three birch drawers, c1954, 78in (198cm) wide.
£5,500–6,500
$8,000–9,500   ⚷ TREA

A mahogany and polished aluminium Direzionali T 96 desk, by Osvaldo Borsani for Techno, manufacturer's label, Italian, 1965, 98½in (250cm) wide.
£3,000–3,500
$4,500–5,000   ⚷ DORO

A jacaranda bureau, by Andreas Hansen for Thorald Madsens, the fall-front over two drawers and a slide, Danish, 1960, 34¼in (87cm) wide.
£400–480
$580–700   ⚷ BUK

A fibreglass Boomerang desk, by Maurice Calka, manufactured by Leleu Deshay, c1970, 69in (175.5cm) wide.
£9,500–10,500
$13,800–15,250   ⊞ MARK

An Art Nouveau carved oak sideboard, with bevelled mirror plates above two drawers and two cabinet doors, one with interior wine box, early 20thC, 59¾in (152cm) wide.
£600–750
$870–1,100 ⚒ Bon(W)

A Hague School oak and ebonized wood sideboard, by J. C. Jansen for LOV Oosterbeek, c1928, 59¾in (152cm) wide.
£3,000–3,500
$4,500–5,000 ⚒ S(Am)

An oak and painted-bronze sideboard, by Jean Royère, c1940, 98in (249cm) wide.
£20,000–24,000
$30,000–35,000 ⚒ S(NY)

An Art Deco mahogany sideboard, c1940, 94½in (240cm) wide.
£1,700–2,000
$2,500–3,000 ⚒ BB(L)

An oak sideboard, by Heal's, with three short drawers above three fielded panel doors, inset label, c1930, 53¾in (136.5cm) wide.
£300–350
$450–500 ⚒ DN

▶ **A mahogany and rosewood-veneered sideboard,** by David Booth for Gordon Russell, the cupboard doors enclosing shelves and a cutlery drawer, trade label, late 1940s, 48in (122cm) wide.
£470–570
$650–850 ⚒ S(O)
David Booth was a freelance designer who made a number of designs for Gordon Russell just after WWII. One of the reasons that the construction and interior fittings of this piece are so simple is the government restrictions on the use of materials at that time.

An oak sideboard, by Robert (Mouseman) Thompson, with five drawers flanked by side cupboards with iron fittings, c1953, 60in (152.5cm) wide.
£3,800–4,500
$5,500–6,500 ⚒ TMA

An oak and rosewood sideboard, by Charles Dudouyt, c1940, 84in (213.5cm) wide.
£4,200–5,000
$6,000–7,250 ➤ S(NY)

A birch sideboard, the removable upper cabinet with sliding glass doors, the lower section with sliding doors of perforated Masonite, on bentwood legs, signed 'Pascoe', 1950s, 54in (137cm) wide.
£200–220
$300–320 ➤ TREA

▶ **A red lacquer sideboard,** with two doors, brass trim and Lucite handle, 1940s, 60in (152.5cm) wide.
£1,250–1,500
$1,800–2,200 ➤ TREA

LOCATE THE SOURCE
The source of each illustration in Miller's can be found by checking the code letters below each caption with the Key to Illustrations, pages 296–298.

◀ **A blonde wood cabinet,** by Jean Royère, on a palisander frame, c1950, 70in (178cm) wide.
£6,000–7,000
$8,700–10,000 ➤ S

A wood and ceramic jewellery cabinet, by Paul McCobb for Winchenden, 1950s, 28in (71cm) wide.
£650–750
$950–1,100 ➤ BB(L)

A walnut and walnut-veneered sideboard, by George Nakashima for Widdicomb, c1958, 72in (183cm) wide.
£2,000–2,200
$3,000–3,200 ➤ BB(L)

A teak sideboard, by Sven Andersen, with brass fittings, Norwegian, 1950, 81½in (207cm) wide.
£1,000–1,200
$1,500–1,750 ➤ DORO

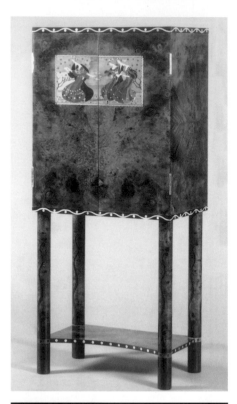

◀ **A Vienna Secessionist burr-walnut-veneered desk/cabinet,** in the style of Koloman Moser, with decorative panels in the style of Maximilian Lenz, the doors with panels of stylized dancing figures in a landscape, opening to reveal a mahogany and bird's-eye elm interior with fall-front desk, drawers and letter compartment, on burr-walnut-veneered legs, with scooped lower shelf, manufactured by Portois & Fix, Austrian, 1905, 27in (68.5cm) wide.
£20,000–24,000
$28,000–35,000 ⚒ S

A **mahogany press cupboard,** in the style of Ambrose Heal, with pewter and ebony inlay, early 20thC, 48in (122cm) wide.
£1,500–1,800
$2,200–2,600 ⚒ L&E

An Art Deco bird's-eye maple cocktail cabinet, by Hille, with shell motif, 1930s, 37in (94cm) wide.
£2,400–2,800
$3,500–4,000 ⚒ Bri

◀ **A sycamore and parchment cabinet,** by Jean-Michel Frank, c1930, 43½in (110.5cm) wide.
£110,000–132,000
$160,000–190,000 ⚒ S(NY)

An Art Deco walnut-cased six-octave mini piano, by Eavestaff, 51in (129.5cm) wide, with matching stool.
£700–900
$1,000–1,300 ⚒ PCh

A **burr-walnut display cabinet,** by Epstein, with etched glazed doors enclosing an etched mirror back panel and glass shelves, c1935, 44in (112cm) wide.
£1,300–1,500
$2,000–2,200 ⚒ B

A **painted softwood kitchen cabinet,** by Margarete Schütte Lihotzky and Ferdinand Kramer, the fall-front opening to reveal eight pull-out compartments, 1930, 38¼in (97cm) wide.
£1,750–2,100
$2,600–3,000 ⚒ BB(L)

◀ **A bureau,** by Ernest Gimson, with elaborately fitted interior, barber's pole inlay, manufactured by Sidney Barnsley, 33in (84cm) wide.
£10,000–12,000
$14,500–17,500 ⚒ C

A rosewood and rosewood-veneered chest, by George Nelson for Herman Miller, with aluminium and plastic-coated iron handles, c1954.
£2,500–3,000
$3,500–5,800 ⚒ BB(L)

A walnut and metal ESU hanging file cabinet, by Charles and Ray Eames for Herman Miller, 1953, 47in (119.5cm) wide.
£12,000–14,000
$17,500–20,500 ⚒ BB(L)
This cabinet was custom-made for the writer Lawrence Strickland.

A transfer-printed and lacquered wood Architectural cabinet, by Piero Fornasetti, fitted for electricity, Italian, 1951, 85¾in (218cm) high.
£11,500–13,500
$16,500–19,500 ⚒ P(Sy)
This design was reissued in the 1980s.

A sycamore linen press, by Peter Behrens, with geometric marquetry decoration, the single door opening to reveal two adjustable shelves, above three drawers, 1910, 31¼in (79.5cm) wide.
£10,800–13,000
$15,500–19,000 ⚒ S

A transfer-printed wood Architectural cabinet, by Piero Fornasetti, on brass legs, Italian, 1950s, 27in (68.5cm) wide.
£2,800–3,300
$4,000–4,700 ⚒ TREA

◄ **A joined oak wardrobe,** with two panelled doors enclosing a hanging rail, dated 1934, 53½in (136cm) wide.
£3,200–3,800
$4,500–5,500 ⚒ TEN

► **An Art Deco ebony six-piece Gaylayde bedroom suite,** by B. Cohen & Sons, with inlaid amboyna bandings, boxwood stringing and frieze inlaid with overlapping geometric circular motifs, 1926, wardrobe 70in (178cm) wide.
£4,500–5,500
$6,500–8,000 ⚒ S(O)

◄ **An Art Deco satinwood and ebonized dressing table and stool,** with hinged drawers, the stool with revolving seat, 74¾in (190cm) wide.
£1,300–1,500
$2,000–2,200 ⚒ S(O)

An oak chest and toilet mirror, by Betty Joel for the Token Works, the chest with hand-written label, one handle missing, chest 46in (117cm) wide, and a side cabinet.
£600–700
$870–1,000 ⚒ B

A wood, wood-veneered and aluminium cabinet, by Eliel Saarinen for Johnson, c1940, 48in (122cm) wide.
£700–850
$1,000–1,250 ⚒ BB(L)

► **A teak and plywood jewellery chest,** by George Nelson for Herman Miller, with rubber-coated steel handles, c1956, 23in (59cm) high.
£6,800–8,000
$9,800–11,800 ⚒ BB(L)

A rosewood-veneered plywood chest, by George Nelson for Herman Miller, with plastic-coated iron handles, c1954.
£2,000–2,400
$3,000–3,500 ⚒ BB(L)

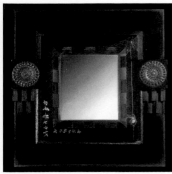

A veneered wood mirror, by Carlo Bugatti, decorated with moulded crenels and two copper *martelé* medallions, with copper banding, 24½in (62cm) wide.
£9,000–10,500
$13,000–15,000 ⚒ S(P)

A Macassar ebony and silvered-bronze waste basket, by Emile-Jacques Ruhlmann, impressed 'Ruhlmann', c1925, 12in (30.5cm) high.
£25,000–28,000
$35,000–40,000 ⚒ S(NY)
Ruhlmann designs are extremely sought after, hence the price.

A silvered-bronze mirror, by Marcel Bergue, c1925, 33½in (85cm) high.
£9,500–11,500
$13,500–15,500 ⚒ S(NY)

A walnut dresser, by Sidney Barnsley, with diamond pattern moulding, 75in (190.5cm) wide,
£8,000–9,500
$11,500–13,500 ⚒ C

A four-panel screen, by Leon Jallot, decorated with polychrome fish motifs, the reverse plain tortoiseshell, incised monogram LJ , 1920s, 74½in (189cm) high.
£8,400–10,000
$12,200–14,500 ⚒ S

A walnut coffer, in the style of Peter Waals of the Cotswold School, with raised fielded panels, the hinged lid with protruding lifts, the front with initials and date 1937, 46in (117cm) wide.
£850–1,000
$1,250–1,500 ⚒ WW

◀ **An oak blanket chest,** by Robert (Mouseman) Thompson, 1950s, 41in (104cm) wide.
£720–800
$1,000–1,200 ⚒ TMA

◀ **A burr-walnut-veneered cocktail bar and stools,** by Epstein, the cabinet with mirror glass top and sliding doors, the stools with upholstered seats and gilt-metal stretchers, c1935, cabinet 67in (170cm) wide.
£750–900
$1,000–1,300
⚒ B

A tubular metal drinks trolley, by Carl Auböck, with two cane-covered metal tiers and wooden wheels, 1950, 25¼in (64cm) wide.
£700–850
$1,000–1,250 ⚒ DORO

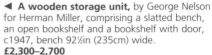

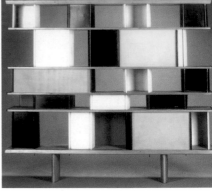

◀ **A wooden storage unit,** by George Nelson for Herman Miller, comprising a slatted bench, an open bookshelf and a bookshelf with door, c1947, bench 92½in (235cm) wide.
£2,300–2,700
$3,300–4,000 🔨 BB(L)

A wooden Mexique bookshelf, by Charlotte Perriand, Jean Prouvé and Sonia Delaunay, manufactured at the Jean Prouvé workshop, Italian, c1953, 72in (183cm) wide.
£33,000–38,000
$47,000–55,000 🔨 BB(L)

◀ **A polished palisander wood and metal E 22 wall unit,** by Osvaldo Borsani for Tecno, with four shelves, the cupboard with two sliding doors, with Tecno label, Italian, 1968, 55¼in (140cm) wide.
£1,600–1,800
$2,300–2,600 🔨 DORO

A Masonite, steel, moulded plywood and zinc ESU 420-N storage unit, by Charles and Ray Eames for Herman Miller, c1963, 47in (119.5cm) wide.
£11,500–13,500
$16,500–19,500 🔨 BB(L)

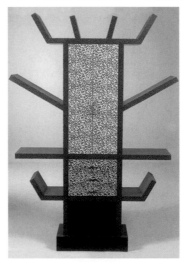

A Casablanca sideboard by Ettore Sottsass for Memphis, decorated with an Abet-Print plastic laminate printed with Sottsass' Bacterio pattern, with plastic label, Italian, 1981, 59½in (151cm) wide.
£3,000–3,500
$4,500–5,000 🔨 DORO

A fibreglass-framed Ultrafragola mirror, by Ettore Sottsass for Poltronova, c1970, 39¼in (99.5cm) wide.
£1,700–2,000
$2,500–3,000 🔨 BUK

A rosewood and aluminium Action Office I bookcase, by George Nelson for Herman Miller, partially painted, with three shelves, the lower shelf divided for paperwork, American, 1964–70, 47¼in (120cm) wide.
£1,100–1,300
$1,600–2,000 🔨 BUK

▶ **A Mini Kitchen,** by Joe Colombo, with laminate pull-out surface, c1963, 44in (113cm) wide.
£2,300–2,600
$3,300–3,800 🔨 S

Insurance values

Always insure your valuable antiques for the cost of replacing them with similar items, regardless of the original price paid. Both dealers and auctioneers can provide a valuation service for a fee.

An Arabia ceramic vase, Francesca Mascitti-Lindh, signed, decorated with a blue-toned glaze, Finnish, 6in (15cm) high.
£100–120
$145–175 ✗ BUKF

A Royal Copenhagen porcelain vase, by Axel Salto, decorated with a blue/black glaze, signed, Danish, c1937, 9½in (24cm) high.
£3,000–3,500
$4,400–5,000 ✗ BUKF

▶ **A Bing & Grøndahl flambé vase,** with mottled brown decoration, Danish, c1950, 5¼in (13.5cm) high.
£125–150
$180–220 ⊞ DSG

A Rörstrand ceramic jug, by Gunnar Nylund, Swedish, 1950s, 7in (18cm) high.
£70–75
$100–110 ⊞ MARK

A Gustavsberg Argenta ware vase, decorated with a snake on a mottle green ground, Swedish, 1925–35, 12½in (32cm) high.
£550–650
$800–950 ✗ G(L)

A Meissen white porcelain vase, German, 1950s, 10in (20.5cm) high.
£30–35
$45–50 ⊞ RCh

A Mougin stoneware vase, moulded in relief with figures before a temple, glazed in cream with brown outlines, slight damage, marked, c1930, 15in (38cm) high.
£1,300–1,500
$2,000–2,200 ⊞ B&B

A Rörstrand stoneware vase, by Carl Harry Stålhane, Swedish, c1950, 4½in (11.5cm) high.
£45–50
$65–75 ✗ SnA

A Gustavsberg earthenware teapot, by Stig Lindberg, decorated in blues, purples, green and yellow with a hand-painted glazed bust of a woman and other motifs, marked, Swedish, 1952, 10in (25.5cm) high.
£230–260
$330–380 ✗ Bon

A Gustavsberg Farstagods vase, by Wilhelm Kåge, with carved decoration, glazed in shades of brown, firing cracks, signed, 1950, 15½in (39.5cm) high.
£2,100–2,500
$3,000–3,500 ⚒ BUK

A Rörstrand pottery jug, by Gunnar Nylund, Swedish, 1950s, 10¼in (26cm) high.
£120–150
$175–220 ⊞ MARK

A Gustavsberg faïence vase, by Stig Lindberg, decorated with painted tear-shaped motifs in pale yellow, black and blue glazed on a white ground, Swedish, c1953, 13¾in (35cm) high.
£280–320
$400–450 ⚒ P(Ba)

A Gustavsberg ceramic candlestick, by Berndt Friberg, Swedish, 1950s, 3in (7.5cm) high.
£85–95
$125–140 ⊞ MARK

A Högenäs miniature cauldron, Swedish, c1960, 3in (7.5cm) high.
£18–20
$20–30 ⊞ MARK

An Upsala-Ekeby black vase, c1955, Swedish, 9in (23cm) high.
£40–45
$60–65 ⊞ MARK

► A Royal Porcelain Factory stoneware vase, by Gerd Bogelund, with diamond-shaped relief decoration in shades of green, brown and beige glazed, signed, Danish, 1967, 11in (28cm) high.
£380–450
$575–650 ⚒ BUK

A Gustavsberg stoneware vase, by Berndt Friberg, with tenmoku glaze, signed, Swedish, 1965, 17¼in (44cm) high.
£2,000–2,200
$2,900–3,250 ⚒ BUK

◄ A Gustavsberg stoneware vase, by Stig Lindberg, with red and black glaze, signed, Swedish, 1966, 17½in (44.5cm) high.
£850–1,000
$1,250–1,500 ⚒ BUK

A Högenäs pottery vase, by Yngve Blixt, with shiny green and beige glaze, Swedish, 1966, 39in (99cm) high.
£1,250–1,500
$1,800–2,200 ⚒ BUK

Bowls – Art Pottery

A Lauder Pottery jardinière, decorated in blue, brown and cream, with sgraffito fish and aquatic foliage, signed, 1880–90, 15¾in (40cm) diam.
£300–350
$450–500 ✠ P(Ba)

A pottery bowl, by William Staite-Murray, decorated with *jun* glaze, impressed seal, c1930, 12in (30.5cm) diam.
£630–700
$900–1,000 ⊞ RUSK

A bowl, by Maija Grotell, decorated with a yellow glaze, signed, American, 1934–46, 6¾in (17cm) diam.
£1,100–1,250
$1,600–1,800 ✠ JMW

Bowls – Studio Pottery

A glazed ceramic bowl, by Glen Lukens, scratched, painted signature, c1955, 18¾in (47.5cm) diam.
£16,000–19,000
$23,000–28,000 ✠ BB(L)

A stoneware bowl, by Katherine Pleydell-Bouverie, covered in a thick dark green dripping glaze with white splashes, impressed mark, c1955, 7¼in (18.5cm) diam.
£250–300
$350–450 ✠ F&C

A stoneware bowl, by Rupert Spira, with all-over graphite grey glaze, with three broad bands of fine vertical inlay, impressed seal, 2002, 17in (43cm) diam.
£2,600–3,000
$3,800–4,400 ✠ B

A stoneware footed bowl, by Dame Lucie Rie, with inlaid criss-cross design and unglazed ring in well, impressed LR seal, c1953, 12½in (32cm) diam.
£12,000–14,000
$17,500–20,500 ✠ P

A tin-glazed earthenware bowl, by James Tower, the exterior mottled green-brown with a white foot, the interior with an abstract bird design, incised and painted marks, 1956, 12½in (31.5cm) diam.
£900–1,100
$1,300–1,600 ✠ B

A porcelain footed bowl, by Dame Lucie Rie, manganese glaze with a blue well with radiating sgraffito design, impressed seal, c1960, 6in (15cm) diam.
£580–700
$850–1,000 ✠ B(B)

A stoneware salad bowl, by Dame Lucie Rie, with brown running flecks on a ground of matt off-white glaze, impressed seal, c1968, 11¼in (28.5cm) wide.
£1,800–2,000
$2,600–3,000 ✠ Bon

A porcelain footed bowl, by Dame Lucie Rie, with inlaid decoration, impressed LR seal, c1974, 7in (18cm) diam.
£1,500–1,750
$2,200–2,500 ✠ Bon

◄ **A bowl,** by Eileen Lewenstein, decorated with a thick drip glaze, on a double knop stem, stamped seal, c1950, 10¼in (26cm) high.
£90–120
$130–175
⚒ P(B)

An earthenware bowl, by John de Burgh Perceval, the exterior with moulded decoration and two stylized lizard handles, signed, dated 1957, 19in (48.5cm) diam.
£1,700–2,000
$2,500–3,000 ⚒ P(Sy)

A ceramic bowl, by Mikael Schilkin, brown-glazed, signed, 4in (10cm) diam.
£100–120
£145–175 ⚒ BUKF

A stoneware bowl, by Annie Fourmanoir, brick-red with a textured surface and a ball in the well, c1970s, 15½in (39.5cm) diam.
£300–350
$450–720 ⚒ Bon

A stoneware footed bowl, by Dame Lucie Rie, white with inlaid criss-cross decoration, impressed seal, c1978, 7¼in (18.5cm) diam.
£4,200–4,800
$6,000–7,000 ⚒ Bon

A pottery bowl, by Elizabeth Fritsch, c1972, 9½in (24cm) diam.
£4,250–5,000
$6,000–7,250 ⚒ P

A pinched stoneware bowl, by Ursula Marley-Price, covered in oatmeal slip, 1990s, 12in (30.5cm) diam.
£400–450
$580–650 ⊞ PGA

◄ **An earthenware bowl-on-stand form,** by Gordon Baldwin, applied coil rim and brightly coloured linear decoration, painted mark, c1978, 9½in (24cm) high.
£750–850
$1,100–1,250 ⚒ Bon

An earthenware vessel, by Gabrielle Koch, with raised pinched rim, incised signature, c1996, 13¼in (34cm) high.
£500–600
$720–870 ⚒ Bon

Bowls – Factories

A Clarice Cliff Fantasque bowl, decorated with Farmhouse pattern, chips, moulded and printed marks and facsimile signature, c1931, 6in (15cm) diam.
£450–550
$650–800 ♪ Hal

A Gustavsberg ceramic bowl, by Wilhelm Kåge, with stylized fish decoration in silver on a turquoise ground, with a silver rim, stamped marks, Swedish, c1948, 11¾in (30cm) diam.
£480–580
$700–850 ♪ BB(L)

A Midwinter Saladware bowl, designed by Terence Conran, decorated with vegetables in yellow and green, c1956, 8½in (21.5cm) wide.
£100–120
$145–175 ♪ AND

A Beswick fruit bowl, decorated with Ballet pattern, 1950s, 9in (23cm) wide.
£20–25
$30–35 ⊞ RAT

A Beswick fruit bowl, by Jim Hayward, painted in black and white with red interior, influenced by Zambezi pattern, c1956, 14in (35.5cm) wide.
£45–55
$65–80 ⊞ RAT

A Rörstrand earthenware footed bowl, by Carl Harry Stålhane, with relief foliate pattern to foot, covered in grey-blue glaze, Swedish, 1950s, 5in (12.5cm) high.
£45–50
$65–75 ⊞ MARK

A Hornsea Pottery bowl, with incised decoration in red, 1950s, 13in (33cm) diam.
£35–45
$50–65 ⊞ RAT

► **A ceramic bowl,** by Birger Kaipiainen, with polychrome decoration on a pale ground, rim chips, signed, Finnish, 14¾in (37.5cm) diam.
£220–260
$320–380 ♪ BUKF

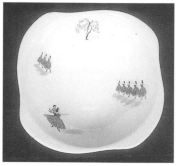

► **A Poole Pottery Delphis bowl,** painted in shades of blue, orange and black, 1960s–70s, 13½in (34.5cm) diam.
£75–100
$110–145 ⊞ HarC

An Upsala-Ekeby black ceramic dish, Swedish, c1955, 13in 933cm) wide.
£55–60
$80–90 ⊞ MARK

◄ **A pair of Gainey ceramic pots,** white-glazed, c1960s, 6¾in (17cm) diam.
£200–240
$300–350 ♪ BB(L)

► **A Gustavsberg bowl,** by Stig Lindberg, decorated in black and white, Swedish, c1950s, 7in (18cm) wide.
£60–65
$90–95 ⊞ MARK

Tablewares – Studio Pottery

A St Ives Pottery earthenware teapot, by Bernard Leach, light brown with yellow slip-trailed design of a bird in flight, impressed marks, c1923, 10¼in (26cm) wide.
£2,800–3,200
$4,000–4,700 ⚒ Bon

A pair of stoneware cups and saucers, by Dame Lucie Rie, the cups with dark brown manganese exteriors and white interiors, the saucers dark brown with white undersides, impressed seals, c1957, cup 3in (7.5cm) high.
£90–100
$130–145 ⚒ G(L)

A stoneware tureen and cover, by Bjorn Wiinblad, decorated with slip-trailed patterns in shades of blue, orange, brown and turquoise, painted marks, retail label for Bollighus, Danish, 1969, 19½in (49.5cm) high.
£200–240
$300–350 ⚒ Bon

◀ **A bronze-glazed coffee set,** by Dame Lucie Rie and Hans Coper, comprising four cups and saucers, four plates, coffee pot and milk jug, impressed LR and HC seals, 1950s.
£3,000–3,500
$4,500–5,000 ⚒ Bon

Tablewares – Factories

An Empire Porcelain Co jam pot and cover, decorated with blue and orange flowers on a yellow ground, 1933, 3½in (9cm) high.
£40–50
$60–75 ⊞ BKK

A Wedgwood mug, by Guyatt, commemorating the Coronation of Queen Elizabeth II, printed in black with a lion and unicorn supporting a crown, gilt rims, 1953, 4in (10cm) high.
£40–50
$60–75 ⚒ SAS

A Clarice Cliff sugar shaker, decorated with Crocus pattern, c1932, 5½in (14cm) high.
£700–800
$1,000–1,150 ⊞ DSG

◀ **A Beswick pottery toast rack,** decorated with Circus pattern in red, blue, black and yellow, 1950, 6in (15cm) long.
£12–15
$15–20 ⚒ P(B)

A Shelley tea service, comprising 22 pieces, decorated with green and silver, c1933.
£250–330
$360–480 ⊞ AJ

A Soho Pottery Solhan Ware biscuit barrel, white-glazed, with cane handle, 1930s, 6¼in (16cm) high.
£35–40
$50–60 ⊞ DEC

A Midwinter Stylecraft plate and cup, by Peter Scott, decorated with Wild Geese series controlled design, c1950, 9in (23cm) wide.
£16–20
£20–30 ⊞ ES

A Midwinter trio, decorated with Red Domino pattern, c1953, cup 3½in (9cm) high.
£15–20
$20–30 ⊞ RAT

◀ **A Midwinter cruet set on a tray,** by Sir Hugh Casson, decorated with Riviera pattern, c1954, tray 5½in (14cm) long.
£65–75
$95–110 ⊞ GIN

A Midwinter gravy boat, saucer and ladle, by Jessie Tait, decorated with Quite Contrary pattern, c1957, gravy boat 8½in (21.5cm) long.
£45–55
$65–80 ⚒ AND

A Ridgway cup and saucer, by Enid Seeney, decorated with Homemaker pattern in black and white, c1955, cup 3¼in (8.5cm) high.
£10–15
$15–20 ⊞ RAT

A Washington Pottery trio, with pale blue polka dot border, c1954, cup 3½in (9cm) high.
£10–15
$15–20 ⊞ RAT

Miller's is a price GUIDE not a price LIST

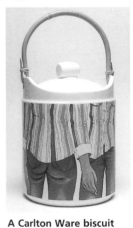

A Carlton Ware biscuit barrel, decorated with Denim pattern in blue and brown on a white ground, with a bamboo handle, 1970s, 12in (30.5cm) high.
£35–40
$50–60 ⊞ StC
Reflecting the contemporary fashion for jeans, Carlton Ware launched their Denim Ware range c1978. The couple featured in the decoration wear matching unisex jeans and cheese-cloth shirts – a classic example of 70s style, accurate down to the open shirt buttons. Denim Ware is becoming increasingly collectable today, particularly the more unusual items such as this biscuit barrel.

A Grindley trio, decorated with stylized lanterns in red and green, 1950s, plate 7in (18cm) diam.
£16–18
$20–30 ⊞ AOS

A Midwinter 22-piece tea set, by Jessie Tait, decorated with Hollywood pattern in yellow and grey, c1956, teapot 6½in (16.5cm) high.
£300–350
$450–500 ⚒ AND

A Ridgway Metro coffee pot, by Enid Seeney, decorated with Homemaker pattern, 1957, 9in (23cm) high.
£150–175
$220–255 ⊞ HarC

A Midwinter cup and saucer, by Sir Hugh Casson, decorated with a village scene in red, blue, yellow and black, 1950s, cup 3in (7.5cm) high.
£16–20
$20–30 ⊞ DBo

A selection of Midwinter Saladware, by Sir Terence Conran, decorated in yellow, green and red, c1956, largest plate 9½in (24cm) diam.
£65–80
$95–115 each ⚒ AND

A Midwinter 28-piece dinner set, by Sir Terence Conran, decorated with Nature Study pattern, 1950s, vegetable dish 10in (25.5cm) wide.
£550–650
$800–950 ⚒ DN

A Midwinter gravy boat, saucer and ladle, by Jessie Tait, decorated with Cherokee pattern in orange, blue and yellow, c1957, gravy boat 8½in (21.5cm) long.
£75–85
$110–125 ⚒ AND

A Midwinter black gravy boat, 1950s, 8½in (21.5cm) long.
£25–30
$35–45 ⊞ BTB

Auction or dealer?

All the pictures in our price guides originate from auction houses and dealers. When buying at auction, prices can be lower than those of a dealer, but a buyer's premium and VAT will be added to the hammer price. Equally, when selling at auction, commission, tax and photography charges must be taken into account. Dealers will often restore pieces before putting them back on the market.

Both dealers and auctioneers can provide professional advice, so it is worth researching both sources before buying or selling your antiques.

An Arthur Wood & Son utensil pot, decorated in green, yellow, black and red, 1960s, 7in (18cm) high.
£20–30
$30–45 ⊞ BTB

▶ **A Portmeirion cup and saucer,** decorated with Jupiter pattern in blue and black, 1960s, 3¼in (8.5cm) high.
£35–40
$50–60 ⊞ LEGE

A Portmeirion coffee set, for six people, decorated with in black and white Greek Key pattern, with plates, 1960s, pot 13in (33cm) high.
£70–80
$100–115 ⊞ GIN

A Robinson Ransbottom Pottery cookie jar, 'A Cow Jumped Over the Moon', 1950s, 9in (23cm) high.
£95–115
$140–170 ⊞ EKK
Cookie jars are a favourite American collectable. The subject received huge publicity when Andy Warhol's famous cookie jar collection was sold after his death in 1987; however, the high prices paid for containers belonging to the pop artist bear little relation to the value of similar pieces without such a glamorous provenance. Cookie jars were made in a huge range of styles, often in novelty figural shapes. Different manufacturers sometimes used identical moulds, so the same design could be produced by several factories. Cookie jars were created as fun, affordable objects (not as fine china) and, given the nature of their contents, were handled by children; hence lids were damaged or broken, and collectors should also check for chips and flaking paint.

A Limoges porcelain tea and coffee set, by Jean Dufy, decorated with Pivoines pattern in cerise, rose and blue on a white ground with gold edging, signed, French, 1925.
£650–750
$950-1,100 ➚ BUK

An Arzberg Porcelain Factory Form 2000 coffee service, by Heinrich Löffelhardt, decorated in red and blue, comprising three settings, 1954–77, coffee pot 8in (20.5cm) high.
£2,500–3,000
$3,500–4,500 ➚ DORO

▶ **A ceramic cheese stand,** signed 'Vallauris', c1950s, 15in (38cm) wide.
£15–18
$20–30 ⊞ LAW

A Winchcombe Pottery coffee jug, c1940, 8in (20.5cm) high.
£90–110
$130–160 ⊞ IW

◀ **A bone china cup and saucer,** decorated with blue and orange flowers, Bavarian, 1930s, saucer 5½in (14cm) wide.
£7–8
$10–15 ⊞ LAW

A porcelain coffee set, decorated with white poodles and polka dots on a black ground, Bavarian, 1950s, coffee pot 7in (18cm) high.
£90–110
$130–160 ➚ LBe

An earthenware five-piece salad set, by Piero Fornasetti, the painted fruit and vegetables incorporating face masks, factory mark, 1955, large bowl 9½in (24cm) diam.
£270–300
$400–450 ➚ WBH

A set of 12 Arabia porcelain coffee cups, signed, Finnish.
£190–230
$275–330 ➚ BUKF

An Arabia porcelain 51-piece dinner service, by Friedl Kjellberg, some pieces stamped Made in Finland, others with impressed mark ARABIA/-F.H.Kj-, Finnish, c1959.
£1,500–1,800
$2,200–2,600 ➚ BB(L)

▶ **A Midwinter 15-piece coffee set,** by Nigel Wilde, decorated with Cherry Tree pattern in red, green and blue, c1966, coffee pot 8in (20.5cm) high.
£120–140
$175–200 ➚ AND

A porcelain three-piece tea service, American, by Raymond Loewy, c1958.
£95–115
$140–165 ➚ BB(L)

A Portmeirion coffee pot, decorated in black and white with Totem pattern, 1960s, 13¾in (35cm) high.
£25–30
$35–45 ⊞ LEGE

Miscellaneous

A Royal Doulton wall tile, by Gilbert Bayes, decorated in relief with a group of four naked water nymphs being carried by three dolphins, in blue, mauve, white and cream, 1930, 8 x 23¾in (20.5 x 60.5cm).
£500–600
$720–870 ➤ B

A Wedgwood pottery trial group by John Skeaping, with straw-coloured glaze, stamped mark, 1927, 8in (20.5cm) high.
£1,100–1,200
$1,600–1,750 ➤ P

A Midwinter black cat, by Colin Melbourne, c1956, 7in (18cm) high.
£180–200
$250–300 ➤ AND

A Rye Pottery vase, modelled as a cockerel, early 1950s, 6in (25cm) high.
£90–100
$130–145 ⊞ NCA

A Royal Dux porcelain figural centrepiece, in the form of a maiden standing on the crest of a wave holding a fishing net, flanked by two scallop-shaped receptacles, marked, Bohemian, c1900, 16¾in (42.5cm) high.
£1,200–1,300
$1,800–2,000 ⊞ B&B

◄ A St Clement pottery model of a panther, glazed in jade green, French, c1920, 22in (56cm) long.
£300–350
$450–500 ⊞ ANO

A Rosenthal porcelain figure of a dancer, by Berthold Boehs, Model No. K201, polychrome-painted, inscribed and impressed marks, German, c1913, 9¼in (23.5cm) high.
£1,000–1,100
$1,500–1,600 ➤ DORO

An Arabia model of a giraffe, by Taisto Kaasinen, signed, Finnish, 6½in (16.5cm) high.
£60–70
$90–100 ➤ BUKF

A Goldscheider ceramic double face mask, decorated in cream, orange and black, Austrian, 1930s, 13½in (34.5cm) high.
£675–750
$1,000–1,100 ⊞ BEV

◄ A Lenci earthenware figure of a girl, white-glazed, highlighted in lilac with green eyes, supported by a cactus., signed and marked, Italian, c1930, 13¼in (24.5cm) high.
£500–600
$720–870 ➤ B

5

A Gustavsberg model of a hippo, by Lisa Larson, Swedish, c1965, 7in (18cm) long.
£85–100
$125–145 ⊞ MARK

A Rörstrand stoneware model of a butterfly, by Birger Kaipiainen, with painted decoration in blue and green, Swedish, 1954–58, 8¼in (21cm) high, on a wooden stand.
£450–550
$650–800 ⚒ BUK

A Carter, Stabler & Adams slip-cast white earthenware candelabra, by John Adams, 1930s, 8½in (21.5cm) high.
£120–150
$175–220 ⊞ ADE

◀ **A Royal Winton Old Mill cheese dish,** decorated in naturalistic colours, c1930, 7in (18cm) wide.
£45–50
$65–75 ⊞ RH

▶ **A pottery ashtray,** advertising Woodbine cigarettes, 1950, 4½in (11.5cm) wide
£10–12
$15–20 ⊞ HUX

A Carlton Ware money box, modelled as a train, decorated in red and orange on a white ground, 1970s, 7in (18cm) wide.
£30–40
$45–60 ⊞ AOS

A Carlton Ware ashtray, decorated with Denim pattern in blue and brown on a white ground, c1978, 6¼in (16cm) diam.
£25–30
$35–45 ⊞ StC

A Poole Pottery Atlantis paperweight, by Guy Sydenham, 1960s–70s, 4½in (11.5cm) diam.
£90–100
$130–145 ⊞ HarC

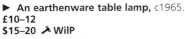

▶ **An earthenware table lamp,** c1965.
£10–12
$15–20 ⚒ WilP

An earthenware inkwell, by Adrien Dalpayrat, with gilt-bronze mount by Edward Colonna, 1898–1903, 6¼in (16cm) diam.
£900–1,000
$1,300–1,600 ⚒ S(Am)

▶ **A glazed ceramic ashtray,** marked, German, 1940s, 6½in (16.5cm) diam.
£120–140
$175–200 ⚒ BB(L)

A Gustavsberg Argenta dish, Swedish, 1920s, 6in (15cm) diam.
£65–80
$95–115 ⊞ OTT

A Leerdam Unica glass vase, by A. D. Copier, internally decorated with a graduated opal layer and with blue coloured powders, engraved marks, Dutch, c1940, 7in (18cm) high.
£500–550
$720–800 ⚒ S(Am)

A Leerdam Unica glass vase, by A. D. Copier, internally decorated with a yellow layer graduating into yellow swirls, engraved marks, Dutch, 1944, 8in (20.5cm) high.
£1,500–1,800
$2,200–2,600 ⚒ S(Am)

A Leerdam Unica glass vase, by A. D. Copier, covered with a blue layer and imprinted with seaweed, air bubbles and a layer of colourless glass, engraved marks, Dutch, 1944, 10¼in (26cm) diam.
£2,800–3,200
$4,000–4,650 ⚒ S(Am)

An Orrefors blue and gold glass vase, by Sven Palmqvist, Swedish, 1946–48, 10½in (26.5cm) high.
£220–250
$320–360 ⚒ Sck

A Leerdam Unica free-blown glass vase, by A. D. Copier, internally decorated with an enclosed opal layer and red coloured powders, Dutch, 1946, 11½in (29cm) high.
£800–900
$1,150–1,300 ⚒ S(Am)

An Iittala mould-blown clear glass Lichen vase, by Tapio Wirkkala, with acid frosted surface, Finnish, c1949, 8¾in (22cm) high.
£650–800
$950–1,150 ⚒ P(Ba)

A Leerdam Unica glass vase, by A. D. Copier, Dutch, 1950, 7in (18cm) diam.
£1,600–1,800
$2,300–2,600 ⚒ S(Am)

An Orrefors glass vase, etched with a mermaid standing in a shell, Swedish, c1950, 12½in (32cm) high.
£340–380
$480–550 ⊞ WeH

An Orrefors glass vase, by Vicke Lindstrand, Swedish, c1950, 4½in (11.5cm) high.
£55–65
$80–95 ⊞ MARK

▶ **A Royal Brierley Rainbow ware blue and green glass vase,** c1950, 8in (20.5cm) high.
£80–100
$115–145 ⊞ RUSK

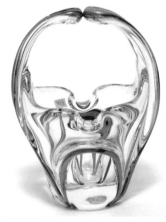

A blue and green glass vase, decorated with an aquarium pattern, Italian, c1950, 11¾in (30cm) high.
£400–450
$580–650 ⚡ SLM

An Iittala red glass ball, by Timo Sarpaneva, Finnish, 1950s, 3½in (9cm) high.
£50–60
$75–90 ⊞ MARK

◀ **A Barbarici glass vase,** by Ecole Barovier, Barovier & Toso, the surface covered with metal oxides, black base, Italian, 1950s, 13¾in (35cm) high.
£1,100–1,300
$1,600–1,900 ⚡ BUK

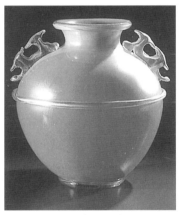

A Seguso Vetri d'Arte glass vase, with everted rim, internally decorated with a pink layer with gold foil inclusions, on applied foot, Italian, 1950s, 13in (33cm) high.
£1,000–1,200
$1,500–1,750 ⚡ S(Am)

A green-tinted glass vase, Italian, 1950s, 7in (18cm) high.
£25–28
$35–45 ⊞ MARK

A Venini Fazzoletto glass handkerchief vase, decorated with white latticino stripes, acid stamped, Italian, c1950, 9in (23cm) high.
£800–900
$1,150–1,300 ⚡ S(NY)

Venini

The glass workshops of Venini have established themselves as the most experimental of the Venetian craftsmen. The progressive tradition began after WWII when the workshop moved away from traditional Venetian forms into more abstract ones with splashed and mottled surfaces.

A Murano glass handkerchief vase, by Paolo Venini, with blue interior and red exterior, etched signature, Italian, 1950, 8in (20.5cm) high.
£830–1,000
$1,200–1,500 ⚡ BUK

A Kosta blue glass vase, Swedish, 1950s, 5¼in (13.5cm) high.
£260–300
$380–440 ⚡ BB(L)

▶ **A Venini acid-etched blue inciso glass vase,** signed, Italian, c1950, 9in (23cm) high.
£4,000–4,600
$5,800–6,800 ⊞ GoW

A Vetreria Aureliano Toso glass vase, by Dino Martens, the clear glass decorated with white and pink threads, Italian, c1950, 10½in (26.5cm) high.
£380–450
$575–650 ⚒ DORO

◀ **An Orrefors glass Stella Polaris vase,** by Vicke Lindstrand, Swedish, 1950s, 8in (20.5cm) high.
£70–80
$100–115 ⊞ MARK

An Aureliano Toso Oriente glass vase, by Dino Martens, entitled Nabucco, with original paper label, Italian, c1952, 9½in (24cm) high.
£5,500–6,000
$8,000–8,700 ⚒ S(NY)

Three Orrefors Graal glass vases, by Edvard Hald, internally decorated in green with fish swimming among seaweed, signed, Swedish, 1952, largest 6in (15cm) high.
£1,500–1,700
$2,200–2,500 ⚒ BB(L)

▶ **An Orrefors Vattenlek glass vase,** by Edwin Ohrström, with stylized decoration of figures on a blue ground, signed, Swedish, 1953, 8¼in (21cm) high.
£1,400–1,600
$2,200–2,300 ⚒ BUK

A Murano glass Pezzato vase, by Fulvio Bianconi, with trangular pattern in blue, red, green and clear glass, etched signature, Italian, 1954, 9¼in (23.5cm) high.
£7,200–8,600
$10,000–12,000 ⚒ BUK

A Kosta glass vase, by Vicke Lindstrand, internally decorated, with a dark purple band to the base, incised marks, Swedish, c1955, 5½in (14cm) high.
£100–120
$145–175 ⚒ P(B)

▶ **An inciso Sommerso glass vase,** by Paolo Venini, with pale olive-green, pale amber and clear glass, paper label, stamped, Italian, c1955, 15¾in (40cm) high.
£950–1,150
$1,400–1,700 ⚒ P(Ba)

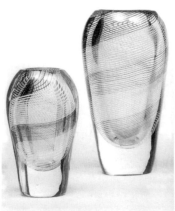

Two Kosta banded glass vases, by Vicke Lindstrand, with diagonal stripes alternately in black and white glass, cased in clear glass, marked, Swedish, c1950, largest 9in (23cm) high.
£600–700
$870–1,000 ⚒ Bon

A Kosta flaring glass vase, by Vicke Lindstrand, on a tall stem with graal technique, vertical lines in brown, acid stamp, Swedish, c1955, 7¾in (19.5cm) high.
£380–420
$570–620 ⊞ FF

▶ **A Kosta glass vase,** by Vicke Lindstrand, with black glass trailed to form an impression of a tree in silhouette within clouded glass, marked, Swedish, c1955, 14in (35cm) high.
£2,000–2,200
$2,900–3,200 ⚒ Bon

An Iittala frosted glass Pot Hole vase, by Tapio Wirkkala, engraved on base, Finnish, 1956, 7in (18cm) high.
£600–650
$870–950 ⊞ FF

A Leerdam Unica glass vase, by Floris Meyham, with yellow, brown and cream layers, covered with a layer of clear glass, Dutch, 1959, 5in (13cm) diam.
£1,300–1,500
$1,900–2,200 ⚒ S(Am)

A set of three bottles, by Nanny Still for Riihimäen Lasi Oy, marked, Finnish, 1959–68, largest 13¼in (33.5cm) high.
£500–600
$720–870 ⚒ Bon

A Holmegaard glass vase, by Per Lutken, Danish, 1950–60s, 7in (18cm) high.
£60–70
$90–100 ⊞ ORI

A Whitefriars blue glass Knobbly series vase, by William Wilson and Harry Dyer, 1960s, 7in (18cm) high.
£65–80
$95–115 ⊞ MARK

An Iittala glass vase, by Tapio Wirkkala, signed, Finnish, 1960s 3¾in (9.5cm) high.
£80–90
$115–130 ⚒ BUKF

Scandinavian glass

The best known of the Scandinavian glass workshops are Orrefors and Holmegaard. These workshops diversified from their traditional forms during the 1950s and began to experiment with form and engraved decoration. Scandinavian glass is widely collected and its organic forms contrast effectively with the more functionally driven aspects of mid-century Modernism. The workshops pioneered the co-operation between craftsmen, fine artists and industry. Edward Hald, artistic director of the workshops, worked with Henri Matisse.

A yellow glass vase, by Gunnel Nyman, with air bubbles, Finnish, 3½in (9cm) high.
£45–55
$65–80 ↗ BUKF

A blue glass vase, by Göran Hongell, signed, Finnish, 6in (15cm) high.
£25–30
$35–45 ↗ BUKF

A clear glass vase, by Tapio Wirkkala, signed, Finnish, 11½in (29cm) high.
£40–45
$60–65 ↗ BUKF

A mushroom-shaped line-cut glass vase, by Tapio Wirkkala, signed, Finnish, 7in (18cm) high.
£450–550
$650–800 ↗ BUKF

A Murano orange glass vase, with pinched lip, Italian, 9¼in (23.5cm) high.
£125–150
$180–220 ⊞ MARK

A Gulluskruf free-blown purple glass vase, by Arthur Carlsson Percy, Swedish, 1951–70, 33½in (85cm) high.
£100–120
$145–175 ↗ Bon

◄ **A yellow glass vase,** with ribbed body, Italian, c1960, 10in (25.5cm) high.
£50–55
$75–80 ⊞ PLB

A Venini clear glass vase, by Barbini, with incised sides, the centre with an aperture opening to a well, signed, Italian, 1960s, 7¼in (18.5cm) high.
£600–700
$870–1,000 ⊞ PLB

A Kosta blue and amber glass vase, by Mona Morales-Schildt, Swedish, 1960, 7¾in (19.5cm) high.
£650–750
$950–1,000 ↗ BUK

◄ **A Kosta amber cased glass vase,** by Mona Morales-Schildt, with three concave cuts, signed, Swedish, 1960, 6½in (16.5cm) high.
£400–480
$580–700 ↗ BUK

► **An Iittala Tree vase,** by Tapio Wirkkala, Finnish, c1960, 9in (23cm) high.
£80–95
$115–140 ⊞ MARK

An Iittala amethyst glass vase, by Tapio Wirkkala, signed, Finnish, 1960s, 11in (28cm) high.
£160–180
$230–260 ⊞ PLB

An Orrefors glass Ariel vase, by Ingeborg Lundin, with geometric design in blue on a clear ground, Swedish, 1960, 6¼in (16cm) high.
£750–900
$1,100–1,300 ✹ BUK

◄ **An optical cut-glass vase,** with internal cutting, Czechoslovakian, 1960s, 11in (28cm) high.
£150–180
$220–260 ✹ Bon

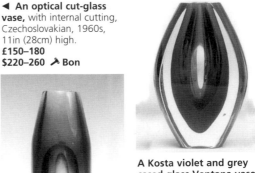

A Kosta violet and grey cased glass Ventana vase, by Mona Morales-Schildt, engraved, Swedish, c1960, 6½in (16.5cm) high.
£300–350
$440–500 ✹ Bon

◄ **A Flygsfors red and white cased glass Coquille vase,** by Paul Kedelv, Swedish, 1961, 10in (25.5cm) high.
£50–60
$75–90 ⊞ REPS

◄ **A green-brown glass vase,** by Mirislav Klinger, two sides cut away to reveal cased clear glass beneath, engraved, Czechoslovakian, 1961, 13¾in (35cm) high.
£250–300
$360–440 ✹ Bon

► **A Holmegaard green glass Flame vase,** by Per Lutkin, marked, Danish, 1961, 9½in (24cm) high.
£120–140
$175–200 ⊞ FF

An Orrefors green glass Ariel vase, by Ingeborg Lundin, signed, Swedish, 1962, 5¾in (14.5cm) high.
£850–950
$1,250–1,400 ⊞ FF

A Stratharn red and black speckled glass vase, c1963, 8½in (21.5cm) high.
£70–80
$100–115 ⊞ TCG

A Stratharn green speckled glass and cloisonné vase, c1963, 7½in (19cm) high.
£60–70
$90–100 ⊞ TCG

A Whitefriars glass Knobbly series vase, 1963, 8in (20.5cm) high.
£65–80
$95–115 ⊞ JHa

A Leerdam Unica cased clear glass vase, by Floris Meydam, the interior trailed and churned in a spiral, the body flecked with green and blue, engraved mark, Dutch, 1964, 8¾in (22cm) high.
£850–1,000
$1,250–1,500 ⚒ **Bon**

A Whitefriars red Textured series glass vase, by Geoffrey Baxter, c1967, 9in (23cm) high.
£50–60
$75–90 ⊞ **JHa**

▶ **A Mdina glass vase,** in the set of an axe, Malta, 1970s, 10½in (26.5cm) high.
£120–150
$175–220 ⊞ **MARK**

Two Holmegaard cased glass bottle vases, one yellow and one red, Danish, 1970s, 8in (20.5cm) high.
£110–130
$160–190 each ⊞ **PLB**

A Whitefriars cinnamon-coloured Textured series glass vase, c1966, 7in (18cm) high.
£50–60
$75–90 ⊞ **JHa**

A James Powell, Whitefriars glass vase, by Geoffrey Baxter, applied with tangerine spots, 1969, 7½in (19cm) high.
£80–100
$115–145 ⊞ **RUSK**

A James Powell, Whitefriars smoked glass triangular vase, by Geoffrey Baxter, 1966, 9½in (24cm) high.
£180–200
$260–290 ⊞ **RUSK**

A Mdina glass vase/ornament, Malta, c1970, 5in (12.5cm) high.
£50–60
$75–90 ⊞ **MARK**

A free-blown studio glass vase, by Sam Herman, engraved mark, American, 1973, 11in (28cm) high.
£200–230
$290–330 ⚒ **Bon**

◀ **An opaque pink-grey glass bottle vase,** by Sam Herman, cased in clear and metallic green, with applied blue-tinted glass rim, engraved mark, American, 1971, 9in (23cm) high.
£220–250
$320–360 ⚒ **Bon**

Two Lassi glass vases,
one green and one red,
Finnish, 1970s,
12in (30.5cm) high.
£40–50
$60–75 each ⊞ PLB

**A blown, cut, polished
and electroplated blue
glass vase,** by Michael
Glancy, inscribed, American,
1980, 5in (12.5cm) high.
£3,300–3,800
$4,750–5,500 ⚲ S(NY)

**A blown glass Venetian
form,** by Dale Chihuly,
brown with a yellow snake
winding around the body,
on a yellow foot, American,
c1900, 34in (86.5cm) high.
£6,500–8,000
$9,500–11,500 ⚲ S(NY)

An Åfors glass vase, by
Bertil Vallien, Swedish,
1970s, 9in (23cm) high.
£45–50
$65–75 ⊞ MARK

An Orrefors blue glass vase, by
Gunnar Cyrén, with green stylized leaf
decoration, signed, Swedish, 1987,
10½in (26.5cm) high.
£1,200–1,400
$1,750–2,000 ⚲ BUK

A Kosta glass Kabale vase, by Ulrica
Hydman-Vallien, decorated with
fantasy figures in violet, grey and
gold, signed, Swedish, 1988,
7¼in (18.5cm) high.
£2,200–2,600
$3,200–3,800 ⚲ BUK

An Åfors glass vase, by
Bertil Vallien, signed, Swedish,
1970s, 4in (10cm) high.
£45–50
$65–75 ⊞ MARK

A Skruf clear glass vase,
by Bengt Edenfalk, Swedish,
1974, 9in (23cm) high.
£70–80
$100–115 ⊞ MARK

◄ **An littala glass Claritas
vase,** by Timo Sarpaneva,
with three white-backed
interior bubbles, engraved
mark, Finnish, 1984,
6in (15cm) high.
£530–600
$750–875 ⚲ S(O)

An littala glass Claritas vase, by Timo
Sarpaneva, internally decorated with a black layer
surrounded by a later of air bubbles, engraved
marks, Finnish, 1988, 8½in (21.5cm) high.
£2,500–3,00
$3,600–4,400 ⚲ S(Am)

An Orrefors lilac glass Sputnik vase, by Lars
Hellsten, Swedish, 2000, 6½in (16.5cm) high.
£225–250
$320–360 ⊞ HaG

Jugs & Bottles

A cranberry glass decanter, in the shape of a goose, the silver-plated pewter top by Kayserzinn, c1900, 11in (28cm) high.
£650–750
$950–1,100 ⊞ ANO

A Charles Schneider blue glass jug, with applied creamy yellow handle and vertical spikes under an acid finish, signed, French, c1918, 14in (35.5cm) high.
£1,000–1,200
$1,500–1,750 🔨 JAA

An Orrefors green glass wine decanter, the stopper in the form of a drinking glass, Swedish, 1950s, 10½in (26.5cm) high.
£350–400
$500–580 🔨 BB(L)

An Iittala blue glass carafe, by Timo Sarpaneva, marked on base, Finnish, c1959, 10¾in (27.5cm) high.
£145–165
$210–240 ⊞ FF

▶ **An Iittala smoky glass bottle,** by Timo Sarpaneva, Finnish, c1960, 7in (18cm) high.
£100–120
$145–175 ⊞ MARK

A Cenedese glass bottle, by Fulvio Bianconi, applied with blue, black and grey pattern, Italian, c1950, 13½in (34.5cm) high.
£2,700–3,300
$4,000–4,800 🔨 S(NY)

A Holmegaard yellow cased glass pitcher, Danish, c1970, 8in (20.5cm) high.
£75–85
$110–125 ⊞ PLB

A Seguso Vetri d'Arte turquoise blue cased glass decanter and stopper, Italian, 1960.
£2,200–2,600
$3,200–3,800 🔨 BUK

A blue glass bottle and stopper, by Salvador Dali, c1960, 12in (30.5cm) high.
£65–75
$95–110 ⊞ MARK

A Holmegaard green cased glass bottle vase, Danish, 1970s, 11¾in (30cm) high.
£70–85
$100–125 ⊞ PLB

Tableware

Two Tiffany Favrile yellow wine glasses, American, early 20thC, 5½in (14cm) high.
£420–480
$600–700 ➤ DuM

Tiffany

Louis Comfort Tiffany was the decorator and designer behind the creation of the glass lamps that are now synonymous with his name. The son of the founder of Tiffany & Co, he travelled to Europe and came under the influence of various Arts and Crafts teachers. His experiments in glass were founded on experimentation and the revival of old techniques. The jewelled effects and leaded lights gave his products a comforting charm that made them perfect for the relatively conservative taste of wealthy Americans. Tiffany lamps are probably the most valuable category of glass objects today.

A Tiffany Favrile champagne glass and a stemmed goblet, American, c1910.
£375–425
$550–620 ➤ DuM

An Orrefors red tulip glass, by Nils Landberg, Swedish, 1950s, 17¾in (45cm) high.
£250–280
$360–420 ➤ Sck

A glass part cocktail set, comprising cocktail shaker and six glasses, with playing card decoration, c1950.
£15–20
$20–30 ➤ WilP

Two Orrefors grey cased tulip glasses, by Nils Landberg, Swedish, 1950, largest 13¼in (33.5cm) high.
£400–480
$580–700 ➤ BUK

A Nuutajärvi red Pop goblet, by Kaj Franck, with a purple and amber stem and iridescent amber foot, engraved, Finnish, c1960, 8in (20.5cm) high.
£280–320
$410–460 ➤ Bon

A Nuutajärvi set of six glasses, by Kaj Franck, harlequin colours, Finnish, 1954–68, 2¼in (5.5cm) high, in presentation box.
£140–160
$200–230 ➤ Bon

▶ **A set of six Smoke glasses,** by Joe Colombo, Italian, 1964, 5½in (14cm) high.
£350–400
$500–580 ⊞ MARK

Bowls

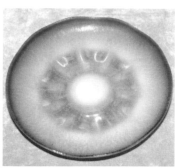

A Tiffany Favrile green glass comport, American, early 20thC, 8¼in (21cm) diam.
£750–850
$1,100–1,250 ⚒ DuM

A Daum orange glass bowl, with wirework metal mount by Louis Majorelle, marked, French, c1925, 12¼in (31cm) diam.
£550–650
$800–950 ⚒ P(Ba)

A Daum *pâte de verre* bowl and cover, by Almeric Walter, decorated with horse chestnuts and leaves, signed, French, c1925, 6½in (16.5cm) diam.
£5,000–5,500
$7,250–8,000 ⚒ S(O)

A blue glass bowl, by Timo Sarpaneva, signed, Finnish, 7¾in (19.5cm) diam.
£125–150
$180–220 ⚒ BUKF

A Cappelin & Co amethyst soda glass, by Vittorio Zecchin, Italian, c1926, 7in (18cm) high.
£300–350
$440–500 ⚒ Bon

An Orrefors red glass Kraka bowl, by Sven Palmqvist, with net decoration on a clear ground, signed, Swedish, 1945, 6½in (16.5cm) diam.
£850–1,000
$1,250–1,500 ⚒ BUK

A Nuutajärvi Notsjö multi-coloured glass plate, by Inkeri Toikka, signed, Finnish, 12¼in (31cm) diam.
£40–50
$60–75 ⚒ BUKF

A Nuutajärvi Notsjö coloured glass plate, by Oiva Toikka, signed, Finnish, 18½in (47cm) diam.
£100–120
$145–160 ⚒ BUKF

A Venini free-blown opaque yellow and white Fazzaletto bowl, by Fulvio Bianconi, marked, Italian, c1950, 10in (25.5cm) diam.
£580–650
$850–950 ⚒ Bon

A Fontana Arte blue glass charger, by Dube, decorated with grey-blue, green and cream enamels with flecks of gold foil, marked, Italian, c1955, 21in (53.5cm) diam.
£1,150–1,350
$1,700–2,000 ⚒ Bon

A Vasart green and pink glass bowl, decorated with blue swirls, signed, Scottish, 1950s, 8in (20.5cm) diam.
£65–75
$95–110 ⊞ SAN

An Orrefors blue glass bowl, by Vicke Lindstrand, Swedish, c1950, 6in (15cm) diam.
£80–90
$115–130 ⊞ MARK

A Holmegaard Freeform glass bowl, by Per Lutken, signed, Danish, 1950–60, 6in (15cm) high.
£100–120
$145–175 ⊞ ORI

A Kosta glass ashtray, by Vicke Lindstrand, Swedish, c1955, 5in (12.5cm) diam.
£70–80
$100–115 ⊞ MARK

A Holmegaard eliptical blue glass ashtray, by Per Lutken, Danish, 1950–60, 7in (18cm) diam.
£80–90
$115–130 ⊞ ORI

A Murano red, yellow blue and green glass ashtray, Italian, 1960s, 6¼in (16cm) diam.
£80–100
$115–145 ⊞ ZOOM

A Venini glass Canette dish, by Ludovico Diaz de Santillana, decorated in red on a smoky ground, Italian, 1960, 17¾in (45cm) diam.
£550–650
$800–950 ♠ BUK

▶ **A Skruf glass bowl,** by Bengt Edenfalk, Swedish, 1970s, 5in (12.5cm) high.
£160–180
$230–260 ⊞ MARK

◀ **An Orrefors green glass bowl,** by Ingeborg Lundin, Swedish, 1967, 6¾in (17cm) diam.
£400–450
$580–650 ♠ Sck

A Riihimäen Lasi Oy red cut-glass dish, by Aimo Okkolin, signed, Finnish, 6in (15cm) diam.
£100–120
$145–175 ♠ BUKF

Two Holmegaard glass bowls, one turquoise blue, one red, each with a white interior, Danish, 1970s, 6¼in (16cm) diam.
£60–75
$90–110 each ⊞ PLB

A Macchia blown glass bowl, by Dale Chihuly, signed, American, 1985, 22in (56cm) wide.
£8,000–9,000
$11,500–13,000 ♠ S(NY)

▶ **A Pilchuk Glass Centre sea form art piece,** by Dale Chihuly, cased and applied blue, shaded brown and red glass, engraved mark, American, 1985, 12in (30.5cm) wide.
£800–900
£1,150–1,300 ♠ Bon

◀ **A Kosta green and red glass bowl,** by Bertil Vallien, with etched decoration of a figure, a mountain and a deer, signed, Swedish, 1985, 7in (18cm) high.
£380–4450
$550–650 ♠ BUK

Miscellaneous

A Tiffany Favrile glass jam pot, with Tiffany Sterling silver cover, early 1900s, 4in (10cm) high.
£480–550
$700–800 ✗ DuM

▶ **A leaded glass window,** depicting flying birds above reeds and water lilies, the sky in shades of amber with pink clouds, American, early 20thC, 47in (119.5cm) high.
£2,500–2,750
$3,600–4,000 ✗ S(NY)

A Royal Copenhagen celadon glass vase, the cover with stylized foliate bronze mount, Danish, 1923–29, 8in (20.5cm) high.
£5,500–6,500
$8,000–9,500 ⊞ GoW

A glass cruet set, with amber glass stoppers and lids, 1930s, 12in (30.5cm) wide.
£100–125
$145–180 ⊞ JAZZ

◀ **A Daum green cut-glass bowl,** French, 1930s, 13in (33cm) diam.
£4,000–4,500
$5,800–6,500 ⊞ GoW

A Fontana Arte glass three-piece desk set, Italian, c1940, tray 10in (25.5cm) wide.
£1,000–1,200
$1,500–1,750 ⊞ GoW

◀ **A Clessidre blue and red hourglass,** by Paolo Venini, Italian, 1950s, 10¼in (26cm) high.
£280–320
$410–460 ⊞ TCG

A Fontana Arte green glass dish, with gilt-metal loop handle, Italian, c1950, 12in (30.5cm) diam.
£1,400–1,650
$2,000–2,400 ⊞ GoW

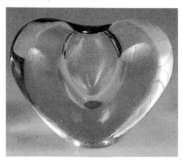

◀ **An Iittala heart-shaped glass ornament,** by Timo Sarpaneva, signed, Finnish, 1950s 4in (10cm) high.
£80–100
$115–145 ✗ BUKF

▶ **A Venini wine red glass Sirena vase,** by Fulvio Bianconi, signed, Italian, 1950, 9¾in (24.5cm) high.
£8,000–9,500
$11,500–13,500 ✗ BUK

A Venini 4040 Zaffiro glass table lamp, by Massimo Vignelli and Paolo Venini, opaque aubergine and white coloured glass cased in clear glass, Italian, c1956, 14in (35.5cm) high.
£280–320
$410–460 ➢ Bon

An Arnolfo di Cambrio glass ashtray, by Joe Colombo, Italian, c1960, 6in (15cm) diam.
£300–350
$440–500 ⊞ MARK

A Strömberg glass ice bucket, Swedish, with sterling silver mounts by Aage Dragsted, Danish, 1960s, 8in (20.5cm) high.
£400–500
$580–720 ⊞ DID

A Kosta glass model of a bird, by Vicke Lindstrand, Swedish, 1964, 8½in (21.5cm) high.
£100–110
$145–160 ⊞ MARK

An Orrefors clear glass triple candle-holder, Swedish, 1970s, 10in (25.5cm) wide.
£65–75
$95–110 ⊞ PIL

A Nuutajärvi multi-coloured glass paperweight, by Oiva Toikka, signed, Finnish, 1979, 3¼in (8.5cm) high.
£160–180
$230–260 ➢ BUKF

◄ **A Murano glass sculpture,** by A. Dona, signed, Italian, 1980s, 21in (53.5cm) high.
£1,600–1,800
$2,300–2,600 ⊞ FMa

A Nuutajärvi red glass sculpture, by Markku Salo, Finnish, 5½in (14cm) high.
£120–140
$175–200 ➢ BUKF

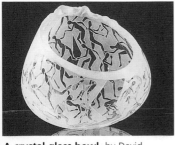

A crystal glass bowl, by David Prytherch, entitled 'Reconcilliation', engraved with figures, the rim carved with figures in relief, signed, 1985, 6in (15cm) wide.
£300–350
$440–500 ➢ AH

A Nuutajärvi brown and opal glass sculpture, by Kerttu Nurminen, signed, Finnish, 1991, 5½in (14cm) wide.
£60–70
$90–100 ➢ BUKF

An Orrefors cut crystal sculpture, by Gunnar Cyrén, surmounted by a silver-gilt model of a horse, signed, Swedish, 1990, 14½in (36.5cm) high.
£2,000–2,400
$3,000–3,500 ➢ BUK
This sculpture was made for the Dressage Committee of Sweden for the World Equestrian Games, Stockholm.

Lighting

A Tiffany Favrile glass and bronze Laburnum lamp, finial replaced, impressed marks, American, 1899–1918, 29½in (75cm) high.
£120,000–140,000
$175,000–200,000 ✒ S(NY)

A Tiffany glass and bronze Greek key lamp, American, c1900, 22in (56cm) high.
£11,000–12,500
$16,000–18,000 ✒ DUM

A Tiffany Favrile glass and bronze Peony lamp, impressed marks, American, 1899–1920, 28½in (72.5cm) high.
£237,000–300,000
$340,000–440,000 ✒ S(NY)

▶ **A Tiffany Favrile glass and bronze 'jewelled' candlestick,** repair to one sphere, impressed marks, American, 1899–1920, 14¾in (37.5cm) high.
£22,500–26,500
$32,500–38,500 ✒ S(NY)

Modern lighting

New ways of applying lighting in the modern home was one of the main characteristics of the 1930s – it was an attempt to get away from the central light fixture in the middle of the ceiling. The idea gathered pace in design circles, but it was only relatively recently that ambient lighting became widespread. The development of low energy halogen lighting has transformed the contemporary interior.

Vintage lighting is rarely as bright as contemporary lighting and there are issues concerning the safety of old electrical products which make retailing them problematic. If you are looking at vintage lighting, only buy from a reputable dealer.

◀ **A Tiffany Favrile glass and bronze Wisteria table lamp,** stamped marks, American, c1900, 26½in (67.5cm) high.
£190,000–220,000
$275,000–325,000 ✒ S

▶ **A Tiffany Pomegranate table lamp,** American, c1900, 21in (53.5cm) high.
£3,800–4,500
$5,500–6,500 ✒ DUM

A Tiffany Favrile glass and bronze Bamboo lamp, impressed marks, American, 1899–1928, 21¼in (54cm) high.
£45,000–55,000
$65,500–80,000 ✒ S(NY)

A Tiffany Oak Leaf table lamp,
American, c1900, 22in (56cm) high.
£11,000–13,000
$16,000–19,000 🔨 DUM

**A Handel reverse-painted glass
and brass Bird of Paradise lamp,**
signed, American, c1919,
23in (58.5cm) high.
£7,500–9,000
$11,000–13,000 🔨 S(NY)

◀ **A *pâte-de-verre* and wrought-
iron Plantes Aquatiques *veilleuse*,**
by Gabriel Argy-Rousseau, moulded mark,
French, c1924, 11¾in (30cm) high.
£7,500–9,000
$11,600–13,000 🔨 S(NY)

▶ **A *pâte-de-verre* La Prairie
veilleuse,** by Gabriel Argy-Rousseau,
in shades of raspberry, sealing wax
red, cobalt blue and sunflower yellow,
with flowering stems among tall
grasses, on a black patinated
wrought-iron base, moulded mark,
French, 1926, 6in (15cm) high.
£9,000–10,500
$13,000–15,250 🔨 S

A pair of Arts and Crafts candlesticks,
early 20thC, 14¼in (36cm) high.
£450–500
$650–720 ⊞ FBG

A bronze and ivory figural lamp, by
Roland Paris, French, c1920,
14in (35.5cm) high.
£2,250–2,500
$3,300–3,600 ⊞ ANO

◀ **An Anglepoise type SS standard
lamp,** by Edouard Wilfried Bouquet,
c1924, 63in (160cm) high.
£4,000–4,800
$5,800–7,000 🔨 DORO

A bronze figural table lamp,
by A. Kelety, early 20thC,
17¼in (43.5cm) high.
£9,000–10,500
$13,000–15,250 ⊞ MI

A PH table lamp, by Poul Henningsen for Louis Poulsen, the tiered opaque glass shade on a patinated brass shaft, stamped mark, Danish, late 1920s.
£3,000–3,500
$4,400–5,000 ⚲ Bon

A table lamp, by Jean-Michel Frank, on an oak cruciform base, french, 8¾in (22cm) high.
£25,750–33,500
$37,500–48,500 ⚲ Pou

◄ **A pair of painted steel adjustable table lamps,** by Christian Dell for Polo Popular, German, 1930s, 16in (40.5cm) high.
£525–625
$750–900 ⚲ BB(L)

A gilt-metal and glass bead chandelier, in the style of Baguès, c1930, 41½in (105.5cm) high.
£5,000–6,000
$7,250–8,700 ⚲ S(NY)

A pair of ceiling light fittings, the frosted glass panels decorated with a stylized fish pattern, 1930s, 15¾in (40cm) high.
£250–300
$360–440 ⚲ P(Ba)

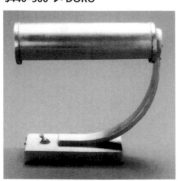

A double table lamp, by Josef Frank for House & Garden, with flexible arms, Australian, c1930, 30¾in (78cm) high.
£300–350
$440–500 ⚲ DORO

A pair of milk glass light covers, by Albert Chase McArthur and Emry Kopta, American, c1930, 6¼in (16cm) high.
£525–625
$750–900 ⚲ BB(L)

A steel Machine Age table lamp, American, c1930, 9in (23cm) high.
£80–95
$115–140 ⚲ BB(L)

A pair of Baccarat table lamps, by Jacques Adnet, the clear glass spheres balancing on stepped silvered bronze bases, stamped mark, French, c1930, 5¼in (13.5) high.
£4,800–5,500
$7,000–8,000 ⚲ S

◄ **A chrome table lamp,** with green glass shade, c1930, 19in (48.5cm) high.
£180–200
$260–290 ⊞ JAZZ

A Modernist aluminium and patinated-metal triple-cone lustre, c1930, 39½in (100cm) high.
£1,500–1,650
$2,200–2,400 ⚒ S

A wood and copper light stand and table, 1930s, 70in (178cm) high.
£250–280
$360–400 ⊞ NET

◀ **A Venini glass Martinuzzi chandelier,** the shades bordered with green thread, the stem with *pulegoso* glass elements, Italian, c1935, 23¾in (60.5cm) high.
£2,200–2,500
$3,200–3,600 ⚒ P(Z)

A pair of bedside lamps, in the style of Desny, comprising a series of glass circles, French, 1930s, 8in (20.5cm) high.
£300–360
$440–525 ⚒ Bon

A double desk lamp, by Christian Dell for Kaiser & Co, model No. 6580 Super, with adjustable black-painted steel and chromed metal stem, designed 1933–34, 21¼in (54cm) high.
£1,150–1,350
$1,650–1,950 ⚒ P(Ba)

A copper table lamp, by Norman Bel Geddes, 1936.
£375–450
$550–650 ⚒ BB(L)

A Bakelite and aluminium executive desk lamp, by Walter Dorwin Teague, model No. 114, with paper label to base, American, 1939–41, 12in (30.5cm) high.
£1,500–1,650
$2,200–2,400 ⚒ TREA

A glass and gilt table lamp, on a tripod base, French, c1940, 25in (63.5cm) high.
£1,000–1,250
$1,500–1,800 ⊞ GoW

◀ **A blue glass table lamp,** by Fontana Arte, Italian, c1940, 21in (53.5cm) high.
£3,300–3,600
$4,750–5,250 ⊞ GoW

▶ **A pair of gilded-metal mirrored wall lights,** c1940, 20in (51cm) high.
£3,400–3,800
$4,800–5,500 ⊞ GoW

A Bakelite and chrome desk lamp, marked Jumo, French, c1945, 5½in (14cm) high.
£850–1,000
$1,250–1,500 ⚒ DORO

A pair of leather and bronze lamps, by Jacques Adnet, with paper and perforated metal shades, French, c1948, 21¾in (55.5cm) high.
£5,000–6,000
$7,250–8,700 ⚒ S(NY)

A two-branch desk lamp, by Karl Hagenauer, with revolving brass supports and marked tinplate shades, c1950, 21in (53.5cm) high.
£850–1,000
$1,250–1,500 ⚒ DORO

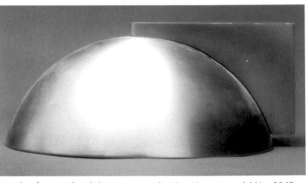

A pair of spun aluminium sconces, by Kurt Versen, model No. 9042, c1950, 12½in (32cm) wide.
£700–840
$1,000–1,250 ⚒ BB(L)

► **A glass table lamp,** by Flavio Poli for Seguso Vetri d'Arte, with a central metal band, maker's mark, slight damage, Italian, c1950, 9¾in (24.5cm) high.
£240–280
$350–400 ⚒ BUK

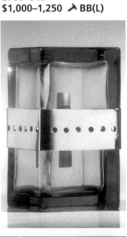

A glass table lamp, by Flavio Poli for Seguso Vetri d'Arte, with green glass over blue, in two parts with a metal connection, small chip, Italian, c1950, 9¾in (24.5cm) high.
£240–280
$350–400 ⚒ BUK

A black-painted three-light floor lamp, by Arteluce, with brown, white and black shades, 1950s, 69in (175.5cm) high.
£1,700–1,850
$2,450–2,600 ⊞ WDG

◄ **A chandelier,** by AVMazzega, with acid-treated glass discs, the metal frame with central fitting for 12 small bulbs, 1950s, 25in (64cm) wide.
£230–260
$330–380 ⚒ S

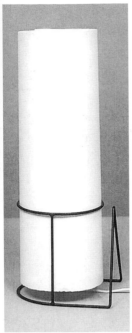

A pair of black and white lacquered aluminium wall lights, by Serge Mouille, lacquer renewed, French, c1950, 12in (30.5cm) high.
£1,400–1,700
$2,000–2,400 ⚒ DORO

A black-lacquered metal table lamp, by Carl Auböck, with hand-made paper shade, c1950, 19¾in (50cm) high.
£160–180
$230–260 ⚒ DORO

▶ **An orange glass hanging lamp,** 1950s, 18in (45.5cm) diam.
£80–100
$115–145 ⊞ ZOOM

A wall light, by Gino Safartti for Arteluce, the red disc supported on a black rod arm, 1950s, 15in (38cm) high.
£250–300
$360–440 ⚒ P(Ba)

A pair of black enamelled aluminium and plastic lamps, c1950, 17¼in (44cm) high.
£280–320
$410–470 ⚒ SLM

A ceiling light, with three orange misted-glass shades, 1950s, 18in (45.5cm) wide.
£65–80
$95–115 ⊞ TWa

An adjustable table lamp, by Karl Hagenauer, with lacquered aluminium shade, c1950, 24¾in (63cm) high.
£1,000–1,200
$1,500–1,750 ⚒ DORO

◀ **A painted steel and brass adjustable desk lamp,** by Clay Mitchie, c1950, 15in (38cm) high.
£280–320
$410–470 ⚒ BB(L)

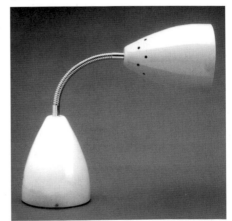

An adjustable lamp, by Max Bill for Novelectric, Swiss, 1950s, 9¼in (23.5cm).
£260–300
$380–440 ⚒ BB(L)

A painted-metal standing lamp, in the shape of a palm tree, with six glass shades modelled as buds and flowers, 1950s, 71in (180.5cm) high.
£500–600
$720–870 ⚒ E

A porcelain table lamp, by Fornasetti, Milan, with polychrome decoration of books, a vase of roses, and scissors, with yellow metal fittings, shade included, Italian, c1950, 16¼in (41cm) high.
£65–80
$95–115 ⚒ BUK

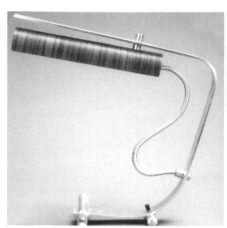

A bentwood and aluminium table lamp, Italian, c1950, 16¼in (41.5cm) high.
£450–540
$650–800 ⚒ BB(L)

A yellow ceramic lamp, by Antonia Campi for Lavenia, stamped, c1952, 11¼in (28.5cm) high.
£460–520
$650–750 ⚒ S

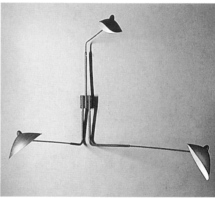

A black and cream painted aluminium three-branch ceiling light, by Serge Mouille, French, designed 1953, 78in (198cm) high.
£15,000–16,500
$21,750–24,000 ⚒ S

◀ **A white-painted metal and brass Handgranate A111 hanging lamp,** by Alvar Aalto for Valaistustyö, Finnish, c1951, 17½in (44.5cm) high.
£1,500–1,700
$2,200–2,400 ⚒ S

A pair of Visor wall sconces, by Arne Jacobsen for Louis Poulsen, 1955, 9¾in (25cm) high.
£650–780
$950–1,150 ⚒ BB(L)

A Venini ceiling lamp, by Massimo Vignelli, decorated with bands of blue, violet, red, green and white, Italian, c1954, 14½in (37cm) high.
£575–700
$850–1,000 ⚒ BUK

◀ **A Venini hanging lamp,** by BBPR Design Group for Olivetti, the opaque glass with purple, lilac, yellow and green decoration and a brass fitting, Italian, 1954, 26¼in (66.5cm) high.
£1,000–1,200
$1,500–1,750 ⚒ Bon

A painted metal three-light floor lamp, by Boris Lacroix, the adjustable shades painted in yellow, grey and lilac, on an iron base, c1954, 67¾in (172cm) high.
£5,750–6,250
$8,400–9,000 ♠ S

A white-lacquered metal PH Globe ceiling light, by Poul Henningsen for Louis Poulsen, Danish, 1958, 25½in (65cm) high.
£550–650
$800–950 ♠ BUK

A hanging lamp, by Arne Jacobsen for Louis Poulsen, Danish, c1955.
£200–240
$290–350 ♠ BB(L)

A green enamel table lamp, by Louis Kalft, after his designs for the Philips Company, marked Philips, Dutch, c1959.
£55–65
$80–95 ♠ WilP

A copper-plated and aluminium ceiling Artichoke lamp, by Poul Henningsen for Louis Poulsen, partially painted white, Danish, 1958, 19¾in (50cm) high.
£750–850
$1,100–1,250 ♠ DORO

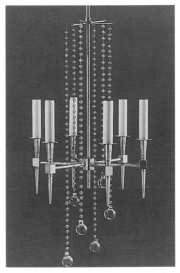

A polished-brass and glass six-light chandelier, by Tommy Parzinger, c1958, 39in (99cm) high.
£2,000–2,200
$2,900–3,200 ♠ S(NY)

▶ **A Visconti spun-fibreglass light shade,** by Achille Castiglioni for Gavina, Italian, 1960, 26in (66cm) high.
£450–500
$650–720 ⊞ MARK

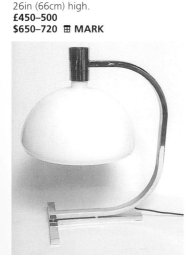

A chrome and white glass table lamp, by Franco Albini, Italian, early 1960s, 26in (66cm) high.
£450–550
$650–800 ⊞ MARK

A glass and steel chandelier, the blue-tinted textured glass cylinders suspended on a series of white-painted asymmetric branches, Italian, c1960.
£500–700
$720–1,000 ♠ Bon

◀ **A pair of handerkchief-shaped glass ceiling lights,** in clear glass with green glass piping to the rim, Italian, c1960, 19¾in (50cm) diam.
£600–700
$870–1,000 ♠ P

A steel and Perspex lamp, the stylized body with nine radiating clear Perspex fans, c1960, 30¾in (78cm) high.
£100–120 🔨 **LJ**

An aluminium and marble Arco adjustable floor lamp, by Achille and Pier Castiglioni for Flos, Italian, 1960s, 60in (152.5cm) high.
£650–750
$950–1,100 🔨 **BUK**

A Vistosi white cased-glass lamp, Italian, late 1960s, 18in (45.5cm) high.
£330–365
$470–530 ⊞ **PAB**

A metal multibranch plant lamp, 1960s, 69in (175.5cm) high.
£400–450
$580–650 ⊞ **ZOOM**

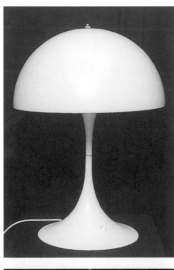

A green resin lamp, with a fibreglass shade, 1960s, 13in (33cm) high.
£25–30
$35–45 ⊞ **REPS**

A black glass Mushroom lamp, by AVMazzega, Italian, late 1960s, 20in (51cm) high.
£340–380
$500–560 ⊞ **PLB**

A Fase chrome lamp, Spanish, c1960, 15in (38cm) high.
£200–225
$290–325 ⊞ **MARK**

◀ **A white plastic table lamp,** by Verner Panton, c1960, 27in (68.5cm) high.
£500–550
$720–800 ⊞ **ZOOM**

A pair of glass wall lights, Italian, c1960, 11in (28cm) high.
£1,100–1,300
$1,600–1,900 ⊞ **GoW**

◀ **A blue glass ceiling light,** by Gino Vistosi for Murano, minor chips, Italian, 1960s, 17in (43cm) diam.
£270–325
$390–470 🔨 **BUK**

A Rosenthal green-glazed porcelain table lamp, with plastic shade, German, c1960, 22½in (57cm) high.
£130–160
$190–230 ⚒ DORO

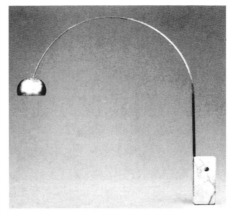

A marble and aluminium floor light, marked Flos, worn, Italian, 1962.
£280–320
$410–460 ⚒ BUK

A brown-patinated copper Model PH exterior light, by Poul Henningsen for Louis Poulsen, Danish, c1966, 17¾in (45cm) diam.
£350–400
$500–580 ⚒ BUK

A pair of Disderot laminated turned-mahogany and frosted opaque glass standing lamps, each with a flaring glass shade, c1965, 62in (157cm) high.
£3,800–4,200
$5,500–6,000 ⚒ S(NY)

A red and white Eclisse lamp, by Vico Magistretti, Italian, 1966, 7in (18cm) high.
£55–65
$80–95 ⊞ PLB

A plastic K9 27 table lamp, by Joe Colombo, for Kartell, 1967, 10in (25.5cm) diam.
£140–155
$200–225 ⊞ PLB

A clear Perspex and white-lacquered cast aluminium King Sun lamp, by Gae Aulenti for Kartell, 1967, 27½in (70cm) high.
£1,200–1,400
$1,750–2,000 ⚒ S

◄ **A lacquered metal and Perspex San Remo floor lamp,** by Archizoom for Poltronova, 1968, 87in (221cm) high.
£1,600–1,800
$2,300–2,600 ⚒ S

► **A chromed plastic Pastillo wall light,** by Studio Tetrach for Valenti, stamped, 1969, 23½in (60.5cm) wide.
£200–220
$290–320 ⚒ DORO

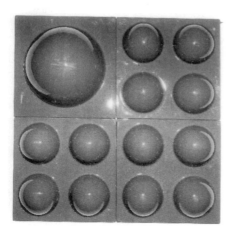

A moulded red plastic wall element, by Verner Panton for Luber, c1971, 23½in (59.5cm) square.
£400–480
$580–700 ⚒ Bon

A table lamp, by Achille Castiglioni for Flos, Italian, 1972, 10in (25.5cm) high.
£125–150
$180–220 ⊞ PLB

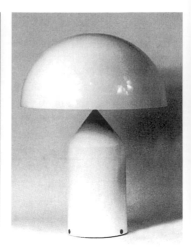

An O-Luce white enamelled aluminium Atollo lamp, designed by Vico Magistretti, Italian, 1977, 27½in (70cm) high.
£180–220
$260–320 ⚒ P(Ba)

◀ **A Sinerpica lamp,** by Michele de Lucchi for Alchimia, with blue, green and pink painted metal, 1979, 28¾in (73cm) high.
£780–880
$1,150–1,300 ⚒ S

▶ **A frosted glass lamp stand,** c1980, 10in (25.5cm) high.
£10–12
$15–20 ⊞ REPS

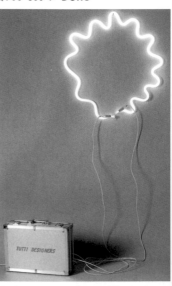

An adjustable aluminium and halogen Chain-Light table lamp, by Udo Maurer, marked.
£470–550
$700–800 ⚒ DORO

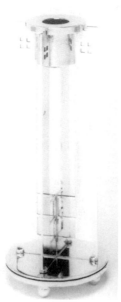

A silver-plated white metal candlestick, by Ettore Sottsass for Swid Powell, stamped marks, c1985, 12½in (32cm) high.
£400–480
$580–700 ⚒ Bon

A silver plated white metal candlestick, by Richard Meier for Swid Powell, stamped marks, 1986, 9¼in (23.5cm) high.
£200–240
$290–350 ⚒ Bon

An iron chain standard lamp, by Franz West for Memphis, 1989, 67in (170cm) high.
£1,000–1,200
$1,500–1,750 ⚒ DORO

A Fluorescent tube wall lamp, by Michelangelo Pistoletto, with an aluminium case, marked, Italian, 1989, case 28in (71cm) wide.
£1,000–1,200
$1,575–1,750 ⚒ DORO

Metalware

A copper charger, by John Pearson, repoussé-decorated with two central birds within flowers and foliage, signed, 1891, 20¼in (51.5cm) diam.
£1,800–2,200
$2,600–3,200 ⚒ B

A pair of Arts and Crafts copper and brass wall sconces, decorated in relief with arched floral panels over planished brass backplates, c1890, 15in (38cm) high.
£360–450
$550–650 ⚒ GH

A copper plant pot, by John Pearson, embossed with leaves and flowers against a hammered ground, marked and numbered 2506, 1900, 9¼in (23.5cm) high.
£600–700
$870–1,000 ⚒ B(B)

Metalwares in the home

The axioms of form and function have tended to limit the use of metals in Modernism to areas where their strength is required. Accordingly, metal features in the structure of the home, in that of furniture, and in a multitude of robust products for the kitchen and workshop.

The history of metal objects is mostly one of lighter weight and more elegant design. Look for aluminium products from the 1940s, which were produced as war production was transferred into the home market. These items are still in abundance at affordable prices.

A Newlyn copper plaque, c1900, 10in (25.5cm) diam.
£340–380
$475–560 ⊞ ANO

► **An anodized metal coal scuttle,** decorated with Ruskin Pottery embellishments and wrought-iron handles, c1900, 20in (51cm) high.
£280–350
$410–500 ⊞ MRW

A WMF pewter flagon, with iris and daffodil design, Austrian, c1900, 14in (35.5cm) high.
£440–485
$650–700 ⊞ ANO

A copper and brass kettle, by W. A. S. Benson, c1900, 8in (20.5cm) high.
£165–185
$240–270 ⊞ RUSK

► **A Birmingham Guild of Handicrafts silver and copper biscuit box,** by Arthur Stanisford Dixon, 1904, 5in (12.5cm) high.
£750–900
$1,100–1,300 ⊞ MoS

A Keswick School of Industrial Art copper vase, c1900, 7in (18cm) high.
£100–125
$145–180 ⊞ ANO

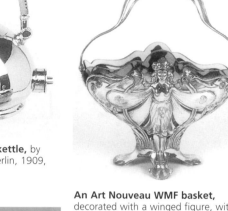

An Arts and Crafts cigarette box, by Omar Ramsden and Alwyn Carr, the cover and sides chased with simulated wave decoration, the cover with an enamel panel depicting a galleon in full sail on a blue and green sea, the base inscribed 'Omar Ramsden et Alwyn Carr Fecerunt', 1907, 3½in (9cm) wide.
£2,800–3,200
$4,000–4,600 ✗ B

A nickel-brass electric kettle, by Peter Behrens for AEG Berlin, 1909, 8¾in (22cm) high.
£500–600
$720–870 ✗ DORO

An Art Nouveau WMF basket, decorated with a winged figure, with flowerhead swing handle, green glass liner, on four trefoil-shaped supports, stamped marks to one foot, Austrian, 10½in (26.5cm) wide.
£580–650
$850–950 ✗ B(B)

A Liberty & Co Tudric pewter and enamel box, the enamelled scene depicting a wooded glade above sides cast with Celtic knots and foliate motifs, enclosing a wooden-lined interior, stamped mark, early 20thC, 12¼in (31cm) wide.
£900–1,000
$1,300–1,500 ✗ S(O)

A copper and silver inlay vase, by Christofle, with foliate decoration, French, 1920, 10in (25.5cm) high.
£1,000–1,200
$1,500–1,750 ⊞ GoW

An Art Deco cocktail unit, comprising chrome mixer, hour-glass-shaped measure, swizzle stick and corkscrew, on a mahogany base, 1930s, 13½in (34.5cm) wide.
£90–100
$130–145 ✗ P(B)

Four gilt-bronze panels, by Edgar Brandt for Au Bon Marché, mounted as two vertical panels, French, 1923–24, 77in (195.5cm) high.
£4,500–5,500
$6,500–8,000 ✗ S(NY)

A wrought-iron firescreen, by Edgar Brandt, French.
£10,500–12,000
$15,250–17,500 ✗ S(NY)

A wrought-iron firescreen, c1925, 31in (78.5cm) wide.
£3,000–3,500
$4,500–5,000 ✗ S

A copper vase, by Jouvenia, French, 1930, 8in (20.5cm) diam.
£750–850
$1,100–1,250 ⊞ GoW

◄ **A Modernist brown patinated-bronze vase,** decorated with a recessed band, with copper liner, on a palmwood base, impressed monogram, c1930, 8¾in (22cm) high, with original watercolour and pencil drawing for a similar vase, French, 10¼ x 7in (26 x 18cm), framed and glazed.
£6,000–7,000
$8,750–10,250 ⚒ S

► **A copper vase,** with brass geometric inlay, signed by Verschneider, French, c1930, 5in (12.5cm) high.
£850–950
$1,250–1,400 ⊞ GoW

A white metal tea strainer and stand, by Bernard Hötger for Franz Bolze, stamped marks, German, Bremen, c1930.
£1,200–1,400
$1,750–2,000 ⚒ P(Ba)

◄ **A wooden-handled kettle,** by Piqot, 1950s, 10in (25.5cm) wide.
£45–50
$65–75 ⊞ BTB

A nickel-plated metal travelling tea for two set, by Rena Dumas for Hermès, comprising teapot and cover with wicker handle, milk jug and sugar and tea bag compartment, stamped, French, 1940s, 4in (10cm) wide, in a brown leather case with shoulder strap.
£5,000–5,500
$7,250–8,000 ⚒ S

A Campden stainless steel seven-piece breakfast set, by Robert Welch for Old Hall, 1956, coffee pot 8¾in (22cm) high.
£55–65
$80–95 ⚒ P(Ba)

◄ **A patinated metal vase,** by Tapio Wirkkala for Hopeakeskusoy Design, Finnish, 1955, 8¼in (21cm) high.
£750–900
$1,100–1,300 ⚒ DORO

A wooden-handled kettle, with fluted sides, French, 1950s, 11in (28cm) high.
£30–35
$45–50 ⊞ ChA

► **A stainless steel coffee pot,** by Arne Jacobsen for Stelton, with wooden handle, Danish, mid-1960s, 8in (20.5cm) high.
£100–120
$145–175 ⊞ MARK

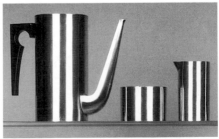

A stainless steel four-piece Cylinda-Line tea service, by Arne Jacobsen for Stelton, with dark brown wooden handles, Danish, 1967, teapot 6¾in (17cm) high.
£250–300
$350–450 ⚒ DORO

Silver

The development of modern furnishings throughout the 20th century has been driven by the impact of metal technology. The transformation of a chair into a sculptural statement, for example. Within the context of a multi-function interior metal objects have not always been at the forefront of modern design. With the emphasis on warmth and comfort in the home, the scope for a wide range of metal products for this domain is simply not there.

The traditions of the great silver workshops continued in the 20th century, supported by patronage and the desire to offer and receive precious objects. The context of Art Deco gave French workshops of the 1930s the opportunity to rediscover the monumental and grandiose, albeit with an angular styling that distinguished it from its organic and belle époque predecessors. After WWII silver design became less formal – mirroring changes in society – with the workshops of Georg Jensen in

Denmark at the forefront of this movement towards a more amorphic range of shapes and forms.

The other great theme in 20th century design has been in the streamlined aesthetic of machine-age production. This has been used to root products in a Functionalist tradition that embraces the speed and efficiencies of modern life. These products are, generally, full of contradictions – static objects made to look faster, a streamlined fridge for example, but they all the more interesting for that.

The sculptural traditions of this period were probably at their height in the 1930s when the combination of contemporary styling and taste afforded the opportunity for many fine commissions. The monumental quality of this work, even in miniature, has tended to make it very much of its time. The most enduringly popular sculptural objects remain those of dancing girls and animals, both of which offer numerous opportunities for collectors.

◀ **A silver box,** by Murrle Bennett & Co, the hinged cover embossed with a heart, London 1903, 2½in (6.5cm) wide, 2oz.
£340–380
$475–575 ➤ DD

A silver cup, by Omar Ramsden and Alwyn Carr, the base with a web of stylized branches forming the stem, martelé finish, inscribed to underside, London 1904, 5in (12.5cm) high, 7oz.
£2,000–2,200
$3,000–3,200 ➤ S(O)

A set of silver cutlery, by Johan Rohde for Georg Jensen, comprising 56 pieces, decorated with Acorn pattern, Danish, 1915.
£5,500–6,500
$8,000–9,500 ➤ LJ

A WMF silver-plated egg cruet, c1905, 7in (18cm) high.
£175–200
$250–300 ⊞ ANO

A silver tazza, by Johan Rohde for Georg Jensen, with openwork stem, designed 1916, manufactured 1920.
£1,650–2,000
$2,400–3,000 ➤ S(NY)

A silver tazza, by Johan Rohde for Georg Jensen, No. 252, with open-work stem centred by a cluster within tiers of beads and foliage, Danish, designed 1917, manufactured 1920.
£13,250–14,500
$19,000–21,000 ➤ S(NY)

◀ **A pair of Wiener Werkstätte repoussé-hammered brass bowls,** by Josef Hoffmann, impressed mark, Austrian, c1920, 13in (33cm) diam.
£16,500–18,500
$24,000–27,000 ➤ S(NY)

A silver tea and coffee service, by Christian Fjerdingstad, comprising eight pieces, with martelé finish and ivory handles, Danish, 1923–25, tray 17¼in (44cm) wide.
£11,300–13,500
$16,500–19,500 ⚘ S(P)

Three silver hors d'oeuvres utensils, by Jean Puiforcat for Cartier, French, c1925.
£825–900
$1,175–1,300 ⚘ BB(L)

◄ **A silver flatware service,** by Johan Rohde for Georg Jensen, comprising 220 pieces, decorated with Scroll pattern, Danish, early 20thC.
£20,000–25,000
$30,000–36,000 ⚘ S(NY)

► **A silver tazza,** by Georg Jensen, with openwork stem, 1925–32, 6½in (16.5cm) diam.
£1,300–1,500
$2,000–2,200 ⚘ BUK

A silver bowl, by Georg Jensen, with drop-ring handles, the foot decorated with Grapevine pattern, marked, Danish, designed 1919, manufactured 1930, 14¼in (36cm) wide, 58oz.
£11,000–14,000
$16,000–20,000 ⚘ S(NY)

A silver sifter spoon, by Georg Jensen, 1915–30, 6in (15cm) long.
£350–375
$500–560 ⊞ SHa

A silver comport, by Jean Puiforcat, with carved wood stem and domed stepped foot, maker's mark, stamped, French, c1930, 8in (20.5cm) diam.
£2,000–2,500
$3,000–3,600 ⚘ S(O)

A silver footed bowl, with gilt interior, 1930.
£75–100
$110–145 ⚘ BUKF

A silver jug, by Hingelberg, with wrapped cane handle, Danish, 1930s, 7in (18cm) high.
£5,500–6,200
$8,000–9,000 ⊞ GoW

► **A silver coffee service,** by Georg Jensen, Danish, 1933–44, coffee pot 6¾in (17cm) high.
£850–1,000
$1,250–1,500 ⚘ BUK

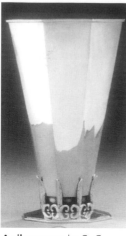

A silver vase, by C. G. Råström, with openwork base, Swedish, Stockholm, 1932, 8½in (21.5cm) high.
£475–575
$700–850 ⚒ BUK

◄ **A silver sugar caster,** by Robinson & Co, with ivory finial, London 1934, 7¼in (18.5cm) high.
£700–850
$1,000–1,250 ⚒ S

A silver shaker, modelled as a milk canister, American, c1930, 11in (28cm) high.
£1,000–1,200
$1,500–1,750 ⊞ GoW

An Art Deco silver cocktail shaker, by Charles Boyton, London 1934, 10in (25.5cm) high.
£675–750
$975–1,100 ⊞ SHa

An Art Deco silver tea service, by E. Viner, comprising three pieces, with composition geometric handle and finial to teapot, Jubilee mark, Sheffield 1934, 21.75oz.
£275–325
$400–470 ⚒ B(B)

Jean Puiforcat (1897–1945)

Puiforcat was a French Art Deco silversmith and designer. His work during the 1920s and '30s has become synonymous with the luxurious taste of the very wealthy in France and America. His achievement was to specialize in costly simplicity. The tea sets and canteens that he designed throughout the 1930s conform to our idea of opulent Art Deco styling – having both shiny surfaces and geometric shapes. The metal is made to contrast with the materials and shapes of the handles, which are often in exotic hardwoods or rock crystal.

A pair of Art Deco silver candlesticks, by Harold Stabler for Mappin & Webb, with incised facsimile signature and BD No. 800198, 1934, 9¾in (25cm) high.
£1,750–2,000
$2,500–3,000 ⚒ SWO

A silver-gilt and ivory chalice, by Jean Puiforcat, with hemispherical bowl and foot, the ivory stem mounted with four silver-gilt fish, marked, French, Paris c1937, 6in (15cm) high, 14oz.
£4,200–5,000
$6,000–7,200 ⚒ S(NY)

A silver bowl and cover, by Jean Puiforcat, set with lapis roundels, the cover with a carved lapis-mounted bud, stamped, French, Paris, 1940s, 7in (18cm) diam.
£3,200–3,800
$4,700–5,500 ⚒ S(O)

A hammered-silver cocktail set, comprising three pieces, Italian, c1940, 10in (25.5cm) high.
£2,300–2,600
$3,400–3,800 ⊞ GoW

A silver ladle, by Georg Jensen, Danish, c1950, 13in (33cm) long.
£400–500
$580–720 ⊞ **ASA**

A silver vase, by Wiwen Nilsson, Swedish, 1948, 8in (20.5cm) high.
£2,000–2,500
$3,000–3,500 ➴ **BUK**

A silver-plated punch bowl, by Lino Sabbatinni, 1950s, 15in (38cm) diam.
£330–400
$475–575 ➴ **BB(L)**

A silver vase, by Sven Arne Gillgren, Swedish, Stockholm, 1948, 11in (28cm) high.
£750–1,000
$1,100–1,500 ➴ **BUK**

A pair of silver salad servers, by Magnuss Stephensen for Georg Jensen, decorated with Argo pattern by, London import marks for 1953, 6¼in (16cm) long.
£160–200
$230–300 ➴ **P(B)**

A silver-plated and glass water jug, Italian, 1950s, 11½in (29cm) high.
£300–350
$440–500 ➴ **BB(L)**

A silver cocktail shaker, by Wiwen Nilsson, Swedish, 1951, 10¾in (27.5cm) high.
£4,250–5,250
$6,250–7,500 ➴ **BUK**

A silver cocktail shaker, by Georg Jensen, dated October 15th 1955, 13½in (34.5cm) high.
£2,500–3,000
$3,500–4,500 ⊞ **SFL**

A silver flatware set, by Gio Ponti for Reed & Barton, comprising 36 pieces, 1957.
£10,250–12,500
$15,000–18,000 ➴ **BB(L)**

Georg Jensen (1866–1935)

Jensen was a Danish silversmith who established his workshop in Copenhagen in the early years of the 20th century. His first designs were inspired by the English Art and Crafts movement. The output of the workshop gradually became characterized by an elegant, simple style that identifies more closely with the narratives of Modernism than with the retrospective objectives of the Arts and Crafts.

During the 1950s the firm Jensen established itself as an internationally acknowledged workshop. The sculptor Henning Koppel's work for Jensen is particularly sought after.

A Pride tea service, by David Mellor for Walker & Hall, comprising teapot with black leather-covered handle, hot water jug, two-handled sugar bowl and cream jug, Sheffield 1961 and 1963, c75oz.
£700–850
$1,000–1,250 ➤ HYD

Two silver vases, by Tapio Wirkkala, Finnish, 1959 and 1960, largest 7½in (19cm) high.
£250–300
$360–440 ➤ BUKI

A silver flatware set, comprising 34 pieces, Danish, 1960s.
£250–300
$380–440 ➤ BB(L)

A silver sugar bowl and milk/cream jug, marked 916, 1964, 3in (7.5cm) high.
£50–60
$75–90 ➤ BUKI

▶ **A silver box,** by Wiwen Nilsson, Swedish, 1965, 3½in (9cm) high.
£275–325
$400–470 ➤ BUK

A silver coffee service, comprising coffee pot, milk jug and sugar bowl, with rosewood cover and handle, hallmarked, 1968, coffee pot 9½in (24cm) high.
£500–600
$720–870 ➤ Bon

A silver four-piece condiment set, by Harald Nielsen for Georg Jensen, comprising a mustard, a salt pot and a pepper pot, on stylized circular feet, pattern Nos. 632 and 632a, the mustard pot with a blue-enamelled interior, with matched Pyramid pattern condiment spoon, on a salver with stylized lug handles, Danish, import marks for London 1970, salver 5½in (14cm) diam, 14oz.
£900–1,100
$1,300–1,600 ➤ Bon

A silver-gilt jardinière, by Wiwen Nilsson, Swedish, stamped, 1971, 8¾in (22cm) diam.
£1,150–1,300
$1,700–2,000 ➤ BUK

◀ **A pair of silver-gilt candlesticks,** with polished silver candle sockets and bases, the shafts comprising a series of articulated rods incorporating silver-gilt nodules, Birmingham assay marks to foot, 1972, 9¼in (23.5cm) high.
£2,800–3,200
$4,000–4,600 ➤ Bon

A silver ladle, by Lindsay Middleton, the hand-worked silver welded in two sections, 1980, 15in (38cm) long.
£300–350
$450–500 ➤ Bon

Colour Review

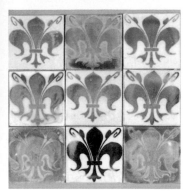

A set of 20 Pilkington's lustre tiles, each painted with a fleur-de-lys, with combed backs, minor damage, some with impressed 'P', early 20thC, each tile 3in (7.5cm) square.
£450–500
$650–725 ✗ S(O)

A set of 21 Pilkington's lustre tiles, painted with a heart motif on a scale ground, with combed backs, some with impressed P, early 20thC, each tile 3in (7.5cm) square.
£850–950
$1,250–1,400 ✗ S(O)

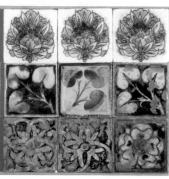

A set of 33 assorted Pilkington's lustre titles, decorated with various leaf and flower designs in colours, mostly combed backs, some mis-fired, minor damage, early 20thC, each tile 3in (7.5cm) square, together with seven other painted tiles and five larger lustre tiles.
£600–700
$875–1,000 ✗ S(O)

Tiles

The widespread use of tiles in the domestic architecture of the 20th century is linked to a project, at the heart of Modernism, for a healthier more efficient life. Tiles make up surfaces that can easily be kept clean. Their use in kitchen and bathroom also place them at the centre of domestic life. The manufacture of tiles is relatively easy and small manufacturers were able to secure a niche. Pilkington were one of a number of tile makers who exploited the taste for Arts and Crafts inspired lustre effects.

A tin-glazed earthenware tile, painted in enamels by Vanessa Bell, inscribed 'Virginia, Dec 25, 1926', 6in (15cm) square.
£3,500–4,000
$5,000–5,800 ✗ G(L)
This tile was given by Vanessa Bell to her sister Virginia Woolf.

Four tiles, designed by Salvador Dali, c1954, 8in (20.5cm) square.
£225–250
$320–360 ⊞ GIN

▶ **A Wedgwood part dinner service,** designed by Eric Ravilious, decorated with Travel Series pattern, comprising tureen, four soup bowls and seven dinner plates, 1940–50, tureen 10in (25.5cm) wide.
£440–500
$650–725 ✗ G(L)

A faïence vase, designed by Pablo Picasso, 'Lampe Femme', scratch-decorated in colour, glazed inside, damage to foot, impressed D'Apres Picasso Madoura Plein Feu, 1955, 13¾in (35cm) high.
£1,800–2,200
$2,600–3,200 ✗ BUK

An earthenware charger, by John Piper, with artist's monogram and dated 1972, 21¼in (54cm) diam.
£1,000–1,200
$1,500–1,750 ✗ Bon

A pottery platter, by John Piper, 'Girl with a Sunflower', painted design with wax resist eyes, the reverse painted 'Fulham Pottery, John Piper' and with title and dated Nov 1982, 22in (56cm) wide.
£1,100–1,300
$1,600–2,000 ✗ P

A Moorcroft bowl, tube-lined with cornflowers, impressed mark, signed in blue 'W. Moorcroft', c1920, 11in (28cm) diam.
£880–1,000
$1,275–1,500 ⚒ S(O)

Six footed bowls, impressed marks and some dates, 1921, 1923, 1924, one with maker's mark.
£500–600
$720–870 ⚒ S(O)

A Pilkington's Lancastrian bowl, with trailed polychrome glaze, early 20thC, 10½in (26.5cm) diam.
£75–90
$110–130 ⚒ G(L)

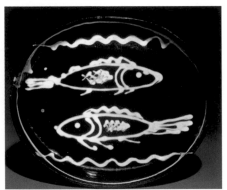

▶ **An earthenware platter,** by Michael Cardew, with a thick glaze over a slip-trailed design, the unglazed rim with cut chevron design, impressed MC and Winchcombe seals, c1928, 14½in (37cm) diam.
£1,400–1,700
$2,000–2,500 ⚒ B

An earthenware dish, by Michael Cardew, with slip-trailed design of two fish on a dark brown ground, impressed MC seal, c1931, 16¾in (42.5cm) diam.
£3,800–4,500
$5,500–6,500 ⚒ B

◀ **A stoneware dish,** by Bernard Leach, with Tree of Life design, reverse with inlaid BL and impressed St Ives seal, dated 1947, 11¼in (28.5cm) diam.
£1,800–2,200
$2,500–3,200 ⚒ P

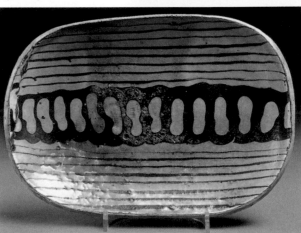

An earthenware dish, by Bernard Leach, with dark brown slip design on a yellow ground, some crawling and foaming of glaze, impressed BL seal, c1935, 11in (28cm) wide.
£800–1,000
$1,150–1,500 ⚒ B

A stoneware plate, by Shoji Hamada, c1930, 10in (25.5cm) diam.
£4,500–5,500
$6,500–8,000 ⚒ Bon

A pair of stoneware dishes, by Shoji Hamada, with a poured design in glazes on unglazed bodies, marked, c1950, 9in (23cm) diam.
£3,500–4,000
$5,000–5,800 ⚒ B

A stoneware dish, by Shoji Hamada, the all-over persimmon glaze with two wax resist stem-leaf designs, one inverted, c1963, 10½in (26.5cm) diam.
£3,000–3,500
$4,500–5,000 ⚒ B

A Hancock's Titian ware bowl, decorated with fruit, 20thC, 12½in (23cm) diam.
£70–85
$100–125 ⚒ G(L)

A Clarice Cliff charger, decorated with Honolulu pattern, the brightly painted ribbed body with a central well, black-printed Bizarre Newport Pottery mark, 1933–35, 18in (45.5cm) diam.
£4,000–4,800
$5,800–7,000 ⚒ S(O)

A Clarice Cliff plate, decorated with Castellated Circle pattern, c1930, 10in (25.5cm) diam.
£1,000–1,200
$1,500–1,750 ⊞ BKK

A Clarice Cliff plate, decorated with Alton pattern, c1930, 9in (23cm) diam.
£180–220
$260–320 ⚒ G(L)

A Poole Pottery Delphis range plate, c1965, in (20.5cm) diam.
£70–85
$100–125 ⊞ ADE

A Rörstrand stoneware plate, painted by Isaac Grünewald, signed, 1943, 14¾in (37.5cm) diam.
£550–650
$800–950 ⚒ BUK

An Arabia stoneware dish, decorated by Rut Bryk, polychrome-painted with an interior with two women, signed, 1945, Finnish, 13¼in (33.5cm) high.
£275–325
$400–470 ⚒ BUK

◄ **A Rörstrand stoneware dish,** decorated by Birger Kaipianinen, with painted decoration of a full table, with women and butterflies, signed, 1955–58, 26¼in (66.5cm) wide.
£1,100–1,300
$1,600–2,000 ⚒ BUK

A Ruskin high-fired vase, with mottled glazes, impressed maker's mark, dated 1933, 6¼in (16cm) high.
£550–625
$800–900 ⚒ S(O)

A Ruskin ginger jar and cover, with running crystalline glazes, impressed maker's mark, 1922–33, 12in (30cm) high.
£1,800–2,200
$2,600–3,200 ⚒ S(O)

A Ruskin souflé-glazed vase, with streaked and mottled glazes, impressed maker's mark and date, c1914, 15in (38cm) high.
£1,300–1,500
$2,000–2,200 ⚒ S(O)

◄ **A Ruskin vase,** with 'tea dust' glaze, impressed marks and date, c1905, 7¼in (18.5cm) high.
£500–600
$720–870 ⚒ S(O)

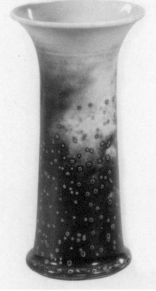

A Ruskin high-fired vase, impressed maker's mark, post-1915, 8in (20.5cm) high.
£820–980
$1,200–1,400 ⚒ S(O)

A Ruskin high-fired vase, restored, impressed maker's mark and dated 1903, 8in (20.5cm) high.
£400–480
$580–700 ⚒ S(O)

Two Moorcroft bowls, tube-lined with stylized yachts, impressed facsimile signatures, one signed in blue 'W.M.', 1934–38, larger 8in (20.5cm) diam.
£280–320
$400–470 ⚒ S(O)

► **A stoneware vase,** by William Staite Murray, the unglazed body decorated with a painted iron-glaze horse, the interior with matt green glaze, impressed M seal, c1930, 9¾in (25cm) high.
£3,000–3,600
$4,500–5,000 ⚒ B

A Winchcombe Pottery earthenware four-handled jar, by Michael Cardew, the rim, foot and interior with a slip-painted design under a glaze, impressed MC and Winchcombe seals, c1935, 10in (25.5cm) high.
£6,200–7,000
$9,000–10,000 ⚒ B

A Winchcombe Pottery earthenware vase, by Michael Cardew, decorated with horizontal bands under glazes, impressed MC and Winchcombe seals, c1938, 11¼in (28.5cm) high.
£2,000–2,400
$3,000–3,500 ⚒ B

A porcelain vase, by Bernard Leach, with a celadon glaze, flanged lip, the lower body with spiral-cut surface, impressed BL and St Ives seals, c1972, 12in (30.5cm) high.
£4,200–5,000
$6,000–7,250 ⚒ B

A stoneware vase, by Betty Blandino, with a small elliptical aperture, impressed BB seal, 12in (30.5cm) high.
£280–340
$400–500 ⚒ B

A stoneware vase, by Shoji Hamada, all-over tenmoku glaze with three incised bands of horizontal lines and repeated criss-cross design, c1950, 11in (28cm) high.
£3,500–4,200
$5,000–6,000 ⚒ B

A St Ives Pottery stoneware Leaping Salmon vase, by Bernard leach, with thick-wiped hakeme glaze over a semi-transparent ash glaze, decorated with glazed leaping salmon with incised detailing, impressed BL and St Ives seals, c1970, 12¼in (31cm) high.
£11,000–13,000
$16,000–19,000 ⚒ B

A raku vase, by David Roberts, with crackle glaze, impressed DR seal, c1990, 21in (53.5cm) diam.
£800–900
$1,150–1,300 ⚒ B

An Abuja Pottery stoneware water pot, by Lami Toto, decorated with incised and inlaid slip design of zoomorphic and abstract motifs, glazed, impressed LT and Abuja seals, c1962, 15½in (39.5cm) high.
£1,400–1,700
$2,000–2,400 ⚒ B
Lami Toto worked as one of ten throwers under Michael Cardew at Abuja during the 1960s.

A stoneware pot, by Janet Leach, impressed JL and St Ives seals, 1993, 18in (45.5cm) high.
£3,000–3,500
$4,500–5,000 ⚒ B

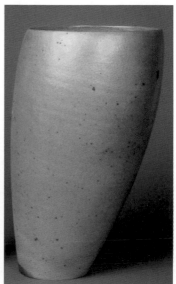

A stoneware pot, by Joanna Constantinidis, impressed C seal, 15¼in (38.5cm) high.
£800–900
$1,150–1,300 ⚒ B

A stoneware vase, by Elizabeth
Fritsch, 11in (28cm) high.
£2,800–3,400
$4,000–5,000 ⚒ B

A stoneware Floating Pillars vase,
by Elizabeth Fritsch, of flattened form,
1975, 11in (28cm) high.
£5,000–6,000
$7,250–8,700 ⚒ P

A stoneware pot, by Hans Coper,
1953, 12¼in (31cm) high.
£45,000–55,000
$65,000–80,000 ⚒ P
**This pot won the Gold Medal at
the Milan Triennale in 1953,
establishing Coper as one the most
gifted ceramic artists worldwide.**

A stoneware candlestick vase, by
Hans Coper, decorated with a matt
black manganese glaze, a candleholder
to the interior, impressed HC seal mark,
c1970, 6¼in (16cm) high.
£3,000–3,500
$4,500–5,000 ⚒ S(O)

A stoneware Cycladic form, by Hans
Coper, the white slip with some
blistering revealing underpainting, the
interior manganese, impressed HC
seal, c1972, 6in (15cm) high.
£13,000–15,000
$19,000–22,000 ⚒ B

A stoneware Cup on Stand form,
by Hans Coper, the interior and stem
with manganese glaze, with a central
cylinder for flowers, impressed HC
seal, c1975, 5in (13cm) high.
£3,000–3,500
$4,500–5,000 ⚒ B

**A stoneware Digswell
form,** by Hans Coper, the
interior manganese,
impressed HC seal, c1962,
17in (43cm) high.
£14,000–16,000
$20,500–23,000 ⚒ P

A stoneware vase, by
Dame Lucie Rie, c1970,
8in (20.5cm) high.
£1,500–1,750
$2,200–2,500 ⚒ SWO

A porcelain vase, by Dame
Lucie Rie, 1964,
5in (13cm) high.
£3,400–3,800
$5,000–5,500 ⚒ Bon

A porcelain vase, by Dame
Lucie Rie, impressed LR,
c1965, 9in (23cm) high.
£2,000–2,500
$3,000–3,500 ⚒ Bon

Discover the world of Clarice Cliff
and all that Jazz

A wide selection of 1920's/30's ceramics by Clarice Cliff, Susie Cooper, Charlotte Rhead, Shelley and others.

Furniture | Mirrors | Lamps | Chrome

Open Tuesday to Friday
10.30am-4.30pm

Saturday
10.30am-5.00pm

Closed
Sundays/Mondays

Clarice Cliff is a registered trademark of Josiah Wedgwood & Sons Limited, Barlaston.

Photography by Keith Paisley

ART DECO ORIGINALS
EMPORIUM

Now celebrating 20 years in business with the opening of a large showroom

Tel/Fax: 01422 347377 www.muirhewitt.com

MUIR HEWITT
Halifax Antiques Centre
Queens Road, Halifax
West Yorkshire HX14LR
England.

A stoneware vase, by Dame Lucie Rie, c1974, impressed LR seal, 8in (20.5cm) high.
£4,500–5,500
$6,500–8,000 ⚒ B

A Carlton Ware ginger jar and cover, decorated with Paradise Bird pattern, W&R mark, c1930, 12½in (32cm) high.
£550–650
$800–1,000 ⚒ B

A Clarice Cliff vase, shape No. 358, decorated with Gibraltar pattern, minor restoration, painted Fantasque Bizarre mark, c1930, 8¼in (21cm) high.
£900–1,000
$1,300–1,500 ⚒ M

A stoneware vase, by Dame Lucie Rie, with all-over matt glaze, impressed LR seal, c1980, 10½in (26.5cm) high.
£3,800–4,500
$5,500–6,500 ⚒ B

A Clarice Cliff vase, decorated with Oranges and Lemons pattern, black printed marks, 1931–32, 7in (18cm) high.
£1,750–2,000
$2,500–3,000 ⚒ S(O)

A Crown Ducal jug, by Charlotte Rhead, pattern No. 4298, c1935, 7½in (19cm) high.
£120–130
$175–200 ⊞ HEW

A Clarice Cliff Bizarre vase, shape No. 356, c1930, 7in (18cm) high.
£800–1,000
$1,150–1,500 ⊞ BDA

A Clarice Cliff vase, decorated with Xavier pattern, 1930–31, 7½in (19cm) high.
£1,700–1,900
$2,500–2,750 ⊞ BEV

◄ **A Clarice Cliff Fantasque single-handed Isis vase,** decorated with Circle Tree pattern, c1930, 9in (24cm) high.
£1,400–1,600
$2,000–2,300 ⚒ AG

A Wedgwood basalt vase, by Keith Murray, shape No. 3818, with horizontal banded decoration, impressed mark and printed facsimile signature, 1934, 8in (20.5cm) high.
£600–700
$870–1,000 ⚒ S(O)

▶ **A Wedgwood earthenware vase,** by Keith Murray, with engine-turned decoration, KM monogram, printed factory marks, c1935, 6¼in (16cm) high.
£1,800–2,000
$2,500–3,000 ⚒ P(Sy)

◀ **A Wedgwood earthenware vase,** by Keith Murray, blue-printed mark, post 1940, 7¼in (18.5cm) high.
£250–300
$350–450 ⚒ S(O)

A Wedgwood earthenware vase, by Keith Murray, red-printed mark and KM monogram, post-1940, 7½in (19cm) high.
£220–250
$320–350 ⚒ S(O)

A Rye Pottery jug, 1950s, 6½in (16.5cm) high.
£30–35
$45–50 ⊞ ADE

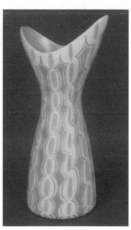

A Carter, Stabler & Adams Freeform vase, decorated by Gwen Haskins, c1955, 14in (35.5cm) high.
£700–800
$1,000–1,200 ⊞ ADE

◀ **A Keramis pottery vase,** small chip to base, blue printed mark, black script mark, impressed 1065, Belgian, c1925, 10½in (26.5cm) high.
£550–650
$800–1,000 ⚒ S(O)

▶ **A Sèvres porcelain vase,** by Emile-Jacques Ruhlmann, the interior decorated in shades of brown with birds on a fruiting vine, heightened with gilding, on gilt-bronze foot, marked, French, 1927, 8¾in (22cm) high.
£4,000–4,500
$5,800–6,500 ⚒ S

A pair of vases, by Siamand Hamage, with stylized floral decoration, French, early 20thC, 10in (20.5cm) high.
£80–100
$115–145 ⚒ G(L)

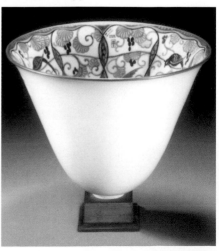

An enamelled ceramic goblet, by Jean Mayodon, decorated with a frieze of satyrs and nymphs, signed with a monogram and Sèvres in gold, 7½in (19cm) high.
£8,000–9,500
$11,500–13,500 ⚒ S(P)

A Sèvres Pâte Nouvelle porcelain vase, by Anne-Marie Fontaine, decorated with cockerels and stylized foliage applied in polychrome slip under a clear glaze, heightened in gilt with horizontal bands, marked, signed, 1933, 16¼in (41.5cm) high.
£6,000–7,000
$8,700–10,000 ⚒ B

A Gustavsberg vase, by Wilhelm Kåge, Swedish, 1940s, 4¼in (11cm) high.
£120–150
$175–220 ⊞ MARK

◄ **A Gustavsberg stoneware vase,** by Stig Lindberg, signed, Swedish, 1966, 17¼in (44cm) high.
£650–750
$950–1,100 ⚒ BUK

A Rörstrand vase, by Ilsa Claesson, Swedish, 1928–32, 7in (28cm) high.
£100–125
$145–180 ⊞ MARK

A Gustavsberg stoneware vase and bowl, by Berndt Friberg, with tenmoku glaze, minor damage to vase, signed, Swedish, 1952 and 1955, vase 6½in (16.5cm) high.
£1,800–2,000
$2,600–3,000 ⚒ BUK

► **A Gustavsberg stoneware vase,** by Anders Bruno Liljefors, with scratched and painted decoration, glazed, signed, Swedish, 1952, 11½in (29cm) high.
£140–165
$200–250 ⚒ BUK

A porcelain Zigzag vase, attributed to Ettore Sottsass, 1980s, 9½in (24cm) high.
£120–140
$175–200 ⚒ BB(L)

A Richard Ginori Il Pellegrino earthenware vase, by Gio Ponti, signed, Italian, c1924, 13¾in (35cm) high.
£14,000–16,000
$20,000–23,000 ⚒ S(NY)

◄ **An Architectural Pottery ceramic planter,** with wrought-iron tripod base, minor chips, impressed mark, American, 1950s, 16in (40.5cm) high.
£350–400
$500–580 ⚒ BB(L)

A porcelain bowl, by Dame Lucie Rie, impressed LR seal, c1983, 10in (25.5cm) diam.
£10,000–12,000
$14,500–17,500 🔨 P

A porcelain bowl, by Dame Lucie Rie, c1978, 7½in (19cm) high.
£10,000–12,000
$14,500–17,500 🔨 Bon

◀ **A stoneware bowl,** by Dame Lucie Rie, c1962, 5½in (14cm) diam.
£2,400–2,800
$3,500–4,000 🔨 Bon

▶ **A porcelain bowl,** by Dame Lucie Rie, the interior with manganese glaze and three bands of sgraffito, impressed LR seal, c1958, 4½in (11.5cm) diam.
£7,000–8,500
$10,000–12,500 🔨 B

A porcelain footed bowl, by Dame Lucie Rie, impressed LR seal, c1980, 6½in (16.5cm) diam.
£6,000–7,000
$8,700–10,000 🔨 B

An Arts and Crafts bowl, decorated with leaves and flowers, TG monogram, 1903, 11¼in (18.5cm) diam.
£220–260
$320–380 🔨 G(L)

An Arts and Crafts bowl, with Celtic inspired centre within a meandering floral border, the exterior similarly decorated with palmette designs, marked, 1914, 14½in (36.5cm) diam.
£2,000–2,400
$3,000–3,500 🔨 G(L)

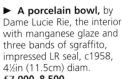

A Clarice Cliff tea service, decorated with Flora pattern, c1930.
£1,100–1,300
$1,600–2,000 🔨 RBB

◀ **A Susie Cooper Kestral shape coffee set,** decorated with pattern No. 1530, c1930, coffee pot 7¼in (18.5cm) high.
£650–750
$950–1,100 ⊞ MAV

A Clarice Cliff Conical teapot, decorated with Appliqué Idyll, moulded and printed marks, 1931–36.
£850–1,000
$1,250–1,500 🔨 S(O)

A Shelley Vogue trio, decorated with Sunray pattern, c1930, plate 7in (18cm) wide.
£270–300
$400–450 ⊞ RH

A Rosenthal porcelain tea service, by Tapio Wirkkala, comprising 26 pieces including covers, maker's mark, German, c1959.
£275–325
$400–470 ↗ BB(L)

An earthenware six-piece coffee set, marked N.190/195/199, Italian, 1950s, coffee pot 7in (18cm) high.
£120–150
$175–220 ↗ WBH

A set of three ceramic coffee cups and saucers, Italian, c1980, saucer 6in (15cm) diam.
£125–140
$180–200 ⊞ PLB

A Steubenville Pottery glazed earthenware dinner service, by Russell Wright, comprising 94 pieces, most pieces impressed and inscribed 'Russell Wright/mfg.by/Steubenville', American, c1938.
£600–720
$870–1,000 ↗ BB(L)

A Poole Pottery galleon, by Harold Stabler, *The Harry Page*, fully rigged, on a plinth, c1925, 20¾in (52.5cm) high.
£1,700–2,000
$2,500–3,000 ↗ B

A ceramic teapot, by Matteo Thun for Memphis, Italian, c1980s, 12in (30.5cm) high.
£200–220
$300–320 ⊞ PLB

A glazed and painted ceramic centrepiece, by Bjorn Winblad, painted marks, Danish, c1963, 10in (25.5cm) high.
£530–630
$765–900 ↗ BB(L)

▶ **A Goldscheider pottery figure of a girl,** by Josef Lorenzl, modelled holding a hat box, with two suitcases at her feet, printed mark and facsimile signature, impressed No. 7064 160 19, c1930.
£1,800–2,200
$2,600–3,200 ↗ B

◀ **A Zsolnay lustre figure,** Hungarian, 1916, 14in (35.5cm) high.
£900–1,000
$1,300–1,500 ⊞ ANO

A Loetz glass jug and six beakers, by Richard Teschner, the jug modelled as a stylized bird, each beaker with a teardrop, slight damage, indistinct etched mark, early 20thC, jug 7in (18cm) high.
£650–750
$950–1,100 ⚒ S(O)

▶ **A Gabriel Argy-Rousseau La Prairie veilleuse,** pâté-de-verre, clear glass decorated in colours, on a black patinated wrought-iron base, 1926, 5½in (14cm) high.
£9,000–11,000
$13,000–16,000 ⚒ S

A Tiffany Favrile Goldfish glass vase, inscribed L.C. Tiffany-Favrile and 1998H, c1913, 16¾in (42.5cm) high.
£350–420
$500–600 ⚒ S(NY)

◀ **A Lalique Bacchantes opalescent glass vase,** moulded with nude maidens, moulded mark, 1930s, 9¾in (25cm) high.
£12,000–14,000
$17,500–20,000 ⚒ BB(L)

A Lalique Danaides glass vase, moulded with a frieze of nudes pouring water, minor damage, stencilled mark, 1930s, 7¼in (18.5cm) high.
£1,700–2,000
$2,500–3,000 ⚒ S(O)

A Lalique Grignon frosted glass vase, moulded with fan motifs, minor damage, stencilled mark, 1932–45, 7in (18cm) high.
£400–480
$580–700 ⚒ S(O)

A Lalique Languedoc frosted glass vase, 1930s.
£6,000–7,000
$8,700–10,000 ⚒ CNY

A Lalique Serpent glass vase, 1930s, 10in (25.5cm) high.
£5,500–6,500
$8,000–9,000 ⚒ CNY

A Lalique Perruches frosted glass vase, on a bronze stand, 1930s, 10½in (26.5cm) high.
£3,000–4,000
$4,500–5,800 ⚒ CNY

▶ **A Lalique Penthièvre glass vase,** stencilled mark, 1930s, 10in (25.5cm) high.
£5,000–6,000
$7,250–8,750 ⚒ Bon

A Lalique moulded and frosted glass Cactus table, inscribed mark, 1947, 60in (152.5cm) diam.
£18,500–22,000
$27,000–32,000 ⚷ S(NY)

A Lalique Etoiles glass scent bottle and stopper, moulded in low relief with scattered stars, the stopper with a crescent moon and the words 'dans la nuit', moulded and engraved marks to base, post-1920, 9½in (24cm) high.
£1,000–1,200
$1,500–1,750 ⚷ S(O)

A Venini glass figural decanter, by Gio Ponti, model No. 3878, Italian, c1948, 11in (28cm) high.
£3,500–4,200
$5,000–6,000 ⚷ S(NY)

◀ **A Venini handkerchief vase,** etched mark, applied paper label, 1950–60, 9½in (24cm) high.
£400–450
$580–650 ⚷ S(O)

A Whitefriars forked vase, by Wilson, c1955, 10in (25.5cm) high.
£100–120
$145–175 ⊞ JHa

◀ **A Whitefriars hooped vase,** by Geoffrey Baxter, c1966, 11in (28cm) high.
£120–140
$175–200 ⊞ JHa

An engraved glass panel, the central sun surrounded by figures blowing pipes, eating grapes and sowing seeds among fruit, vegetables, animals and birds, minor chips, 1930s, 44¾ x 60¼in (113.5 x 153cm).
£4,800–5,800
$7,000–8,400 ⚷ S(O)

A Schott & Gen Jenaer Glassworks glass teapot with inserts, by Wilhelm Wagenfeld, 1932, 5½in (14cm) high.
£160–200
$230–300 ⚷ BB(L)

▶ **A Savoy glass vase,** by Alvar Aalto, No. 3031, engraved mark, designed 1936, manufactured 1954–55, 11½in (29cm) high.
£3,500–4,000
$5,000–5,800 ⚷ S

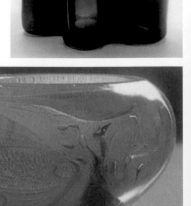

A Leerdam Unica glass vase, by A. D. Copier, imprinted with fishes and seaweed, c1942, 11in (28cm) diam.
£5,000–6,000
$7,250–8,750 ⚷ S(Am)

An Orrefors glass vase, by Simon Gate, with pressed relief geometric design, Swedish, 1930, 6¼in (16cm) high.
£300–360
$450–500 ✦ BUK

An Orrefors glass vase, by Edward Hald, decorated with flowers, Swedish, c1944, 4¼in (11cm) high.
£200–220
$300–320 ✦ BUK

An Orrefors Ariel glass vase, by Edvin Ohrström, Swedish, 1950, 3¾in (9.5cm) high.
£2,000–2,200
$3,000–3,200 ✦ BUK

◄ **An Orrefors Ariel glass vase,** by Edvin Ohrström, entitled 'The Girl and the Dove', Swedish, 1970, 6¾in (17cm) high.
£820–1,000
$1,000–1,500 ✦ BUK

An Orrefors Graal glass vase, by Gunnar Cyrén, decorated with a rowing boat and fish, signed, Swedish, c1989, 9in (23cm) high.
£840–1,000
$1,250–1,500 ✦ BUK

An Orrefors Ariel glass vase, by Ingeborg Lundin, engraved mark, Swedish, c1975, 6½in (16.5cm) high.
£6,000–7,000
$8,700–10,000 ✦ P(Sy)

► **An Orrefors Mali II glass vase,** by Gunnar Cyrén, signed, Swedish, 1990, 8½in (21.5cm) high.
£500–600
$720–870 ✦ BUK

An Orrefors Ariel glass vase, by Ingeborg Lundin, Swedish, c1960, 7in (18cm) high.
£2,500–3,000
$3,500–4,500 ✦ S(NY)

A Kosta glass vase, Swedish, 1970s, 5in (12cm) high.
£80–100
$115–145 ⊞ PIL

A set of three Riihimaen glass vases, Finnish, 1970s, 6in (15cm) high.
£140–155
$200–225 ⊞ PAB

A Barovier & Toso glass vase, by Ercole Barovier, Italian, c1951, 9¾in (25cm) high.
£2,000–2,200
$3,000–3,200 ⚒ P(Z)

A glass vase, by Ercole Barovier, c1960, 13½in (31cm) high.
£1,500–1,750
$2,200–2,500 ⚒ DORO

A Venini glass vase, by Fulvio Bianconi, Italian, signed, 1950, 21½in (54.5cm) high.
£525–625
$750–900 ⚒ BUK

A Murano glass vase, Italian, 1950s, 19½in (50cm) high.
£215–240
$300–350 ⊞ DSG

A Fili Policromi glass vase, by Seguso Vetri d'Arte, Italian, 1952, 11¾in (30cm) high.
£1,300–1,600
$2,000–2,300 ⊞ FF

A Venini Pezzato glass bottle, by Fulvio Bianconi, etched signature, Italian, 1950s, 14½in (37cm) high.
£4,750–5,500
$7,000–8,000 ⚒ BUK

◄ **A Cenedese sommerso glass vase,** by Antonio da Ros, Italian, c1960, 15½in (39.5cm) high.
£850–1,000
$1,200–1,500 ⚒ Bon

An Avem glass vase, by Giulio Radi, c1950, 10½in (26.5cm) high.
£4,000–4,500
$5,800–6,500 ⚒ S

A Venini glass vase, by Fulvio Bianconi, c1960, 6in (15cm) high.
£5,000–5,500
$7,250–8,750 ⊞ GoW

A seven-piece cadmium Red Sea form set, by Dale Chihuly, signed, American, 1994, 20in (51cm) wide.
£14,000–16,500
$20,000–24,000 ⚒ S(NY)

A Vistosi blown glass chick, by Alessandro Pianon, with copper legs, Italian, 1960, 8¼in (21cm) high.
£950–1,150
$1,400–1,600 ⚒ BUK

Sculpture

Three gilt-bronze and ivory figures, after models by A. Gory, Exotic Dancer, Flower Girl and Flower Seller, French, early 20thC, largest 15in (38cm) high.
£1,000–2,500
$1,500–3,600 each ⚒ C

A pair of bronze and ivory figures of clowns, by Bruno Zach, one signed Zach, one missing left hand, Austrian, 1918–30, largest 11½in (29cm) high.
£4,200–5,000
$6,000–7,250 ⚒ S(O)

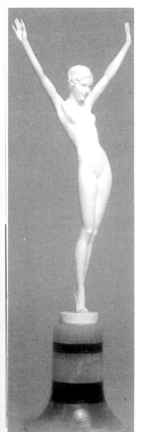

► **A silver-plated stylized model of a boat,** by Hagenhauer, with an African maiden, Austrian, Vienna 1920s, 14in (35.5cm) high.
£670–750
$1,000–1,100 ⊞ ANO

A bronze figure of a dancing girl, from a model by Lorenzl, with gilt-coloured and green patination, on a marble base, Austrian, c1925, 7in (18cm) high.
£600—700
$870–1,100 ⚒ P

A patinated-brass reclining female figure, by Hagenauer, stamped mark, WHW monogram, Austrian, 1930s, 21in (53.5cm) long.
£10,000–12,000
$14,500–17,500 ⚒ S

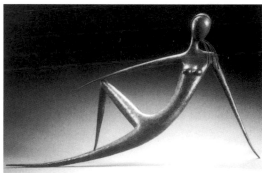

A carved ivory figure of a woman, Nude, after Ferdinand Preiss, German, early 20thC, 17½in (44.5cm) high.
£5,000–6,000
$7,250–8,750 ⚒ C

► **A study of a standing bison,** by Max Le Verrier, c1930, 9in (23cm) wide.
£3,600–4,400
$5,000–6,500 ⊞ MI

A lapis lazuli and jade table clock, with gilded face, Swiss, c1925, 10in (25.5cm) wide.
£5,000–6,000
$7,250–8,750 ➶ CNY

A brass gravity clock, c1919, 10in (25.5cm) high.
£180–220
$250–320 ➶ SWO

An Art Deco brass-cased eight-day timepiece, with separate ink pot, on a marble base, c1920, 24in (61cm) wide.
£180–200
$250–300 ➶ TPA

An Art Deco-style mantel timepiece, by Jaeger Le Coultre, the Perspex case with gilt chinoiserie decoration, 6¼in (16cm) high.
£350–420
$500–600 ➶ WW

A boudoir mantel clock, by Cartier, in an orange-painted case with Art Deco-style brass decoration, on a black stepped base, 1930s, 4in (10cm) high.
£680–750
$1,000–1,100 ➶ TMA

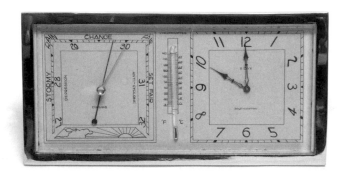

An Art Deco-style chrome-plated barometer clock and thermometer, by Dimmer, Southampton, c1935, 9in (23cm) wide.
£250–280
$350–410 ⊞ RTW

> **Cross Reference**
> See Colour Review (page 241)

An Art Deco-style chrome desktop barometer, by Zeiss Ikon, German, c1930, 7in (18cm) high.
£400–450
$580–650 ⊞ RTW

▶ **A leather-covered desk clock,** by Jaeger, c1940, 5in (12.5cm) high.
£1,000–1,200
$1,500–1,750 ⊞ GoW

A metal and plastic battery-operated table clock, by Metamec, 1950s, 8in (20.5cm) wide.
£8–10
$10–15 ⊞ REPS

A pink plastic electric alarm clock, by Metamec, c1950, 6½in (16.5cm) wide.
£8–10
$10–15 ⊞ REPS

A wood and metal table alarm clock, by Metamec, 1960s, 11in (28cm) wide.
£8–10
$10–15 ⊞ REPS

A plastic clock, by Metamec, c1960, 7in (18cm) high.
£10–12
$15–18 ⊞ REPS

A plastic space-age alarm clock, German, 1960s, 8½in (21.5cm) high.
£35–40
$50–60 ⊞ MARK

A plastic mantel clock, modelled as a sailing boat, Chinese, mid-1960s.
£25–30
$35–45 ⚒ WilP

A metal alarm clock, by Golden Clock, 1970s, 8in (20.5cm) wide.
£7–8
$8–10 ⊞ REPS

▶ A digital electric bedside alarm clock, by Braun, 1980s, 7in (18cm) wide.
£15–20
$20–30 ⊞ REPS

A laminated rosewood and chrome desk clock, by Howard Miller, American, stamped, 6¾in (17cm) high.
£160–180
$230–260 ⚒ BB(L)

A plastic digital bedside President Timelite radio alarm clock, c1970, 5in (12.5cm) high.
£23–25
$30–35 ⊞ REPS

Wall Clocks

◄ **An Art Deco wall clock,** with steel hands, the electric movement by Tyme, c1930, 12¼in (31cm) diam.
£200–250
$300–350 ✗ P(F)

▶ **An electric star wall clock,** by Metamec, 1950s–60s, 18in (45.5cm) diam.
£18–20
$25–30 ⊞ REPS

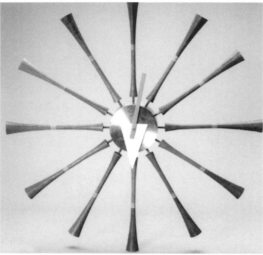

A Spool clock, by George Nelson for Howard Miller Clock Co, American, c1952, 23in (58.5cm) diam.
£700–900
$1,000–1,300 ✗ BB(L)

A wood and metal battery-operated quartz wall clock, by Metamec, 1960s, 13in (33cm) diam.
£10–12
$15–18 ⊞ REPS

◄ **A metal and plastic battery-operated star wall clock,** 1960s, 13in (33cm) diam.
£11–12
$15–18 ⊞ REPS

▶ **A wall clock,** by George Nelson for Howard Miller Clock Co, American, c1970, 14in (35.5cm) diam.
£400–450
$580–650 ✗ BB(L)

◄ **An electric ball clock,** by George Nelson for Howard Miller Clock Co, the cylindrical brass drum radiating spokes terminating in wooden spheres, black enamelled hands, remnants of manufacturer's label to underside, American, 1947, 13¼in (33.5cm) diam.
£450–550
$650–800 ✗ B(Ba)

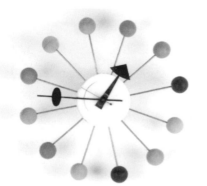

◄ **An electric ball clock,** by Howard Miller for George Nelson Associates, impressed Howard Miller Clock Co/Zeeland Mich., label, American, designed c1948, 13¼in (33.5cm) diam.
£650–800
$950–1,150 ✗ BB(L)

Wristwatches

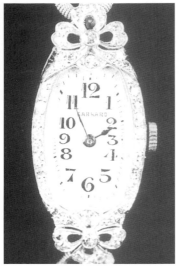

An Art Deco-style cocktail watch, by Garrard, the dial with Arabic numerals, surrounded by pavé-set diamonds with ribbon-tie terminals, on a wire mesh double bracelet with a diamond-set clasp.
£450–550
$650–800 ✗ HYD

An Art Deco platinum and diamond cocktail watch, with Swiss movement, on a platinum expandable bracelet, 1930s–40s, with presentation case.
£500–600
$720–870 ✗ G(L)

An Art Deco silver wristwatch, by Mappin.
£750–850
$1,100–1,250 ⊞ TEM

A 18ct gold wristwatch, by Le Coultre, with winder at back, c1930.
£5,000–5,500
$7,250–8,000 ⊞ AGR

Collecting wristwatches

The market in wristwatches is organized around traditional lines with a premium being placed on quality of workmanship and materials. Approaching the market from the perspective of design offers some huge possibilities for collectors. The most stylistically extravagant watches will often be those associated with the fashion end of the market, rather than with the classic market epitomized by Swiss production. Fashion watches will, ironically, be harder to find because of their ephemeral nature. A fashion watch should probably look lived-in.

A stainless steel asymmetrical wristwatch, by Acutron, 1960s.
£375–450
$550–650 ✗ BB(L)

A Heuer Carrera manual wind chronograph, with 45-minute indicators, c1965.
£1,00–1,200
$1,500–1,750 ⊞ HARP

A Heuer Camaro manual wind chronograph, with date, in a gold-plated cushion case, c1965.
£650–800
$950–1,150 ⊞ HARP

◄ **A Heuer Monaco automatic chronograph,** with 30-minute and 12-hour registers, date indication by self-winding movement, in a waterproof steel case, c1969.
£2,000–2,500
$2,900–3,600 ⊞ HARP

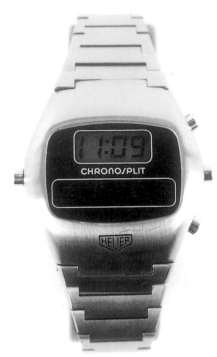

An Omega Speedmaster Mk III chronograph, automatic movement, 24-hour dial and calendar, diving case, limited edition, 1970s, with original box.
£550–600
$800–880 ⊞ JoV

A Spaceman stainless steel wristwatch, 1970s.
£250–300
$350–450 🪓 BB(L)

◄ **A Heuer Chronosplit wristwatch,** with quartz LED/LCD, steel case and bracelet, c1971.
£800–900
$1,150–1,300 ⊞ HARP

► **A Heuer Leonidas Easy-Rider chronograph,** Jacky Ickx edition, 1971.
£500–600
$720–870 ⊞ HARP
Jacky Ickx was a Formula 1 driver sponsored by Heuer.

A Heuer chronograph, with 30-minute marker and date, c1971.
£500–600
$720–870 ⊞ HARP

A Heuer Chronosplit Manhatten wristwatch, with quartz digital and analogue displays, c1973.
£700–800
$1,000–1,150 ⊞ HARP

◄ **A Heuer manual wind chronograph,** with 45-minute marker and date indicator, c1978.
£600–700
$870–1,000 ⊞ HARP

Auction or dealer?

All the pictures in our price guides originate from auction houses and dealers. When buying at auction, prices can be lower than those of a dealer, but a buyer's premium and VAT will be added to the hammer price. Equally, when selling at auction, commission, tax and photography charges must be taken into account. Dealers will often restore pieces before putting them back on the market.

Both dealers and auctioneers can provide professional advice, so it is worth researching both sources before buying or selling your antiques.

Jewellery

The evolution of jewellery design during the 20th century has been driven by a desire to reflect the increasingly informal relations of modern life. The desire to offer, receive and commemorate continue to be fundamental psychological motives for the importance of jewellery but there are now a much wider range of materials and forms through which these may be expressed.

The informalities of modern life, based on a more egalitarian outlook, have allowed designers and makers to experiment with less precious materials. The creation of costume jewellery offers a vast array of stylish and affordable pieces which have taken different forms throughout the century, beginning with the small-scale production of Arts and Crafts workshops using ceramic and enamels, and moving on to larger-scale studio lines manufacturing accessories for the fashion industry. These costume pieces, of course, do not have the intrinsic value of precious materials, but are still very collectable and have increased dramatically in price over the last five years.

The stylistic developments of the mass market are very different from the relatively conservative tastes that continue to demand quality materials and workmanship from the best jewellery workshops. These big names, such as Georg Jensen, are the ones that, through the quality of their work, the scale of their creations and the use of precious materials, command the highest prices.

There is an enormous quantity of costume jewellery available to the collector. Some of it, like the home-made jewellery from WWII, is more interesting than valuable. The main markets in jewellery will continue to be dominated by the traditional and the precious. The more ephemeral and socially interesting pieces will have to be found outside the mainstream market place and hunted down by enterprising collectors.

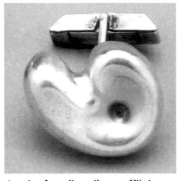

A pair of sterling silver cufflinks, American, c1950.
£350–420
$500–600 ✗ BB(L)

A pair of garnet earrings, by Tom Scott, the double-tiered openwork drops randomly set with rose-cut garnets, maker's mark, c1975.
£130–150
$200–220 ✗ Bon

A pair of sterling silver and gilt cufflinks, by Atelier Borgila, Swedish, Stockholm, 1976.
£200–220
$300–320 ✗ BUK

Rings

A garnet and diamond cluster ring, the step-cut garnet within an openwork and textured square pattern surround, randomly set with brilliant-cut diamonds, one diamond missing, c1965.
£250–300
$350–450 ✗ Bon

► **A silver ring,** by Björn Weckström for Lapponia, Swedish, 1970.
£450–550
$650–800 ✗ BUK

► **An 18ct gold and tourmaline pendant and ring,** by Andrew Grima for the H. J. Co, set with diamonds, 1966, pendant 3in (7.5cm) long.
£3,500–4,500
$5,000–6,500 ⊞ DID

A silver ring, by Kristian Nilsson, set with an amethyst, Swedish, Stockholm, 1982.
£550–600
$800–870 ✗ BUK

Brooches

A brown enamel and sterling silver abstract brooch, by Henning Koppel for Georg Jensen, Danish, c1847, 1¼in (3cm) wide.
£600–700
$870–1,000 ⊞ DID

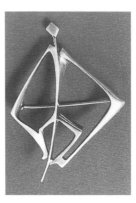

A 14ct gold brooch, by Bent Gabrielsen Pedersen for Hans Hansen, c1955. 2¾in (7cm) wide.
£450–500
$650–720 ⊞ DID

A sterling silver brooch, in the form of an abstract human figure, for J. Tostrup, c1920, 2¼in (5.5cm) high.
£350–400
$500–580 ⊞ DID

◄ **A brooch,** with green baguette-cut stones and green rhinestone drops, on a gilt setting, 1950s, 2¼in (5.5cm) long.
£60–70
$90–100 ⊞ PGH

► **A gold and diamond scrolled feather brooch,** London import marks for 1957, French control marks, in a Wartski fitted leather case.
£2,000–2,200
$3,000–3,200 ⚒ Bon

A japanned metal brooch, by Capri, in the shape of a flower, set with a white diamanté, with round green and marquise blue diamanté, signed, c1960, 2in (5cm) long.
£35–40
$50–60 ⊞ PKT

► **A silver brooch,** by Georg Jensen, with eight cut diamonds, marked, 1963.
£175–200
$250–300 ⚒ Bea(E)

A yellow metal brooch, by Miriam Haskell, the flower design with *faux* turquoise blue centres, c1955, 2in (5cm) diam.
£100–125
$145–175 ⊞ PKT

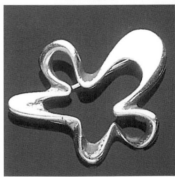

A brooch, by Eisenberg Ice, set with various shades of pink round and baguette-cut diamanté with small white stone leaves, signed, c1965, 2in (5cm) wide.
£240–280
$350–400 ⊞ PKT

A yellow metal brooch, by Kramer, with open centre, surrounded by four rows of yellow diamanté, c1960, 2in (5cm) diam.
£75–85
$110–125 ⊞ PKT

► **A steel, gold and coral brooch,** by Eva Dora Lamm for Anton Michelsen, c1980, 1½in (4cm) high.
£130–150
$200–220 ⊞ DID

Necklaces

A sterling silver bracelet and earrings set, by Henning Koppel for Georg Jensen, import marks, Danish, after 1945, bracelet 7½in (19cm) long.
£425–475
$620–700 ⚒ BUK

A sterling silver heart pendant, by Georg Jensen, No. 126, Danish, after 1945, 31¼in (79cm) long.
£200–250
$300–350 ⚒ BUK

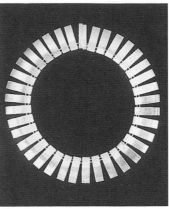

A silver-coloured metal necklace, by Arno Malinowski for Georg Jensen, No. 136, stamped marks, Danish, 1950s, 15½in (39.5cm) long.
£800–900
$1,150–1,300 ⚒ S

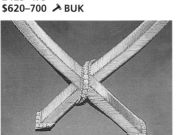

A gold and diamond necklace, designed as a woven crossed ribbon, with lines of brilliant-cut diamonds, c1950, 16½in (42cm) long.
£1,500–1,800
$2,200–2,600 ⚒ S(Am)

A silver-coloured metal choker, by Torun Vivianna Bülow-Hübe, hung with pendant drops with lapis lazuli beads, stamped mark, Danish, 1950s, 4in (10cm) diam.
£3,200–3,500
$4,600–5,000 ⚒ S

A diamanté and cabochon necklace, by Kenneth Lane, 1960s.
£200–220
$300–320 ⊞ FMa

A sterling silver necklace and earrings set, by Bent K, Danish, 1950–60, necklace 14¼in (36cm) long.
£180–230
$250–330 ⚒ BUK

A sterling silver pendant and chain, by Tony White, with suspended oval agate, hallmarked, Australian, c1960.
£160–180
$230–260 ⚒ LJ

Two silver pendants, by Elis Kauppi for Kupittaan Kulta Oy, one set with rose quartz, the other with clear quartz, each with maker's stamp, Finnish, 1960 and 1966.
£220–260
$320–380 ⚒ Bon

An enamel and silver pendant, by Norman Grant, Edinburgh, c1960.
£150–200
$220–300 ⊞ DID

A pewter necklace, by Jorgen Jensen, comprising 12 concave square plaques, each connected by a circular ring and fitted with a T-bar clasp, the reverse hallmarked, Danish, c1960, 16½in (42cm) long.
£120–140
$175–200 ✗ LJ

A yellow metal necklace, by Christian Dior for Henkel & Grosse, set with autumn-coloured diamanté, with small pearl drops, c1962, 14in (35.5cm) long.
£200–220
$300–320 ⊞ PKT

A silver pendant, by Nanna Ditzel for Georg Jensen, Danish, 1963, 2¼in (5.5cm) diam.
£300–350
$450–500 ⊞ ASA

A silver chain, by Wiwen Nilsson, Swedish, 1968, 42½in (108cm) long.
£1,275–1,525
$1,800–2,300 ✗ BUK

An aquamarine and diamond pendant, by John Donald, the aquamarine within an 18ct white gold textured radiating surround, set with brilliant-cut diamonds, maker's mark, 1969.
£700–800
$1,000–1,150 ✗ Bon

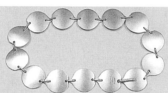

A silver necklace, by Hans Hansen, with 15 stylized tulip panel links, Danish, c1970, 15in (38cm) long.
£400–500
$580–720 ✗ P(L)

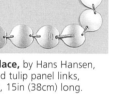

A silver and agate necklace, by MP, London 1960, Swedish import marks for 1969, pendant 8in (20.5cm) long.
£350–400
$500–580 ⊞ DID

▶ **A white metal collar and wide bangle,** by Hubert Taylor-Rose, each hinged and pierced with fretwork asymmetrical decoration, 1970s.
£250–300
$350–450 ✗ RTo

A sterling silver torque, by Bent Gabrielsen Pedersen for Hans Hansen, the pendant set with black enamel, Danish, c1970.
£200–250
$300–350 ⊞ DID

A silver and quartz collar necklace, by Torun for Georg Jensen, the quarter drop suspended from a tapering silver collar, signed, Danish, 1970.
£1,500–1,800
$2,200–2,600 ✗ Bon

A sterling silver pendant and earrings set, Half Moon and Crescent Moon, by Tapio Wirkkala, Finnish, 1972.
£500–600
$720–870 ✗ BUK

Bracelets

A diamond bracelet, by Mauboussin, designed as four tapered bands of flattened gas-pipe linking, the front decorated with brilliant-cut diamonds, 1950s.
£3,200–3,600
$4,650–5,250 ↗ S

A blue-enamelled bracelet, by Atelier Borgila, Swedish, Stockholm, 1950, 7in (18cm) long.
£200–220
$300–320 ↗ BUK

A 9ct gold bangle, by Elis Kauppi for Kupittaam Kulta, set with an amethyst, Finnish, Turku, c1953.
£550–650
$800–950 ⊞ DID

A silver bangle, by Georg Jensen, No. 117, Danish, c1960.
£200–250
$300–350 ↗ WilP

◄ **A diamond bracelet,** the tapering woven herringbone design with a central tie motif set with graduated brilliant-cut diamonds, c1960, 7in (18cm) long.
£800–900
$1,150–1,300 ↗ S(Am)

A sterling silver bangle, by Bent Gabrielsen Pedersen for Hans Hansen, Danish, 1960s, 3in (7.5cm) diam.
£300–350
$450–500 ⊞ DID

A silver bracelet, by Georg Jensen, No. 188, 1960s.
£300–330
$450–480 ⊞ DAC

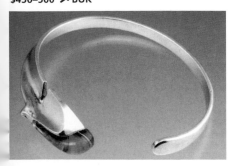

A steel bracelet, by Sigurd Persson, Swedish, Stockholm, 1966.
£300–350
$450–500 ↗ BUK

◄ **A silver and acrylic bracelet,** Salamander, by Björn Weckström for Lapponia, Swedish, 1974.
£200–250
$300–350 ↗ BUK

A sterling silver cuff bracelet, by Elsa Peretti for Tiffany & Co, signed, Italian, 1975.
£320–380
$450–550 ↗ SK

Textiles

Over the course of the last 50 years, the fashion industry has become one of the main engines of the consumer society. Inexpensive garments are now manufactured in record time, and distributed around the globe to be sold in markets on every continent. Contemporary clothing has become ephemeral.

At the beginning of the 20th century the industry served a wealthy élite and the expensive garments they produced were works of art that had several lives as they were continually reused and transformed in the process. The advent of ready-to-wear was a consequence of growing prosperity, advancing industrial techniques and the impact of WWI. The production of large quantities of military uniforms for the troops was beyond the capability of military tailors and consequently mass production of clothing was developed, in part at least, to serve the fighting machine.

The mass market in fashion took off during the 1920s and '30s and was driven by marketing in the popular press, and the celebrity endorsement of Hollywood. The characteristics of the mass market are always towards informality, and fashion is no exception. The trends have been towards convenience, expressed through rising hemlines and a general loosening up, reflecting the evolution of society towards more democratic and horizontal structures. A core theme of the 20th century, the emancipation of women, is evident in a range of dramatic and dynamic transformations of the look, and the momentum is maintained by the emergence of street style during the 1970s and '80s.

A wide variety of printed textiles is available to the collector, although not always in large pieces! Lucienne Day curtains were often transformed, through a desire to reuse materials, into something smaller. Printed furnishing fabrics, especially those of the 1950s, '60s and '70s, offer an interaction between art and home, and textiles and wall hangings were positioned as a possible alternative to paintings within the context of the modern interior.

A piano shawl, hand-embroidered with coloured silks, Chinese, 1920s, 48in (122cm) square.
£140–160
$200–230 ⊞ JPr

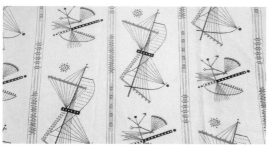

A pair of Nautilus curtains, by Mary Warren, printed with black on a yellow ground, slight fading, 1950s, 46 x 84in (117 x 213.5cm).
£35–40
$50–60 ⊞ DE

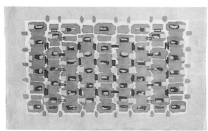

A wool carpet, by Paul Leleu, with woven tag, French, c1950, 68 x 100¾in (172.5 x 254.5cm).
£5,750–7,000
$8,000–10,000 ⚲ S(NY)

A machine-stitched Comfy quilt, with a paisley pattern, 1920–30, 88 x 69in (223.5 x 175.5cm).
£65–80
$95–115 ⊞ JJ

A Californie tapestry, by F. Robert, woven in colours with stylized exotic birds and foliage, on a yellow ground, signed, 1950s, 45¼ x 117¼in (115 x 298cm).
£500–550
$720–800 ⚲ DN

A pair of curtains, with an abstract design in red, blue, cream and green on a beige ground, 1950s, 53in (134.5cm) long.
£55–65
$80–95 ⊞ HSt

Fashion

A **natural-coloured straw hat,** decorated with a band of artificial poppies, daisies and buttercups, c1910.
£90–100
$130–145 ⊞ CCO

A **wire-framed black lace hat,** with silk flowers, 1910.
£85–95
$125–140 ⊞ CCO

A **cream hat,** decorated with an embroidered linen insert, 1920s.
£50–55
$75–80 ⊞ CCO

A **cream linen cloche hat,** decorated with appliquéd and embroidered stylized flowers in shades of pink, 1920s.
£50–55
$75–80 ⊞ CCO

A **pair of brown leather lace-up boots,** 1920s, 24in (61cm) high.
£220–225
$300–325 ⊞ SPT

▶ A **pair of brown kid leather and snakeskin shoes,** 1920s.
£55–65
$80–95 ⊞ DE

A **black devoré coat,** with cut sleeves, 1920.
£80–90
$115–140 ⊞ DE

▶ A **georgette rose print dress,** 1920s.
£45–55
$65–80 ⊞ DE

A **peach drop-waisted acetate dress,** 1920–30.
£65–80
$95–115 ⊞ DE

A pair of cream suede peep-toe shoes, by Lotus, 1930s.
£35–40
$50–60 ⊞ DE

A pair of red suede and leather shoes, by J. Miller, American, 1930s.
£20–25
$30–35 ⊞ DE

A black straw hat, decorated with a black velvet band and flowers, c1930.
£40–45
$60–65 ⊞ CCO

Three school caps, brown and blue, black and green and black with red crest, 1930s.
£25–30
$35–45 each ⊞ SPT

▶ **A straw boater,** 1930s.
£35–40
$50–60 ⊞ SPT

▶ **A two-piece acetate evening dress,** decorated with yellow and white flowers on a green ground, c1930.
£65–80
$95–115 ⊞ DE

A satin wedding dress, with beaded decoration around the neck and waist, late 1930s.
£120–140
$175–200 ⊞ TT

▶ **A georgette dress,** with woven detail in red, yellow and green on a dark blue ground, 1930s.
£40–50
$60–75 ⊞ DE

A light blue net lace dress, 1930s.
£65–75
$95–110 ⊞ DE

A black crêpe evening dress, decorated with gold and turquoise sequins, 1930s.
£65–75
$95–110 ⊞ DE

A black crêpe long-sleeved evening dress, decorated with sequins, 1930s.
£95–110
$140–160 ⊞ DE

An acetate tea dress, with red and yellow flowers on a cream ground, 1930s.
£45–55
$65–80 ⊞ DE

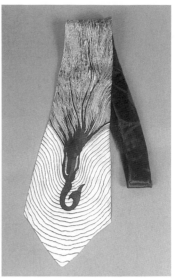

A black and white tie, decorated in the manner of Salvador Dali with a mermaid pattern, 1940s.
£65–70
$95–110 ⊞ SpM

A Shakespeare scarf, decorated in colours on a white ground within a red border, 1940s.
£70–80
$100–115 ⊞ REN

Headscarves

The printed silk square has its origins in the tradition of printed cotton handkerchiefs produced throughout the 19th century. The handkerchiefs were printed using copper engraving – a slow and expensive process. Scarves have usually been printed using the silk screen process.

During the 20th century the scarf became symbolic of women's emancipation and integration into the world of work. Scarves became popular after the impact of the Ballets Russes when they were associated with the public expression of a liberated sexuality. These associations were confirmed, in the popular imagination, by the circumstances of Isadora Duncan's death.

During WWII the scarf became a staple of fashion at every level in society. It was symbolic of women entering the workforce and achieving their first steps of economic independence. The scarf also became a token of exchange between sweethearts during the war. The popularity of the scarf has endured throughout the post-war period and is still very collectable today.

A pair of brown and tan snakeskin shoes, with utility mark, 1940s.
£25–30
$35–45 ⊞ DE
Wartime shortages in Britain led to the Utility scheme, which included clothing. Designers had to use less material, fewer fastenings and simpler techniques. Regulations stipulated no more than three buttons to a jacket, the heels of shoes could be no more than 2in (5cm) and peep-toe shoes were banned. Utility wear was marked with the trademark CC41, CC standing for Civilian Clothing, and 41 for the year Utility was introduced.

◄ A pair of black suede shoes, by Russell & Bromley, with ribbon trim, late 1940s.
£20–25
$30–35 ⊞ CCO

A gentleman's brown felt hat, 1940s.
£25–30
$35–45 ⊞ DE

◄ A black felt and net hat, 1940s.
£35–40
$50–60 ⊞ L&L

◀ **A cotton peek-a-boo midriff swimsuit,** decorated with blue and cream flowers on a red ground, 1940s.
£40–45
$60–65 ⊞ SpM

A gentleman's fawn wool two-piece suit.
£60–65
$90–95 ⊞ DE

A blue sarong-style dress, of the type worn by Dorothy Lamour, with gold glitter decoration, 1940s.
£65–75
$95–110 ⊞ SpM

A satin evening dress, with a black bodice, the skirt decorated with pink, white and blue flowers on a black ground, 1940s.
£45–65
$65–95 ⊞ DE

A brown wool crêpe suit, by Fitzwear, with utility mark on skirt, 1940s.
£45–50
$65–75 ⊞ TT

Two Hawaiian resort outfits, comprising yellow, green and purple gown with peplum and matching jacket, labelled Kamahemeha for Watmulis, and a kaftan printed with lilies on a red ground, labelled Surf'n' Sand, Honolulu, 1940s and 1950s.
£235–280
$335–400 ⚒ S(O)

A peach nylon hat with net trim, by New Look, 1940–50.
£35–40
$50–60 ⊞ DE

A pair of cotton swimming trunks, with a geometrical design in blue, brown, black and yellow, 1950s.
£8–10
$12–15 ⊞ DE

A pair of stockings, by Bluebird, in original coloured box, 1950s.
£12–15
$15–20 ⊞ YR

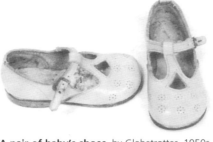

A pair of baby's shoes, by Globetrotter, 1950s.
£12–15
$15–30 ⊞ Ech

A yellow hat, by Marie Modern for John Lewis, with black piping, 1950.
£25–30
$35–45 ⊞ DE

A scarf, decorated in blue, green, beige and pink on a white ground, 1950s, 30in (76cm) square.
£5–6
$8–12 ⊞ HSt

▶ **A cotton swimsuit,** with elasticized back, decorated in colours on a black ground, 1950s.
£10–12
$15–18 ⊞ DE

A cream and green felt and straw hat, by Mitzi Lorenz of London, 1950.
£25–30
$35–45 ⊞ DE

▶ **A cotton bikini,** by Orchider, with lace-up sides.
£30–35
$45–50 ⊞ SpM

A red and white polka-dot cotton one-piece swimsuit, by Kittiwake, with bone bodice. c1950.
£18–20
$20–30 ⊞ DE

▶ **A black and white taffeta evening dress,** with pink and white butterfly decoration, c1950.
£35–40
$50–60 ⊞ DE

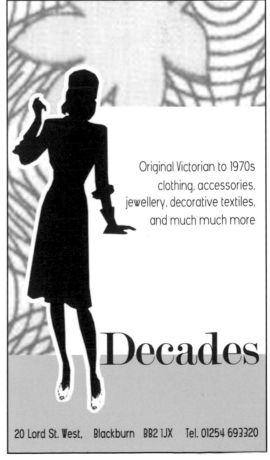

A gold-sequinned nylon ball gown, made for Harrods, Swiss, c1950.
£85–100
$125–145 ⊞ DE

A black pleated tulle cocktail gown, by Jean Dessès, the boned bodice with velvet straps and bow, late 1950s.
£700–850
$1,000–1,250 🔨 S(O)

A green satin evening dress, 1950s.
£30–35
$45–50 ⊞ DE

A grey floral silk two-piece suit, by Robark, London, late 1950s.
£35–45
$50–65 ⊞ DE

A lilac linen two-piece with appliqué flowers, by Alison, American, 1950s–60s.
£40–50
$60–75 ⊞ DE

◄ **A pair of kitten-heeled brown and tan snakeskin shoes,** by Stilo Venice Girl, c1960.
£25–30
$35–45 ⊞ DE

► **Two dresses,** by Rudi Gernreich, one woven in lilac and beige with nuclear symbol to the front and a small triangular ground, the reverse with large triangle repeats, the other woven with purple Maltese crosses on an olive green ground, with matching scarf, American, late 1960s.
£470–550
$680–800 🔨 S(O)

A Mary Quant-style black bathing suit, with cutaway sides and daisy motif, 1960s.
£20–25
$30–35 ⊞ HarC

A brown, green and orange plaid suit, by Chanel, with green collar and cuff edges, c1960.
£1,100–1,200
$1,600–1,750 S(LA)

A blue and white floral cotton mini jacket dress, 1960s.
£15–20
$20–30 DE

A gold-sequinned and beaded woollen dress, by Dianna Warren, early 1960s.
£60–70
$90–100 DE

A silk long-sleeved dress, by Emilio Pucci, with abstract design in shades of blue and turquoise, the tie belt with beaded ends, Italian, 1960s, with letter of authenticity from Eleanor 'Babe' Goddard.
£3,300–4,000
$4,700–5,800 CO
This dress was owned and worn by Marilyn Monroe hence the value.

A black and white three-piece suit, by Chanel, 1960s.
£1,500–1,700
$2,200–2,600 SBT

A printed cotton mini beach dress, c1960.
£15–20
$20–30 DE

► **A pair of brown land cream patent leather shoes,** by Gina, Italian, 1970s.
£14–16
$18–20 HSt

A pair of blue land white platform shoes, by High Brow, 1970s.
£25–30
$35–45 DE

A Pucci-style one-piece swimsuit, by Bernard Altmann, Austrian, 1970s.
£22–27
$32–40 ⊞ SpM

A green-checked woollen two-piece suit, by Pierre Cardin, with flared trousers, 1970.
£60–65
$90–95 ⊞ DE

A cotton dress, by Bernard Frères, 1970s.
£30–35
$45–50 ⊞ DE

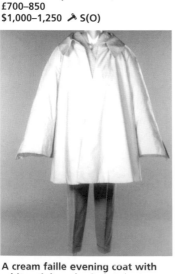

A printed chiffon backless gown, by Ossie Clark and Celia Birtwell, with padded shoulders, together with a cream moss crêpe long-sleeved gown with broad key-hole back, c1970.
£700–850
$1,000–1,250 ⚒ S(O)

A pair of black satin above-the-knee platform boots, by Biba, early 1970s.
£200–240
$300–350 ⚒ S(0)

A black velvet hat, by Vivienne Westwood, printed in gold foil 'Bride of Fortune', c1986.
£100–125
$145–180 ⊞ ID

A red tweed Armour jacket, by Vivienne Westwood from the Time Machine collection, with denim gauntlet-style sleeves and orb motif on shoulder, c1988.
£250–300
$360–440 ⊞ ID

◀ **A chartreuse green taffeta Femme evening ensemble,** by Jean-Paul Gaultier, comprising underwired taffeta bra, long full skirt, jacket with mandarin collar and matching evening bag, c1990.
£2,350–2,800
$3,400–4,000 ⚒ S(O)

A cream faille evening coat with white mink under-jacket, by Jean Lanvin, with matching camel trousers and belt, 1990.
£580–650
$850–950 ⚒ S(O)

A brown wool and black braid trimmed Femme ensemble, by Jean-Paul Gaultier, the fitted jacket with black bobble and petersham braid, the trousers with braid and ribbon decoration, mid-1990s.
£300–350
$440–500 ⚒ S(O)

A vinyl raincoat, by Koji Tatsuno, decorated with autumn leaves on a gold ground, 1998.
£500–550
$720–800 ⚒ S(O)

A blue goffered satin coat and pair of trousers, by Koji Tatsuno, the coat with basket weave effect and the trousers with overall scale effect, 1998.
£300–350
$440–550 ⚒ S(O

Pop Fashion

An Apple label olive green lady's jacket, 1960s.
£150–175
$230–255 ⊞ BTC
The Apple Boutique in London was opened by the Beatles in the 1960s.

A Jimi Hendrix shirt, in mustard polyester mix, with ruched front and cuffs, 1967, with statement of provenance.
£820–900
$1,200–1,300 ⚒ S(O

An Afghan coat, decorated with brown and gold embroidery, 1960s–70s.
£50–60
$75–90 ⊞ HarC
The Afghan coat became a favourite hippy garment in the 1960s and 1970s. Buyer beware, however, the sheep or goat skin was often imperfectly cured, and even after 20 to 30 years coats can still be smelly, especially in the rain.

A Seditionaries printed red silk and black muslin bondage shirt and pair of Sex black bondage trousers, the trousers with towelling bum flap and Anarchy label, 1976–677.
£1,400–1,600
$2,000–2,300 ⚒ S(O)

Street fashion

The development of youth culture during the 1960s and the interest in alternative life styles fuelled a pick-and-mix approach to dressing up. The end of the 1960s also witnessed the beginnings of various stylistic revivals that have come to characterize the fashion system at the end of the 20th century. The advent of Punk in the mid-1970s helped to establish a new logic of antagonism in street fashion. This logic has helped to identify street fashion as the avant-garde element of the fashion system. London's status as the capital of experimentation in fashion is now assured.

▶ **A pair of Bluebird 15 denier nylons,** including a card with a picture of Robert Wagner inscribed 'The stockings sponsored by the stars', 1950s.
£9–10
$12–15 ⊞ RAD

A pair of Beatles nylon stockings, by Vroom & Dressmann, in original packaging, German, 1960s.
£20–25
$30–35 ⊞ BTC

A Savage collection sweater, by Vivienne Westwood, with Savage pattern on back and blue front with tubes attached to breasts, 1981–82.
£250–300
$360–440 ⊞ ID

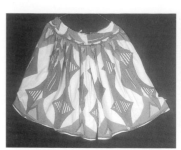

A pair of Savage collection shorts, by Vivienne Westwood, printed with red, green and yellow on a white ground, 1981–82.
£100–150
$145–220 ⊞ ID

A pair of Mary Quant ribbed tights, Wild Lilac colour, 1960s, in original packaging.
£5–8
$7–10 ⊞ HarC

▶ A Hobo collection green chequered cotton suit, by Vivienne Westwood, the jacket with batwing sleeves, the skirt with men's ties threaded through, c1983.
£900–1,000
$1,300–1,500 ⊞ ID

A Buffalo collection brown cotton skirt, by Vivienne Westwood, with a green medieval print border with embroidered detail, 1982–83.
£220–250
$320–360 ⊞ ID

Romilly McAlpine Collection

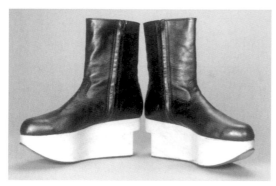

A pair of black leather rocking horse boots, by Vivienne Westwood, with yellow soles, 1990s.
£240–280
$350–400 ⚲ S(O)

▶ A Grand Hotel collection satin rainbow-striped Circle skirt and waistcoat, by Dior, 1993.
£470–530
$680–750
⚲ S(O)

A Dressing Up collection apple green Harris tweed jacket and skirt, the jacket with faceted stones bursting through pinked slashes, the skirt with side split, with pink Syrian stripe codpiece blouse, show sample, 1991.
£470–530
$680–750 ⚲ S(O)

An Ancient Bruce of Kinnaird tartan Super DB coat, waistcoat and trousers, by Vivienne Westwood, with striped cotton Hals shirt from Always on Camera collection and a matching mohair shawl, show samples, 1992–93.
£2,000–2,400
$3,000–3,500 ⚲ S(O)

A Grand Hotel collection brown Duchesse satin Grand Circle skirt, by Dior, together with a black satin bustier, 1993.
£1,300–1,500
$1,900–2,150 ↗ S(O)

Vivienne Westwood

The Punk movement in Britain has been mythologized by its main protagonists into something which was both anarchic and avant-garde. Vivienne Westwood established herself as the creative driving force behind the development of a quirky, idiosyncratic and particularly English vision. Post-punk Westwood has moved into more elevated circles of cultural production. Among her most important patrons has been Romilly McAlpine whose collection was recently sold. Westwood's achievement has been to position street fashion as a serious cultural resource.

▶ A pair of red gingham platform shoes, c1993.
£500–550
$720–800 ↗ S(O)

A pair of green moc croc Super Elevated platform shoes, by Anglomania, 1993.
£1,000–1,200
$1,500–1,750 ↗ S(O)

◀ A pair of printed and woven calico platform shoes, 1993.
£240–280
$350–400 ↗ S(O)

An On Liberty collection grey and red tartan Super DB jacket, waistcoat and Super MD trousers, the three different weave effects playing with the orb motif of the tartan, the fitted jacket with accentuated lapels, the trousers with large turn-ups, 1994.
£3,500–4,200
$5,000–6,000 ↗ S(O)

A tartan silk Domino cape, with large hood and train, show sample, 1994.
£1,100–1,300
$1,600–1,900 ↗ S(O)

An On Liberty collection Highland ensemble, consisting of Astrakhan Dunbar jacket and McPoiret Tartan Experience skirt with draped swags, together with a knitted silk jabot sweater from Les Femmes collection, 1996, and an Astrakhan handbag.
£3,300–3,900
$4,800–5,800 ↗ S(O)

A Storm in a Teacup collection patchwork tartan trouser suit, the Krall jacket, fitted waistcoat, trousers and belt of multi-coloured tartan woven by Ian Sutherland, together with a soft blue tartan blouse and Boucher print silk tie, 1996.
£700–850
$1,000–1,250 ↗ S(O)

Posters

The poster as we understand it – a large coloured print for advertising, information or decoration and characterized, stylistically, by an integration of text and image – was itself a product of the late 19th century Industrial Revolution and of the metropolitan expansion that was a characteristic of its urban development.

The poster evolved into its modern form in Paris during the last quarter of the 19th century. Its production was made possible by the development of colour lithography without the attendant difficulties of letterpress and engraving. The display of these posters became integrated into the architectural and urban development of the rapidly expanding metropolis, to accommodate its increasing population, and through the extensions of its transport systems that became a natural space for their organized display. By the end of the century the poster had become established as the primary form of advertising for commercial products, and artists such as Jules Cheret, Alphonse Mucha and Toulouse-Lautrec had assured the poster of its status as art for advertising. The poster was widely collected during the 1890s and it is the case that, ironically, it is sometimes easier to source a late 19th century poster than one of a more recent origin.

The 20th century development of poster art has continued throughout the century and offers the collector a bewildering choice of poster images by content, so that propaganda, travel, advertising, film or even Modernist posters exist as separate fields. The organization of poster images in this section continues this. No such distinction is made on the grounds of technology and the market includes images that are created by hand-drawn lithography, photolithography, screen printing and by stencil.

In Britain the status of the poster as a collectable work of art has only recently been revised upward. In part this reflects the growing realization that these ephemeral and fragile pieces of paper have status as both aesthetic images and documents of social history. The late 20th century has also seen a much wider acceptance of the economic, political and social values of cultural production, reflected in the growing importance of the creative economy in business and education. As more people are drawn into the creative economy an interest in the history of its evolution becomes more widespread. The tendency for recent posters to be photographic or electronic in origin has also drawn attention to the hand-made and craft qualities of the poster as work of art in the first half of the 20th century.

More recently there has been a revival in the Modernist tradition, which stretches throughout the 20th century, of artists seeking new audiences by making work in forms that reach beyond the gallery. This chimes with the contemporary political rhetoric of access and the poster has been an important part of this recent activity.

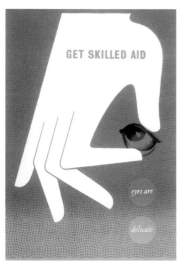

Silk screen

During the 1950s silk screen printing became a possibility in Britain. In America it had been widely used throughout the 1930s and was associated with the New Deal images of the WPA. Silk screen printing has its origins in stencil, or *pochoir*, printing.

Its relatively low tech process made it suitable for groups without access to large publicity budgets and where small print runs were required. The entertainment posters associated with the developing youth culture of the 1960s are almost all printed using silk screen.

The development of new printing inks and photo-optical processes have assured silk screen a bright future.

A Royal Society for the Prevention of Accidents poster, by Manfred Reiss, 'Get Skilled Aid', printed in red, blue and white, 1948, 29¾ x 19¼in (75.5 x 49cm).
£275–325
$400–475 ⊞ REN

► **An Art Directors Club of New York poster,** by McKnight Kauffer, advertising the 28th Annual National Exhibition of Advertising and Editorial Art, printed in red and black, 1949, 44½ x 29½in (113 x 75cm).
£5,250–6,250
$7,500–9,000 ⚡ SWAN

► **A poster,** advertising a Gene Pitney concert at the Gaumont, Wolverhampton, printed in black, white, yellow and red lettering on same colour background, damaged, 17 November 1965, 29½ x 39¼in (75 x 101cm).
£120–150
$175–225 ⚡ Bon(C)

A poster, advertising a Yardbirds concert in Bishop's Stortford, printed in red and black lettering on a white background, damaged, 9 April 1966, 29¼ x 19¾in (74.5 x 50cm).
£350–420
$500–600 ⚒ Bon(C)

◀ **A poster,** advertising a Hendrix and the Move concert at the Royal Albert Hall, sellotape on borders, 14 November 1967, 20 x 15in (51 x 38cm).
£850–1,000
$1,250–1,500 ⚒ Bon(C)

▶ **A poster,** advertising *100 Rifles/100 Pusek*, Czechoslovakian, 1969, 33 x 23in (84 x 58.5cm).
£100–125
$145–180 ⊞ REEL

A poster, by Robert Indiana, '3', printed in red, white and blue, 1968, 19 x 38in (48.5 x 96.5cm).
£170–200
$250–300 ⊞ CJP

Propaganda

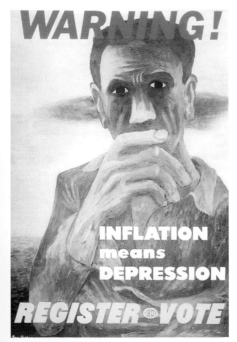

A poster, by Ben Shahn, 'Warning! Inflation Means Depression', American, 1946, 41 x 27½in (104 x 70cm).
£2,000–2,500
$3,000–3,500 ⚒ SWAN

Cross Reference
See Colour Review (page 248–256)

▶ **An ATS recruitment poster,** by Abram Games, 1941, 30 x 20in (76 x 51cm).
£4,000–5,000
$5,800–7,250 ⊞ REN
Games designed three posters for this campaign. This, the first, was banned by Winston Churchill, and very few survive.

Propaganda

The enfranchisement and emancipation that are the engines of progressive social change and Modernism have transformed the nature of communications between the State and its citizenry. These communications are identified by the generic propaganda. This class of communication is held to be crude, heavy-handed and fundamentally dishonest – especially in times of war. Furthermore, the aesthetics of propaganda, with their appeal to sentimentality, are considered banal, literal and reactionary. While a good deal of propaganda conforms to this view there are many examples to the contrary. A distaste for the overtly political has resulted in these images being undervalued. The counter cultural propaganda and lifestyle politics of the 1960s and '70s produced by activist groups are also important social documents.

Travel

A Cunard Line *Lusitania* poster, 1910, 12 x 10in (30.5 x 25.5cm).
£1,000–1,200
$1,500–1,750 ✗ HAld

A Cunard Line travel poster, by E. Sanderson & Co, 'Europe – America', chromolithograph, early 20thC, 39 x 24½in (99 x 62cm).
£400–450
$580–650 ✗ ELR

A Ste Croix Les Rasses poster, with monogram RH, Swiss, 1922, 40¼ x 25in (102 x 63.5cm).
£1,600–1,800
$2,300–2,600 ✗ VSP

A poster, after Edward McKnight Kauffer, advertising St Albans Route 84 from Golders Green, colour lithograph, dated 1929, 39¼ x 25in (99.5 x 63.5cm).
£400–500
$580–720 ✗ S(S)

An LMS poster, Best Way Series No. 58, printed by McCorquodale & Co, c1925, 40¼ x 50in (102 x 127cm).
£1,000–1,200
$1,500–1,750 ✗ ONS

A poster, by Tom Purvis, 'Continent via Harwich' printed in yellow, green and black on linen, c1925, 40 x 24in (101.5 x 61cm).
£550–650
$800–950 ⊞ Do

▶ A Southern Railway poster, by Leslie Carr, 'Canterbury', printed by McCorquodale & Co, 1929, 25¼ x 50in (64 x 127cm).
£800–950
$1,150–1,400 ✗ ONS

A Red Star Line poster, by Henri Cassiers, 'Dover – New York', Belgian, 1909, 45 x 61in (114.5 x 155cm).
£2,500–2,750
$3,600–4,000 ✗ VSP

An LMS poster, by Christopher Clark, printed by Horrocks on linen, c1924, 40¼ x 50in (102 x 127cm).
£650–750
$950–1,150 ✗ ONS

An LMS poster, by Maurice Greffenhagen, 'Piccadilly Circus by Night', 1926, 40¼ x 46in (102 x 117cm).
£5,000–6,000
$7,250–8,750 ✗ ONS

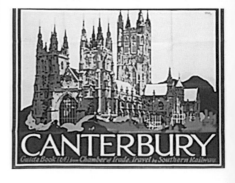

◄ An LMS poster, by Norman Wilkinson, 'Garston, The LMS Merseyside Port', c1930, 50 x 40in (101.5 x 127cm).
£1,700–1,900
$2,500–2,750 ⊞ BSL

An LMS poster, by Norman Wilkinson, c1930, 40 x 50in (101.5 x 127cm).
£6,500–8,000
$9,500–11,500 ⊞ REN

◄ A poster, after Jean Dupas, Richmond Station for the River, lithograph, 1930s, 39¾ x 25in (101 x 63.5cm).
£1,500–1,650
$2,200–2,400 ⚒ S(S)

Richmond Station for the River

An Australian National Travel Association poster, by Percy Trompf, No. 1, The Landing of Captain Cook at Botany Bay 1770, c1930, 40 x 50in (101.5 x 127cm).
£800–950
$1,150–1,400 ⚒ P(Sy)

A Hamburg-Amerika Linie poster, c1935, 38½ x 26¾in (98 x 68cm).
£120–150
$175–225 ⚒ VSP

An Aberdeen Line poster, by E. J. Kealey, 'To England & South Africa', colour lithograph, c1930, 40 x 24¾in (101.5 x 63cm).
£350–420
$500–600 ⚒ P(Sy)

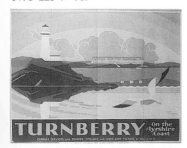

A poster, by W. T. N., McCorquodale Studio, 'Turnberry, on the Ayrshire Coast', in green, yellow and orange, lithograph, printed by Wellington Printers, London, 1930s, 40 x 50in (101.5 x 127cm).
£1,000–1,200
$1,500–1,750 ⚒ S

A London Transport poster, by Clive Gardner, 'At London's Service', printed by Vincent Brooks-Day, 1934, 40¼ x 25¼in (102 x 64cm).
£200–240
$300–350 ⚒ ONS

Lithography

The process of lithography and the development of colour lithography during the 19th century made the modern poster a practical, if not entirely economic, possibility. The origins of the poster are part social, part technical and part artistic. The lithographic process is based on the antipathy of grease and water and allows a print to be taken from a flat surface of limestone which has been marked with grease. Ink will adhere to the grease and a print may be taken.

The possibility of printing lettering without the constraints of letterpress made the closer integration of text and image a practical possibility. The craft of lithography, particularly the many colour separations required in artistic printing, resulted in a drive towards simplification in poster design. This has its origins in the flat colours and perspective effects of Japanese wood-block prints which were available in Europe after the 1850s. The posterization of commercial art reached its climax in the images of Tom Purvis, who designed for LNER, during the 1920s and '30s.

An LMS poster, by Bryan de Grineau, 'The Irish Mails', printed in orange, blue and black on a beige ground, c1930, 40¼ x 50in (102 x 127cm).
£1,800–2,000
$2,600–3,000 ⚒ ONS

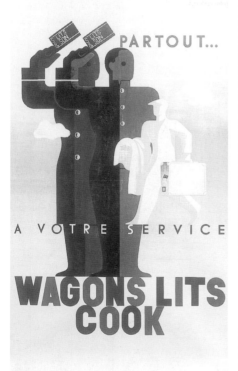

A poster, by Adolphe Mouron Cassandre, 'Wagons Lits Cook', coloured lithograph, French, 1933, 39 x 24½in (99 x 62cm).
£4,000–4,500
$5,800–6,500 ⊞ BSL

An LNER poster, by Doris Zinkeisen, printed in green and brown, 1937, 40¼ x 50in (102 x 127cm).
£2,700–3,000
$4,000–4,400 ⚒ ONS

An LMS poster, by Austin Cooper, 'Lowestoft', in green, red and blue, printed by McCorquodale & Co, London, minor damage, 1930s, 40 x 49in (101.5 x 124.5cm).
£600–700
$870–1,000 ⚒ S

A poster, by Jarvis, 'Cunard White Star Cruises', coloured lithograph, c1934, 40 x 25in (101.5 x 63.5cm).
£800–950
$1,150–1,400 ⊞ BSL

An LNER poster, by Fred Taylor, 'Richmond on the London & North Eastern Railway', printed by Adams Bros, c1930, 40 x 25in (101.5 x 63cm).
£380–420
$575–625 ⚒ ONS

A London Transport Poster, by Austin Cooper, 'London's Leisure Hours', printed in yellow, red, blue and brown, 1933, 40 x 25in (101.5 x 63.5cm).
£120–150
$175–225 ⚒ ONS

An Orient Line Cruises poster, by Kalvert Booth, 'Norway', printed in orange, yellow, green and black, c1935, 40 x 24in (101.5 x 61cm).
£475–525
$700–725 ⊞ Do

A British Railways poster, 'St. Ives, Cornwall', printed in blue, yellow, red and green, on linen, 1930s, 40 x 25in (101.5 x 63.5cm).
£375–425
$560–620 ⚒ ONS

A British Railways poster, by Christopher Clark, 'Trooping the Colour', coloured lithograph, c1950, 40 x 50in (101.5 x 127cm).
£1,300–1,500
$2,000–2,200 ⊞ BSL

A British Railways coloured lithographic poster, by Leonard Russell Squirrell, 'Yorkshire', printed by Jordison & Co, London, coloured lithograph, some damage, 1954, 40 x 25in (102 x 64cm).
£240–280
$350–400 ⚒ S

A British Railways poster, by Gyrth Russell, 'Cornwall', printed by Jordison & Co, coloured lithograph, c1950, 40 x 50in (101.5 x 127cm).
£650–700
$950–1,000 ⚒ ONS

A travel poster, 'Middelkerke', printed in blue, green, yellow and brown, Belgian, early 1950s, 39 x 24in (99 x 61cm).
£120–140
$175–200 ⚒ RAR

A British Railways poster, by Terence Cuneo, 'Progress, Every Week British Railways' Modernisation Plan Goes Further Ahead', printed by Waterlow, c1960, 40¼ x 50in (102 x 127cm).
£450–500
$650–720 ⚒ ONS

Advertising

A Hermann Scherrer poster, by Ludwig Hohlwein, in red, brown and white, printed by G. Schuh & Co, German, some creasing, 1907, 47 x 31½in (119.5 x 80cm).
£6,250–7,250
$9,200–10,500 ⚒ SWAN

A Fine Monis poster, by Clerice Frères, printed in yellow, red and black, on linen, French, 1911, 17 x 13in (43 x 33cm).
£130–160
$200–230 ⊞ Do

A Marco Polo Tee poster, by Ludwig Hohlwein, in black, blue and green, printed by G. Schuh & Co, German, minor damage, 1910, 42¾ x 29in (108.5 x 73.5cm).
£3,600–4,400
$5,300–6,300 ⚒ SWAN

A poster of Mistinguett, by Daniel de Losques (David Thoroude), linen-backed, French, 1911, 63¼ x 40¼in (160.5 x 102cm).
£700–950
$1,000–1,400 ♪ BB(L)

A Cognac Monnet poster, by Leonetto Cappiello, linen-backed, French, 1927, 79 x 51in (200.5 x 129.5cm).
£3,800–4,200
$5,500–6,000 ♪ BB(L)

A Veuve Amiot poster, by Leonetto Cappiello, French, 1922, 64 x 47½in (162.5 x 120.5cm).
£1,200–1,300
$1,750–2,000 ♪ BB(L)

A poster, by Otto Ernst, 'Kulm Hotel', coloured lithograph, French, 1925, 39 x 27in (99 x 68.5cm).
£2,000–2,200
$3,000–3,200 ⊞ BSL

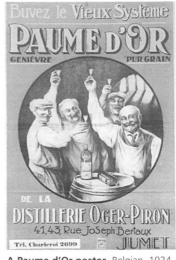

A Paume d'Or poster, Belgian, 1924, 38¼ x 24¾in (97 x 63cm).
£120–140
$175–200 ♪ VSP

A Siemens poster, 'Siemens Gasfilled Lamps, The Light of Purity', printed in red, yellow and black, on linen, c1925, 18 x 12in (45.5 x 30.5cm).
£145–165
$200–240 ⊞ Do

An Eno's Fruit Salt poster, by Claud Lovat Fraser, printed by Curwen Press, London, minor damage, coloured lithograph, 1920s, 30 x 20in (76 x 51cm).
£240–280
$350–400 ♪ S

▶ A Chapeaux Mossant poster, by Olsky, coloured lithograph, c1928, 62 x 47in (157.5 x 119.5cm).
£2,200–2,500
$3,200–3,600 ⊞ BSL

An Archidur poster, printed in red, green and black, on linen, Belgian, c1935, 12 x 33in (30.5 x 84cm).
£150–175
$220–255 ⊞ Do

Typo-photo

The term typo-photo was first coined by Laszlo Moholy-Nagy in Berlin c1926, to describe the integration of text and image in mechanical processes of graphic reproduction. The mechanization of printing processes at the beginning of the 20th century made communications possible with a new mass audience. This was reflected in the spread, throughout the 1930s, of photographically illustrated fashion and news magazines.

Nowadays, typo-photo is associated with the typographic experimentation of the Bauhaus School in Germany and in the spread of Modernism from Europe to America. Moholy-Nagy escaped from Germany, c1935, travelled to Britain and continued to the USA where he was a member of the new Bauhaus in Chicago. After WWII colour printing became more widespread and typo-photo's austerity was replaced by a concern for narrative and art direction.

A Favor poster, by Bellenger, printed in red, blue, orange and black, French, 1937, 15 x 23in (38c x 58.5cm).
£170–200
$250–300 ⊞ Do

A Socovel poster, printed in red, yellow, green and black, Belgian, 1930s, 24 x 33in (61 x 86.5cm).
£275–325
$400–470 ⊞ Do

A poster, by Abram Games, advertising *The Financial Times*, 1951, 30 x 20in (76 x 51cm).
£2,500–3,000
$3,500–4,500 ⊞ REN

A Guinness poster, by R. Pepé, coloured lithograph, minor damage, c1962, 61 x 41in (155 x 104cm).
£240–280
$350–400 ⚒ CSK

Film

An RKO poster, *The Sin Ship*, printed in red, green and brown, American, 1930, 41 x 27in (104 x 68.5cm).
£350–400
$500–580 S

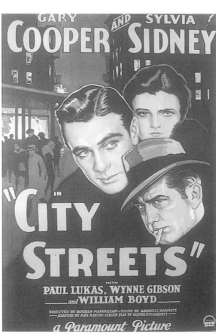

A Paramount poster, *City Streets*, printed in green, pink and black, American, 1931, 41 x 27in (104 x 68.5cm).
£3,500–4,000
$5,000–5,800 S

An RKO poster, by Roland Coudon, *King Kong*, printed in red and brown, American, 1933, 63 x 47in (160 x 119.5cm).
£8,000–8,500
$11,500–12,500 S

A Paramount poster, *Angel*, printed in pink, blue and black, Danish, 1937, 35 x 27in (89 x 68.5cm).
£1,500–1,700
$2,200–2,500 S

An MGM poster, *Dr Jekyll and Mr Hyde*, printed in red, yellow, blue and black, Swedish, 1941, 40 x 54in (101.5 x 137cm).
£400–450
$580–650 S

A British Gaumont poster, *The Lady Vanishes*, printed in pink, green and black, 1938, 40 x 27in (101.5 x 68.5cm).
£4,300–4,800
$6,250–7,000 S

A Tobis poster, *Titanic*, printed in red, blue and black, Swedish, 1943, 39 x 28in (99 x 71cm).
£550–600
$800–870 S

▶ An Ealing Films poster, by John Piper, *Pink String Sealing Wax*, c1946, 30 x 40in (76 x 101.5cm).
£2,000–2,500
$3,000–3,500 REN

A **Universal poster,** by William Reynold Brown, *Creature from the Black Lagoon*, 1954, 22 x 28in (56 x 71cm).
£3,000–3,500
$4,500–5,000 ✗ S(NY)

A **Paramount poster,** by Saul Bass, *Vertigo*, 1958, 22 x 28in (56 x 71cm).
£1,200–1,350
$1,750–2,000 ✗ S(NY)

A **United Artists poster,** *The Magnificent Seven*, printed in red, yellow and brown, on linen, 30 x 40in (76 x 101.5cm).
£450–500
$650–720 ✗ S

A **Paramount poster,** *Breakfast at Tiffany's*, printed in red and black, American, 1961, 81 x 41in (206 x 104cm).
£1,200–1,400
$1,750–2,000 ✗ S

A **Paramount insert,** *Funny Face*, American, 1950s, 36 x 14in (91.5 x 35.5cm), framed and glazed.
£100–120
$145–175 ✗ Bon

▶ A **Universal poster,** *Frankenstein*, printed in red and green, linen-backed, Belgian, 1950s, 22 x 14in (56 x 35.5cm).
£500–600
$720–870 ✗ S

A **poster,** by Saul Bass, *Exodus*, printed in yellow, orange and blue, 1960, 30 x 40in (76 x 101.5cm).
£200–250
$300–350 ⊞ REEL

A **United Artists special première poster,** by Renato Fratini, *From Russia With Love*, printed in pink, blue and black, 1963, 30 x 40in (76 x 101.5cm).
£850–950
$1,250–1,400 ✗ S
This very rare poster was used at a regional première screening.

A **20th Century Fox poster,** *Love Me Tender*, printed in blue and red on a yellow ground, American, 1956, 30 x 20in (76 x 51cm).
£200–240
$300–350 ✗ Bon(C)

A **United Artists poster,** *Goldfinger*, printed in black, yellow and orange, American, 1964, 41 x 27in (104 x 68.5cm).
£450–500
$650–720 ⊞ REEL

A poster, by Jan Lenica, *Repulsion*, printed in blue, green and black, 1965, 30 x 40in (76 x 101.5cm).
£350–400
$500–580 ⊞ REEL

A Hammer poster, *Slave Girls*, printed in pink and black, 1966, 30 x 40in (76 x 101.5cm).
£80–90
$115–130 ⚒ Bon(C)

A poster, *One Million Years BC*, printed in pink brown and grey, 1966, 30 x 40in (76 x 101.5cm).
£130–150
$200–220 ⚒ Bon(C)

A United Artists poster, *You Only Live Twice*, 1967, 30 x 40in (76 x 101.5cm).
£225–250
$325–350 ⚒ RBB

An MGM coloured poster, *Blow Up*, 1967, 30 x 40in (76 x 101.5cm).
£350–400
$500–580 ⊞ REEL

A Walt Disney poster, *The Jungle Book*, printed in green, brown and blue, American, 1967, 41 x 27in (104 x 68.5cm).
£250–300
$350–450 ⚒ S

A United Artists poster, *The Graduate*, printed in red, black and green, 1968, 30 x 40in (76 x 101.5cm).
£370–420
$550–600 ⚒ S

A United Artists poster, *Midnight Cowboy*, printed in brown, yellow, black and white, 1969, 40 x 30in (101.5 x 76cm).
£100–120
$145–175 ⊞ SEY

A Paramount coloured poster, *Barbarella*, American, 1968, 41 x 27in (104 x 68.5cm).
£250–300
$350–450 ⊞ REEL

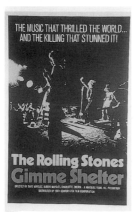

◀ **A 20th Century Fox poster,** *The Rolling Stones Gimme Shelter*, printed in black, yellow and red, American, 1971, 41 x 27in (104 x 68.5cm).
£300–350
$450–500 ⊞ REEL

A United Artists poster, *Diamonds Are Forever*, printed in red, blue, yellow and black, 1971, 40in (101.5cm) square.
£170–200
$250–300 ⊞ REEL

A Hammer poster, *Scars of Dracula,* c1971, 40 x 27in (101.5 x 68.5cm).
£90–110
$130–160 ⚲ Bon

Cross Reference
See Colour Review (page 252–253)

▶ **A United Artists poster,** *One Flew Over The Cuckoo's Nest,* printed in red and black, American, 1975, 41 x 27in (104 x 68.5cm).
£250–300
$350–450 ⊞ REEL

A Warner Bros poster, *Enter The Dragon,* printed in red, yellow and blue, 1973, 41 x 27in (104 x 68.5cm).
£200–250
$300–350 ⊞ REEL

A Salt-Pan Films poster, *The Cars that Ate Paris,* printed in pink, black and white, 1974, 40 x 30in (101.5 x 76cm).
£55–65
$80–95 ⊞ VEY

A poster, by Richard Amsel, *The Sting,* printed in red, orange and brown, American, 1974, 41 x 27in (104 x 68.5cm).
£130–150
$200–220 ⊞ REEL

A Universal poster, *Jaws,* printed in red, blue and black, 1975, 50 x 40in (152.5 x 101.5cm).
£250–300
$350–450 ⚲ S

A Warner Bros poster, *The Outlaw Josey Wales,* printed in orange and brown, American, 1976, 41 x 27in (104 x 68.5cm).
£300–350
$450–500 ⊞ REEL

A British Lion poster, *The Man Who Fell To Earth,* 1977, 11¾ x 15¾in (30 x 40cm).
£80–100
$115–145 ⊞ CTO

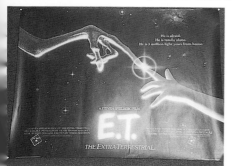

◀ **A Universal poster,** *E.T.,* printed in brown, blue and white, 1982, 40 x 30in (101.5 x 76cm).
£50–60
$75–90 ⊞ SEY

▶ **An Orion Pictures poster,** *Robocop,* printed in red, blue and black, American, 1987, 41 x 27in (101.5 x 68.5cm).
£65–75
$95–110 ⊞ REEL

Collectables

The main story of design and Modernism presented in this book is that of creative activity engaged with technology to service a mass market and consumer society. A large part of this process is supported by the mass media and the formal structures that define the contemporary content of film, television and magazines.

The development of collectors' markets that place value in the association between objects and celebrity is a reflection of our contemporary fascination with the famous. Auction houses have been at the forefront of marketing the collections of wealthy entertainers and of cult personalities such as Jacqueline Kennedy Onassis and of Diana,

Princess of Wales. The markets that support celebrities are often a reflection of the fan base of that celebrity and values of these items often reflect the growing affluence of that fan base.

The interest in recent history is often fuelled by nostalgia. The curent increase in the popularity of the Festival of Britain among collectors is partly due to its 50th anniversary and partly due to its relation to our recent attempts to commemorate the millennium.

The popularity, in collecting terms, of these ephemeral objects is testimony to the potential of small things to remain of interest. The archaeology of the past begins with the everyday.

Household

A stained and painted wood tray, attributed to Omega Workshops, c1915, 26½in (67.5cm) diam.
£800–1,000
$1,150–1,500 ➤ P

▶ **An ABS plastic water decanter,** by Gustavsberg, 1950s, 13¼in (33.5cm) high.
£125–150
$180–220 ➤ BB(L)

l. A glued 'aeroplane' veneered bowl, by Tapio Wirkkala, signed, Finnish, c1950, 7½in (19cm) wide.
£750–900
$1,100–1,300 ➤ BUK
c. A glued 'aeroplane' veneered bowl, by Tapio Wirkkala, signed, Finnish, c1950, 9¾in (25cm) wide.
£2,100–2,600
$3,000–3,800 ➤ BUK
r. A glued 'aeroplane' veneered bowl, by Tapio Wirkkala, signed, edge damaged, Finnish, c1950, 7¼in (18.5cm) wide.
£1,000–1,200
$1,500–1,750 ➤ BUK

A chrome bottle opener, in the form of a hand, decorated with toasts in various languages, 1950s, 9½in (24cm) long.
£10–15
$15–20 ⊞ BTB

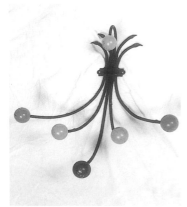

A metal coat hook, with red, yellow and green knobs, 1950s, 19in (48.5cm) wide.
£35–40
$50–60 ⊞ BTB

▶ **A roll of wallpaper,** by Storeys, with a blue and green pattern on a white ground, 1960, 20in (51cm) wide.
£18–20
$25–30 per roll ⊞ TWI

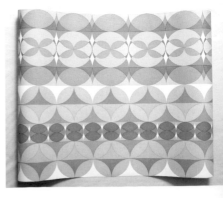

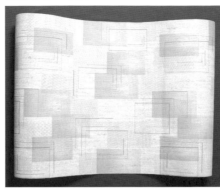

◀ **A red-enamelled roasting pan,** by Timo Sarpaneva, with a loose teak handle, with original label, minor chips, Finnish, 1960, 6½in (16.5cm) high.
£180–220
$250–320 ✯ BUK

A roll of embossed wallpaper, with pink and beige rectangles on a cream ground, 1970, 21in (53.5cm) wide.
£45–50
$65–75 per roll ⊞ TWI

Two Nagel Variante sculptures, S70 and S71, with silvered-plastic spheres, on chrome bases, West German, early 1970s, 33in (84cm) high.
£100–120
$145–175 ⊞ PAB

A blue acrylic photograph frame, by Felice Antonio Botta, probably Italian, 1970s, 6in (15cm) square.
£80–95
$115–140 ⊞ MARK

A roll of wallpaper, with a red, orange and yellow pattern, 1970s, 21in (53.5cm) wide.
£20–25
$30–35 per roll ⊞ MARK

◀ **A black-painted metal candle-holder,** by Dansk Designs, Danish, 1970s, 4in (10cm) diam.
£20–25
$30–35 ⊞ PLB

A red plastic Wall-All organizer, 1970s, 26½in (67.5cm) high.
£150–180
$220–260 ⊞ PLB

Technology

A nickel and brass electric kettle, by Peter Behrens for AEG, with braided cane handle, the lid with a turned wood finial, AEG mark and 3590 to base, slight damage, c1909, 9in (23cm) high.
£2,000–2,500
$3,000–3,500 ✯ BUK

An Ecko 'sad face' radio, model AD36, in a brown Bakelite case, 1935, 14in (35.5cm) high.
£550–600
$800–870 ⊞ GAD

▶ **An RCA book radio,** with yellow lettering, in a brown Bakelite case, Chilean, 1938, 4in (10cm) high.
£1,300–1,500
$2,000–2,200 ⊞ GAD

A blue plate-glass Sparton-Radio, by Walter Dorwin Teague, model No. 558, with chrome bands, on a black base, American, 1936.
£3,750–4,500
$5,500–6,500 ✯ DORO

A Fada Temple radio, model No. 652, in a butterscotch Catalin case, damaged, American, 1930s, 11in (28cm) wide.
£225–250
$325–360 ✦ SK(B)
Catalin is cast phenolic resin.

A Fada Streamliner or Bullet radio, model No. 200, in a pale green Catalin case, American, 1945, 10in (25.5cm) wide.
£1,000–1,200
$1,500–1,750 ⊞ GAD

A Bendix radio, model No. 526C, in a green Catalin case, American, 1946, 11in (28cm) wide.
£600–700
$870–1,000 ⊞ GAD

A Wurlitzer jukebox, 1948, 58in (147.5cm) high.
£6,000–7,200
$8,700–10,500 ⊞ TRA

A Sonorette radio, in a brown Bakelite case, French, 1950, 8in (20.5cm) high.
£450–500
$650–720 ⊞ GAD

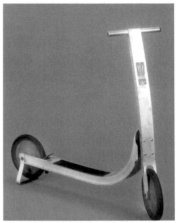

An aluminium scooter, American, c1950, 29¼in (74.5cm) high.
£70–85
$100–125 ✦ BB(L)

◄ **A Crosley Bullseye radio,** in an orange Bakelite case, American, 1951, 9in (23cm) wide.
£225–250
$325–350 ⊞ GAD

▶ **A UNIC radio,** in a chrome case, c1955, 12in (30.5cm) high.
£550–600
$800–870 ⊞ MARK

A Braun Phonosuper phonograph and radio, by Dieter Rams and Hans Gugelot, German, 1956, 22in (56cm) wide.
£350–400
$500–600 ✦ BB(L)

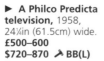

An Ice-O-Matic ice crusher, 1950s, 9in (23cm) high.
£35–40
$50–60 ⊞ BTB

▶ **A Philco Predicta television,** 1958, 24¼in (61.5cm) wide.
£500–600
$720–870 ✦ BB(L)

A Bush valve television, with a brown Bakelite case, 1950s, 12in (30.5cm) high.
£200–220
$300–320 ✗ SWO

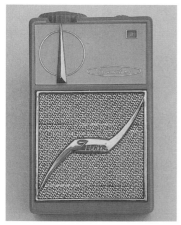

A Zephyr pocket transistor radio, model No. AR600, in a pale grey case, Japanese, 1961, 4½in (11.5cm) high.
£90–100
$130–145 ⊞ OVE

A Spica pocket transistor radio, model No. ST600, in a blue case, Japanese, 1965, 5in (13cm) high.
£50–60
$75–90 ⊞ OVE

An Olivetti Valentine typewriter, by Ettore Sottsass Jr, Italian, 1969, 14in (35.5cm) high.
£90–110
$130–160 ✗ BB(L)

A Roberts transistor radio, model No. R300, finished in brown leather, 1960, 9in (23cm) wide.
£70–80
$100–115 ⊞ PPH

A Realtone Comet pocket transistor radio, model No. TR1088, Japanese 1962, 4½in (11.5cm) high.
£90–100
$130–145 ⊞ OVE

A radio, incorporating a lavatory roll holder, 1960s, 8in (20.5cm) wide.
£15–20
$20–30 ⊞ ZOOM

► **A JVC Videosphere television set,** incorporating an alarm clock and radio, in a white case, 1970, 10in (25.5cm) diam.
£350–400
$500–580 ⊞ MARK

An Aephelion space-age design television, 1961, damaged, 37in (94cm) wide.
£720–800
$1,000–1,150 ⊞ MARK

An Imperial pocket transistor radio, in a black case, Japanese, 1963, 4½in (11.5cm) high.
£20–25
$30–35 ⊞ OVE

◄ **A Citroën DS-21 automobile,** 1972.
£11,500–14,000
$16,500–20,500 ✗ BB(L)

Luggage

A Louis Vuitton vanity case, No. 84831, with reinforced brass corners and catches, French, 1930, 16in (40.5cm) wide, with a Louis Vuitton handbag.
£750–900
$1,100–1,300 ✗ S(O)

A basket weave handbag, with brass fittings, 1950s, 10in (25.5cm) wide.
£70–80
$100–115 ⊞ LBr

▶ A gold hard plastic handbag, with clear Lucite lid and handle, American, c1950, 8in (20.5cm) wide.
£180–200
$250–300 ⊞ LBr

A Koch snakeskin two-piece luggage set, 1950s, largest 19in (48.5cm) high.
£140–170
$200–250 ✗ BB(L)

A Koch fibreglass three-piece luggage set, 1950s, largest 25in (63.5cm) wide.
£200–250
$300–350 ✗ BB(L)

◀ A Louis Vuitton suitcase, with solid frame, French, 31½in (80cm) wide.
£800–950
$1,150–1,400 ✗ S(O)

A white hard plastic handbag, with clear Lucite lid, 1950s, 10in (25.5cm) wide.
£160–180
$230–260 ⊞ LBr

Festival of Britain

A Bryant & May Festival of Britain book of matches, printed in black and white on a red and yellow ground, 1951, 2 x 1½in (5 x 4cm).
£3–4
$5–8 ⊞ HUX

A Festival of Britain glass paper-weight, 1951, 5 x 3in (12.5 x 7.5cm).
£35–45
$50–65 ⊞ MURR

A Poole Pottery Festival of Britain plate, decorated with flowers in red and yellow, 1951, 10in (25.5cm) diam.
£90–100
$130–145 ⊞ FBS

Television

◀ **A Hovis Coronation Periscope,** 1953, 14½in (37cm) high.
£20–22
$30–35 ⊞ HUX

The Flintstones Big TV Bumper Book, the cover printed in blue, yellow, mauve and green, 1962, 12 x 9in (30.5 x 23cm).
£5–7
$10–12 ⊞ YR

A set of Dutch Milk Premium plastic Beatles figures, in brown, pink and black, 1964, 4½in (11.5cm) high.
£85–100
$125–145 ⊞ TBoy

The Girl From U.N.C.L.E. **annuals,** with full-colour covers, 1967 and 1968, 10 x 8in (25.5 x 20.5cm).
£5–8
$10–12 each ⊞ YR

A Bendy blue and yellow Smurf, 1960s, 8½in (21.5cm) high.
£8–10
$12–15 ⊞ CMF

▶ **A** *Land Of The Giants* **Picture Card Bubble Gum,** in a red, blue and yellow wrapper, 1968, 2 x 3in (5 x 7.5cm).
£8–10
$12–15 ⊞ YR

Lady Penelope **annual,** the red leather-effect cover embossed in gold, with inset full-colour picture of Lady Penelope, 1968, 11 x 9in (28 x 23cm).
£5–7
$10–12 ⊞ YR

A Corgi *Magic Roundabout* **Playground,** No. 853, comprising an oval playground with hand-operated roundabout and train track, a clockwork musical see-saw, a train with carriage and truck, Mr Rusty and various other figures in the locomotive, Brian, Dougal, Dylan, Ermintrude and Zebedee, trees, shrubs and flowers, in original box, inner packing missing, 1970s.
£320–360
$450–500 ➶ DN
Created by Frenchman Serge Danot and narrated by Eric Thompson (father of actress Emma), the *Magic Roundabout* **first appeared on British TV in 1965. The Technicolour series became an instant hit, with both children and adults, particularly students, who appreciated the surreal and occasionally spaced-out quality of the story and characters. This playground set is among the most collectable of all** *Magic Roundabout* **merchandise and it is rare to find it complete.**

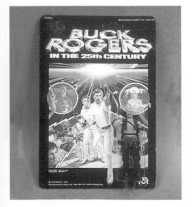

◀ **A** *Buck Rogers in the 25th Century* **action figure,** Tiger Man, 1979, card 9 x 6in (23 x 15cm).
£30–35
$45–50 ⊞ OW

Focus on Style: Pre-Modern

The emergence of a Modernist style, after WWI, that considered itself radical and socially progressive and that looked to a design ethic that was driven by a logical Functionalism, or rationalism, has fostered an enduring mythology of Modernism. The words Modernism and revolution are always closely linked – along with the idea that Modernist styling breaks decisively with its immediate predecessors – in an attempt to position the Modernist designer among the avant-garde.

This powerful mythology needs to be examined and called into question. The roots of Modernist thinking and practice can be traced back to the origins of the Industrial Revolution and in the factory organization of the Victorians. The historian and collector of 20th-century Modernism should understand and acknowledge the roots and antecedents of Modernism.

A beech bentwood rocking chair, by Thonet, with foot rest rail, stamped Thonet, with remains of paper label, early 20thC
£1,200–1,400
$1,750–2,000 ⚒ S(O)

A set of 21 Pilkington's lustre tiles, painted with a heart motif on a scale ground, with combed backs, some with impressed P, early 20thC, each tile 3in (7.5cm) square.
£850–950
$1,250–1,400 ⚒ S(O)

Thonet
(1796–1871, German)

The bentwood furniture of Michel Thonet marks the beginning of the industrial mass-production of furniture. His experiments bending wood allowed him to design a dining or café chair that could be made out of just six pieces of wood bolted together. The chair became a staple of the industrial metropolis and was closely associated, in continental Europe, with the emergence of café society and of the lounge lizard as a Modernist intellectual archetype. By the end of the 19th century over 50 million café chairs had been manufactured and exported from the factory as flat-packs. Thonet continued his experiments and created a range of furniture designs that became progressively more self-conscious, even baroque, in their design.

A pair of brown-painted wicker armchairs, the curved backs leading to rolled arms above caned seats, on circular banded legs joined by a X-stretchers, c1900.
£1,500–1,600
$2,000–2,300 ⚒ S(NY)

Paxman (1803–65, British)

The Great Exhibition of 1851 was decisive evidence of the pre-eminence of Great Britain as the workshop of the world. Furthermore, it marked the evolution of the idea of national identity as configured beyond military power and political influence and by productive and manufacturing output.

The Exhibition also began a tradition of trade fair displays that continue to this day. The International exhibition became, through its development during the 19th-century, an important indicator of both traditional manufacturing craft and expertise and of technological and scientific advance. The Exhibition provided a narrative of material and social progress founded on the resources, both material and human, of the exhibitor nations.

These exhibitions became an important indicator of the direction of national progress. Not surprisingly, it was important for the architecture and planning of the exhibition to reflect these ambitions. The Crystal Place, in London was designed by Sir Joseph Paxman and constructed entirely from cast-iron and glass. Paxman was the gardener at Chatsworth for the Duke of Devonshire and it is no accident that his design for the Palace resembles a gigantic greenhouse. Indeed, the logic of construction was such that the Palace could have been extended almost indefinitely in a succession of cast-iron hoops and glass. The Palace was later successfully dismantled and moved, piece by piece, to South London. It was destroyed by fire in 1932.

A Stiller shoe poster, by Bernhard, printed by Hollerbaum & Schmidt, Berlin, restored losses, 1908, 26½ x 36½in (67.5 x 92.5cm).
£7,000–8,500
$10,000–12,500 ⚒ SWAN

Creating a collection

Opportunity exists to contextualize items in a collection by association with earlier, related objects. This is a sort of curatorial process and is probably part of a collecting project that requires some experience.
The pricing structure of the markets in 19th-century objects is clearly more advanced than that in 20th-century design. That does not mean, however, that such items are always more expensive, and bentwood chairs, for example, may be very inexpensive in their simpler forms.

► **A bentwood side chair,** by Thonet, c1870.
£400–480
$580–700
⚒ BB(L)

Focus on Style: Timber-Framed Modern

The extension of the metropolis through the development of the garden suburb and the metropolitan railway turned Greater London into the first extended city. It is characterized by its leafy, ordered suburban layout. This has been seen as both a source of delight, as in John Betjeman's *Metroland*, or as a plague, as in Osbert Lancaster's *Subtopia* – being neither city nor countryside. The retro styling of much suburban development reflected the conservative nature of both the speculative builder and his market. The great expansion of the city took place in the 1920s with the desire to build homes fit for heroes. It is hardly surprising that the returning soldiers and their families should choose a comfortable, familiar and bucolic style of contemporary architecture as opposed to the austere rationalism associated with Modernist ideas.

An oak trestle dining table, by Gustav Stickley, model No. 631, top revarnished, c1904, 96in (244cm) wide.
£14,750–17,750
$21,500–25,500 ⚒ S(NY)

A walnut library bookcase, by Peter Wals, with ebony and boxwood stringing, early 20thC, 76in (193cm) wide.
£12,000–15,000
$17,500–22,000 ⊞ L

An oak wardrobe, by Robert 'Mouseman' Thompson, with beaten iron fittings, 48in (122cm) wide.
£3,000–4,000
$4,000–5,800 ⚒ C

◄ **A mahogany press cupboard,** in the style of Ambrose Heal, with pewter and ebony inlay, early 20thC, 48in (122cm) wide.
£1,500–1,800
$2,200–2,600 ⚒ L&E

London & Empire Exhibition 1924

The period after WWI was as traumatic for the victorious powers as for those defeated in war. Great Britain saw its traditional identity as industrial and Imperial Superpower questioned, and began a project, exemplified in the Empire Exhibition of 1924, to reconfigure national identity beyond traditional Imperial relations and to begin the transition towards an economy of communications, services and creativity. The resulting networks of communications and transport infrastructure, comprising the efforts of roadbuilders, Imperial Airways and of the General Post Office, created the conditions for the extension of community beyond its traditional limits as set by village, town and city. These efforts should be acknowledged as significant precursors to the contemporary globalization of the internet and wireless communities.

The vernacular styling of much suburban development has its roots in a romanticized ideal of pre-industrial society. This has tended to be seen as an attempt to resist modernity and to retreat towards a bucolic, pastoral ideal. The foundations for this analysis are to be found in both William Blake's notion of Albion and in the political and aesthetic ideas of the Arts and Crafts movement. This reflects a desire to read the bucolic as a more culturally authentic representation of Englishness than that afforded by 19th century industrialization. It is therefore entirely understandable that the favoured expression of this new England should be as Timber-Framed Modern.

The furnishings and design of this extended community are rooted in the simplifications of the later Arts and Crafts movement which draw on the austere simplifications and ethics of the 19th-century Shaker movement in the USA. These traditions, long overlooked by middle class Victorian and Edwardian taste, were appropriated by the garden suburbs of Hampstead and Letchworth. The resulting Modernism is low-key, but high-tech, and comfortable rather than dislocating. The focus on the garden and seaside as important elements within this version of Modernism is peculiarly English and is testimony to an environmental concern that was probably ahead of its time.

▶ **An Arts and Crafts coromandel and ebony cabinet-on-stand,** by Charles Spooner, c1910, 37½in (95.5cm) wide.
£9,500–10,500
$13,750–15,250 🔨 P

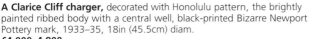

A Clarice Cliff charger, decorated with Honolulu pattern, the brightly painted ribbed body with a central well, black-printed Bizarre Newport Pottery mark, 1933–35, 18in (45.5cm) diam.
£4,000–4,800
$5,800–7,000 🔨 S(O)

▶ **A Carter, Stabler & Adams pottery vase,** painted in buff, grey, black and blue with stylized flower and leaf motifs, marked with artist's initial H and pattern code LJ, c1925, 11¾in (30cm) high.
£1,300–1,500
$1,500–2,200 🔨 RTo

◄ **A Wedgwood pottery trial group** by John Skeaping, with straw-coloured glaze, stamped mark, 1927, 8in (20.5cm) high.
£1,100–1,200
$1,600–1,750
⚒ P

A Clarice Cliff plate, decorated with Alton pattern, c1930, 9in (23cm) diam.
£180–220
$260–320 ⚒ G(L)

An Art Deco dining room suite, by Heal's, comprising table, four single chairs, two carvers and a sideboard, c1930, table 60¼in (153cm) wide.
£2,600–3,000
$3,800–4,400 ⚒ B(B)

A burled wood-veneered cocktail table, by Russel Wright for Heywood-Wakefield, with chrome-plated handles, c1934, 21in (53cm) high.
£2,500–3,000
$3,500–4,500 ⚒ BB(L)

◄ **A limed-oak refectory dining table,** with twin-barrel turned end supports, 1950s, 78in (198cm) wide, and six limed-oak dining chairs.
Table   **£2,700–3,000 / $4,000–4,500**
Chairs   **£2,500–2,800 / $3,500–4,000** ⚒ WW

Market update

The idea of Timber-Framed Modernism is particularly English. It carries with it an association with the suburban and, at a more modest level, the shed, beach hut and artist's studio. The personal and idiosyncratic nature of these spaces contrasts powerfully with the rationalist logic of Continental Modernism or with the austere minimalist style of 20th-century design.

The 'comfy Modernism' style allows for an eclectic mixture of objects and for their display in the home. The style is perfectly suited to collectors who are furnishing a home rather than creating a museum display. Always take care to identify pieces that are genuinely 20th-century in design rather than reproductions of earlier styles.

The fact that this strand of design history has tended to be marginalized makes the pricing structure sensible. A later, and historically significant, form of this tradition is the 'utility' furniture produced during and after WWII under the guidance of Gordon Russell. This furniture is generally considered interesting but valueless, offering many opportunities to acquire pieces at modest prices.

A Poole Pottery plate, decorated by Gwen Haskins after a 1930s design by Arthur Bradbury, c1974, 15½in (39.5cm`) diam.
£500–600
$720–870 ⊞ HarC

Colour Review

A sterling silver brooch, by Georg Jensen, designed as a dove within a foliate border, pattern No. 70, 1904–45.
£160–190
$230–275 ↗ G(L)

A gold pendant, by Tapio Wirkkala for N. Westerback, Finnish, 1970.
£2,300–2,800
$3,300–4,000 ↗ BUK

A 14ct yellow gold bracelet, by Paloma Picasso for Tiffany & Co, composed throughout with kiss and hug symbols, 1983.
£1,500–1,800
$2,200–2,600 ↗ SLN

▶ An Eye clock, by George Nelson for Howard Miller, in brass, wood and painted metal, retains paper label and impressed Howard Miller, c1954, 30in (76cm) wide.
£8,000–9,500
$11,750–14,000 ↗ BBL

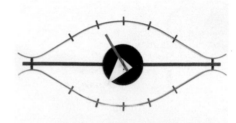

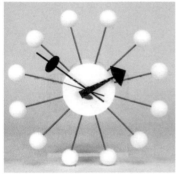

A Ball clock, by George Nelson for Howard Miller, white painted wood and aluminium, with Howard Miller label, 1947, 13in (33cm) diam.
£550–650
$800–950 ↗ BB(L)

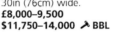

A Spike clock, by George Nelson for Howard Miller, 1948, 19in (48.5cm) diam.
£375–450
$560–650 ↗ BB(L)

◀ A clock, by Dieter Rams for Braun, German, 1960s, 5¾in (14.5cm) diam.
£250–300
$360–440 ↗ BB(L)

A silver and white onyx tray, by Jean E. Puiforcat, the scalloped ends threaded with an undulating onyx band, the centre engraved JMC, stamped on reverse, Mexican, mid-20thC, 16in (40.5cm) square, 81oz.
£22,000–26,000
$32,000–38,000 ↗ S(NY)

A silvered-metal two-handled coupe, by Josef Hoffman for Wiener Werkstätte, impressed Wiener Werkstätte JH, Austrian, c1924, 7¼in (18.5cm) diam.
£20,000–23,000
$29,000–33,000 ⊞ S(NY)

◀ A set of eight enamelled bowls, by Krenit, 1953, largest 4½in (11.5cm) high.
£275–350
$400–500 ↗ BB(L)

A cold-painted bronze and ivory figure, by Professor Otto Poertzel, 'The Aristocrats', on an onyx and marble base, signed, impressed PK foundry mark, German, 1920s, 18¾in (47.5cm) high.
£10,800–12,500
$15,500–18,000 ⚒ S(NY)

A patinated bronze group, by Mario Korbel, 'Andante', signed, inscribed, further inscribed Roman Bronze Works NY, American, 1917, 29½in (75cm) high.
£12,000–15,000
$17,500–22,000 ⚒ S(NY)

A cold-painted bronze and ivory figure, by D. H. Chiparus, in the form of a Pierrot, signed, French, 1920s, 16in (40.5cm) high.
£3,000–3,600
$4,400–5,200 ⚒ S(NY)

▶ **A cold-painted bronze and ivory figure,** cast and carved from a model by Ferdinand Preiss, 'Cabaret Girl', 1920–30, 15¾in (40cm) high.
£9,500–12,000
$13,800–17,400 ⊞ ASA

A gilt bronze and ivory figure, by D. H. Chiparus, 'Cleopatra', on a marble base with a gilt plaque inscribed 'Cleopatre pas D. H. Chiparus Lauréat des Beaux-Arts', signed, French, 1920s, 19in (48.5cm) high.
£12,500–15,000
$18,000–22,000 ⚒ S(NY)

A patinated bronze and ivory figure, by D. H. Chiparus, 'Antinea', signed, French, 1920s, 26½in (67.5cm) high.
£55,000–65,000
$80,000–95,000 ⚒ S(NY)

▶ **A silvered-bronze female nude torchère,** by Alexandre Kéléty, on a marble base, signed, Hungarian, c1930, 22¼in (56.5cm) high.
£9,000–10,000
$13,000–14,500 ⚒ S

▶ **A bronze figure of a nude,** by Georges Chauvel, on a marble plinth, signed, stamped with Alexis Rudier Paris foundry mark, French, early 20thC, 22in (56cm) wide.
£3,200–3,800
$4,500–5,500 ⚒ S(O)

◀ **A gilt, green-patinated and cold-painted bronze figure,** by Pierre Le Faguays, entitled 'Dancer with Thyrsus', on a stepped beige-veined black marble base, c1920, 22in (56cm) high.
£4,500–5,000
$6,500–7,250 ⚒ S

► **A parcel-gilt bronze group,** by Raymond Delamarre, 'La Tentation', inscribed, French, c1925, 37½in (95.5cm) high.
£35,000–42,000
$50,750–61,000 ✠ S(NY)

An Art Deco bronze figure, by Marcel-André Bouraine, a nude throwing a spear, signed, inscribed 'Etling, Paris', 1918–35, 14¾in (37.5cm) high.
£3,500–4,000
$5,000–5,800 ✠ S(O)

A bronze and ivory figure, by F. Preiss, on a marble base, 'Diana', bow and arrow replaced, signed, c1925, 9¾in (24.5cm) high.
£7,000–8,000
$10,200–11,600 ✠ P

A silvered-bronze figure, by Maurice Guiraud-Rivière, 'La Comète', on a marble base, signed, inscribed 'Etling, Paris', French, early 20thC, 20in (51cm) high.
£13,000–15,000
$19,000–22,000 ✠ S(NY)

A patinated bronze model, by Rembrandt Bugatti, 'Petite Leopard Marchant', signed, impressed, c1911, 7in (18cm) high.
£110,000–130,000
$159,000–188,500 ✠ S(NY)

A pair of nickle-plated brass heads, by Franz Hagenhauer, impressed, Austrian, mid-20thC, 15¼in (38.5cm) high.
£15,000–18,000
$21,750–26,000 ✠ S(NY)

A cold-painted bronze figure, by Bruno Zach, depicting an Indian riding a horse, signed 'Zach, Argentor-Vienna', 1918–35, 15¾in (40cm) high.
£3,800–4,500
$5,500–6,500 ✠ S(O)

A patinated bronze model, by Maurice Prost, entitled 'Panthère', inscribed 'M. Prost/Susse Frès/Edits. Paris', French, 1920s, 26in (66cm) long.
£4,200–5,000
$6,100–7,250 ✠ S(NY)

► **An ebonized wood model of a dachshund,** by Hagenauer, 'DOG', on a nickel-plated base, underside stamped Atelier Hagenauer Wien, Handmade and with WHW monogram, Austrian, 1930s, 11in (28cm) high.
£3,800–4,500
$5,500–6,500 ✠ S

An enamelled steel, Plexiglass and wood constructivist sculpture, by Derek Carruthers, c1950.
£2,000–2,500
$2,900–3,600 ✠ BB(L)

A bronze sculpture, by Dame Elizabeth Frink, 'Firebird', signed, marked on the base, 1962, 16½in (42cm) high.
£5,000–5,500
$7,250–8,000 ✠ RTo

◀ **A hammered copper vase,** by Frans Zwollo Sr, set with turquoise stones, with original pewter liner, stamped mark, c1905, 5in (12.5cm) high.
£1,500–1,650
$2,150–2,350 ⚒ S(Am)

▶ **A beaten copper and gilt amphora vase,** by Jean Dunand, with ribbed decoration and a frieze of hearts at the rim, signed, early 20thC, 7in (18cm) high.
£5,000–6,000
$7,250–8,700 ⚒ S(P)

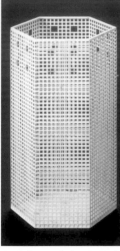

A perforated sheet steel waste basket, by Josef Hoffman, designed 1902, manufactured c1970, 19¼in (49cm) high.
£300–350
$440–500 ⚒ BB(L)

A white metal charger, by Claudius Linossier, with star motif, the *martelé* finish patinated in dark brown and inlaid in shades of brass, grey and rust, the rim inlaid with lozenges, signed, 1920s, 19¾in (50cm) diam.
£14,500–17,500
$21,000–25,500 ⚒ S

A copper ball vase, by Claudius Linossier, with *martelé* finish, patinated in shades of mottled rust, red, brown and black, inlaid with a frieze of geometric motifs at the rim, cut mark 'Linossier' to base, 1930s, 5½in (14cm) high.
£4,800–5,500
$7,000–8,000 ⚒ S

An enamelled metal umbrella stand, by Piero Fornasetti, 'A Moor', marked Fornasetti Milano, Made in Italy, 1960s, 22½in (57cm) high.
£680–750
$1,000–1,100 ⚒ S(O)

A gilt-iron grille, by Edgar Brandt for Au Bon Marché, now mounted for use as a fire screen, impressed 'Pierre Quidon', French, 1923–24, 37½in (95.5cm) high.
£9,000–11,000
$13,000–16,000 ⚒ S(NY)

A metal waste-basket, by Piero Fornasetti, Italian, 1950s, 19¾in (50cm) high.
£575–700
$850–1,000 ⚒ DORO

▶ **A pair of perforated aluminium waste-baskets,** 1950s, American, 14in (35.5cm) high.
£700–800
$1,000–1,150 ⚒ BB(L)

▶ **A wire clothes stand,** by Verner Panton, Danish, 1959, 50¾in (152cm) high.
£620–750
$900–1,100 DORO ⚒

A Daum glass mushroom lamp, the shade and base with a white and yellow ground decorated with red and maroon poppies, the base and the shade signed Daum Nancy, 16¼in (41cm) high.
£23,000–25,500
$33,500–37,000 ↗ S(P)

A Tiffany Favrile glass and bronze lamp, the shade with a dogwood border, the base and finial with dark brown patina, shade and base impressed, 1899–1918, 22¼in (56.5cm) high.
£16,000–17,500
$23,000–25,500 ↗ S(NY)

A silver-bronze and alabaster lamp, by Albert Cheuret, inscribed mark, French, c1925, 16in (40.5cm) high.
£12,000–15,000
$17,400–21,750 ↗ S(NY)

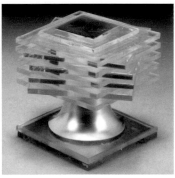

A glass and aluminium table lamp, by Desny, formed from stacked square glass plates with a central tapering column, small chips, c1926, 4½in (11.5cm) high.
£600–700
$870–1,000 ↗ S(O)

A pair of aluminium and glass light fittings, by Henry Dreyfuss for the 20th Century Limited, American, 1938, 12½in (32cm) diam.
£700–850
$1,000–1,250 ↗ BB(L)

▶ **A brown Bakelite table lamp,** by Jumo, with chromium-plated metal jointed arm, French, c1945, 5½in (14cm) high.
£1,200–1,500
$1,750–2,150 ↗ DORO

A table lamp, Italian, 1950s, 23in (58.5cm) high.
£325–350
$470–500 ⊞ ZOOM

A floor lamp, by Arredoluce for Raymor, model No. 12128, c1954, 71in (180.5cm) high.
£7,000–8,000
$10,000–11,500 ↗ BB(L)

◀ **A brown-painted copper outside light,** by Poul Henningsen for Louis Poulsen, Danish, 1966, 11¾in (30cm) high.
£375–450
$550–650 ↗ BUK

A mother-of-pearl hanging lamp, by Verner Panton, 1970, 21¾in (55cm) high.
£700–850
$1,000–1,250 ↗ DORO

◀ **A standing Visor lamp,** by Arne Jacobsen for Louis Poulsen, Danish, 1955, 49½in (125.5cm) high.
£1,300–1,800
$1,900–2,750 BB(L) ↗

An Art Deco wool carpet, c1930, 132½ x 98in (336.5 x 249cm).
£2,800–3,400
$4,000–4,500 ⚘ S(NY)

A wool carpet, by Paule Leleu, woven mark, 1940s, 98 x 137in (249 x 348cm).
£5,200–6,200
$7,500–9,000 ⚘ S(NY)

A wall hanging, by AB Märta Måås-Fjetterström and Marianne Richter, slightly worn, minor stains, fringes worn, Finnish, 1959, 84 x 52¾in (213.5 x 134cm).
£550–650
$800–950 ⚘ BUK

An Art Deco wool carpet, by Ashley Havinden, with woven monogram, c1930, 97½ x 78½in (247.5 x 199.5cm).
£5,800–7,000
$8,400–10,000 ⚘ S(NY)

A rug, by AB Märta Måås-Fjetterström and Barbro Nilsson, slightly worn, stained, damage to ends, fringes missing, signed, 1943, 69¾ x 52in (177 x 132cm).
£750–900
$1,100–1,300 ⚘ BUK

A tapestry, by A. Toussaint, 1950s, 77 x 55in (195.5 x 139.5cm).
£2,500–3,000
$3,500–4,500 ⚘ S

▶ **A length of linen Palio fabric,** by Alexander Girard for Herman Miller, silkscreen-printed with a geometric design, signed, 1964, 86 x 51in (218.5 x 129.5cm).
£185–220
$270–320 ⚘ TREA

An Aubusson tapestry, by Jean Lurçat, with inscription 'au seul bruit du soleil', signed, manufacturer's label, French, 1943, 101¼ x 120in (257 x 300cm).
£8,300–10,000
$12,000–14,500 ⚘ S(P)

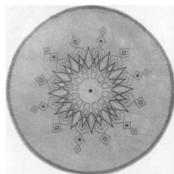

A wool carpet, by Paule Leleu, 1950s, woven mark, 106½in (270.5cm) diam.
£6,200–7,500
$9,000–10,200 ⚘ S(NY)

A wool shag rug by Paul Wieland for Monsanto, label, c1960, 72 x 51½in (183 x 131cm).
£600–720
$870–1,000 ⚘ BB(L)

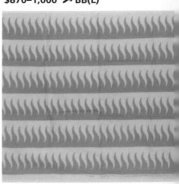

◄ **A pair of Checks and Rectangular fabric panels,** by Alexander Girard, with silkscreen-printed geometric design, signed, 1971, 54½ x 25½in (138.5 x 66cm).
£125–150
$180–220 ⚒ TREA

A Snake fabric panel, by Alexander Girard, silkscreen-printed, 1972, approx 30in (76cm) square.
£185–220
$270–320 ⚒ TREA

A length of Motus fabric, by Gaetano Pesce for Collezione Expansion, 1970, 787in (2000cm) long.
£950–1,100
$1,400–1,600 ⚒ S

► **A Wave fabric panel,** by Verner Panton for Mira-X, 1974, 47 x 59in (119.5 x 150cm).
£750–850
$1,100–1,250 ⊞ MARK

A Ribbons linen fabric panel, by Alexander Girard, silkscreen-printed with geometric design, signed, 1972, 25½ x 82in (65 x 208.5cm).
£200–240
$300–350 ⚒ TREA

An Oriented wool rug, by Alessandro Mendini for Alchimia, designed 1980, 94 x 66in (239 x 186cm).
£1,400–1,600
$2,000–2,300 ⚒ S

A Love rug, by Robert Indiana, c1975.
£95–115
$140–170 ⚒ BB(L)

◄ **A wool dress,** possibly by Ossie Clark, with bias-cut curved stripes, c1970.
£500–600
$720–870 ⚒ S(O)

► **A maxi dress,** by Rudi Gernreich, with short sleeves and floral appliqué skirt, c1973, together with a necklace of dyed chicken feathers.
£350–420
$500–600 ⚒ S(O)

A Kabuki-style mini dress, by Rudi Gernreich for Harmon Knitwear, with obi band, c1963.
£470–580
$650–850 ⚒ S(O)

A cotton Anarchy Karl Marx shirt, by Westwood/McLaren, c1976.
£2,500–3,000
$3,500–4,500 ⚒ S(O)

A poster, 'Nach Südamerika' by Ottomar Anton, German, c1926, 41¼ x 27½in (105 x 70cm).
£300–350
$450–500 ➚ VSP

▶ **A Boston and North Eastern Railway poster,** 'The Night Scotsman', by Alexander Alexeïeff, 1932, 40 x 50in (101.5 x 127cm).
£35,000–40,000
$50,000–58,000 ➚ SWAN

A poster, 'Zwitserland', by Herbert Matter, 1936, 40½ x 25in (103 x 63.5cm).
£1,600–2,000
$2,300–3,000 ➚ SWAN

A Swissair poster, 'Nice', by Henry Ott, printed by 'indicolodruck' Bollman, Swiss, c1950, 40¼ x 25¼in (102 x 64cm).
£115–130
$165–200 ➚ VSP

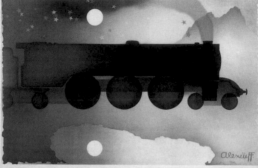

A BOAC poster, by Abram Games, printed by The Baynard Press, 1950, 40¼ x 25in (102 x 63.5cm).
£600–720
$870–1,000 ➚ VSP

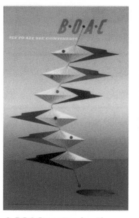

◀ **A London Underground linen poster,** by Bainbridge, 1962, 40 x 25in (101.5 x 63.5cm).
£325–375
$470–570 ⊞ Do

◀ **An LMS poster,** 'Sunny Rhyl', by Septimus Scott, lithograph, c1925, 40 x 50in (101.5 x 127cm).
£4,000–4,500
$5,800–6,500 ⊞ BSL

A poster, 'San Marco Venedig', by Giuseppe Riccobaldi del Bava, c1935, 39½ x 24¼in (100.5 x 61½cm).
£575–675
$850–975 ➚ VSP

A poster, 'Ski in Aspen', by Herbert Bayer, repaired tears and restoration to edges and image, American, 1946, 40 x 29¾in (101.5 x 75.5cm).
£3,500–4,000
$5,000–5,800 ➚ SWAN

A poster, 'Venezia', by A. M. Cassendre, printed by Calcografia & Cartefalori, Italian, 1951, 39½ x 24½in (100.5 x 62cm).
£1,700–2,000
$2,500–3,000 ➚ VSP

A poster, 'Harwich Hook of Holland, day and night services', by Huveneers, printed by The Haycock Press, London, c1955, 39¾ x 25in (101 x 63.5cm).
£300–350
$450–500 ➚ VSP

VINTAGE POSTERS

A poster, by E. Gaud, advertising Saint Tropez, printed by Imprimerie a. Karcher, c1965, 30¾ x 23in (78 x 58.5cm).
£130–160
$200–230 ⚒ VSP

A poster, advertising Acapulco, c1970, 36 x 25¼in (91.5 x 64cm).
£115–130
$170–200 ⚒ VSP

An SNCF poster, by Bernard Villemot, 'Visitez La Côte d'Azur', printed by Hubert Baille, Paris, 1968, 39½ x 24½in (100.5 x 62cm).
£300–350
$450–500 ⚒ VSP

A Stiller shoe poster, by Bernhard, printed by Hollerbaum & Schmidt, Berlin, restored losses, 1908, 26½ x 36½in (67.5 x 92.5cm).
£7,000–8,500
$10,000–12,500 ⚒ SWAN

A linen poster, 'A Country Girl', by Dalys, 1920s, 28 x 19in (71.x 48.5cm).
£175–225
$250–350 ▦ Do

An Alf Cook linen theatre poster, 'Robinson Crusoe' by Jim Affleck, 1920s, 30 x 20in (76 x 51cm).
£225–250
$325–360 ▦ Do

A poster, 'PKZ', by Herbert Matter, lithograph, 1928, 50 x 36in (127 x 91.5cm).
£3,500–4,000
$5,000–5,800 ▦ BSL

A linen poster, 'Cognac Quevedo', Spanish, 1930s, 33 x 24in (84 x 61cm).
£325–375
$470–570 ▦ Do

▶ **A poster,** 'Heilig', by Pokorny Hofbauer, lithograph, c1930, 49½ x 36½in (125 x 92cm).
£1,000–1,200
$1,500–1,750 ▦ BSL

A poster, 'Bonal Gentiane-Quina', by A. M. Cassandre, French, 1935, (160 x 120cm).
£2,600–3,000
$3,800–4,400 ⚒ VSP

A set of five subway cards, by Shepard, advertising Wrigley's Juicy Fruit, some staining, 1940, 11 x 28in (28 x 71cm).
£1,000–1,200
$1,500–1,800 ↗ SWAN

A D. H. Evans poster, 'Fashion Wise', by Elfer, c1950, 40 x 30in (101.5 x 76cm).
£120–140
$175–200 ↗ VSP

A Lilliput poster, 'Such a nice change', by Arpad Elfer, c1950, 40 x 30in (101.5 x 76cm).
£300–350
$450–500 ↗ VSP

A GPO poster, 'Please pack parcels very carefully, by Tom Eckersley, c1955, 35¾ x 29in (91 x 73.5cm).
£75–85
$110–125 ↗ VSP

An Amsterdam Fashion Week poster, by Eppo Doeve, 1953, 29¼ x 19¾in (74.5 x 50cm).
£200–250
$300–350 ↗ VSP

A Cinzano poster, possibly by Paul Colin, discolouration in margins, 1950, 28 x 46½in (71 x 118cm).
£700–850
$1,000–1,250 ↗ SWAN

A Guinness poster, c1940, 60 x 40in (152 x 102cm).
£600–700
$870–1,000 ↗ CSK

◀ **A Guinness poster,** 1956, 60 x 40in (152 x 102cm).
£300–350
$450–500 ↗ CSK

▶ **A Guinness lithograph poster,** 1936, 60 x 40in (152 x 102cm).
£475–575
$700–850 ↗ CSK

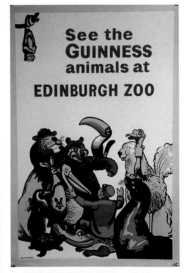

A Guinness linen poster, 1960s, 30 x 20in (76 x 51cm).
£300–350
$450–500 ⊞ Do

◀ **A Guinness poster,** by Abram Games, c1960, 30 x 20in (76 x 51cm).
£275–325
$400–470 ↗ VSP

LOCATE THE SOURCE
The source of each illustration in Miller's can be found by checking the code letters below each caption with the Key to Illustrations, pages 296–298.

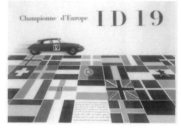

A poster, 'ID 19 Championne d'Europe', 1960, 44 x 34in (112 x 86.5cm).
£125–150
$180–220 ⚒ VSP

A poster, 'Foyer Charbon, confort familial', c1955, 23½ x 15¾in (59.5 x 40cm).
£75–100
$110–145 ⚒ VSP

A Holland festival poster, by Dick Elffers, Dutch, 1960, 39½ x 24½in (100 x 62cm).
£100–120
$145–175 ⚒ VSP

▶ **A Morris poster,** 'So oder so – ein Wunderauto', c1960, 34¾ x 25in (88.5 x 63.5cm).
£200–220
$300–320 ⚒ VSP

A Montreux Jazz festival silkscreen poster, by Roger Bornand, 1968, 39½ x 27½in (100.5 x 70cm).
£60–80
$90–115 ⚒ VSP

A Perrier poster, by Bernard Villemot, 1980, 22¾ x 18¼in (58 x 46.5cm).
£185–200
$270–300 ⚒ VSP

A Loto poster, 'Super cagnotte des vacances', by Bernard Villemot, 1989, 69 x 46½in (175.5 x 118cm).
£135–160
$200–230 ⚒ VSP

▶ **An RKO poster,** advertising *King Kong*, by René Peron, 1933, 63 x 47in (160 x 119.5cm).
£6,000–7,000
$8,700–10,200 ⚒ S

A Dear Film linen-backed poster, advertising *Femmina*, 1958, 55 x 39in (139.5 x 99cm).
£160–200
$230–300 ⚒ BB(L)

◀ **An ICI linen-backed poster,** advertising *Ossessione*, 1942, 19¾ x 28in (50 x 71cm).
£160–200
$230–300 ⚒ BB(L)

A linen-backed film poster, advertising *La tête contre les murs,* 1958, 62 x 45in (157.5 x 114.5cm).
£600–720
$870–1,000 ⚒ BB(L)

A Zenith International linen-backed poster, advertising *The 400 Blows,* Polish, 1959, 33 x 23in (84 x 58.5cm).
£700–850
$1,000–1,250 ⚒ BB(L)

A film poster, advertising *TinTin et le mystère de la toison d'or,* French, c1960, 23¾ x 15¾in (60.5 x 40cm).
£70–85
$100–125 ⚒ VSP

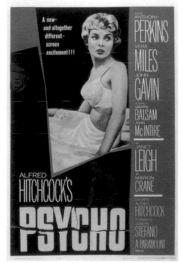

A Paramount poster, by Saul Bass, advertising *Psycho,* 1960, 41 x 27in (104 x 68.5cm).
£600–720
$870–1,000 ⚒ BB(L)

A Metro-Goldwyn-Mayer linen-backed poster, advertising *Lolita,* Italian, 1962, 55 x 39in (139.5 x 99cm).
£400–480
$580–700 ⚒ BB(L)

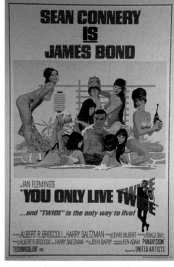

A United Artists poster, advertising *You Only Live Twice,* 1967, 41 x 27in (104 x 68.5cm).
£350–400
$500–580 ⊞ REEL

A Rank film poster, advertising *Blade Runner,* 1982, 41 x 27in (104 x 68.5cm).
£200–250
$300–350 ⊞ REEL

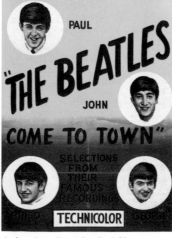

A dayglow linen-backed film poster, advertising *The Beatles Come to Town,* 1964, 42 x 28in (106.5 x 71cm).
£850–950
$1,250–1,380 ⚒ S

Bob Dylan, silkscreened poster, 'Blowing in the Mind' by Martin sharp, printed in red and gold metallic, 1967, 30 x 20in (76 x 50cm).
£300–325
$440–470 ⊞ ASC

A Bob Dylan poster, by Milton Glaser, 1967, 36 x 26in (91.5 x 66cm).
£250–300
$350–450 ⊞ CJP

A John Lennon silkscreen poster, 1967, 29 x 19in (73.5 x 48cm).
£250–300
$350–450 ⊞ CJP

A Jimi Hendrix silkscreen poster, for the Riki-Tik Club, c1967, 29 x 19in (73.5 x 48cm).
£200–220
$300–320 ⊞ CJP

A Miller Blues Band poster, 1967, 19¾ x 14¼in (50 x 36cm).
£100–120
$145–175 ⚒ VSP

A Beatles poster, designed by The Fool, published by Apple to promote The Beatles' shop in Baker Street, 1967, 29 x 21¾in (73.5 x 55.5cm).
£150–180
$220–260 ⚒ Bon(C)

A Saville Theatre poster, 'The Jimi Hendrix Experience', by Hapshash and the Coloured Coat, 1967, 29 x 19in (73.5 x 48cm).
£450–550
$650–800 ⊞ CJP

A rock concert poster, 'Trips Festival featuring Jefferson Airplane', signed in silver by Bob Masse, 1969, 20½ x 14in (52 x 35.5cm).
£60–70
$90–100 ⚒ Bon(C)

A poster, 'Summer is a Tape Thing', by Peter Max, 1971, 36 x 24in (91.5 x 61cm).
£125–150
$180–220 ⊞ CJP

A silkscreen poster, advertising the Verve and Massive Attack concert, by Emek, signed, 1998, 30¼ x 22in (77 x 56cm).
£120–150
$175–225 ⚒ Bon(C)

An Army advertising poster, by Abram Games, restored, 1951, 40 x 25½in (101.5 x 65cm).
£1,400–1,600
$2,000–2,300 ⚒ SWAN

A Ministry of Information poster, advertising the 'Off the ration exhibition', by Frederic Henri Kay Henrion, 1951, 25 x 20in (63.5 x 51cm).
£500–600
$700–870 ⚒ SWAN

A poster, 'Che hoy y siempre', by Niko, 1983, 30 x 19¾in (76 x 50cm).
£165–200
$240–300 ⚒ VSP

A poster, 'Dada soirée', by Kurt Schwitters and Théo van Doesburg, 1923, 12in (30.5cm) square.
£6,200–7,400
$9,000–10,500 ⚒ VSP

A silkscreen poster, by Walter Dexel, 1929, 24 x 13¼in (61 x 33.5cm).
£350–420
$500–600 ⚒ BB(L)

A poster, 'Poteries' by Jean Cocteau, c1955, 24¾ x 19in (63 x 48.5cm).
£270–320
$400–450 ⚒ VSP

> Miller's is a price GUIDE not a price LIST

A poster, 'Love', by Robert Indiana, 1967, 29in (73.5cm) square.
£100–120
$145–175 ▦ CJP

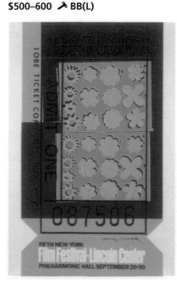

A Lincoln Center poster, advertising the fifth New York film festival, by Andy Warhol, 1967, 29¼ x 45in (74.5 x 114.5cm).
£600–720
$870–1,000 ⚒ VSP

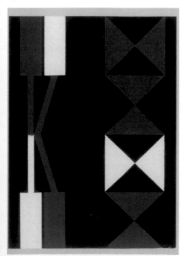

A Knoll International artwork collage, 'K' signed on reverse 'Matter', 8½ x 12in (21.5 x 30.5cm).
£550–650
$800–950 ⚒ BB(L)

▶ **A poster,** 'Nude on the Music Hall Floor', by Milton Glaser, two sheets, 1978, 48 x 36in (122 x 91.5cm).
£100–120
$145–175 ⚒ VSP

A Steendrukkerij de Jong poster,
'J', by Otto Treumann, c1957,
41 x 27¼in (104 x 69cm).
£85–100 / $125–145 ⚒ VSP

A Kröller-Müller Museum poster,
by Otto Treumann, c1957,
20in (51cm) square.
£85–100 / $125–145 ⚒ VSP

A pair of Beatles curtains, Dutch,
1960s, 40in (101.5cm) long.
£120–140 / $175–200 ⚒ S(O)

A poster, 'autographie, 100 jaar
vondelpark', by Willem H. Crouwel,
1965, 39½ x 27½in (100.5 x 70cm).
£125–150
$180–220 ⚒ VSP

An advertising poster, 'bauhaus',
by Herbert Bayer, 1968, 23½ x 16½in
(59.5 x 42cm).
£120–140
$175–200 ⚒ VSP

◀ **The Beatles,** an autographed
pull-out from *Boyfriend* magazine,
1963–64, 12 x 20in (30.5 x 51cm).
£5,200–6,200
$7,500–9,000 ⚒ S(O)

▶ **A magazine clipping,** signed
by the Beatles, 1963, 9¾ x 9¼in
(25 x 23.5cm).
£2,300–2,700
$3,300–4,000 ⚒ S(O)

A Stedelijk Museum poster,
'Zeefdrukaffiches', by Willem H. Crouwel,
1966, 37½ x 25¼in (95.5 x 64cm).
£85–100
$125–145 ⚒ VSP

An Israel Museum poster,
'De Stijl', 1977, 40 x 28¼in
(101.5 x 72cm), framed.
£100–120
$145–175 ⚒ BB(L)

◀ **The Beatles,** an
autographed copy
of *Sgt. Pepper's
Lonely Hearts Club
Band* first mono
pressing, complete
with insert, 1967.
£40,000–48,000
$58,000–70,000
⚒ S(O)

Focus on Style: Deluxe Modern

A silver bowl, by Georg Jensen, with drop-ring handles, the foot decorated with Grapevine pattern, marked, Danish, designed 1919, manufactured 1930, 14¼in (36cm) wide, 58oz.
£11,000–14,000
$16,000–20,000 ⚒ S(NY)

Three silver hors d'oeuvres utensils, by Jean Puiforcat for Cartier, French, c1925.
£825–900
$1,175–1,300 ⚒ BB(L)

◄ **A silver bowl and cover,** by Jean Puiforcat, set with lapis roundels, the cover with a carved lapis-mounted bud, stamped, French, Paris, 1940s, 7in (18cm) diam.
£3,200–3,800
$4,700–5,500 ⚒ S(O)

► **A silver-gilt and ivory chalice,** by Jean Puiforcat, with hemispherical bowl and foot, the ivory stem mounted with four silver-gilt fish, marked, French, Paris c1937, 6in (15cm) high, 14oz.
£4,200–5,000
$6,000–7,200 ⚒ S(NY)

◄ **A Wedgwood Vase,** by Keith Murray, finished in green matt glaze, 1930s, 7in (18cm) high.
£175–200
$250–300 ⊞ BET

Paris Exhibition 1925

The French attempt to reconfigure national identity after the trauma of WWI was expressed in the style and decorations of the *Exposition des Arts Décoratifs et Industriels Modernes*. The Exhibition, held in Paris in 1925, gave the name Art Deco to a luxurious style characterized by angular geometry and shiny surfaces. The resulting designs, whether for architecture, furniture or metals, have a solidity that gives them a monumental character. A natural expression of this style was in the architecture and furnishings of the great French Line transatlantic ocean liners – *Normandie and France*.

The style was unashamedly aimed at the wealthy in France and America. It carried none of the ideologies associated with progressive Modernism elsewhere in Europe. Indeed, the social character of Art Deco was rooted in its appeal to the tradition, established by Napoleon, of the *arts et métiers*. This was a system of technical and craft education that allowed for national examinations and for the creation of accepted bench marks of quality in handiwork. The system had two aims: the first was to maintain quality as an identifiably French characteristic, the second was to assure the consumer of accredited standards of production and, as a consequence, to establish notions of value beyond price point.

Ruhlmann (1879–1933, French)

In furniture design, appeal was made to the French tradition of cabinet makers. This line stretched back to before the Revolution and was associated with the opulent furnishings of the royal palaces. The most important 1920s workshops were those of Emile Jacques Ruhlmann.

Ruhlmann was a decorator in the grandest traditions, creating a complete co-ordinated interior for the connoisseur. These schemes were carried out to the very highest standard and required a prodigious organization of labour and materials to make them possible, even at the very high prices demanded by Ruhlmann. His designs for furniture are characterized by the development of the tapering leg so that the chair

or table seems to be on tip-toe. Ruhlmann's choice of timber was generally of the exotic hardwood variety – Macassar ebony or amboyna – with a rich dark colour that could be contrasted by ivory inlay.

Ruhlmann's work was a central feature of the Paris Exhibition in 1925 where his furnishings were complemented by the neo-classical paintings of Jean Dupas and the sculptures of Joseph Bernard. The style of Ruhlmann's work was extensively copied and Art Deco styling continued to be popular in France throughout the 1930s. Ruhlmann died in 1933, and although the workshops remained open they lost influence in the more socially progressive ethos of the 1930s.

A Sèvres porcelain vase, by Emile-Jacques Ruhlmann, the interior decorated in shades of brown with birds on a fruiting vine, heightened with gilding, on gilt-bronze foot, marked, French, 1927, 8¾in (22cm) high.
£4,000–4,500
$5,800–6,500 ⚒ S

A Sèvres Pâte Nouvelle porcelain vase, by Anne-Marie Fontaine, decorated with cockerels and stylized foliage applied in polychrome slip under a clear glaze, heightened in gilt with horizontal bands, marked, signed, 1933, 16¼in (41.5cm) high.
£6,000–7,000
$8,700–10,000 ⚒ B

A Lalique pale amber glass Tourbillon vase, moulded in high relief with spiralling shapes, engraved mark, French, c1926, 8in (20.5cm) high.
£8,500–10,000
$12,500–14,500 ⚒ B

A Lalique Serpent glass vase, 1930s, 10in (25.5cm) high.
£5,500–6,500
$8,000–9,000 ⚒ CNY

A Lalique Bacchantes opalescent glass vase, moulded with nude maidens, moulded mark, 1930s, 9¾in (25cm) high.
£12,000–14,000
$17,500–20,000 ⚒ BB(L)

◄ A Lalique Languedoc frosted glass vase, 1930s.
£6,000–7,000
$8,700–10,000 ↗ CNY

► A Lalique Grignon frosted glass vase, moulded with fan motifs, minor damage, stencilled mark, 1932–45, 7in (18cm) high.
£400–480
$580–700 ↗ S(O)

A Lalique Danaides glass vase, moulded with a frieze of nudes pouring water, minor damage, stencilled mark, 1930s, 7¼in (18.5cm) high.
£1,700–2,000
$2,500–3,000 ↗ S(O)

A Lalique Penthièvre glass vase, stencilled mark, 1930s, 10in (25.5cm) high.
£5,000–6,000
$7,250–8,750 ↗ Bon

A Lalique Perruches frosted glass vase, on a bronze stand, 1930s, 10½in (26.5cm) high.
£3,000–4,000
$4,500–5,800 ↗ CNY

A Lalique moulded and frosted glass Cactus table, inscribed mark, 1947, 60in (1525cm) diam.
£18,500–22,000
$27,000–32,000 ↗ S(NY)

Market update

The values of Deluxe Modern place it at the very top of the market. This is hardly surprising when one considers the quality of materials and craftsmanship that are associated with the best in this category. Furthermore, the best pieces of Art Deco have the great advantage of looking expensive, even from a distance.

The furniture from the Ruhlmann workshops is probably the most expensive 20th-century furniture of all. The market for Art Deco is well established among collectors. Indeed, the appreciation of the quality and refinement of 1920s and 1930s design dates back to the early 1970s.

The original Art Deco style was quickly copied, in less expensive form, and pieces such as dining room suites, made by commercial furniture manufacturers, are more affordable.

◄ A pair of Ours Polaire armchairs, by Jean Royère, French, 1951.
£30,000–36,000
$43,000–53,000 ↗ S(P)

Focus on Style: Functionalist Modern

The logic of a design aesthetic based on machine production, materials and a belief in the axiomatic 'form follows function' has created one of the most powerful and important strands in the evolution of Modernism during the 20th century. This logic is associated, in its origins, with the Bauhaus School in Germany and is usually presented as a rationally-driven programme of design solutions to specific social and material problems. This has helped to establish the 20th-century creative, especially in the figure of the architect, as an archetype of the social engineer as technician.

An orange-lacquered bentwood and plywood armchair, designed by Josef Hoffman or Adolf Schneck, made by Thonet-Mundus AG, remains of Thonet paper label, 1925.
£1,200–1,400
$1,750–2,000 ↗ DORO

A tubular metal and fabric armchair, by Ludwig Mies van der Rohe for Thonet, model No. MR20, 1927.
£7,250–8,500
$10,500–12,500 ↗ BB(L)

◀ **A chromium-plated tubular steel and wood table,** by Marcel Breuer for Thonet, with orange-painted top, designed 1927, manufactured 1930, 29½in (75cm) square.
£1,750–2,000
$2,500–3,000 ↗ DORO

▶ **A tubular steel Wassilly chair,** designed by Marcel Breuer for Habitat, c1960.
£110–125
$160–180 ⊞ MARK

The Bauhaus (established 1919)

The Bauhaus School was established as an evolution of the German werkbund system of artistic and design education. The founder of the School was the architect Walter Gropius and its principal aim was to train artists and designers for industrial production. The School was established in Weimar and Gropius quickly recruited a full complement of teaching staff. Among the names associated with the School are those of Mies van der Rohe, Marcel Breuer, Paul Klee, Johannes Itten and Wilhelm Wagenfield.

The School became a hot-house of design education and was identified by conservatives as dangerously progressive. The School moved to Dessau and was eventually forced to close by the Nazi authorities. Its closure and the emigration of the main protagonists has become an important part of the cultural history of Modernism in the 20th century. The Bauhaus refugees were enthusiastically welcomed in Britain and in the USA. The widespread use of machine production and the size of the American market offered much greater opportunities for the more established protagonists such as Gropius, Breuer and Rohe. The refugees arrived at the precise moment when American cultural interests had begun a project to move the centre of cultural production from Europe to New York.

Barcelona Exhibition 1929

The design logic of the Bauhaus may be read as a pragmatic response to the material shortages and economic uncertainties of post-war Germany. The resulting minimalist interior has become a key element in Modernism and is expressed by the axiomatic 'less is more'. The style was used in the German Pavilion at the International Exhibition in Barcelona in 1929. The minimal interior of marble, glass and steel created an architecture that used light as a defining element. The furnishings for the house included the Barcelona chair designed by Mies van der Rohe (see p69). The chair is still in production and has become the most important signifier of rationalist, functionalist, modern.

A set of six chromed tubular steel and Rexine SP9 dining chairs, by Rowland Wilton-Cox for PEL, stamped brass labels, 1932–34.
£700–800
$1,000–1,150 ✎ P(Ba)

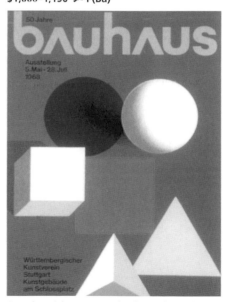

An advertising poster, 'bauhaus', by Herbert Bayer, 1968, 23½ x 16½in (59.5 x 42cm).
£120–140
$175–200 ✎ VSP

A Schott & Gen Jenaer Glassworks glass teapot with inserts, by Wilhelm Wagenfeld, 1932, 5½in (14cm) high.
£160–200
$230–300 ✎ BB(L)

A painted softwood kitchen cabinet, by Margarete Schütte Lihotzky and Ferdinand Kramer, the fall-front opening to reveal eight pull-out compartments, 1930, 38¼in (97cm) wide.
£1,750–2,100
$2,600–3,000 ✎ BB(L)

Market update

The Functionalist tradition is accepted as the defining narrative of 20th-century design and Modernism. Its origins in the architectural avant-garde and the Bauhaus School in Germany ensure that the products of first-period Modernism command the highest prices for 20th-century pieces.

The metal furniture associated with this tradition is only now receiving the recognition it deserves. The market has been slow to appreciate the qualities of mass-produced objects, especially those in new materials. The relative rarity of these first-period objects is only now becoming clear and prices are rising as a result. Later examples of the classic designs remain in production and are readily available, making them much more affordable.

In identifying the value of modern design in the 1930s, great store is set by provenance. An association with a particular individual, or house, will increase the desirability, and hence the value, of a piece.

Focus on Style: Plywood Modern

The development of plywood laminates made the bending and moulding of timber a practical possibility. Furniture designers and architects were quick to adopt the material in the hope that it would make machine-produced mass production furniture a possibility. Experiments with plywood began in the 1920s and continued throughout the 1930s, '40s and '50s. The use of organic materials also allowed for the development of a modern style that was more acceptable to standard European taste than the machine aesthetic of tubular metal furniture. The results were able to embrace the Modernist demands of practicality and mass production and also to establish a continuity with the past. The results

have been identified as humanist rationalist and are certainly less austere than machine aesthetic or rationalist-driven designs of the period.

This second organic strand in the Functionalist tradition of modern design offers an interesting counterpoint to the austere leather and chrome styling of the Bauhaus. The designs of Aalto, Isokon and other pioneers are both useful and beautiful and recognized as such, with the most successful remaining in production.

The experimental structure of some bentwood and moulded furniture makes it fragile and unsuitable for domestic use, but the tried-and-tested designs remain practical and aesthetically pleasing.

◀ **A laminated wood chair,** by Gerald Summers for Makers of Simple Furniture, c1935.
£1,800–2,000
$2,600–3,000 ⚒ S

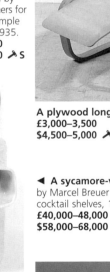

A plywood long chair, by Marcel Breuer for Isokon, 1936.
£3,000–3,500
$4,500–5,000 ⚒ RBB

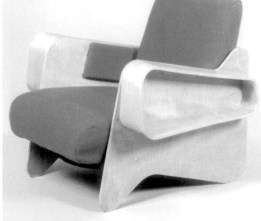

◀ **A sycamore-veneered plywood prototype armchair,** by Marcel Breuer for Isokon, the armrests with integral cocktail shelves, 1935.
£40,000–48,000
$58,000–68,000 ⚒ S

Isokon (established 1931)

The appeal to tradition, implicit in the use of timber, made plywood furniture an acceptable form of Modernism for the British market. This was recognized by Jack Pritchard who established Isokon. Isokon was an important conduit for the introduction of Continental design ideas into Britain. Pritchard was instrumental in welcoming Marcel Breuer to Britain and in manufacturing his bent plywood lounger. This was a progression from the aluminium lounger designed while Breuer was at the Bauhaus.

A plywood nesting table, by Marcel Breuer for Isokon, c1938, 24in (61cm) wide.
£700–850
$1,000–1,250 ⚒ BB(L)

Gerald Summers

Gerald Summers established his workshops under the title Makers of Simple Furniture. During the 1930s he produced a series of designs – mostly tables and chairs – which made a visible virtue of the fact that sheets of plywood could be bent, or folded, into three-dimensional shapes. The results were aimed at sophisticated city dwellers in London and were scaled for the smaller rooms and spaces of Modernist apartments.

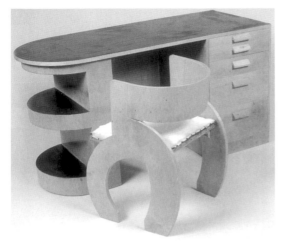

A moulded birch plywood LCW chair, by Charles and Ray Eames for Evans Products Co, distributed by Herman Miller, American, with original wide mount, and Evans label.
£750–900
$1,100–1,300 ➤ TREA

◀ **A birch-veneered plywood desk and chair,** by Gerald Summers for Makers of Simple Furniture, the desk with original linoleum top, 1936, desk 53¼in (135.5cm) wide.
£9,500–11,500
$13,800–16,800 ➤ DORO

A moulded plywood high-back chair, designed by Gerald Summers for makers of Simple Furniture, c1938.
£4,000–5,000
$5,800–7,200 ➤ P(Ba)

A birch-veneered pressure-formed plywood Paimio armchair, by Alvar Aalto for Artek, Finnish, some wear, 1945–55.
£2,800–3,300
$4,000–4,800 ➤ BUK

Market update

This second, organic strand, in the Functionalist tradition of Modern design makes for an interesting counterpoint to the austere leather and chrome styling of the Bauhaus. The designs of Aalto, Isokon and other pioneers are both useful and beautiful and recognized as such.

Aalto furniture, manufactured by Artek and Finmar, survives in relatively large quantities. Some pieces, like the stacking stool (see p66), may be found inexpensively. The armchairs and standing furniture will cost more. A good first-period example of the Paimio chair will be in the region of £3,000–3,500 ($4,500–5,000).

Gerald Summers' furniture is much rarer and the values of his pieces are considerably higher since they are judged to have been at the leading edge of experiment, and design during the 1930s.

The experimental structure of some bentwood and moulded furniture makes it fragile and unsuitable for domestic use. The tried-and-tested designs remain practical and aesthetically pleasing and the most successful designs remain in production.

Focus on Style: Big Modern

The enthusiastic embracing of industrial production and scientific management, required to serve the people and geography of the USA, has helped the American economy grow to unchallenged status. The productive capacity of the American economy was so huge that, by the 1920s, American manufacturers were searching for new export markets in post-war Europe and the British Empire. The progressive and democratic social policies of the 20th century made free trade and the end of 19th-century-style imperialism inevitable. The two great European wars of the 20th century can be explained, in part at least, as part of this process. The evolution of American Modern towards a global style associated with corporate interests and mass consumerism begins in the 1920s and 1930s.

The development of a mass market is one of the foundations of American consumer society. The secondary development of the mass media – films and magazines especially – during the 1930s enabled manufacturers to promote their products as up-to-date. The American design tradition is, in consequence, rooted in mass production, machine aesthetics and consumption. These are very different from the roots of the European design movement. The rhetoric of Modernism refers endlessly to speed, or time-and-motion, as a defining characteristic of industrial society. This finds expression in the axiomatic 'time is money' and in the streamlined look of American industrial products of the 1930s. The pioneers of the streamlined look were Raymond Loewy, Henry Dreyfus and Walter Dorwin Teague. They produced a process of styling that could be applied as equally successfully to a steam engine as to a paper clip. The range of streamlined products produced in America is enormous. The monumentality of many of the resulting products, from fridges to trailers, gives a powerful impression of scale. American Modern is Big Modern.

◀ **A wooden storage unit,** by George Nelson for Herman Miller, comprising a slatted bench, an open bookshelf and a bookshelf with door, American, c1947, bench 92½in (235cm) wide.
£2,300–2,700
$3,300–4,000 ⚒ BB(L)

A rosewood and rosewood-veneered chest, by George Nelson for Herman Miller, with aluminium and plastic-coated iron handles, American, c1954.
£2,500–3,000
$3,500–5,800 ⚒ BB(L)

◀ **An ebonized birch and glass coffee table,** by Isamu Noguchi for Herman Miller, model No. IN-50, 50¼in American, (127.5cm) wide.
£1,600–2,000
$2,300–3,000
⚒ BB(L)

A Masonite, steel, moulded plywood and zinc ESU 420-N storage unit, by Charles and Ray Eames for Herman Miller, American, c1963, 47in (119.5cm) wide.
£11,500–13,500
$16,500–19,500 ⚒ BB(L)

New York World's Fair 1939

The New York World's Fair was the last of its kind before WWII. The design of the fair with its saucer and obelisk has become synonymous with mid-century American Modern. The Fair attempted to create a vision of the future – and of the sights, sounds and experiences of that future. The advent of WWII transformed the immediate outlook but also powered the American economy to new levels of output. This output sustained the American economy in growth throughout the 1940s and 1950s.

The contrast between American affluence and European austerity is engraved in the popular mythology of the American soldier with cigarettes, chewing gum and nylons. Post-war Europe lay in ruins and the primary economic activity was that of reconstruction rather than consumption. Throughout the 1950s America continued to develop its model of consumer society. This model of consumption required the careful nurturing of desire rather than need as the primary instinct before purchase. This version of the consumer society has been described as the 'affluent society'. The process of design is transformed by this model into a combination of both improvement and styling. The resulting systems have planned obsolescence built into them.

◄ **An Eye clock,** by George Nelson for Howard Miller Clock Co, in brass, wood and painted metal, retains paper label and impressed Howard Miller, American, c1954, 30in (76cm) wide.
£8,000–9,500
$11,750–14,000 ↗ BBL

Market update

In the USA the practice of design has always been accepted as part of the larger industrial process that serves the consumer society. Successful design is therefore distinguished by its commercial success and by its large-scale manufacture.

The idea that design can be an esoteric, detached and intellectual activity, rather than a practical one, is essentially European. The commercial pragmatism of American design and manufacturing place it at the centre of the emerging market in 20th-century design, especially in the 1930s, when industrial mass production began to be applied to furniture manufacture. It became even more evident after WWII when new materials and the manufacturing capacity and marketing skills of Herman Miller and Knoll gave American designers a worldwide market.

The expansive characteristics of American style capitalism have under-written the production of a huge volume of furniture and design in the 20th century, a volume that has fuelled the emerging collectors' market. Prices in general reflect this availability and abundance.

A rosewood-veneered plywood Lounge Chair and Ottoman, by Charles and Ray Eames, with leather upholstery, American, 1956.
£1,500–1,800
$2,200–2,600 ↗ S(O)

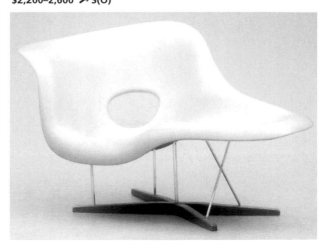

► **A metal-framed La Chaise easy chair,** by Charles and Ray Eames for Vitra, with moulded fibreglass shell, American.
£2,000–2,400
$3,000–3,500 ↗ BUK

Focus on Style: Welfare Modern

The economic legacies of the 1930s and of WWII accelerated the drive to create the political and social structures of welfare provision. In Europe, the progressive ideas of the Modern Movement architects were put to the service of reconstruction and to the articulation of a new public space.

The 1951 Festival of Britain was conceived as a tonic to the nation and set out to be a hybrid of celebration and exhibition, trade fair and cultural event. The varied functions of the Festival were given expression in the architecture of the South Bank site in London. The Exhibition pavilions were linked by a series of promenade spaces that spoke of fun fairs, markets and the seaside.

The graphic design of the Festival abandoned the rigid sans serif typefaces associated with 1930s machine Modernism and replaced them with a diversity of typographic elements taken from the play-bills, notices and alphabets of early industrial Britain. Their use in exaggerated italic form and in blow-up scale helped to define the graphic tone of the Festival. Beyond the South Bank the design of housing, hospitals, schools and their equipment provided a vivid example of Modernism, design, architecture and mass production in the service of a progressive political agenda.

The Festival architects worked in collaboration with industrial, graphic and exhibition designers to present the narratives set out in the Festival project. The widespread use of artists to decorate and embellish the public spaces of the exhibition was enthusiastically taken up in cities and towns around the country. The escape of art from the gallery context and its values had been an objective of the artistic avant-garde since the beginning of the century. The context of reconstruction provided its most promising chance of realization.

Across Europe modern design and architecture were pressed into serving the twin objectives of reconstruction and social progress. The result was the emergence of a distinctive European variant of modern design, its ethos driven by a concern for materials, economy and scale. 1950s European modern design appears surprisingly small scale and modest. This is certainly true of the contrast between, say, the scale of American and European cars during the period. The European distaste for over-scaled or expansionist modern was provoked by the memory of the excessive design statements of the regimes that had led Europe into war.

The post-war period's austerity is reflected in the choice and use of materials, and also in the utilitarian styling of many of its products. The revival of fantasy as an element in design, began as austerity came to an end in the mid 1950s. This was a reaction to the intellectual high-mindedness of the modern tradition in Europe. It was also an indication of the excitement offered by the rediscovery of popular arts and vernacular styles.

A wooden side chair, by Jean Prouvé, c1950.
£2,000–2,400
$3,000–3,500 ⚘ BB(L)

A child's wooden chair, by Kit Nicholson for the Pioneer Health Centre, c1935.
£400–480
$580–700 ⚘ BB(L)

A laminated wood occasional table, by Gerald Summers for Makers of Simple Furniture, c1934, 20in (51cm) high.
£1,200–1,400
$1,750–2,000 ⚒ BB(L)

A birch-veneered two-tier table, No. 70, 1930s, 21¾in (55.5cm) high.
£1,800–2,200
$2,600–3,200 ⚒ S

Market update

The significance of post-WWII European design is linked to its association with the political and social projects of reconstruction. This ideological connection is part of what defines Modernism in the 20th century. This belief in the political and social dimension of objects is unfashionable at present, at least within the limits of consumer society.

The utilitarian nature of much of this design and the failure, in political terms, of the planned State, undermine the status of much of this design. The market is simply not very good at locating value through context rather than materials and workmanship. The project of contextualising European Modernism and its products is not so well advanced as that to locate American products at the centre of 20th century life, a project undertaken from the 1930s onwards by the museum establishment in the USA. Consequently, European Modernism appears, in its scale and localized objectives, as more modest than its American counterparts. Accordingly, with the exception of the most famous names, prices are realistic.

A wooden stacking stool, by Alvar Aalto for Artek, model No. 60, Finnish, 1930–33.
£1,000–1,200
$1,500–1,750 ⚒ BB(L)

▶ **An Army advertising poster,** by Abram Games, restored, 1951, 40 x 25½in (101.5 x 65cm).
£1,400–1,600
$2,000–2,300 ⚒ SWAN

◀ **A white-painted metal rod rocking chair,** by Ernest Race for Race Furniture, with mahogany armrests, 1948.
£350–400
$500–580 ⚒ S

A pair of aluminium BA chairs, by Ernest Race, 1945.
£600–700
$870–1,000 ⚒ BB(L)

Focus on Style: Pop Modern

The arrival of television as the defining media of cultural exchange, during the 1950s, introduced British consumers to American popular culture in ever increasing quantities. The emerging youth culture of the late 1950s appropriated the style and values of American popular culture to service its requirement for specific consumer goods.

The Pop sensibility to popular culture was also an expression of the impatience, among young Britons, with the entrenched values of the establishment. The self-conscious excitement in the ephemeral abundance of consumer society helped define the tone of swinging London. The austere social progress of the 1950s was turned into a more hedonistic and permissive project.

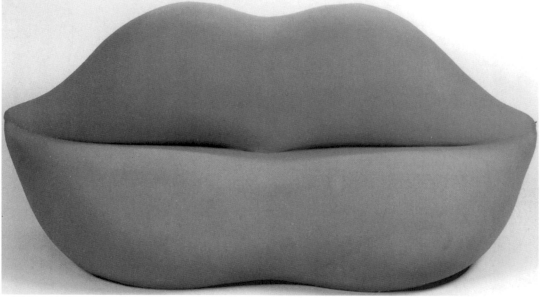

A polyurethane foam Marilyn sofa, by Studio 65 for Gufram, Turin, 1972.
£3,200–3,700
$4,700–5,400 🔨 **DORO**

Pop Art

Pop Art developed in Britain and America at the end of the 1950s and throughout the 1960s. It was marked by the use, in painting and design, of a framework of cultural references that extended beyond the traditional limits of fine art and good taste. Artists also began to explore the possibilities of industrial methods in cultural production – embracing the use of printing techniques associated with the mass media for example. The dynamic energy of Pop Art found another outlet, beyond the fine arts, in the new art direction of fashion magazines and in the increased prominence of designer names.

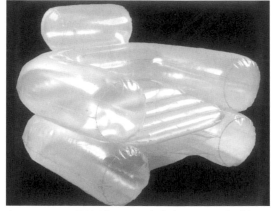

A transparent PVC Blow Armchair, by Donato d'Urbino, Paolo Lomazzi and Jonathon De Pas for Zanotta, Italian, 1967.
£700–850
$1,000–1,250 🔨 **DORO**

◀ **A chromed-steel Papegojan armchair,** by Ib Arberg for Rocksjöverken, with black lacquered metal support and upholstered in beige corduroy, Swedish, c1970, 63¾in (162cm) high.
£650–720
$950–1,000 🔨 **BUK**

▶ **A red fibreglass garden Egg chair,** by Peter Ghyczy for Reuter Product, with orange fabric interior, designed 1968.
£250–300
$360–440 ⊞ **W**

New Domestic Landscape

Modern design embraced the new materials and manufacturing processes, plastic chief among them, to create products that were radical in their use of materials, forms and in their social functions. In Italy, architects and designers helped to define a new domestic landscape. The products, driven by ideas expressed in vocabulary of articulate political radicalism, were experimental more than practical. The stagnation of the social-democratic project in much of Europe during the 1970s led to a questioning of the political ambitions appropriate to the design activity.

The hedonism and fun expressed in the late Pop designs of the Memphis design group (1981) are a perfect expression of post-Modern design disengaging from the political agenda that had been a characteristic of European Modern design up to that point. They aspire to be anti-Modern without being reactionary or conservative.

A leather chair, in the shape of a boxing glove, 1960s.
£450–500
$650–720 ⊞ MARK

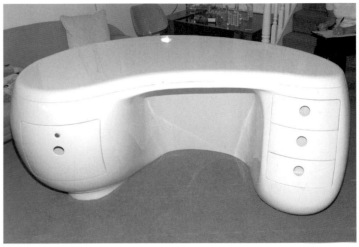

A fibreglass Boomerang desk, by Maurice Calka, manufactured by Leleu Deshay, c1970, 69in (175.5cm) wide.
£9,500–10,500
$13,800–15,250 ⊞ MARK

This is Tomorrow Exhibition 1956

The exhibition at the Whitechapel gallery was presented as an attempt to establish a pluralistic set of design references. The exhibition was work by artists, architects and designers associated with the Independent Group – a cultural group that met at the Institute of Contemporary Art to discuss the changing relations between artist and society. The presentation of exhibits, assembled from parts drawn from a wide and varied range of sources, emphasized the ephemeral quality of contemporary design and cultural production. This perception, radical in the late 1950s, became a commonplace of the 1960s.

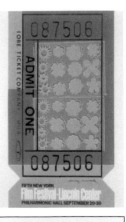

▶ **A Lincoln Center poster,** advertising the fifth New York film festival, by Andy Warhol, 1967, 29¼ x 45in (74.5 x 114.5cm).
£600–720
$870–1,000 ⚒ VSP

A Wave fabric panel, by Verner Panton for Mira-X, 1974, 47 x 59in (119.5 x 150cm).
£750–850
$1,100–1,250 ⊞ MARK

Market update

This form of Modernism is distinguished by its throwaway, fashionable nature, kitsch styling and identification with youth culture. It is not surprising that Pop has been the entry point into the market for collectors of 20th-century design. Prices and values for most Pop objects are quite modest – the rejection of established taste in favour of Pop makes the project hard to sustain and collectors simply grow out of it. In printmaking, a field not included in this book, Pop was distinguished by the development of its own style associated with photographic methods of mechanical reproduction. Screen printing, introduced into Britain during the 1950s and '60s, was the choice for Pop artists. Numbered prints by artists from the 1960s may still be found at under £1,000 ($1,500). Perhaps only those by Andy Warhol are routinely beyond this level.

Focus on Style: Post-Modern

A crisis of Modernism became evident during the 1970s. It manifested itself in different ways in response to different cultural traditions. The term post-Modernism is a catch-all that describes the eclectic styling and cultural references of design during the 1980s.

The appeal of post-Modernism has its origins in the growing awareness of the limits set on modern design by its reliance on Functionalism. Politically, the social-democratic project which had structured post-war European planning had become stagnant. The response, in European design, was to disengage design from the political agendas that had underpinned the development of Modernism throughout the 20th century. In America, the crisis was described in relation to a stifling corporate conservatism in design. The conformist rhetoric of modern design gave way to a playful and eclectic use of materials and styles.

A characteristic of post-Modern design is that the assembly of diverse elements in a design draws attention to the role of designer. The designer transparency of Modernist design, where the designer aspired to the anonymity of technical assistant, was replaced by a self-conscious promotion of the designer as life-style consultant and brand.

Post-Modernism in design was identified by reference to a group of individual star designers and to their products as limited edition or specially designed. The popular understanding of the term 'design' changed so that it became synonymous with a self-conscious styling that distinguished it from the purely functional.

The decorative character of post-Modernism is established by the iconic aspirations of much post-Modern design. The iconic signature pieces were usually arranged so that they became a gallery of life-style signifiers rather than functionalist or utilitarian objects. The rejection of any classical notion of unity, or integration in the whole, was further evidence of a widespread suspicion of established notions of good taste, whether modern or otherwise.

The iconoclastic aspirations of post-Modern design have tended to place it at the margins of mainstream consumer culture. The products of such design are often limited editions and, although using industrial materials, are assembled in conditions associated with the organization of craft workshops rather than factories. The significations of such objects reflect well on their owners who aspire to be bohemian, radical and successful.

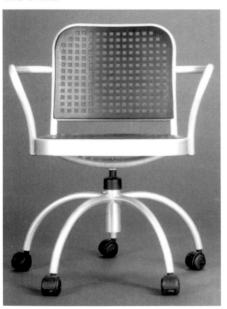

A Silver chair, by Vico Magistretti, for de Padova, Italian, 1989.
£95–110
$140–150 ✤ BB(L)

A polyester cast and moulded Samsone table, by Gaetano Pesce for Cassina, 1980, 63in (160cm) wide.
£7,000–8,000
$10,000–11,500 ✤ Bon

▶ **A steel mesh How High the Moon armchair,** by Shiro Kuramata for Vitra, Japanese, 1986.
£4,500–5,500
$6,500–8,000 ✤ DORO

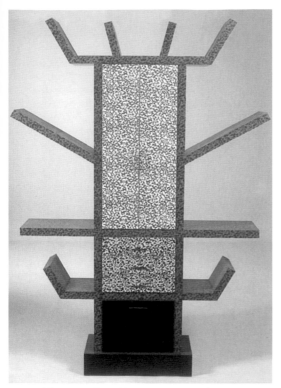

A Casablanca sideboard by Ettore Sottsass for Memphis, decorated with an Abet-Print plastic laminate printed with Sottsass' Bacterio pattern, with plastic label, Italian, 1981, 59½in (151cm) wide.
£3,000–3,500
$4,500–5,000 ✗ DORO

A welded mild steel Paris chair, by André Dubreuil, 1998.
£1,800–2,200
$2,600–3,200 ✗ S(O)

◀ **A polished sheet steel Well Tempered chair,** by Ron Arad for Vitra, 1986–93.
£7,500–9,000
$11,000–13,000 ✗ DORO

Market update

The post-Modern aesthetic was a designer- and architect-led response to the crisis of Modernism during the 1970s. The project was marked by the disengagement of Modernists from the political objectives traditionally associated with the broader Modernist project. The result was a form of Modernism that was both populist in styling, like Pop, but more substantial and refined in its execution. This allowed a generation of designers to become celebrities in their own right and to market their products as limited edition collectors' pieces.

The prices associated with these kinds of objects are artificially high and reflect the bogus economics of limited-edition marketing. The epitome of this is Ron Arad's big easy chair, a hugely expensive limited edition object – but every sale has at least one!

The idea of the 'cult' object, a fashionable accessory, is at the heart of post-Modern consumption. It is probably too early to say whether these sorts of objects will ever be collected beyond the limited framework of their original conception.

Focus on Style: Eclectic Modern

By the end of the 20th century, Modernism in design had been an identifiable phenomenon for most of the century. The most successful and iconic products had remained in production since their first creation and there was more Modernist design in the year 2000 than in the heyday of international, Functionalist-style Modernism. In such circumstances it is difficult to recall that Modernism, by its appeal to the radical and new, is usually located at the margins of mainstream taste.

Planet design was a much smaller place in the 1950s and '60s. The provision of art education was more limited and the range of products much smaller. The iconic status of, say, the Eames Lounge Chair and Ottoman was assured from the first. It is sustained by its continuing production and by its ubiquity in art-directed commercials and home-style journalism. The Eames chairs form a very significant part of the story of this book. It is testimony to the cultural significance that we accord the Modernist project and its objects, that we have witnessed the emergence of a market where this significance is organized in a collector's value system. It is this system that this book attempts to describe.

Of course, the creation of a pantheon of design classics is also a reflection of the mythologies that surround and contextualize each of these objects. Some of these objects are located in a specifically 20th century tradition, others make appeal to longer-established craft traditions. The idea of a monolithic, or single, idea of design has given way to an understanding of different Modernisms.

The cultural contexts of 20th century design are more varied than those of design in the previous centuries. Before the Industrial Revolution the concentration of consumptive power, in design terms, was held entirely within the aristocracy. The Industrial Revolution transferred some of that power to the emerging middle, or professional class. The 20th century has seen, through progressive politics and political upheaval, the creation of a globalized mass market in products, services and ideas. It is not surprising that modern design should be used as a powerful symbol of this emancipatory project and that it should be more widely recognized by collectors.

The enormous ambition of the Modernist project, in its late 20th century manifestation, is reflected in the contemporary abundance of material goods. The divergence of styles and the eclecticism of its terms of reference give contemporary Modernism an eclectic quality that distinguish it from its overtly programmatic antecedents. The narrative of modern design and the trajectory of its ideas is so appealing that the objects associated with that narrative have become part of our shared cultural heritage.

Eclectic modern is a core theme of this book and represents the rejection of an idea of Modernism as a single, unified or monolithic project. Instead, we construct our own version of Modernism out of the available resources. Most of these are material, but some are related to the ideas, places and people that shaped the original manifestations of the project.

A stained beech bentwood and cane rocking chair, in the style of Antonio Volpe, Italian, c1910.
£5,250–6,250
$7,500–8,750 ↗ S(NY)

A DAR chair, by Charles and Ray Eames for Herman Miller, 1951.
£260–300
$380–440 ↗ BB(L)

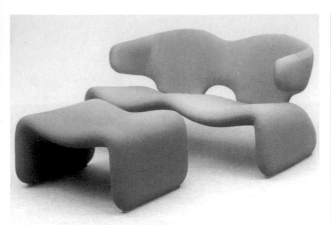

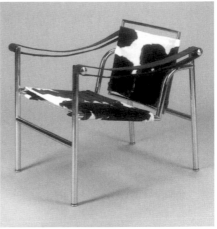

A steel-framed Djinn sofa and footstool, by Oliver Mourgue for Airborne, covered in nylon jersey, colour faded, c1960.
£575–650
$850–950 ✦ BUK
The Djinn series can be seen in the interior of Stanley Kubrick's film *2001: A Space Odyssey*.

A metal-framed Basculant chair, by Le Corbusier, Charlotte Perriand and Pierre Jeanneret for Cassina, model No. B301, c1960.
£950–1,150
$1,400–1,700 ✦ BB(L)

A beech and deal Red/Blue chair, by Gerrit Rietveld, designed 1918, manufactured 1919.
£30,000–35,000
$43,000–50,000 ✦ S(NY)

An Art Deco leather-upholstered club chair, French, early 20thC.
£600–700
$870–1,000 ✦ NOA

An enamelled tubular-steel and fabric Wassily chair, designed by Marcel Breuer for Thonet, model No. B3, c1928.
£12,500–15,000
$18,000–22,000 ✦ S(NY)

A metal-framed Barcelona Chair, by Ludwig Mies van der Rohe, model No. MR90, c1931.
£60,000–80,000
$87,000–115,000 ✦ C(Am)

Focus on Designers: Sir Ambrose Heal

The Heal family store had its beginnings in mattress and bed manufacturing. The store in London's Tottenham Court Road also has workshops and the business developed as suppliers to Britain's 19th-century middle class. The firm diversified into producing other types of furniture such as wardrobes and sideboards. Early catalogues show that the furniture was of traditional Victorian design and was available in a variety of timbers and finishes. The roots of Heal's origins are firmly in trade and this has tended to obscure their contribution to modern design in Britain during the 20th century.

Ambrose Heal was a furniture designer, retailer and design establishment figure. As a young man he came into contact with William Morris and the design reform movement at the end of the 19th century. Heal's trade background distinguished him from other Morris acolytes who were generally from an intellectual or aesthetic background. The reform movement was an attempt to define an English vernacular style that could claim simplicity and authenticity. His objective was to break decisively from the prevailing over-decoration and superficial complexity of much high Victorian design.

Ambrose Heal began to design furniture in the 1890s and launched a series of designs aimed at the new Garden suburbs. The resulting pieces, with their simple construction, plain finishes and modest proportions were an austere counterpart to the prevailing taste. The staff at Heal's referred to the pieces as prison furniture. Heal's work as a designer drew on traditions of design and craftsmanship that owed much to the past. However, his desire for authenticity, honesty and other Arts and Crafts values anticipate the doctrines of fitness for purpose associated with high Modernism.

Heal was a founding member of the Design and Industries Association and developed his store into a showcase for the best of British and international Modern design during the 1920s and '30s. He was among the first to discover Scandinavian Modernism and to present it to the London public. Heal became an influential figure in design circles along with Gordon Russell and Frank Pick. The creation of the Mansard Gallery on the top floor of the store established a showcase for artists and craftspeople working in Britain. The presentation of textiles, posters and pottery extended the scope of Heal's activities beyond furniture. They became furnishers to Betjeman's metroland – and favoured a comfy, timber-framed Modernism.

During the 1950s and '60s Heal's established a reputation for presenting the best in contemporary design. They became champions of Anglo-Scandinavian Modernism and of bright, modern textile designs. In the relatively conservative world of furniture manufacturing and retailing Heal's enjoyed a reputation as innovative and modern and of having a sure taste.

By the 1970s Heal's had begun to face competition – notably Terrence Conran's Habitat store. The more difficult trading conditions required more capital and the family retreated from the front line of management. The firm continues to enjoy a reputation for quality and for distinctive modern design.

◀ **An Art Nouveau coffee table,** by Heal's, with undershelf, on six triangular-section legs, c1900, 28½in (72cm) wide.
£400–500
$580–720 ↗ P

An Art Deco dining room suite, by Heal's, comprising table, four single chairs, two carvers and a sideboard, c1930, table 60¼in (153cm) wide.
£2,600–3,000
$3,800–4,400 ↗ B(B)

◀ **A limed-oak part dining room suite,** by Heal's, London, comprising eight dining chairs, a sideboard and side table, early 20thC, side table 36in (91.5cm) wide.
£2,300–2,750
$3,350–4,000 ↗ S(S)

A limed-oak wardrobe, by Heal's, with central mirrored door flanked by panelled doors enclosing hanging space and drawers, c1930, 72½in (184cm) wide.
£480–520
$700–750 🔨 P

Market update

Heal's furnishings are surprisingly difficult to find at auction. The later Arts and Crafts pieces by Russell, Gimson and the Barnsleys attract more attention for their rejection of machinery in favour of handiwork. The machine powered and commercial workshops of Heal's have tended to marginalize their furniture in relation to the narrative of the Arts and Crafts movement in Britain. It is possible that the Heal's market, based as it was on the suburban expansion of London, has none of the aristocratic appeal that collectors find so appealing. Whatever, Heal's furniture should not be underestimated. It is often of superb quality and its scale and colour make it suitable for modern interiors. The very best pieces stand comparison with anything produced by the Arts and Crafts movement.

When pieces appear at auction private collectors often buy them. Prices vary with bedroom suits from the 1930s selling in the £1,000–1,500 ($1,500–2,000) range. Dining furniture is more expensive, with sets of chairs at about £1,000 ($1,500) for four and refectory tables at £2,500–3,000 ($3,500–4,500). Look for the ivory label in the drawer marked Heals. During the 1950s and '60s the firm was at the forefront of producing interesting textile designs. These are not yet too expensive and lengths may be bought for £100 ($145) or less.

A limed-oak refectory dining table, with twin-barrel turned end supports, 1950s, 78in (198cm) wide, and six limed-oak dining chairs.

Table	£2,700–3,000 / $4,000–4,500	
Chairs	£2,500–2,800 / $3,500–4,000	🔨 WW

An oak writing desk, by Ambrose Heal for Heal's, with fall flaps at each end, enclosing six file trays, printed label, 60in (152cm) wide.
£8,000–10,000
$11,500–14,500 🔨 C

An oak cabinet, by Ambrose Heal for Heal & Sons, manufacturer's label, 44in (113cm) wide.
£2,500–3,000
$3,500–4,500 🔨 C

◀ An Arts and Crafts oak chest, attributed to Heal's, the cupboard doors with fielded chestnut panels, over three long drawers.
£1,500–1,800
$2,200–2,600 🔨 P

Focus on Designers: Alvar Aalto

The Finnish architect and designer Alvar Aalto is one of the most significant figures in 20th-century design. Aalto was the designer of the Finnish pavilions at the Paris Exhibition in 1937 and of the New York World's Fair in 1939. He was instrumental in introducing the concept and styling of Scandinavian Modern to a wider, international audience.

Aalto trained as an architect in Finland. His architecture and design work managed to combine the material integrity of Arts and Crafts, the flow of Art Nouveau and the minimalist rigour of Modernism. During the 1920s Aalto received an important architectural commission – for a sanatorium at Paimio, Finland. The unified interior that Aalto preferred, and was reflected in this project, gave him the opportunity to begin designing furniture. He began to experiment with the techniques of laminating and bending wood. He was able to work in collaboration with Otto Korhonen to perfect the process for the manufacture of his designs. The chair design numbers 31 and 41 were immediately recognized as important stages in the evolution of Functionalist Modernism towards a softer, more humane, aesthetic.

In 1935 Aalto established the Artek firm to manufacture and retail his furniture designs, along with glassware and lighting. The commercial manufacture of his designs has continued to this day. His wife Aino was a partner in the venture together with a manufacturing expert and a public relations specialist. The range of talents assembled by Aalto to support Artek reveal his understanding of the requirements of modern business. They opened the Helsinki shop in 1936.

Aalto's furniture designs could be economically manufactured and transported. His designs became associated with the furnishings of the Finnish educational establishments and in the furnishings of healthcare environments. The use of timber made for a more comfortable form of functionalist modernism than that associated with metal or machine-age styling. Artek exported furniture to Britain, through Finmar Ltd, and to America in the 1950s – Harvard University Library purchased Aalto tables for its reading rooms.

The stacking three-legged stool, designed in 1933, is one of the simplest pieces of furniture ever designed. The bentwood leg allows for the stools to be stacked in a distinctive spiral tower. During the 1930s a range of glass vases was launched. These were moulded into a distinctive amorphic, or organic, shape, and were unusual for having no surface decoration. They are a perfect synthesis of organic form and Functionalist logic. The chairs, stool and Aalto's organic glass vase shapes are functional, utilitarian products that exemplify a Modernist approach to design that is reassuring in the integrity of its values.

An ebonized plywood and birch-framed 403 side chair, by Alvar Aalto for Finmar, model No. 51, with Finmar retail label, c1930.
£600–720
$870–1,000 ➤ Bon

▶ **A set of six wooden stacking chairs,** by Alvar Aalto for Artek, c1932.
£5,250–6,250
$7,500–9,000 ➤ BB(L)

A set of four dark-stained pine garden chairs, by Alvar Aalto, Finnish, 1938–39.
£5,000–5,500
$7,250–8,000 🔨 S

A birch-veneered pressure-formed plywood Paimio armchair, by Alvar Aalto for Artek, Finnish, some wear, 1945–55.
£2,800–3,300
$4,000–4,800 🔨 BUK

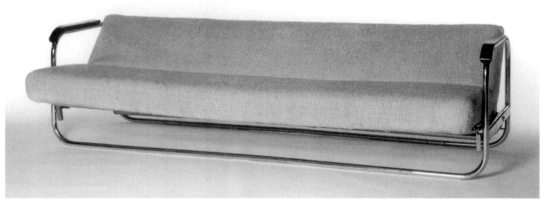

A chrome-plated tubular metal-framed convertible sofa, by Alvar Aalto, with ebonized wooden armrests and adjustable seat and back, Finnish, c1948, 25¼in (64cm) high.
£18,000–21,000
$26,000–30,000 🔨 P(PL)

◄ **A wood and webbing lounge chair,** by Alvar Aalto, model No. 406, Finnish, 1946.
£400–450
$580–650 ⊞ PLB

► **A blue glass Savoy vase,** by Alvar Aalto, Finnish, designed 1937, manufactured 1950s, 4in (10cm) high.
£80–100
$115–145 ⊞ MARK

Market update

Aalto is recognized as one of the big names of design history. Vintage pieces from the 1930s are sought after and command high prices. A good Paimio chair could be in the £4,000–6,000 ($5,800–8,800) range. This is Aalto's best known chair and others, even rarities, command lower prices. There are utilitarian pieces that can be bought for £200–£300 ($300–450). Aalto pieces have usually had a hard life. Be careful of condition and watch out for splits in the laminate. Aalto pieces remain in production.

Focus on Designers: Jean Prouvé

The French architect Jean Prouvé was born in 1901. He began to design furniture during the 1920s and was first drawn to investigate the possibilities for mechanical transformations in chair design. The results of these early experiments are often over complex. The difficulties of resolving these problems simply and in ways that could be manufactured economically and in large numbers provoked Prouvé into considering a more low-tech approach to materials and design. He looked to motor manufacturing for inspiration.

The Ateliers Jean Prouvé was set up in 1931. This design studio was part laboratory, part factory and part social experiment. Prouve's political sympathies lay to the left and he sought, in his designs, to appeal to that constituency through economy and an austere Functionalism that suited the student houses and municipal buildings he furnished. After WWII the projects of reconstruction and post-imperial reform, particularly its infra-structure and design elements, were the key market for Prouve's designs. The moral high-mindedness attached to the socially progressive, democratic,

project has tended to lend Prouve's work a moral gravitas. This is particularly true in its contrast to the larger scaled American Modernism or to the later, hedonistic, rationale of Pop Modern.

Prouvé borrowed manufacturing techniques from the developing assembly lines of the motor and aviation industries. These industries also manifest themselves in the box-section steel and wing-shapes used in his designs.

The Prouvé look is derived from his Functionalist concerns and his desire for economic use of materials. His designs are very different from those of his Bauhaus contemporaries for he finds expression in even cheaper materials and they are assembled using realtively low-tech spot welding and bending technologies. The technical sophistications associated with Bauhaus design engineering are replaced by Prouvé using a system which requires relatively low levels of investment in plant, materials and craft. It is not surprising, then, that Prouvé's clients tended to be public sector establishments rather than the corporate clients that supported American design.

An aluminium and painted steel swivel stool, by Jean Prouvé, French, c1950.
£2,400–2,800
$3,500–4,000 ⚚ BB(L)

A wood and metal Standard chair, by Jean Prouvé, French, 1930.
£1,500–1,800
$2,200–2,600 ⚚ BB(L)

An oak and metal wardrobe, by Jean Prouvé, French, c1945, 62½in (159cm) wide.
£9,500–11,500
$13,800–16,800 ⚚ P(PL)

Market update

Prouvé furniture is unique. It has an authentic industrial quality that sets it apart from the chromed-metal and leather output of Modernism. The utilitarian context of most of Prouvé's work indicates large-scale production, but original pieces in good condition are rare, and consequently command high prices. French and American collectors already recognize Prouvé as a significant Modernist designer and prices range accordingly. Chairs and tables are priced in thousands – not for the faint-hearted!

◄ **A wood and metal Compass desk,** by Jean Prouvé, with three ABS plastic drawers, incised mark, French, c1950.
£6,500–8,000
$9,500–11,500 ⚚ BB(L)

Focus on Designers: George Nelson

George Nelson (1908–86) was a key figure in the development of modern design in America. Although he trained as an architect, he is best known as a designer of furniture, a writer, and mentor. In the early 1930s Nelson travelled to Europe and discovered the architecture of the Modern movement called International Style. This was the second stage in the development of rationalism – that is, a design strategy of problem solving based on clear principles of materials, engineering and function. Nelson became an enthusiastic convert and, upon his return to the USA, began to introduce the personalities of European Modernism to the American public. He wrote a series of articles on Le Corbusier, Walter Gropius and Mies van der Rohe which were published in the journal *Pencil Points*. The New York Museum of Modern Art's exhibition of International Style Architecture gave the movement further momentum in America.

Nelson became interested in the Modernist ideal of domestic architecture as embodying the convenience and efficiencies of modern life. In 1945 he was able to publish his work under the title *Tomorrow's House*. His writing brought him to the attention of the Herman Miller Company and he was invited to join them as design director. One of his first decisions was to develop the design ideas of the young Charles Eames and hence began his long association with Herman Miller in 1946.

Nelson was able to combine his role at Herman Miller with an independent design practice. He was fascinated with the possibilities of space-saving storage in the modern house and designed furniture with open-plan spaces in mind. His sideboards have the distinctive long, low look of the 1950s. His Home Desk of 1946 exemplifies his concern for convenience and functionalism in the modern home. The marshmallow sofa of 1956 is now highly sought-after as an early example of a pop sensibility in design.

Nelson's best known designs are probably the range of clocks that use atomic patterns and star shapes to represent the clock face. These clocks are perfectly matched to the scientific optimism of the 1950s. Nelson was a major contributor to the New York World's Fair in 1964.

Nelson-designed furniture is appealing to collectors. It has a distinctive American look and its design is unmistakably of its time. It is less obvious than much of the Eames furniture and is not obviously office furniture brought into the home. His role as spokesperson and Modernist philosopher in the USA assured him of a following among the design community.

◀ **An electric ball clock,** by George Nelson for Howard Miller Clock Co, the cylindrical brass drum radiating spokes terminating in wooden spheres, black enamelled hands, remnants of manufacturer's label to underside, American, 1947, 13¼in (33.5cm) diam.
£450–550
$650–800 ↗ B(Ba)

A walnut-framed Home Desk, by George Nelson for Herman Miller, model No. 4658, with a leather top, with typewriter compartment, storage unit with sliding doors and a steel mesh Pendaflex basket, on tubular metal legs, American, c1946, 54in (137cm) wide.
£12,500–15,000
$18,000–22,000 ↗ P(PL)

Market update

Nelson-designed furniture is appealing to collectors. It has a distinctive American look and its design is unmistakably of its time. His role as spokesperson and Modernist philosopher in the USA assure him of a following among the design community. Nelson also has the great virtue of being less fashionable that, say, the Eames. A Nelson wall clock may be priced at about £400–500 ($580–650). A sideboard or chest at about £2,500–3,000 ($3,500–4,500) and the iconic marshmallow sofa at £11,000–13,000 ($16,000–19,000).

▶ **A black-enamelled metal and chrome-framed Marshmallow sofa,** by George Nelson for Herman Miller, 18 round cushions upholstered in black leather, signed with paper label, re-upholstered, American, 1950s, 53in (134.5cm) long.
£5,500–6,000
$8,000–8,700 ↗ TREA

Focus on Designers: Charles & Ray Eames

The design office of husband and wife Charles and Ray Eames passed into the folklore of modern design during the 20th century. They are rightly considered to be among the greatest designers of the century. Their achievements in furniture design are remarkable enough but they were also architects, graphic designers, exhibition designers and film makers.

Charles Eames was born in 1907 and trained as an architect in his home town of St Louis, Missouri. He was awarded a fellowship at the Cranbrook Academy of Art in Michigan in 1936 and was appointed head of the department of experimental design. He met Ray at Cranbrook and in 1941 they married and moved to California.

The Eames House at Pacific Palisades in California was built as part of the Case Study House programme. The American journal *Art and Architecture* sponsored a design and building programme that it presented in the journal. The Eames House was constructed using prefabricated and easily available components. The design featured a double-height multi-function space which was filled with an eclectic selection of objects from Latin America, Africa and Japan. It suggested a technologically progressive yet humane Modernism that engaged happily with the abundant diversity of craft and industrial production. This richly textured and eclectic display provided a richly rewarding visual experience. The Eames House featured in one of their later films.

Charles Eames had begun experimenting with the application of new materials and industrial production to furniture manufacturing. His experiments were conducted with Eero Saarinen and the results were submitted to the 1940–41 Organic Design in Home Furnishings Exhibition held at the Museum of Modern Art in New York. The pieces shown were experimental and they remained prototypes. The experiments with moulded plywood bore fruit during WWII when Eames was invited, in collaboration with Evans Manufacturing, to produce contoured-shell form in moulded plywood for use as traction splints. The medical departments of the American military provided the first practical use for the experimental work at Cranbrook and in California.

In 1946 Eames was introduced to the Michigan-based furniture industrialist Herman Miller. The company began to produce Eames furniture and the relationship continued throughout the booming 1950s and '60s. The productive capacity of the Herman Miller Company, together with the fact that the furniture quickly became a staple of their output, means that there is a wide range of Eames furniture available to collectors. The premium is on iconic pieces or experimental prototypes in unusual materials. The quantity of Eames furniture should not be allowed to obscure the quality and precision of its design and manufacture. In the late 1950s and in the '60s Eames developed systems of furniture that could be extended to furnish the vast spaces of corporate offices and airport terminals.

Charles and Ray Eames were enthusiastic supporters of the idea that design could make a better world and that it should be a fun and rewarding experience – for both designers and consumers. Charles and Ray Eames made a series of short films, as a kind of recreation, which provide entertaining testimony to these ideals.

A fibreglass La Chaise chair, by Charles and Ray Eames, with iron rods on a wooden base, c1990.
£3,200–3,500
$4,650–5,000 ✗ Bon
This chair was originally designed in 1948 as a proposal for the Museum of Modern Art International Competition for Furniture Design. Although La Chaise was not one of the prize-winning designs, its elegant form made it one of the most notable competition entries, appearing in both the catalogue and the exhibition of 1950.

◀ **A bent plywood LCW chair,** by Charles and Ray Eames, designed 1947, manufactured c1970.
£700–800
$1,000–1,150 ⊞ MARK

◄ **A set of four fibreglass DSR chairs,** by Charles and Ray Eames for Herman Miller, on tubular metal Eiffel Tower bases, marked Herman Miller, c1950.
£620–700
$900–1,000
⚒ BUK

◄ **A steel and moulded plywood ESU storage unit,** with painted Masonite panels, c1950, 47in (119.5cm) wide.
£5,500–6,000
⚒ S(NY)

A rosewood 670 lounge chair, by Charles and Ray Eames for Herman Miller, with black leather-covered padding, on an aluminium pedestal, armrests restored, American, 1956.
£1,150–1,300
$1,650–1,900 ⚒ Bon

A wire rod and vinyl DKR chair, by Charles and Ray Eames, first edition, c1953.
£280–350
$400–500 ⊞ MARK

Market update

The furniture designs of Charles and Ray Eames dominate the market in modern design furniture. This is a reflection of their status as design pioneers in America and the world and also of the enduring quality of their work. The Lounge Chair and Ottoman (see p25) is a classic and has had iconic status since its launch.

Eames furniture is still in production, so there is no shortage of material for collectors. The office furniture range in particular has been produced in enormous quantities, therefore keeping prices within certain limits defined by the retail cost of new furniture.

The Lounge Chair and Ottoman is priced at £2,000–3,000 ($3,000–4,500) at auction. The selectivity of the auction market is reflected in the desire for sales to present pieces in rare or unusual colours and of studio prototypes. The limited numbers of these items, and their provenance, make them very desirable. Remember that most of the Eames furniture on the market will be of relatively recent origin.

► **An Aluminium Group armchair,** by Charles Eames for Herman Miller, with ribbed red fabric on a five-support swivel base with casters, c1958.
£500–575
$720–820 ⚒ Bri

Focus on Designers: Robin & Lucienne Day

Within the context of post-war austerity Robin and Lucienne Day provided clear evidence of a young, talented and ambitious generation of designers eager to embrace Modernism to the service of social and material reconstruction.

Both Robin and Lucienne had trained at the Royal College of Art in London. They were married in 1942 and Robin's early career was as a graphic artist and poster designer. He entered the furniture competition at New York's Museum of Modern Art, in collaboration with Clive Latimer, and was awarded first prize for a storage unit in moulded plywood and aluminium. He was spotted by Lesley and Rosamund Julius, directors of the British furniture manufacturing company Hille. Robin became their design director in 1950 and continued to work with them throughout his professional life. In 1963, Hille launched a one-piece moulded-plastic stacking chair on steel legs. The polypropylene chair was a low cost, colourful success and it quickly became ubiquitous in the public spaces of Britain. The chair was recently reissued in association with Habitat.

Lucienne's career was as a textile artist and designer. She was able to provide, as both partner and colleague, a backdrop of contemporary-style decoration that showed Robin's furniture to great effect. The use of textiles as a defining feature in the architecture of post-war Britain sets it apart from other forms of Modernism that prioritize the use of glass. Lucienne and Robin worked together on a display for the 1951 Festival of Britain. Her Calyx design for the project was to be her most successful and brought her international recognition. Lucienne Day quickly established herself, during the 1950s and in partnership with Heal's, as the most talented and productive of designers. Her designs quickly became a characteristic of the contemporary interior in Britain. The use of Day fabric in ceiling-to-floor curtains was quickly promoted to badge-of-honour status among Britain's design community. She continued to work with Heal's until the 1970s – extending her output to wallpapers and carpet design. In the mid-1970s she turned to a more craft-based production of silk mosaic panels. The Days were the first designers in post-war Britain to enjoy celebrity status as Moderns.

A birch and rosewood-veneered ebonized sideboard, attributed to Robin Day for Hille, on black-enamelled steel uprights, c1955, 84in (213.5cm) wide.
£550–650
$800–950 ↗ Bon

A Form Group unit four-seat seating system, by Robin Day for Hille, each with ebonized plywood back with grey, cream and black striped tweed fabric, with a coffee table and pad seat, on black-enamelled squared steel frames, 1961, each frame 83in (211cm) wide.
£1,000–1,200
$1,500–1,750 ↗ P(Ba)

Market update

The furniture and textiles of Robin and Lucienne day are surprisingly difficult to collect. The 1950s British context must have tended to limit supply and the furniture, recognized as uncompromisingly modern, can only have been found in a certain kind of architect or designer's house. Remember that, in Britain, the prevailing taste in the furniture market has been for the conservative – in repro-duction or antique form.

The ambiguities of British Modernism limit its appeal on the international market and there is no doubt that, relative to its rarity, Day furniture is still affordable The recent revivals of these designs by retail giant Habitat will tend to make original pieces more desirable and help the market in vintage Day furniture.

Finding good lengths of textile, by any good designer, remains difficult – finding examples by Lucienne Day especially so. This is because furnishing textiles have an ambiguous place in the market. They count as marginal in both the furniture and vintage fashion markets. Also, the post-war ethos of economy has tended to mean that curtain lengths have been transformed into smaller items – perhaps even into shoe bags and dusters. The premium has to be on good lengths of textile that can be displayed as wall hangings. Expect to pay about £500–£1,000 ($720–1,500) for a good length of 1950s fabric – not expensive for wall art.

A pair of lounge chairs, by Robin Day for Hille, with slatted stick backs and shaped single-piece back and arm rails, on turned uprights, with white vinyl-covered squab cushions, designed 1950, manufactured 1956.
£700–850
$1,000–1,250 ↗ B(Ba)

Focus on Designers: Piero Fornasetti

The work of the Italian designer Piero Fornasetti offers a maverick contrast to the prevailing mood of considered restraint in European post-war Modernism. Fornasetti was born in 1913 and educated at the Brera Academy. During WWII he lived in exile in Switzerland and began an association with the architect Gio Ponti. Together the two would create a uniquely Italian version of post-war design. Ponti was a Functionalist working in the traditions of pre-war European Modernism. Ponti's architecture and furnishings were presented as a rational counterpoint to Fornasetti's exotic, whimsical and dramatic decorations based on the trompe l'oeil techniques of operatic and theatrical scene painters.

The roots of Fornasetti's design are in the eclectic appropriation of images from the past. These were used to cover every surface of his furniture designs and were later to embellish ceramic and other home furnishings. Fornasetti worked from his house in Milan, where his son continues the studio. The art-direction of home furnishings provided an opportunity for elements of surrealism and fun to enter the narrative of Modernism. The frames of reference of Fornasetti's graphic appropriations are historically eclectic – 19th century engravings are a staple ingredient – and richly decorated in colour and with gold.

In Britain and America the Pop sensibility was directed, through class antagonisms, towards recent popular culture. In Italy, Fornasetti provided compelling evidence of the potential beyond such narrow limits.

Fornasetti produced cabinet pieces and screens, but these larger pieces of furniture are quite rare. The ceramics, boxes and other objects that he produced survive in greater quantity. He also designed fabrics, ties and scarves and even a bicycle.

◀ A transfer-printed and lacquered wood Architectural cabinet, by Piero Fornasetti, fitted for electricity, Italian, 1951, 85¾in (218cm) high.
£11,500–13,500
$16,500–19,500
⚲ P(Sy)
This design was reissued in the 1980s.

▶ A transfer-printed wood side chair, by Piero Fornasetti, designed c1950.
£2,200–2,600
$3,200–3,800
⚲ BB(L)

◀ An earthenware five-piece salad set, by Piero Fornasetti, factory mark, 1955, large bowl 9½in (24cm) diam.
£270–300
$400–450 ⚲ WBH

Market update

Fornasetti's unique style is instantly recognizable. The visual excitement of his designs and the density of decoration have placed his work at the forefront of decorator's mise-en-scene for almost 20 years. Big furniture by Fornasetti is rare and commands high values, £10,000–£15,000 ($14,500–22,000) for standing cabinets.

The ceramic designs are more easily available and are priced in the £100–£300 ($145–440) range. Boxes are about the same. The workshop is still in operation.

Focus on Designers: Arne Jacobson

The Ant, Swan and Egg chairs that Arne Jacobsen designed for the Danish furniture manufacturer Fritz Hansen helped define a characteristic Danish version of Modern and to continue a Scandinavian tradition of combining Functionalism with softer, more organic shapes.

Jacobsen trained as an architect and began his career in that capacity during the 1930s. He was a Functionalist by nature and began to extend his design activities towards what Alvar Aalto had described as architectural accessories.

Jacobsen had first spoken with Fritz Hansen during the 1930s but nothing had come of it. The post-war context of an international mass market provided an opportunity for collaboration between the two. The new technologies of furniture manufacturing were used to create the Ant dining chair (1951), and the more ample Swan (1958), and Egg (1958) chairs. The two later designs used a fibreglass shell and aluminium frame to create a complex, sophisticated and yet comforting shape. The Egg chair has achieved iconic status among the design cognoscenti.

Jacobsen's career as an architect developed towards the realization of a complete vision. The ideal of architectural and design unity carried through from the building to all its furnishings is a powerful force in the history of design. The commission for St Catherine's College in Oxford gave Jacobsen the opportunity to design buildings and furniture into a harmonious whole. The Oxford high back chair is an extended relative of the Ant. Its sensual form contrasts with the square geometry of the buildings and spaces.

An Ant chair, by Arne Jacobsen for Fritz Hansen, Series 3103, 1955.
£90–110
$130–160 ⊞ ORI

▶ **A chrome-plated tubular steel Drop side chair,** by Arne Jacobsen, with vinyl-covered padded seat and back, 1958.
£900–1,100
$1,300–1,600 ⋏ Bon
This is one of 300 chairs designed and manufactured exclusively for the SAS Royal Hotel, Copenhagen.

An aluminium-framed Swan sofa, by Arne Jacobsen for Fritz Hansen, with moulded fibreglass shell, Danish, 1957–58.
£2,200–2,600
$3,200–3,800 ⋏ BB(L)

Market update

Of all 1950s Modernists Jacobsen is probably the one with the most contemporary appeal. His designs combine elegance and functionalism with a quality of materials and organic form. The leather Egg chair is probably the only serious contender to the Eames lounger for the status of most-wanted design classic, and classic Jacobsen designs remain in production. The potential of leather for patination and changes in colour gives the chair a unique aesthetic potential. The price range for an Egg chair in good condition is £2,000–3,000 ($3,000–4,500).

An aluminium-framed and leather-covered Egg chair, by Arne Jacobsen for Fritz Hansen, with moulded fibreglass shell, damaged, the leather stamped in white with the initials FH, with label, marked, Danish, c1960.
£1,500–1,800
$2,200–2,600 ⋏ BUK

Focus on Designers: Hans Wegner

Hans Wegner created some 500 chair designs during his career as a cabinet maker and furniture designer. Wegner is unusual, among Modernists, in having first been apprenticed to a cabinet maker. It was through this that he learnt the skills which allowed him to be so productive.

Wegner subsequently trained as an architect and worked as assistant to Arne Jacobsen who introduced him to an uncompromising Modernism. The desire for Modernist spaces to be flexible was reflected in their requirement for light-weight, comfortable furniture. Wegner began a project to reduce traditional chair forms to their essentials. The result was a series of chair archetypes that were both traditional and new. They confirmed the tendency of Scandinavian Modernism to acknowledge its origins in the crafts and materials of the region.

Wegner's first design success came with the Chinese chair (1944). This dining or side chair was an evolution of a traditional Oriental design. It was produced by Johannes Hansen and was characterized by a modern elegance and minimalism while also – through the material and its structure – recalling traditional chair types. Wegner produced Modernist versions of the vernacular stick back and Windsor-type chairs. Wegner also experimented with woven cane seating, rope and deck-chair patterns for folding 'holiday' furniture. These latter chairs were popular as modern architecture continued to experiment with flexible living spaces and alfresco openings.

Wegner established relations with several furniture manufacturers in Denmark – Fritz Hansen, PP Møbler, Carl Hansen and Planmobel. Like his contemporary Jacobsen, he extended his design activities towards metalwares and lighting in pursuit of harmonious unity of design. Wegner's early chair designs remain an archetype of civilized modernity and continue to be produced today.

A teak and woven cane The Chair armchair, by Hans J. Wegner for Johannes Hansen, cane renovated, 1949.
£600–720
$870–1,000 ↗ BUK

An oak-veneered pressure-formed plywood armchair, by Hans J. Wegner for Carl Hansen & Sons, with branded stamp, Danish, designed 1951, manufactured 1955.
£1,200–1,400
$1,750–2,000 ↗ DORO

An ash and teak Peacock chair, by Hans J. Wegner for Johannes Hansen, Danish, c1947.
£4,500–5,000
$6,500–7,250 ↗ WDG

Market update

The multitude of chair designs by Hans Wegner afford him a special place in the collectors' market for 20th-century design. His attention to tradition, detail and materials place him in a continuity of design. This is at odds with the prevailing narrative of Modernism that has prioritized the new and revolutionary over the traditional. The best of his designs remain unaffected by changes in fashion and have classic status. Chairs by Wegner are modestly priced in the £400–600 ($575–875) range.

An ash-framed Hoop Chair, by Hans J. Wegner for PP Møbler, the seat and backrest covered with wool, the back legs with casters, marked, Danish, 1965.
£750–900
$1,100–1,300 ↗ BUK

Focus on Designers: Verner Panton

The Danish-born architect and designer Verner Panton has, since the mid-1950s, lived and worked in Switzerland. This exile has allowed him to develop a series of design ideas that avoid both the rigorous rationalism of Swiss Modern or the traditional craft orientation of Danish Modern. The result, always unmistakably Panton, is a form of 'pop' hybrid that extends to space-age materials and to a radical redefinition of the living space.

Panton was trained in design in Denmark and graduated from the Copenhagen Academy in 1951. He worked in the experimental studio of Arne Jacobsen and was introduced to the work of Charles Eames and Eero Saarinen. The futuristic experimentation of these designers convinced Panton to extend this activity. The result was a series of futuristic chair designs which would bring him international recognition. The Cone chair (1958) is made of sheet metal covered in upholstery with a drop-in seat. The Heart (1959) also combined a metal frame and a stretch-knit covering. His most innovative design was the stacking chair made from a single form of cantilevered plastic. This was the first single-piece plastic chair. Originally manufactured by Hansen in glass-reinforced polyester, it was taken up by the American firm of Herman Miller who began mass production in 1968.

Panton continued to experiment with design but became increasingly concerned with the idea of the living environment as an area of ambiguous, soft spaces. These radical ideas formed the basis of a new domestic landscape which promised to liberate traditional roles within the family. The social progressiveness of these designs was perfectly matched to the mood of sexual liberation and of gender equalities at the end of the 1960s. The limits of design radicalism became evident in the 1970s as the socially progressive element in design slipped away and was replaced by self-conscious 'whimsical' response post-modern anxiety.

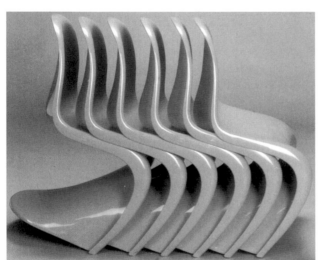

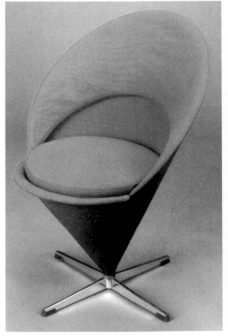

◄ **A set of six Panton chairs,** by Verner Panton for Herman Miller, 1959–60.
£2,600–3,000
$3,800–4,000 ⨯ BB(L)

A Cone chair, by Verner Panton for Plus-Line, Danish, 1958.
£700–800
$1,000–1,150 ⨯ BB(L)

◄ **An injection moulded black plastic stacking chair,** by Verner Panton for Herman Miller, designed c1960, manufactured 1968–79.
£300–350
$440–500
⊞ MARK

Insurance values

Always insure your valuable antiques for the cost of replacing them with similar items, regardless of the original price paid. Both dealers and auctioneers can provide a valuation service for a fee.

◄ A moulded-steel and foam **Living Tower,** by Verner Panton for Panton Design, 1968.
£4,200–5,000
$6,000–7,250 ♪ BUK

Market update

The designs of Verner Panton reflect those aspects of the 1960s and early '70s that are most appealing to contemporary tastes. The use of new materials and the articulation of new spaces as an indicator of new lifestyle choices place him in the vanguard of fashion, hedonism and '60s idealism. It is precisely these associations that render original Panton environments so fragile. Nowadays, we may collect the design without engaging the complicating politics implicit in Panton's work.

The plastic cantilever remains his most enduring designs. The foam spaces are quite rare; they have a sculptural quality and architectural scale that take them beyond the usual limits of furniture design. Panton textile designs may be purchased in lengths for £200–400 ($300–580).

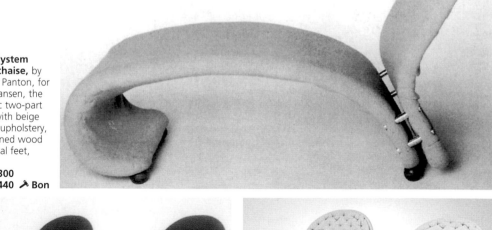

► A System 1-2-3 chaise, by Verner Panton, for Fritz Hansen, the organic two-part form with beige tweed upholstery, on stained wood spherical feet, 1970s.
£250–300
$360–440 ♪ Bon

A pair of System 1-2-3 chairs, by Verner Panton for Fritz Hansen, with black removable seat covers, on a chrome steel foot, stained, Danish, 1973.
£500–600
$720–870 ♪ BUK

A pair of System 1-2-3 de Luxe armchairs, by Verner Panton for Fritz Hansen, upholstered in beige fabric and with aluminium bases, 1970s.
£800–900
$1,150–1,300 ♪ BUK

Focus on Designers: The Memphis Group

The emergence of the Milan-based Memphis design group during the 1980s was part of a process which, in Italy at least, had begun in the anti-design movements of the 1960s and '70s. The potential for political radicalism in design had always existed in Italy and now it attached itself to the figure of Ettore Sottsass as leader of the iconoclastic design group.

Sottsass was born in Austria into a family of design Modernists. They moved to Turin and Sottsass began to study architecture. He graduated in 1939 and, after three years in the military, established his own studio in Milan. Sottsass worked on the design of interiors and furniture for the new domestic spaces, often quite small, of post-war apartment blocks. His contemporaries in these projects were Marco Zanuso and Vico Magistretti. Sottsass came into contact with the Olivetti firm in the early 1960s and became their design director. Throughout the 1960s he designed typewriters and computers for the firm – rejecting the streamlined aesthetic favoured by his predecessors and creating his own expressive design language.

Visits to America and to the Far East opened up new possibilities for Sottsass and he was encouraged to distance himself from a European anxiety in design and to question the rationalist agenda at the heart of high-Modernist projects. The result was the creation of a personal design language around which an anti-design movement (Superstudio, Archizoom and Gruppo Strum) began to cluster. In 1976 he was instrumental in the creation of a loose group of designers in Milan under the title Studio Alchimia. The group rejected the Bauhaus logic of good design in favour of witty, anarchic forms.

Sottsass deployed design as a form of cultural criticism. He attacked the prevailing notion of good taste in design by the use of kitsch and populist decoration and produced bookcases, lights and tables, often in Formica materials. The creation of the Memphis group in 1980 and the display, at the Milan Fair in 1981, of their anarchic designs created an international sensation and brought Sottsass and his followers into the international design establishment. Memphis and Sottsass defined a post-modern response, expressed with witty humour, to the prevailing anxieties of the modernist project. The group helped define a more individually expressive response to the design brief than was possible through the rationalist logic of Moderism.

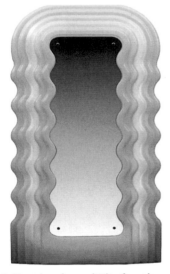

A fibreglass-framed Ultrafragola mirror, by Ettore Sottsass for Poltronova, c1970, 39¼in (99.5cm) wide.
£1,700–2,000
$2,500–3,000 ⚈ BUK

A lacquered wood D'Antibes cabinet, by George J. Sowden for Memphis, with blue top and yellow sides, American, 1981, 23in (58.5cm) wide.
£2,200–2,500
$3,200–3,500 ⚈ Bon

A ceramic teapot, by Matteo Thun for Memphis, Italian, c1980s, 12in (30.5cm) high.
£200–220
$300–320 ⚈ PLB

▶ **A Palm Springs dining table,** by Ettore Sottsass, and a set of six First dining chairs by Michele de Lucchi for Memphis, 1983 and 1984, Italian, table 84in (213.5cm) wide.
£4,500–5,000
$6,500–7,250
⚈ B&B

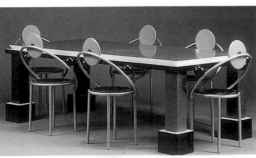

Market update

The ironic humour and self-consciously arch design aesthetic of Memphis immediately placed it within the most fashionable circles of the design establishment. This was evident from the very beginning when the Memphis Studio launched its design range with a catwalk-style show at the Milan Furniture Fair. The fashion association and limited production of Memphis designs have placed them at the top of the market for 1980s design.

Consultant's Note

Many wonderful and extraordinary things were made during the 20th century, but it has not been possible to include them all in this book. We have tried, within the limits of the format, to trace the developing themes of design through the 20th century. This is such a huge story, and the wealth and variety of objects so great, that there cannot but be much that is left out. However, we hope that the presentation, within the logic of this book, will allow readers to recognize the objects and, through their styling, place them in a context that begins to explain their value and meaning. It should be remembered that much of what is discussed in this book was mass produced and is not particularly old. These items require a different appreciation from that traditionally afforded to objects within the world of art, antiques and collectables.

The stories of Modernism presented in these pages are shaped around the cultural forces of politics, scientific and technological progress and educational emancipation. The intellectual projects of which these objects are part can be traced to political, social and technological traditions which go much further back than the 20th century.

Whatever the limits of this book, it should be remembered that this is essentially an introduction for beginners to an enormous subject. More specialized information is available within any of the fields we have looked at. Further titles by Mitchell Beazley and Miller's may be of help and are included in the bibliography below.

Bibliography

Atterbury, Paul, *Twentieth-Century Ceramics,* Miller's, 1999.

Baker, Fiona and Keith, *20th Century Furniture,* Carlton Books, 2000.

Benton, Tim and Campbell-Cole, Barbie (eds.), *Tubular Steel Furniture*, conference paper, Art Book Co, 1979.

Collins, Michael, *Post-Modern Design* (ed.), Andreas Papadakis, Academy Editions, 1989.

Conway, Hazel, *Ernest Race*, The Design Council, 1982.

Crow, Thomas, *The Rise of the Sixties*, Everyman Art Library, 1996.

Fiell, Charlotte and Peter, *Modern Furniture Classics since 1945*, Thames & Hudson, 1991.
1000 Chairs, Taschen, 1997.
60s Decorative Art, (eds.), Taschen, 2000.

Fitoussi, Brigitte, *Memphis*, Thames & Hudson, 1998.

Fukuyama, Francis, *The End of History and the Last Man*, Penguin,1992.

Galbraith, J. K., *The Affluent Society*, Mariner Books, Houghton Mifflin, 1998.

Garner, Philippe, *Sixties Design*, Taschen 1996.

Gilbert, Anne, *60s and 70s Designs and Memorabilia*, Avon Books, 1994.

Gowing, Christopher and Rice, Paul, *British Studio Ceramics in the 20th Century*, Barrie & Jenkins, 1989.

Greenberg, Cara, *Mid-Century Modern Furniture of the 1950s*, Thames & Hudson, 1995.

Hayes, Jennifer, *Lucienne Day A Career in Design*, Whitworth Art Gallery, 1993.

Hoban, Sally, *Collecting Modern Design*, Miller's, 2001.

Jackson, Lesley, *The New Look – Design in the Fifties*, Thames & Hudson, 1991.
Contemporary, Phaidon, 1994.
The Sixties, Phaidon, 1998.
20th Century Factory Glass, Mitchell Beazley, 2000.

Julien, Guy, *The Dictionary of 20th Century Design and Designers*, Thames & Hudson, 1993.

Kirkham, Pat, *Charles and Ray Eames, Designers of the 20th Century,* MIT Press, 1998.

Klein, Dan and Ward,Lloyd, *The History of Glass*, Little, Brown & Co., 1993.

Marcus, George, *Functionalist Design*, Prestel, 1995.

Marsh, Graham and Norand, Tony, (eds.), *Film Posters of the 1960s*, Avrum Press, 1997
Collecting the 1950s, Miller's, 1997.
Collecting the 1960s, Miller's, 1999.
Collecting the 1970s, Miller's, 2001.

Sollo, John, *An Insider's Guide to Twentieth-century Furniture*, Miller's, 2002.

Sparke, Penny, *A Century of Design*, Mitchel Beazley, 1998.
Ettore Sottsass Jnr, Design Council, 1982.

Waal, Edmund de, *Bernard Leach*, Tate Gallery Publishing, 1998.

Watson, Oliver, Studio Pottery, Phaidon, 1993.

Whitford, Frank, *The Bauhaus*, Thames & Hudson, 1984.

Woodham, Jonathan, *Twentieth Century Design*, Oxford University Press, 1997.

Glossary

ABS plastic: Tough plastic used for making moulded articles.

acetate: Man-made fabric created in Germany in the 19th century.

acid etching: Cold decoration technique in which the surface of the glass is partially covered with a wax or resin then submerged in acid which bites into the exposed areas.

adzed: Wooden surface that is patterned with ridges. It is created by the wood having been faced with an adze.

Aesthetic Movement: English literary and artistic movement of the late 19th century founded on the ethos of 'art for art's sake'. The group was dedicated to the ideal of beauty and rejected the idea that art should have a social or moral purpose, in contrast to the Arts and Crafts Movement.

amphora: Greek or Roman oil or wine-storage vessel with a bulbous body and large strap handles from the shoulder to the neck.

anodized: Metalwork given a final tough protective coating by means of electrolysis.

appliqué: Decorative application of a second fabric to the main fabric ground.

Ariel: Technique of creating air-bubble designs in glass by sandblasting a pattern in deep relief onto a clear or multicoloured **blank**, then reheating and casting the blank in a layer of clear glass so that the design is captured in trails of air. Developed by Orrefors in 1937.

Art Deco: Term widely used to describe the architectural and decorative arts style that emerged in France in the 1920s. It took its name from the 1925 Exposition Internationale des Arts Décoratifs et Industriels Modernes in Paris. Geometric forms and patterns, bright colours, sharp edges, and the use of expensive materials, such as enamel, ivory, bronze and polished stone are well-known characteristics of this style, but the use of other materials such as chrome, coloured glass and **Bakelite** also enabled Art Deco designs to be made at low cost.

Art Nouveau: Style of decorative art and architecture popular in Europe in the late 19th and early 20th centuries which is characterized by stylized curvilinear designs and organic forms. In Germany the style was called *Jugendstil*. Art Nouveau developed along two distinct lines: the rectilinear style pioneered by C. R. Mackintosh and seen in the work of the members of the Vienna Secession, and the intricate curvilinear style of French and Belgian designers, such as Hector Guimard. Mackintosh's style of Art Nouveau was to influence the Wiener Werkstätte.

Arts and Crafts Movement: English aesthetic and social movement of the later 19th century, led by John Ruskin, William Morris, C. R. Ashbee and others, which sought to revive the importance of craftsmanship in a time of increasing mechanization and mass production. The ideal of the movement was to make well-designed and crafted objects available to all people, but because the objects were made by hand in workshops only wealthy patrons could afford to buy them. However, the movement did stimulate a drive for better standards in mass-production at the time, while its belief that good art and design could reform society, and its practice of rejecting showy decoration to concentrate on the simplicity of an object was to have a significant influence on exponents of the Modern Movement, such as the designers associated with the German Bauhaus. The movement also influenced some 20th century designers in Sweden, Finland and Germany to revive their own national styles.

avante-garde: Term used to describe art that is especially innovative.

Bakelite: Trade name of a plastic invented in 1907 by the chemist Leo H. Baekeland. It was the first plastic to be entirely synthetic.

blank: Partially-formed vessel or sculpture which has been allowed to cool so that it can be treated to various cold decoration techniques, such as cutting, **acid etching** or sandblasting. With **Ariel** and **Graal**, the blank is then reheated and cased with another layer of glass.

cabochon: Jewel cut into a dome shape, especially popular in 19thC jewellery.

cantilever: The practice whereby a floor or horizontal structure projects out of a wall or vertical structure without a visible means of support. In design the term is used to describe a style of chair that has no back legs: the back of the seat is supported by the frame as the weight is distributed at the front of the chair. This style has been explored in the 20th century through the use of bent plywood, tubular steel and plastic.

chinoiserie: Chinese-style ornamentation on porcelain, wall-papers, fabrics, furniture and garden architecture.

chromolithograph: Commercial type of colour-printed lithograph from the late 19th century.

classical: Term used broadly to describe a style of architecture, art and design that is created in, or that follows, the restrained style of classial antiquity and its adherence to accepted standards of form and craftsmanship.

codpiece: Protuberant box to protect the genitals and groin.

Constructivism: Russian movement of artists, architects and designers who abandoned fine art traditions after the 1917 Russian Revolution in order to create art to serve the new social and political order. The exponents linked their work with mass production and industry, but although they designed furnishings and objects their ideas were never put into mass production. The main artists were Alexander Rodchenko, El Lissitzsky and Kasimir Malevich. Avoiding the use of traditional art materials, they strove to make new art works by bringing different elements together, seen to strong effect in their posters created out of photomontage. The movement was to have a strong influence on groups which the Modern Movement, such as De Stijl and the Bauhaus.

crackle glaze (*craquelure*): Deliberate cracked effect achieved by firing ceramics to a precise temperature.

CTM: Coffee table metal

De Stijl: Group composed of architects, designers, painters, thinkers and poets founded in the Netherlands around a

magazine of the same name in 1917.
Under the leadership of the painter and architect Theo van Doesburg, the group aimed to break down the divisions between fine and applied arts in order to create a pure style of art, design and architecture that rejected natural forms in favour of abstract geometric forms.

Deutscher Werkbund: an organization formed in Germany in 1907 to bridge the gap between industry and design. Composed of manufacturers, architects, designers and politicians, it campaigned for a style of design that it believed to be appropriate to the new industrial age, and argued for the moral and aesthetic importance of design, underlining its belief that practicality was the basis for expressing contemporary cyltural values. It carried through some of the ideas of Art Nouveau and applied them to industrial design.

DTM: dining table metal

electroplate: The process of using an electrical current to coat a base metal or alloy with silver, invented in 1830s and gradually superceding Sheffield plate.

ESU: Eames storage unit.

faïence: Tin-glazed earthenwares named after the town of Faenza in Italy, but actually used to describe products made anywhere in Italy, where they are called maiolica.

feldspar: Hard rock-forming minerals consisting of aluminium silicates of potassium, sodium, calcium or barium.

finial: Decorative turned knob.

flambé: Glaze made from copper, usually deep crimson, flecked with blue or purple, and often faintly cracked.

fluted: Border resembling a scalloped edge, used as a decoration on furniture, glass silver and porcelain items.

'form follows function': Phrase used widely to denote the Modernist principle that the form of an object or building should reflect the construction principles and materials from which it is made. This maxim was coined by the American architect Louis Sullivan in an essay of 1896 in reference to architecture. As a maxim for the Modern Movement, its original meaning has been adapted to suggest that the idea of 'utility' should determine an object's appearance.

Functionalism: Term used broadly to refer to the principle that nothing is included in a design that does not enhance the object's purpose. The American architect Louis Sullivan is usually cited as the "founder" of Functionalism with his maxim "form follows function".

goffered: Pattern usually achieved by passing material through a pair of rollers; raised on one side, incised on the other

Graal: Technique of creating a coloured pattern within the wall of a vessel, developed by Orrefors in 1916. The process involves making a small cased **blank**, which is then cut, engraved or acid etched with a pattern. The **blank** is then reheated, cased with clear glass, and blown into its final form, leaving the expanded pattern suspended inside the wall.

gravity clock: Any type of clock which, suspended from a chain or ratchet, is powered by its own weight.

hickory: American wood which is similar to ash but a little darker in colour.

'industrial style': Term used broadly to refer to the development in the Modern Movement when designers began using new materials, such as glass, bricks, metals and plastics in favour of traditional materials. In the 1980s and 1990s the style was interchangeable with that referred to as High-Tech.

iridescence: Rainbow-like surface effect created with lustre colours, or by exposing the piece to hot vapours of metal oxides.

Jun: Named after the town in ancient China where an opalescent blue glaze was used from the 11thC.

Lapis: Artificial stone or paste made by grinding silicates of bright ultramarine blue.

LCW: low coffee table wood

LTR: low table rod

Lucite: Another term for **Plexiglass** or **Perspex**.

martelé: Term for metalware with a fine, hammerered surface, first produced in France but later revived during the Art Nouveau period.

Masonite: Trade name of a dark brown hardboard commonly used for partitions and linings.

melamine: Plastic often used for laminate coatings, particularly on wooden kitchen surfaces, and to make tableware.

minimal: Descriptive term for designs of the Modern Movement that are characterized by a rejection of ornamentation in favour of simple elemental forms and structures.

Modern Movement: General term originally used by the architectural historian Nikolaus Pevsner in his influential book *Pioneers of the Modern Movement* (1936), to describe an international movement in architecture and design that emerged in Europe in the early decades of the 20th century. It was originally underpinned by a desire for a design ethos that reflected ideals of democracy and social reform, and a belief that the world of art and the manufacturing industry could be reconciled in order to provide all levels of society with well-designed, mass-produced goods. Early groups that were instrumental in the development of the Modern Movement include the Deutscher Werkbund in Germany before World War I, and the De Stijl group in the Netherlands after 1917. These principles were put into practice most notably, and with the most lasting influence, at the Bauhaus in Germany in the 1920s and early 1930s. The movement rejected the use of historical styles and unnecessary decoration, instead adhering to the principle "form follows function". It is more or less interchangeable with the term "Modernism".

neoclassicism: Style of decorative arts and architecture that originated in the second half of the 18th century. With its rejection of the earlier Rococo, it marked a revival of interest in the art and design of Classical antiquity and the qualities of restraint, harmony, proportion and reason. It is distinctive for its simple geometric forms, subdued colours and restrained decoration. The term is sometimes used broadly to describe designs that are created in, or that follow, this style.

obi: Waist sash for a Japanese costume.

pâte-de-verre: Translucent glass created by melting and applying powdered glass in layers or by casting it in a mould.

patinated: noble and desirable dull green colour of ancient bronze, caused by oxidization of the metal.

PEL: Practical Equipment Limited

Perspex: Trade name of a tough, light and translucent solid plastic which became commercially available in the later 1930s. It has great flexibility and a strong resisance to weathering, and is often used instead of glass. It can also be opaque.

planish: Initial stage in finishing the surface of plate metal before polishing, to reduce the hammer marks which occur during raising, by using a special flat-headed hammer.

Plexiglass: Trade name of a tough, light and solid plastic that can be manufactured as a translucent or opaque material.

Pop: Art and design movement that developed during the 1960s responding to the general level of economic and technological optimism and finding inspiration in mass consumerism and popular culture. Rejecting Modernism, it sought to express the democratic spirit of the age, replacing Modernist values with its own aspirations of fun, change, variety, irreverence, and disposability.

rattan: Stripped inner bark of a palm grown in the Malay Penninsula, used for caning.

repoussé: Term for embossing. Relief decoration on metal is made by hammering from the reverse so that the decoration projects, then is finished from the front by chasing.

Rexine: Strong, coated cloth often appearing as imitation leather. The base cloth of cotton or a cotton/rayon mix is applied with a cellulose nitrate or PVC coating. Embossing is done with steel rollers, often in a geometric or leather grain pattern.

sans serif: Term used for any typeface that does not have serifs, the small lines at the extremities of a main stroke in a type character.

scalloped: Decoration consisting of a series of depressions resembling the shape of a scallop shell, usually of rims on silver or earthenware vessels.

Secession: Name taken by several groups of artists in Germany and Austria who broke away from the official academies in the 1890s to pursue their own artistic aims and organize their own exhibitions. The first Secession was in Munich in 1892. This was followed by the Vienna Secession in 1897, and by the Berlin Secession in 1899.

sgraffito: Form of ceramic decoration incised through a coloured slip, revealing the ground beneath.

slip: Smooth dilution of clay and water used in the making and decoration of pottery.

socle: Block or slab that forms the lowest part of the pedestal of a sculpture or decorative vase.

Swedish Modern: Tradition-based yet essentially modern style, it is characterized by the use of natural materials in preference to those such as tubular steel, a material synonymous with the Modern Movement. The objects were well-designed, inexpensive to manufacture and affordable for most people. This style dominated international taste in domestic interior design after WWII.

tazza: Wide but shallow bowl on a stem with a foot.

tenmoku: A high-temperature firing brown/black feldspathic stoneware glaze. It is deeply stained using iron oxide. It originated in china during the T'ang Dynasty, but the technique of firing was perfected during the Sung Dynasty, enabling a much thicker glaze to be applied to the ware.

torchère: Portable stand for a candlestick, candelabrum or lamp.

trefoil: Three-cusped figure which resembles a symmetrical three-lobed leaf or flower.

'truth to materials': The edict of the Arts and Crafts Movement that the forms of objects should reflect the materials from which they are made. It was to influence designers of the Modern Movement, including those at the Bauhaus in Germany and Gordon Russell in Britain.

tube-lining: Type of ceramic decoration in which thin trails of slip are applied as outlines to areas of coloured glaze.

Vitrolite: Pigmented structural glass for both interior and exterior use which could be cut, laminated, curved and textured. Its versatility and affinity with early 20th-century design made it a popular building material of the period.

WMF: Short for Württembergische Metallwarenfabrik, a German foundry that was one of the principal producers of Art Nouveau metalware.

WPA: Works Progress Administration, a massive employment relief programme launched in 1935, the largest and most important of Franklin Roosevelts's New Deal Cultural Programmes of the 1930s, which marked the US government's first direct investment in cultural development.

Index to Advertisers

Directory of Specialists

If you would like to contact any of the following specialists, we would advise readers to make contact by telephone before a visit, therefore avoiding a wasted journey.

Auctioneers

London
Bonhams, 101 New Bond Street, W1S 1SR
Tel: 020 7629 6602
www.bonhams.com

Christie, Manson & Wood Ltd, 8 King Street, St James's, SW1Y 6QT
Tel: 020 7839 9060

Sotheby's, Hammersmith Road, W14 8UX
Tel: 020 7293 5000
www.sothebys.com

Australia
Leonard Joel Auctioneers, 333 Malvern Road, South Yarra, Victoria 3141
Tel: 03 9826 4333
decarts@ljoel.com.au or jewellery@ljoel.com.au
www.ljoel.com.au

Austria
Dorotheum, Palais Dorotheum, A-1010 Wien, Dorotheergasse 17
Tel: 0043 1 515 60 455

Canada
Ritchies Inc, Auctioneers & Appraisers of Antiques & Fine Art, 288 King Street East, Toronto, Ontario, M5A 1K4
Tel: (416) 364 1864
auction@ritchies.com
www.ritchies.com

Finland
Bukowskis, Horhammer, Iso Roobertink, 12 Stora Robertsg, 00120 Helsinki, Helsingfors
Tel: 00 358 9 668 9110
www.bukowskis.fi

Sweden
Bukowskis, Arsenalsgatan 4 Stockholm
Tel: 00 46 (0)8 614 08 00
info@bukowskis.se
www.bukowskis.se

Stockholms Auktionsverk, Jakobsgaten 10, PO Box 16256, S-103 25 Stockholm
Tel: 0046 8 453 67 00

USA
Butterfields, 7601 Sunset Boulevard, Los Angeles, CA 90046
Tel: 00 1 323 850 7500
Christie, Manson & Woods

International Inc. 502 Park Avenue, (including Christie's East), New York 10022
Tel: 001 212 636 2000

William Doyle Galleries, 175 East 87th Street, New York 10128
Tel: 212 427 2730

Du Mouchelles, 409 East Jefferson, Detroit, Michigan 48226
Tel: 001 313 963 6255

Jackson's Auctioneers & Appraisers, 2229 Lincoln Street, Cedar Falls, IA 50613
Tel: 00 1 319 277 2256

Los Angeles Modern Auctions, PO Box 462006, Los Angeles, CA 90046
Tel: (323) 904 1950
www.lamodern.com

Skinner Inc, 357 Main Street, Bolton, MA 01740
Tel: 00 1 978 779 6241

Skinner Inc, The Heritage On The Garden, 63 Park Plaza, Boston, MA 02116
Tel: 001 617 350 5400

Sloan's Auctioneers & Appraisers, 2516 Ponce de Leon Boulevard, Coral Gables, Florida 33134
Tel: 305 447 0757
www.sloansauction.com

Sloan's Auctioneers & Appraisers, 4920 Wyaconda Road, North Bethesda, MD 20852
Tel: 00 1 301 468 4911/800 649 5066
www.sloansauction.com

Sotheby's, 1334 York Avenue, New York, NY 10021
Tel: 00 1 212 606 7000
www.sothebys.com

Swann Galleries, Inc, 104 East 25th Street, New York
Tel: 00 1 212 2544710

Treadway Gallery, Inc, 2029 Madison Road, Cincinnati, Ohio 45208
Tel: 001 513 321 6742
www.treadwaygallery.com

Books

USA
Thomas G. Boss Fine Books, 234 Clarendon Street, Boston, MA 02116
Tel: 617 421 1700
www.bossbooks.com
Art Deco, Arts & Crafts and Art Nouveau books.

Ceramics

East Sussex
Art Deco Etc, 73 Upper Gloucester Road, Brighton, BN1 3LQ
Tel: 01273 329268
poolepottery@artdeco.co.uk

Hampshire
Bona Art Deco Store, The Hart Shopping Centre, Fleet, GU13 8AZ
Tel: 01252 616666
artdeco@bona.co.uk
www.claricecliff.co.uk
Clarice Cliff.

Rick Hubbard Art Deco, 3 Tee Court, Bell Street, Romsey, SO51 8GY
Tel: 01794 513133
Mobile: 07767 267607
rick@rickhubbard-artdeco.co.uk
www.rickhubbard-artdeco.co.uk
Large selection of Clarice Cliff, Shelley, Susie Cooper plus many more and furniture.

Kent
Delf Stream Gallery, 14 New Street, Sandwich, CT13 9AB
Tel: 01304 617684
oastman@aol.com
www.delfstreamgallery.com
19th–20th century European and American art pottery.

London
Beth, GO 43–44, Alfies Antique Market, 13-25 Church Street, Marylebone, NW8 8DT
Tel: 020 7723 5613

Beverley, 30 Church Street, Marylebone, NW8 8EP
Tel: 020 7262 1576

Wiltshire
Martra Decorative Arts, Salisbury Antiques Market, 37 Catherine Street, Salisbury, SP1 2DH
Tel: 01722 326033
Mobile: 07887 722043

sales@martra.co.uk
mark@martra.co.uk
tracy@martra.co.uk
www.martra.co.uk
Dealers in late 19th & 20th century ceramics, glass, compacts, etc. Specialists in Susie Cooper.

Yorkshire
Muir Hewitt Art Deco Originals, Halifax Antiques Centre, Queens Road Mills, Queen's Road/Gibbet Street, Halifax, HX1 4LR
Tel: 01422 347377
Clarice Cliff.

USA
Antik, 104 Franklin Street, New York, NY 10013
Tel: 212 343 0471
www.antik-nye.net

Cincinnati Art Galleries, 225 E. Sixth Street, Cincinnati, Ohio 45202
Tel: 513 381 2128
www.cincinnatiartgalleries.com
Rookwood pottery, American and European art pottery and art glass, Art Nouveau, Arts & Crafts, Art Deco.

Mood Indigo, 181 Prince Street, New York, NY 10012
Tel: 212 254 1176
info@moodindigonewyork.com
www.moodindigonewyork.com
American dinnerware, Barware, 1939 New York Fair items and Art Deco accessories.

Decorative Arts

Dorset
Altamira, 14 Seamoor Road, Westbourne, Bournemouth, BH4 9AR
Tel: 01202 766444

Greater Manchester
A. S. Antiques, 26 Broad Street, Pendleton, Salford, M6 5BY
Tel: 0161 737 5938
Mobile: 07836 368230
as@sternshine.demon.co.uk

Lancashire
Jazz Art Deco
Tel: 07721 032277
jazzartdeco@btinternet.com
www.jazzartdeco.com

London
Art Nouveau Originals,
Unit 31, 290 Westbourne
Grove, W11 2PS
Tel/Fax: 01733 244717
Mobile: 07774 718 096
anoc1900@compuserve.com

Republic of Ireland
Mitofsky Antiques,
8 Rathfarnham Road,
Terenure, Dublin 6
Tel: 00 353 1 492 0033
info@mitofskyartdeco.com
www.mitofskyartdeco.com

Scotland
decorative arts @ doune,
Stand 26, Scottish Antique
and Arts Centre,
By Doune, Stirling,
FK16 6HD
Tel: 01786 461 439
Mobile: 07778 475 974
decorativearts.doune@bt
internet.com

Shropshire
Decorative Antiques,
47 Church Street,
Bishop's Castle, SY9 5AD
Tel: 01588 638851
enquiries@decorative-
antiques.co.uk
www.decorative-
antiques.co.uk
*Decorative objects of the
19th & 20th centuries.*

Yorkshire
Briar's C20th Decorative
Arts, Skipton Antiques
& Collectors Centre,
The Old Foundry,
Cavendish Street,
Skipton, BD23 2AB
Tel: 01756 798641
*Art Deco ceramics and
furniture, specialising in
Charlotte Rhead pottery.*

USA
JMW Gallery, 144 Lincoln
Street, Boston, MA02111
Tel: 001 617 338 9097
www.jmwgallery.com
*American Arts & Crafts,
decorative arts, American
art pottery, mission
furniture, lighting, colour
block prints, metalwork.*

Fireplaces
Greater Manchester
Twentieth Century Fires,
2nd Floor, Bankley House,
Bankley Street,
Manchester, M19 3PP
Tel: 0161 225 1988
sales@c20fires.co.uk
www.c20fires.co.uk

Furniture
Bedfordshire
Graham Mancha,
Design for Modern Living

Tel: +44 (0) 1296 682994
graham@mancha.demon.
co.uk
www.mancha.demon.co.uk

East Sussex
Chemosphere
Tel: 07946 277555
mail@chemosphere.co.uk
www.chemosphere.co.uk
*50s, 60s, 70s retro, mid-
century design furniture
by Charles Eames, Arne
Jacobsen and Danish design.*

Gloucestershire
Ruskin Decorative Arts,
5 Talbot Court,
Stow-on-the-Wold,
Cheltenham, GL54 1DP
Tel: 01451 832254
william.anne@ruskindecarts.
co.uk
*Specialists in the Arts &
Crafts movement and the
decorative arts.*

Kent
20th Century Marks,
12 Market Square,
Westerham, TN16 1AW
Tel: 01959 562221
Mobile: 07831 778992
lambarda@btconnect.com
www.20thcenturymarks.
co.uk
*20th century furniture
and design.*

London
Art Furniture, 158 Camden
Street, NW1 9PA
Tel: 020 7267 4324

Bent Ply, Unit G1, Alfie's,
13 Church Street, NW8 8DT
Tel/Fax: 020 8346 1387
Shop 020 7724 2544
Mobile: 0771 1940 931
brunanaufal@msn.com
www.bentply.com
*Original furniture and design
from the 20th century.*

Eat My Handbag Bitch,
6 Dray Walk, The Old
Truman Brewery,
91-95 Brick Lane, E1 6QL
Tel: 020 7375 3100
contact@eatmyhandbag
bitch.co.uk
www.eatmyhandbagbitch.
co.uk
*Post-war design, furniture,
glass, small decorative
items, ceramics, lighting.*

Fandango, 50 Cross Street,
Islington, N1 2BA
Tel: 020 7226 1777
shop@fandango.uk.com
www.fandango.uk.com
*Post-war design lighting
and furniture.*

Le Style 25, Unit 1(A)
Riverbank Business Park,

Dye House Lane,
off Wick Lane, Bow,
E3 2TB Tel: 020 8983 4285
Mobile: 07778 310 293
info@lestyle25.com
www.lestyle25.com
*Original Art Deco furnishings
and decorative items.*

New Century, 69 Kensington
Church Street, W8 4BG
Tel: 020 7376 2810 or
020 7937 2410

Planet Bazaar,
149 Drummond Street,
NW1 2PB
Tel: 0207 387 8326
Mobile: 07956 326301
info@planetbazaar.co.uk
www.planetbazaar.co.uk

The Target Gallery,
Windmill Street, W1P 1HF
Tel: 020 7636 6295

Themes & Variations,
231 Westbourne Grove
Tel: 020 7727 5531

Gordon Watson Ltd, 50
Fulham Road, SW3 6HH
Tel: 020 7589 3108
Art Deco furniture, lighting.

Nottinghamshire
Fears & Kahn, Nottingham
Antiques Centre,
British Rail Goods Yard,
Nottingham, NG2 3AE
Tel: 0115 9818501
Mobile: 07947 557 127
info@fearsandkahn.co.uk
www.fearsandkahn.co.uk

Oxfordshire
The Country Seat,
Huntercombe Manor Barn,
Henley-on-Thames, RG9
5RY Tel: 01491 641349
ferry&clegg@thecountryseat.
com
www.thecountryseat.com
*17th–20th century
architect-designed furniture,
post-war furniture, art
pottery, metalwork,
Whitefriars glass.*

Suffolk
Puritan Values at the
Dome, St Edmunds
Business Park,
St Edmunds Road,
Southwold, IP18 6BZ
Tel: 01502 722211
sales@puritanvalues.com
www.puritanvalues.com
*Specialising in the Arts &
Crafts movement.*

Surrey
Avalon Design
Tel: 01737 557 975/
01737 554 764/
07985 420462
avalondesign@btinternet.com

www.avalondesign.co.uk
*Wide range of furniture
from designers such as
Eames, Kjaerholm, Panton
& Jacobsen. Lighting from
manufacturers such as
Artemide, O-Luce & Flos,
also glass, art, etc.*

Yorkshire
Domane, Union House,
No 5 Bridge Street,
Leeds, LS2 7RF
Tel/Fax: 0113 245 0701
www.domaneinteriors.com

Pure Design Classics, 20–21
Chatham Place, off Seven
Dials, Brighton, BN1 3TN
Tel: 01273 735331
info@pure2k.com
www.pure2k.com
*From Arne Jacobsen to
Verner Panton, we sell next
generation antiques,
furniture, lighting, glass,
ceramics and other items
of original twentieth
century design. We offer
a sourcing service if you
require specific items or a
certain look, and supply
reproduction items of
some classics to order.
Open Mon & Tues by appt.
Weds–Sat 10am–6pm,
Sun 12pm–4pm.*

Denmark
Dansk Mobelkunst,
Bredgade 32, DK-1260
Copenhagen, Denmark
Tel: +45 33323837
info@dmk.dk

USA
John Alexander Furniture
& Decorative Arts
1860-1920,
10–12 West Gravers Lane,
Philadelphia,
Pennsylvania 19118
Tel: 215 242 0741
info@JohnAlexanderltd.com
www.johnalexanderltd.com

Collage Classics, 1300
N. Industrial Boulevard,
Dallas, TX 75207
Tel: 214 828 9888
txcollage@aol.com
www.collageclassics.com

Deco Deluxe, 993 Lexington
Avenue, New York, NY
10021 Tel: 212 472 7222

Deco Deluxe II, 1038
Lexington Avenue,
New York, NY 10021
Tel: 212 249 5066

Daniel Donnelly,
520 North Fayette Street,
Alexandria, VA 22314
Tel: (703) 549 4672
info@danieldonnelly.com

www.danieldonnelly.com
Mark Frisman, 74 Varick
Street, Suite 202,
New York, NY 10013
Tel: (212) 925 8344
www.markfrisman.com

Karl Kemp & Associates Ltd
Antiques, 34 & 36 East
10th Street, New York, NY
10003 Tel: 212 254 1877
info@KarlKemp.com
www.karlkemp.com

Maison Gerard Art Deco,
53 East 10th Street,
New York, NY 10003
Tel: 212 674 7611
www.maisongerard.com

Skyscraper, 237 East 60th
Street, New York, NY
10022 Tel: 212 588 0644
info@skyscraperny.com
www.skyscraperny.com

Glass
London
20th Century Glass,
Nigel Benson, Kensington
Church Street Antique
Centre, 58-60 Kensington
Church Street, W8 4DB
Tel: 020 7938 1137
Tel/Fax 020 7729 9875
Mobile: 07971 859848
*Open Thurs, Fri & Sat
12–6pm or by appt.*

Origin 101, Gateway
Arcade, Islington High
Street, N1
Tel: 07769 686146/
07747 758852
david@origin101.co.uk
www.origin101.co.uk

USA
Glasstiques, PO Box 6177,
Vacaville, CA 95696
Tel: 707 451 3688
glass@glasstiques.com
www.glasstiques.com

Jewellery
London
Shapiro & Co, Stand 380,
Gray's Antique Market,
58 Davies Street, W1Y 5LP
Tel: 020 7491 2710

Posters
London
Barclay Samson Ltd,
65 Finlay Street, SW6 6HF
Tel: 020 7731 8012
richard@barclaysamson.com

Liz Farrow T/As Dodo,
Stand F073/83,
Alfie's Antique Market,
13–25 Church Street,
NW8 8DT
Tel: 020 7706 1545
*Tues–Sats only
10.30–5.30pm.*

Charles Jeffreys Posters
& Graphics,
12 Octavia Street, SW11
3DN Tel: 020 7978 7976
Mobile: 07836 546150
charlie@cjposters.com
www.cjposters.com

Onslow's, The Depot,
2 Michael Road,
SW6 2AD
Tel: 020 7371 0505
Mobile: 078 31 473 400

The Reel Poster Gallery,
72 Westbourne Grove,
W2 5SH
Tel: 020 7727 4488
www.reelposter.com

Paul & Karen Rennie,
13 Rugby Street,
WC1N 3QT
Tel: 020 7405 0220
info@rennart.co.uk
www.rennart.co.uk
*Specialists in 20th century
British art and design.*

Netherlands
Van Sabben Poster
Auctions, PO Box 2065,
1620 EB Hoorn
Tel: 31 229 268203
uboersma@sabbenposter
auctions.nl
www.vsabbenposter
auctions.nl

USA
Vintage Posters, 28241
Crown Valley Parkway
Suite F-612, California
Tel: (717) 249 1961

Silver
London
The Silver Fund, 40 Bury
Street, St James's,
SW1Y 6AU
Tel: 020 7839 7664
dealers@thesilverfund.com
www.thesilverfund.com

USA.
The Silver Fund,
1001 Madison Avenue at
77th Street, New York,
NY10021
Tel: 001 212 794 4994
dealers@thesilverfund.com
www.thesilverfund.com

Textiles
Lancashire
Decades, 20 Lord St West,
Blackburn, BB2 1JX
Tel: 01254 693320

London
Steinberg & Tolkien
Vintage & Designer
Clothing, 193 Kings Road,
SW3 5EB
Tel: 020 7376 3660

Key to Illustrations

Each illustration and descriptive caption is accompanied by a letter code. By referring to the following list of auctioneers (denoted by ⌁) and dealers (⊞) the source of any item may be immediately determined. Inclusion in this edition in no way constitutes or implies a contract or binding offer on the part of any of our contributors to supply or sell the goods illustrated, or similar articles, at the prices stated. Advertisers in this year's directory are denoted by †.

If you require a valuation for an item, it is advisable to check whether the dealer or specialist will carry out this service and if there is a charge. Please mention Miller's when making an enquiry. Having found a specialist who will carry out your valuation it is best to send a photograph and description of the item to the specialist together with a stamped addressed envelope for the reply. A valuation by telephone is not possible.

Most dealers are only too happy to help you with your enquiry; however, they are very busy people and consideration of the above points would be welcomed.

A&C No longer trading

ADE ⊞ Art Deco Etc, 73 Upper Gloucester Road, Brighton, East Sussex BN1 3LQ Tel: 01273 329268 poolepottery@artdeco.co.uk

AG ⌁ Anderson & Garland (Auctioneers), Marlborough House, Marlborough Crescent, Newcastle-upon-Tyne, Tyne & Wear NE1 4EE Tel: 0191 232 6278

AGR ⊞ Anthony Green Antiques, Unit 39, The Bond Street Antique Centre, 124 New Bond Street, London W1S 1DX Tel: 020 7409 2854 vintagewatches@hotmail.com www.anthonygreen.com

AH ⌁ Andrew Hartley, Victoria Hall Salerooms, Little Lane, Ilkley, Yorkshire LS29 8EA Tel: 01943 816363 info@andrewhartleyfinearts.co.uk www.andrewhartleyfinearts.co.uk

AHL ⊞ Adrian Hornsey Ltd, Brook Manor, Buckfastleigh, Devon TQ11 0HR Tel: 01364 642324 sales@a-h-antique.com

AJ No longer trading

AL ⊞ Ann Lingard, Ropewalk Antiques, Rye, East Sussex TN31 7NA Tel: 01797 223486 ann-lingard@ropewalkantiques.freeserve.co.uk

AND No longer trading

ANO ⊞ Art Nouveau Originals Tel: 07774 718 096 anoc1900@compuserve.com

AnSh No longer trading

AOS ⊞ Antiques on the Square, c/o Grays Market, London W1Y 2LP

AOT ⊞ Annie's Old Things, PO Box 6, Camphill, Queensland 4152, Australia Tel: 0061412353099 annie@fan.net.au

APO ⊞ Apollo Antiques Ltd, The Saltisford, Birmingham Road, Warwick CV34 4TD Tel: 01926 494746

ARF ⊞ Art Furniture, 158 Camden Street, London NW1 9PA Tel: 020 7267 4324

ASA ⊞ A. S. Antiques, 26 Broad Street, Pendleton, Salford, Greater Manchester M6 5BY Tel: 0161 737 5938 Mobile: 07836 368230 as@sternshine.demon.co.uk

B ⌁ Bonhams, 101 New Bond Street, London W1S 1SR Tel: 020 7629 6602 www.bonhams.com

B(B) ⌁ Bonhams, 1 Old King Street, Bath, Somerset BA1 2JT Tel: 01225 788 988

B(Ba) ⌁ Bonhams, 10 Salem Road, Bayswater, London W2 4DL Tel: 020 7313 2700 www.phillips-auctions.com

B(Ch) ⌁ Bonhams, 65–69 Lots Road, Chelsea, London SW10 0RN Tel: 020 7393 3900 www.bonhams.com

B(Ed) ⌁ Bonhams, 65 George Street, Edinburgh, Scotland EH2 2JL Tel: 0131 225 2266

B(Kn) ⌁ Bonhams, Montpelier Street, Knightsbridge, London SW7 1HH Tel: 020 7393 3900 www.bonhams.com

B(WM) Bonhams, The Old House, Station Road, Knowle, Solihull, West Midlands B93 0HT Tel: 01564 776151

B(Z) ⌁ Bonhams, Kreuzstrasse 54, 8008 Zurich, Switzerland Tel: 00 41 1 254 2400

B&B ⊞ No longer trading.

BB(L) ⌁ Butterfields, 7601 Sunset Boulevard, Los Angeles, CA 90046, USA Tel: 00 1 323 850 7500

BDA ⊞ Briar's C20th Decorative Arts, Skipton Antiques & Collectors Centre, The Old Foundry, Cavendish Street, Skipton, Yorkshire BD23 2AB Tel: 01756 798641

Bea(E) ⌁ Bearnes, St Edmund's Court, Okehampton Street, Exeter, Devon EX4 1DU Tel: 01392 422800

BET ⊞ Beth, GO 43-44, Alfies Antique Market, 13-25 Church Street, Marylebone, London NW8 8DT Tel: 020 7723 5613

BEV ⊞ Beverley, 30 Church Street, Marylebone, London NW8 8EP Tel: 020 7262 1576

BKK ⊞ Bona Art Deco Store, The Hart Shopping Centre, Fleet, Hampshire GU13 8AZ Tel: 01252 616666

Bon ⌁ See B(Kn)

Bon(C) ⌁ See B(Ch)

Bri ⌁ Bristol Auction Rooms, St John's Place, Apsley Road, Clifton, Bristol, Gloucestershire BS28 2ST Tel: 0117 973 7201 www.Bristolauctionrooms.co.uk

BrL ⊞ The Brighton Lanes Antique Centre, 12 Meeting House Lane, Brighton, East Sussex BN1 1HB Tel: 01273 823121 Mobile: 07785 564337 peter@brightonlanes-antiquecentre.co.uk www.brightonlanes-antiquecentre.co.uk

BSL ⊞† Barclay Samson Ltd, 65 Finlay Street, London SW6 6HF Tel: 020 7731 8012

BTB ⊞ Behind the Boxes, 98 Kirkdale, Sydenham, London SE26 4BG Tel: 020 8291 6116

BTC ⊞ Beatcity, PO Box 229, Chatham, Kent ME5 8WA Tel: 01634 200444 Darrenhanks@beatcity.co.uk www.beatcity.co.uk

BUK ⌁ Bukowskis, Arsenalsgatan 4, Stockholm, Sweden-SE111 47 Tel: 00 46 (0)8 614 08 00 info@bukowskis.se www.bukowskis.se

BUKF ⌁ Bukowskis, Horhammer, Iso Roobertink, 12 Stora Robertsg, 00120 Helsinki, Finland Tel: 00 358 9 668 9110 www.bukowskis.fi

BW ⌁ Brightwells Fine Art, The Fine Art Saleroom, Ryelands Road, Leominster, Herefordshire HR6 8NZ Tel: 01568 611122 fineart@brightwells.com www.brightwells.com

C ⌁ Christie, Manson & Wood Ltd, 8 King Street, St James's, London, SW1Y 6QT Tel: 020 7839 9060

C20F ⊞ Twentieth Century Fires, 2nd Floor, Bankley House, Bankley Street, Manchester M19 3PP Tel: 0161 225 1988 sales@c20fires.co.uk www.c20fires.co.uk

CAu ⌁ The Cotswold Auction Company Ltd, inc. Short Graham & Co and Hobbs and Chambers Fine Arts, The Coach House, Swan Yard, 9-13 West Market Place, Cirencester, Gloucestershire GL7 2NH Tel: 01285 642420 info@cotswoldauction.co.uk www.cotswoldauction.co.uk

CAu ⌁ The Cotswold Auction Company Ltd, inc. Short Graham & Co and Hobbs and Chambers Fine Arts, Chapel Walk Saleroom, Cheltenham, Gloucestershire GL50 3DS Tel: 01242 256363 info@cotswoldauction.co.uk www.cotswoldauction.co.uk

CAu ⌁ The Cotswold Auction Company Ltd, inc. Short Graham & Co and Hobbs and Chambers Fine Arts, 4–6 Clarence Street, Gloucester GL1 1DX Tel: 01452 521177 info@cotswoldauction.co.uk www.cotswoldauction.co.uk

CAV ⊞ Rupert Cavendish Antiques, 610 King's Road, London SW6 2DX Tel: 020 773 17041 www.rupertcavendish.co.uk

CCO ⊞ Collectable Costume Tel: 07980 623926

ChA No longer trading

CHU ⊞ Church Street Antiques, 2 Church Street, Wells Next the Sea, Norfolk NR23 1JA Tel: 01328 711698

CJB ⊞ Classic Juke Boxes, London N1 Tel: 020 7493 1849

CJP ⊞ Charles Jeffreys Posters & Graphics, 12 Octavia Street, London SW11 3DN Tel: 020 7978 7976 Mobile: 07836 546150 charlie@cjposters.com www.cjposters.com

CMF ⊞ Childhood Memories Tel: 01252 793704 maureen@childhood-memories.co.uk www.childhood-memories.co.uk

CNY ⌁ Christie, Manson & Woods International Inc., 502 Park Avenue, (including Christie's East), New York 10022, USA Tel: 001 212 636 2000

CO ⌁ Cooper Owen, 10 Denmark Street, London WC2H -8LS

COHU ⊞ Stephen Cohu Antiques, The Village Gallery, Ville de l'Eglise, St Ouen, Jersey, Channel Islands JE3 2LR Tel: 01534 485177/630845

COLL ⊞ Collinge Antiques, Old Fyffes Warehouse, Conwy Road, Llandudno Junction, Wales LL31 9LU Tel: 01492 580022

CSA ⊞ Church Street Antiques, 10 Church Street, Godalming, Surrey GU7 1EH Tel: 01483 860894

CSK ⌁ Christie's South Kensington Ltd, 85 Old Brompton Road, London SW7 3LD Tel: 020 7581 7611 christies.com

CTO ⊞ Collector's Corner, PO Box 8, Congleton, Cheshire CW12 4GD Tel:01260 270429 dave.popcorner@ukonline.co.uk

DAC ⊞ David Cardoza Antiques, Lewes Road, Laughton, Lewes, East Sussex BN8 6BN Tel: 01323 811162 Mobile: 07855 835991 sales@davidcardozaantiques.co.uk www.davidcardozaantiques.co.uk

DAD ⊞ decorative arts @ doune, Stand 26, Scottish Antique and Arts Centre, By Doune, Stirling, Scotland FK16 6HD Tel: 01786 461 439 Mobile: 07778 475 974 decorativearts.doune@btinternet.com

DAL ⊞ Dalkeith Auctions Ltd, Dalkeith Hall, Dalkeith Steps, Rear of 81 Old Christchurch Road, Bournemouth, Dorset BH1 1YL Tel: 01202 292905 how@dalkeith-auctions.co.uk www.dalkeith-auctions.co.uk

DBo ⊞ Dorothy Bowler, Ely Street Antique Centre, Stratford-on-Avon, Warwickshire CV37 6LN Tel: 01789 204180

DD ⚒ David Duggleby, West End Salerooms, Whitby, Yorkshire YO23 3DB Tel: 01723 507111 auctions@davidduggleby.freeserve.co.uk www.davidduggleby.com

DDM ⚒ DDM Auction Rooms, Old Courts Road, Brigg, Lincolnshire DN20 8JD Tel: 01652 650172

DE ⊞† Decades, 20 Lord St West, Blackburn, Lancashire BB2 1JX Tel: 01254 693320

DEC ⊞ Decorative Antiques, 47 Church Street, Bishop's Castle, Shropshire SY9 5AD Tel: 01588 638851 enquiries@decorative-antiques.co.uk www.decorative-antiques.co.uk

DID ⊞ Didier Antiques, 58–60 Kensington Church Street, London W8 4DB Tel: 020 7938 2537/078 36 232634

DJH ⊞ David J Hansord & Son, 6 & 7 Castle Hill, Lincoln LN1 3AB Tel: 01522 530044 Mobile: 07831 183511

DN ⚒ Dreweatt Neate, Donnington Priory, Donnington, Newbury, Berkshire RG14 2JE Tel: 01635 553553 fineart@dreweatt-neate.co.uk

Do ⊞ Liz Farrow T/As Dodo, Stand F073/83, Alfie's Antique Market, 13-25 Church Street, London NW8 8DT Tel: 020 7706 1545

DORO ⚒ Dorotheum, Palais Dorotheum, A-1010 Wien, Dorotheergasse. 17, 1010 Austria Tel: 0043 1515 60 455

DSG ⊞ Delf Stream Gallery, 14 New Street, Sandwich, Kent CT13 9AB Tel: 01304 617684 www.delfsstreamgallery.com

DuM/ DUM ⚒ Du Mouchelles, 409 East Jefferson, Detroit, Michigan 48226, USA Tel: 001 313 963 6255

E ⚒ Ewbank, Burnt Common Auction Rooms, London Road, Send, Woking, Surrey GU23 7LN Tel: 01483 223101 www.ewbankauctions.co.uk

Ech ⊞ Echoes, 650a Halifax Road, Eastwood, Todmorden, Yorkshire OL14 6DW Tel: 01706 817505

ELG ⊞ Enid Lawson Gallery, 36a Kensington Church Street, London W8 4DB Tel: 020 7937 8444

ELR ⚒ ELR Auctions Ltd, The Nichols Building, Shalesmoor, Sheffield, Yorkshire S3 8UJ Tel: 0114 281 6161

ES ⊞ Ernest R Sampson, 33 West End, Redruth, Cornwall TR15 2SA Tel: 01209 212536

F&C ⚒ Finan & Co, The Square, Mere, Wiltshire BA12 6DJ Tel: 01747 861411

F&F ⊞ Fenwick & Fenwick, 88-90 High Street, Broadway, Worcestershire WR12 7AJ Tel: 01386 853227/841724

FA ⊞ Fagin's, Old Whiteways Cider Factory, Hele, Exeter, Devon EX5 4PW Tel: 01392 882062

FBG ⚒ Frank H Boos Gallery, 420 Enterprise Court, Bloomfield Hills, Michigan 48302, USA Tel: 001 248 332 1500

FBS § Festival of Britain Society, c/o Martin Packer, 41 Lyall Gardens, Birmingham, West Midlands B45 9YW Tel: 0121 453 8245 martin@packer34.freeserve.co.uk www.packer34.freeserve.co.uk

FF ⊞ Freeforms, Unit 6 The Antique Centre, 58-60 Kensington Church Street, London W8 4DB Tel: 020 7937 9447

FMa ⊞ Francesca Martire, Stand F131-137, Alfie's Antique Market, 13-25 Church Street, London NW8 0RH Tel: 020 7724 4802 Mobile: 07990 523891

G(L) ⚒ Gorringes inc Julian Dawson, 15 North Street, Lewes, East Sussex BN7 2PD Tel: 01273 472503 auctions@gorringes.co.uk www.gorringes.co.uk

GAA ⊞ Gabrian Antiques Tel: 01923 859675 gabrian.antiques@virgin.net

GAD ⊞ Decodence Tel: 07831 326326 gad@decodence.demon.co.uk

GAK ⚒ Keys, Aylsham Salerooms, Off Palmers Lane, Aylsham, Norfolk NR11 6JA Tel: 01263 733195 www.aylshamsalerooms.co.uk

GH ⚒ Gardiner Houlgate, The Bath Auction Rooms, 9 Leafield Way, Corsham, Nr Bath, Somerset SN13 9SW Tel: 01225 812912 gardiner-houlgate.co.uk www.invaluable.com/gardiner-houlgate

GIN ⊞ The Ginnell Gallery Antique Centre, 18-22 Lloyd Street, Greater Manchester M2 5WA Tel: 0161 833 9037

GOH ⊞ Goya Hartogs, SO01 Alfie's Antique Market, Church Street, London NW8 8DT Tel: 0788 7714477

GoW ⊞ Gordon Watson Ltd, 50 Fulham Road, London SW3 Tel: 020 7589 3108

GRM Graham Mancha, Design for Modern Living Tel: +44 (0) 1296 682994 graham@mancha.demon.co.uk www.mancha.demon.co.uk

HaG ⊞ Harington Glass, 2–3 Queen Street, Bath, Somerset BA1 1HE Tel: 01225 482179

Hal ⚒ Halls Fine Art Auctions, Welsh Bridge, Shrewsbury, Shropshire SY3 8LA Tel: 01743 231212

HALd ⚒ Henry Aldridge & Son, Unit 1, Bath Road Business Centre, Devizes, Wiltshire SN10 1XA Tel: 01380 729199 andrew.aldridge@virgin.net www.henry-aldridge.co.uk

Har/ HarC ⊞ Hardy's Collectables, 862 Christchurch Road, Boscombe, Bournemouth, Dorset BH7 6DQ Tel: 01202 422407/473744 Mobile: 07970 613077

HARP ⊞ Harpers Jewellers Ltd, 2/6 Minster Gates, York YO1 7HL Tel: 01904 632634 harpers@talk21.com www.vintage-watches.co.uk

HEW ⊞† Muir Hewitt, Halifax Antiques Centre, Queens Road Mills, Queen's Road/Gibbet Street, Halifax, Yorkshire HX1 4LR Tel: 01422 347377

HSt ⊞ High Street Antiques, 39 High Street, Hastings, East Sussex TN34 3ER Tel: 01424 460068

HUM ⊞ Humbleyard Fine Art, Unit 32 Admiral Vernon Arcade, Portobello Road, London W11 2DY Tel: 01362 637793 Mobile: 07836 349416

HUN ⊞ The Country Seat, Huntercombe Manor Barn, Henley-on-Thames, Oxfordshire RG9 5RY Tel: 01491 641349

HUX ⊞ David Huxtable, Basement Stall 11/12, 288 Westbourne Grove, London W11 Sats at Portobello Road Tel: 07710 132200 david@huxtins.com

HYD ⚒ Hy Duke & Son, Dorchester Fine Art Salerooms, Dorchester, Dorset DT1 1QS Tel: 01305 265080

ID ⊞ Identity, 100 Basement Flat, Finsborough Road, London SW10 9ED Tel: 020 7244 9509

IW ⊞ Islwyn Watkins, Offa's Dyke Antique Centre, 4 High Street, Knighton, Powys, Wales LD7 1AT Tel: 01547 520145

JAA ⚒ Jackson's Auctioneers & Appraisers, 2229 Lincoln Street, Cedar Falls, IA 50613, USA Tel: 00 1 319 277 2256

JAZZ ⊞ Jazz Art Deco Tel: 07721 032277 jazzartdeco@btinternet.com www.jazzartdeco.com

JHa ⊞ Jeanette Hayhurst Fine Glass, 32a Kensington Church Street, London W8 4HA Tel: 020 7938 1539

JJ ⊞ Jen Jones, Pontbrendu, LLanybydder, Ceredigion, Wales SA40 9UJ Tel: 01570 480610

JMW ⊞ JMW Gallery, 144 Lincoln Street, Boston, MA02111, USA Tel: 001 617 338 9097 www.jmwgallery.com

JoV ⊞ Joe Vickers, Bartlett Street Antiques Market, Bath, Somerset BA1 2QZ Tel: 01225 466689

JPr ⊞ Joanna Proops Antique Textiles & Lighting, 34 Belvedere, Lansdown Hill, Bath, Somerset BA1 5HR Tel: 01225 310795 antiquetextiles@uk.online.co.uk www.antiquetextiles.co.uk

L ⚒ Lawrence Fine Art Auctioneers, South Street, Crewkerne, Somerset TA18 8AB Tel: 01460 73041

L&E ⚒ Locke & England, 18 Guy Street, Leamington Spa, Warwickshire CV32 4RT Tel: 01926 889100 www.auctions-online.com/locke

L&L ⊞ Linen & Lace, Shirley Tomlinson, Halifax Antiques Centre, Queens Road/Gibbet Street, Halifax, Yorkshire HX1 4LR Tel: 01422 366657

L&T ⚒ Lyon & Turnbull, 33 Broughton Place, Edinburgh, Scotland EH1 3RR Tel: 0131 557 8844

Law/ LAW ⊞ Malcolm Law Collectables, Greenways Garden Centre, Bethersden, Kent Tel: 0777 3211603

LBe ⊞ Linda Bee Art Deco, Stand L18–21, Grays Antique Market, 1–7 Davies Mews, London W1Y 1AR Tel: 020 7629 5921

LBr ⊞ Lynda Brine, Assembly Antiques, 6 Saville Row, Bath, Somerset BA1 2QP Tel: 01225 448488 lyndabrine@yahoo.co.uk www.scentbottlesandsmalls.co.uk

LEGE ⊞ Legend Tel: 0117 926 4637

LJ ⚒ Leonard Joel Auctioneers, 333 Malvern Road, South Yarra, Victoria 3141, Australia Tel: 03 9826 4333 decarts@ljoel.com.au or jewellery@ljoel.com.au www.ljoel.com.au

M ⚒ Morphets of Harrogate, 6 Albert Street, Harrogate, Yorkshire HG1 1JL Tel: 01423 530030

MAR ⚒ Frank R Marshall & Co, Marshall House, Church Hill, Knutsford, Cheshire WA16 6DH Tel: 01565 653284

MARK ⊞† 20th Century Marks, 12 Market Square, Westerham, Kent TN16 1AW Tel: 01959 562221 Mobile: 07831 778992 lambarda@btconnect.com www.20thcenturymarks.co.uk

MAV ⊞ May Avenue Tel: 07710 424033

MI ⊞ Mitofsky Antiques, 8 Rathfarnham Road, Terenure, Dublin 6, Republic of Ireland Tel: 00 353 1 492 0033 info@mitofskyartdeco.com www.mitofskyartdeco.com

MoS ⊞ Morgan Stobbs Mobile: 0402 206817 By appointment

MTay ⊞ Martin Taylor Antiques, 323 Tettenhall Road, Wolverhampton, West Midlands WV6 0JZ Tel: 01902 751166/07836 636524 enquiries@mtaylor-antiques.co.uk www.mtaylor-antiques.co.uk

MURR ⊞ Murrays' Antiques & Collectables Tel: 01202 309094

NAW ⊞ Newark Antiques Warehouse, Old Kelham Road, Newark, Nottinghamshire NG24 1BX Tel: 01636 674869 enquiries@newarkantiques.co.uk

NCA ⊞ New Century, 69 Kensington Church Street, London W8 4BG Tel: 020 7376 2810/020 7937 2410

NET ⊞ Nettlebed Antique Merchants, 1 High Street, Nettlebed, Henley-on-Thames, Oxfordshire RG9 5DA Tel: 01491 642062

NP ⊞ The Neville Pundole Gallery, 8A & 9 The Friars, Canterbury, Kent CT1 2AS Tel: 01227 453471 www.pundole.co.uk

ONS ⚒ Onslow's, The Depot, 2 Michael Road, London SW6 2AD Tel: 020 7371 0505 Mobile: 078 31 473 400

OOLA ⊞ Oola Boola, 139–147 Kirkdale, London SE26 4QJ Tel: 0208 291 9999 Mobile: 07956 261252 oola.boola@telco4u.net

ORI ⊞ Origin 101, Gateway Arcade, Islington High Street, London N1 Tel: 07769 686146/ 07747 758852 David@origin101.co.uk www.origin101.co.uk

OTT ⊞ Otter Antiques, 20 High Street, Wallingford, Oxon OX10 0BP Tel: 01491 825544

OVE No longer trading

OW ⊞ Off World, Unit 20, Romford Shopping Halls, Market Place, Romford, Essex RM1 3AT Tel: 01708 765633

P ⚒ See B

P(B) ⚒ See B(B)

P(Ba) ⚒ See B(Ba)

P(Ed) ⚒ See B(Ed)

P(F) No longer trading

P(PL) ⚒ Phillips, de Pury & Luxembourg, 3 West 57 Street, New York, NY 10019, USA Tel: 212 570 4830 phillips-auctions.com

P(Sy) ⚒ See SHSY

P(WM) ⚒ See B(WM)

P(Z) ⚒ See B(Z)

PAB ⊞ Paolo Bonino, Stand SO01, Alfies Antique Market, 13–25 Church Street, London NW8 8DT Tel: 077 674 98766/020 7624 2481

PCh ⚒ Peter Cheney, Western Road Auction Rooms, Western Road, Littlehampton, West Sussex BN17 5NP Tel: 01903 722264 & 713418

PGA ⊞ Paul Gibbs Antiques, 25 Castle Street, Conwy, Gwynedd, Wales LL32 8AY Tel: 01492 593429 teapot@marketsite.co.uk

PGH No longer trading

PIL ⊞ Pilgrim Antique Centre, 7 West Street, Dorking, Surrey RH4 1EL Tel: 01306 875028

PKT ⊞ Glitter & Dazzle, Pat & Ken Thompson, Hampshire Tel: 01329 288678

PLB ⊞ Planet Bazaar, 149 Drummond Street, London NW1 2PB Tel: 0207 387 8326 Mobile: 07956 326301 info@planetbazaar.co.uk www.planetbazaar.co.uk

PLY ⚒ The Plymouth Auction Rooms, Edwin House, St John's Rd, Cattedown, Plymouth, Devon PL4 0NZ Tel: 01752 254740

PPH ⊞ Period Picnic Hampers Tel: 0115 937 2934

PR ⊞ Prime Parts, 85 Gloucester Road, Bishopston, Bristol BS7 8AS Tel: 0117 9830007

PrB ⊞ Pretty Bizarre, 170 High Street, Deal, Kent CT14 6BQ Tel: 07973 794537

PVD ⊞ Puritan Values at the Dome, St Edmunds Business Park, St Edmunds Road, Southwold, Suffolk IP18 6BZ Tel: 01502 722211 sales @puritanvalues.com www.puritanvalues.com

Rac/ ⊞ Field, Staff & Woods, 93 High Street, Rochester, Kent
RAC ME1 1LX Tel: 01634 846144

RAD ⊞ Radio Days, 87 Lower Marsh, Waterloo, London SE1 7AB Tel: 020 7928 0800

RAR No longer trading

RAT ⊞ Room at the Topp, 1st Floor, Antiques Warehouse, Glass Street, Hanley, Stoke on Trent, Staffordshire ST1 2ET Tel: 01782 752310

RBB ⚒ See BWL

RCh ⊞ Rayner & Chamberlain Tel: 020 8293 9439

RDG ⊞ Richard Dennis Gallery, 144 Kensington Church Street, London W8 4BN Tel: 020 7727 2061

REEL ⊞ The Reel Poster Gallery, 72 Westbourne Grove, London W2 5SH Tel: 020 7727 4488 www.reelposter.com

REN ⊞† Paul & Karen Rennie, 13 Rugby Street, London WC1N 3QT Tel: 020 7405 0220 info@rennart.co.uk www.rennart.co.uk

REPS ⊞ Repsycho, 85 Gloucester Road, Bishopston, Bristol BS7 8AS Tel: 0117 9830007

RGe ⊞ Rupert Gentle Antiques, The Manor House, Milton Lilbourne, Nr Pewsey, Wiltshire SN9 5LQ Tel: 01672 563344

RH ⊞ Rick Hubbard Art Deco, 3 Tee Court, Bell Street, Romsey, Hampshire SO51 8GY Tel: 01794 513133 Mobile: 07767 267607 rick@rickhubbard-artdeco.co.uk www.rickhubbard-artdeco.co.uk

RIC ⊞ Rich Designs, Unit 1, Grove Farm, Bromyard Road, Worcester WR2 5UG Tel: 01905 748214

RTo ⚒ Rupert Toovey & Co Ltd, Star Road, Partridge Green, West Sussex RH13 8RJ Tel: 01403 711744

RTT ⊞ Rin Tin Tin, 34 North Road, Brighton, East Sussex BN1 1YB Tel: 01273 672424

RTW ⊞ Richard Twort Tel: 01934 641900 Mob: 07711 939789

RUSK ⊞† Ruskin Decorative Arts, 5 Talbot Court, Stow-on-the-Wold, Cheltenham, Gloucestershire GL54 1DP Tel: 01451 832254 william.anne@ruskindecarts.co.uk

S ⚒ Sotheby's, 34–35 New Bond Street, London W1A 2AA Tel: 020 7293 5000 www.sothebys.com

S(Am) ⚒ Sotheby's Amsterdam, De Boelelaan 30, 1083 HJ, Amsterdam, Netherlands Tel: 00 31 20 550 22 00

S(LA) ⚒ Sotheby's, 9665 Wilshire Boulevard, Beverly Hills, California 90212, USA Tel: (310) 274 0340

S(NY) ⚒ Sotheby's, 1334 York Avenue, New York, NY 10021, USA Tel: 00 1 212 606 7000

S(O) ⚒ Sotheby's Olympia, Hammersmith Road, London W14 8UX Tel: 020 7293 5534

S(P) ⚒ Sotheby's France SA, 76 rue du Faubourg, Saint Honoré, 75008 Paris, France Tel: 00 33 147 42 22 32

S(S) ⚒ Sotheby's Sussex, Summers Place, Billingshurst, West Sussex RH14 9AD Tel: 01403 833500

SAN ⊞ Steven F. Anton Antiques & Collectables, Scottish Antique and Arts Centre, Carse of Cambus, Doune, Perthshire, Scotland FK16 6HD Tel: 01786 841203/01383 860520

SAS ⚒ Special Auction Services, The Coach House, Midgham Park, Reading, Berkshire RG7 5UG Tel: 0118 971 2949 www.invaluable.com/sas/

SBT ⊞ Steinberg & Tolkien Vintage & Designer Clothing, 193 Kings Road, London SW3 5EB Tel: 020 7376 3660

Sck ⚒ Stockholms Auktionsverk, Jakobsgaten 10, PO Box 16256, S-103 25 Stockholm, Sweden Tel: 0046 8 453 67 00

SEA ⊞ Mark Seabrook Antiques, PO Box 396, Huntingdon, Cambridgeshire PE28 0ZA Tel: 01480 861935 Mobile: 07770 721931 enquiries@markseabrook.com www.markseabrook.com

SEY ⊞ The Directors Cut, Mike Seymour, The Antiques Centre, Ely Street, Stratford-upon-Avon, Warwickshire CV37 6LN Tel: 07931 345784 mike@seymour.gsbusiness.co.uk

SFL ⊞ The Silver Fund, 40 Bury Street, St James's, London SW1Y 6AU Tel: 020 7839 7664 dealers@thesilverfund.com www.thesilverfund.com

SHa ⊞ Shapiro & Co, Stand 380, Gray's Antique Market, 58 Davies Street, London W1K 5LP Tel: 020 7491 2710

SHSY ⚒ Shapiro Auctioneers, 162 Queen Street, Woollahra, Sydney, NSW 2025, Australia Tel: 00 612 9326 1588

SK ⚒ Skinner Inc, The Heritage On The Garden, 63 Park Plaza, Boston, MA 02116, USA Tel: 001 617 350 5400

SK(B) ⚒ Skinner Inc, 357 Main Street, Bolton, MA 01740, USA Tel: 00 1 978 779 6241

SLM ⚒ Sloan's Auctioneers & Appraisers, 2516 Ponce de Leon Boulevard, Coral Gables, Florida 33134, USA Tel: 305 447 0757 www.sloansauction.com

SLN ⚒ Sloan's Auctioneers & Appraisers, 4920 Wyaconda Road, North Bethesda, MD 20852, USA Tel: 001 301 468 4911 or 800 649 5066 www.sloansauction.com

SnA ⊞ Snape Maltings Antique & Collectors Centre, Saxmundham, Suffolk IP17 1SR Tel: 01728 688038

SpM ⊞ Sparkle Moore, The Girl Can't Help It!/Cad Van Swankster, G100 & G116 Ground Floor, Alfies Antique Market, 13–25 Church Street, Marylebone, London NW8 8DT Tel: 020 7724 8984/0208 809 3923 sparkle.moore@virgin.net www.grays.clara.net

SPT ⊞ Sporting Times Gone By Tel: 01903 885656 Mobile: 07976 942059 www.sportingtimes.co.uk

StC § Carlton Factory Shop, Carlton Works, Copeland Street, Stoke-on-Trent, Staffs ST4 1PU Tel: 01782 410504 www.stclere.co.uk

SWAN ⚒ Swann Galleries,Inc, 104 East 25th Street, New York 10010, USA Tel: 00 1 212 2544710

SWN ⊞ Swan Antiques, Stone Street, Cranbrook, Kent TN17 3HF Tel: 01580 712720

SWO ⚒ Sworders, 14 Cambridge Road, Stansted Mountfitchet, Essex CM24 8BZ Tel: 01279 817778 www.sworder.co.uk

TBoy ⊞ Cloud Cuckoo Land, 12 Fore Street, Mevagissey, Cornwall PL26 6UQ Tel: 01726 842364 inkquest@dial.pipex.com www.inkquest.dial.pipex.com

TCG ⊞ 20th Century Glass, Nigel Benson, Kensington Church Street Antique Centre, 58–60 Kensington Church Street, London W8 4DB Tel: 020 7938 1137/020 7729 9875 Mobile: 07971 859848

TEM ⊞ Tempus, Union Square, The Pantiles, Tunbridge Wells, Kent Tel/Fax: 01932 828936 www.tempus-watches.co.uk

TEN ⚒ Tennants, The Auction Centre, Harmby Road, Leyburn, Yorkshire DL8 5SG Tel: 01969 623780 enquiry@tennants-ltd.co.uk www.tennants.co.uk

TMA ⚒ Tring Market Auctions, Brook Street, Tring, Herts. HP23 5EF Tel: 01442 826446 sales@tringmarketauctions.co.uk www.tringmarketauctions.co.uk

TPA ⊞ Times Past Antiques, 59 High Street, Eton, Windsor, Berkshire SL4 6BL Tel: 01753 857018

TRA ⊞ Tramps, Tuxford Hall, Lincoln Road, Tuxford, Newark, Nottinghamshire NG22 0HR Tel: 01777 872 543 info@trampsuk.com

TREA ⚒† Treadway Gallery, Inc., 2029 Madison Road, Cincinnati, Ohio 45208, USA Tel: 001 513 321 6742 www.treadwaygallery.com

TRL ⚒ Thomson, Roddick & Medcalf, Coleridge House, Shaddongate, Carlisle, Cumbria CA2 5TU Tel: 01228 528939

TT ⊞ Treasures in Textiles, 53 Russian Drive, Liverpool, Merseyside L13 7BS Tel: 0151 281 6025

TWa ⊞ Time Warp, c/o Curioser & Curioser, Sydney Street, Brighton, East Sussex BN1 Tel: 01273 821243

TWI ⊞ Twinkled, High St Antiques Centre, 39 High Street, Hastings, East Sussex TN34 Tel: 01424 460068 info@twinkled.net www.twinkled.net

UC ⊞ Up Country, The Old Corn Stores, 68 St John's Road, Tunbridge Wells, Kent TN4 9PE Tel: 01892 523341 www.upcountryantiques.co.uk

UTP ⊞ Utility Plus, 66 High Street, West Ham, Pevensey, East Sussex BN24 5LP Tel: 01323 762316

V&S No longer trading

VEY ⊞ Paul Veysey Tel: 01452 790672 www.drivepast.com

VSP ⚒ Van Sabben Poster Auctions, PO Box 2065, 1620 EB Hoorn, Netherlands Tel: 31 229 268203 uboersma@sabbenposterauctions.nl www.vsabbenposterauctions.nl

W&S ⊞ Pat Woodward and Alma Shaw, Unit G43, Grnd Floor, Gloucester Antiques Centre, In The Historic Docks, Severn Road, Gloucester GL1 2LE

WaH ⊞ The Warehouse, 29–30 Queens Gardens, Worthington Street, Dover, Kent CT17 9AH Tel: 01304 242006

WBH ⚒ Walker, Barnett & Hill, Cosford Auction Rooms, Long Lane, Cosford, Shropshire TF11 8PJ Tel: 01902 375555 wbhauctions@lineone.net www.walker-barnett-hill.co.uk

WDG ⚒ William Doyle Galleries, 175 East 87th Street, New York 10128, USA Tel: 212 427 2730

WeH ⊞ Westerham House Antiques, The Green, Westerham, Kent TN16 1AY Tel: 01959 561622/562200

WilP ⚒ W&H Peacock, 26 Newnham Street, Bedford MK40 3JR Tel: 01234 266366

WW ⚒ Woolley & Wallis, Salisbury Salerooms, 51–61 Castle Street, Salisbury, Wiltshire SP1 3SU Tel: 01722 424500

YR ⊞ Yorkshire Relics of Haworth, 11 Main Street, Haworth, Yorkshire BD22 8DA Tel: 01535 642218

ZOOM No longer trading

Index

Italic page numbers denote colour pages; **bold** numbers refer to information and pointer boxes.